D0872128

Stupidity

Stupidity

AVITAL RONELL

University of Illinois Press

Urbana and Chicago

Publication of this book was supported by a grant
from the Faculty of Art and Science Humanities
Deans' Discretionary Fund of New York University.
♾ THIS BOOK IS PRINTED ON ACID-FREE PAPER.

Library of Congress Cataloging-in-Publication Data
Ronell, Avital.
Stupidity / Avital Ronell.
p. cm.
Includes bibliographical references and index.
ISBN 0-252-02613-6 (alkaline paper)
1. Stupidity in literature.   2. Literature, Modern –
History and criticism.   I. Title.
PN56.S737R66   2002   809'.93353   00-010294

Contents

Slow Learner

THE TEMPTATION is to wage war on stupidity as if it were a vanquishable object — as if we still knew how to wage war or circumscribe an object in a manner that would be productive of meaning or give rise to futurity. One could not easily imagine circumstances in which an agency of state or government, even a U.S. government, would declare war on stupidity in the manner it has engaged a large-scale war on drugs. Though part of a politically suspect roundup, the presumed object of the drug wars offered a hint, at least, of materiality. Stupidity exceeds and undercuts materiality, runs loose, wins a few rounds, recedes, gets carried home in the clutch of denial — and returns. Essentially linked to the inexhaustible, stupidity is also that which fatigues knowledge and wears down history. From Schiller's exasperated concession that even the gods cannot combat stupidity, to Hannah Arendt's frustrated effort, in a letter to Karl Jaspers, to determine the exact status and level of Adolf Eichmann's *Dummheit*, to current psychoanalytical descriptions of the dumb interiors of the despotic mind (heir to the idiot-king of which Lacan has written), stupidity has evinced a mute resistance to political urgency, an instance of an unaccountable ethical hiatus.[1] In fact, stupidity, purveyor of self-assured assertiveness, mutes just about everything that would seek to disturb its impervious hierarchies.

Neither a pathology nor an index as such of moral default, stupidity is nonetheless linked to the most dangerous failures of human endeavor. I hesitate to say here what stupidity is because, eluding descriptive analysis, it switches and regroups, turns around and even fascinates, as it fascinated Flaubert's Saint Antoine.[2] While stupidity is "what is there," it cannot be simply located or evenly scored. Not since Nietzsche pulled the switch and got the powerful forces of alternative valences going. Typically for the genealogist, stupidity, in the end, is extolled for promoting life and growth. To the extent that morality teaches hatred of too great a freedom, it implants the need for limited horizons and immediate tasks, teaching the narrowing of perspectives "and thus in a certain sense stupidity, as a condition of life and growth." Not without consequence, Nietzsche distributes the tyranny and discipline of stupidity equally among slave morality, Christian values, and scholarship. Narrowing perspective and limiting freedom,

3

these forces of historical moment—tyrannical and arbitrary in the way they have regulated human affairs — are viewed by Nietzsche as instances of "this rigorous and grandiose stupidity [that] has educated the spirit." Stupidity, in Nietzsche's estimation, does not lack rigor but, on the contrary, is responsible for discipline and breeding, for education ("the indispensable means for spiritual discipline and breeding").[3] Benevolent and disdainful at once, Nietzsche reserves a place for stupidity that, after all is said and done, puts it on the side of life, of discipline and education. However devalued and Christian, grandiose or enslaved, stupidity belongs among the powerfully determining forces with which it enjoys shared custody of our destiny.

Because it generates so many startling contradictions, stupidity, for philosophy or for the end of philosophy, acquires a status that needs to be claimed, if not entirely understood. What does stupidity have to do with thought or the affiliated branches of knowledge or scholarship? Where does it belong on the map of dogmatic philosophy, which continues to divide the territories of thought into empirical and transcendental sectors? Nietzsche does not say where to locate it, how to read it, or whether or not stupidity properly belongs where philosophy reigns. Raising it , he more or less forgets stupidity, like an umbrella. But then he remembers; it comes back to him when he affirms the protective values of deception and self-doubting: "One of the subtlest ways of deceiving, for as long as possible, at any rate of successfully posing as more stupid than one is — which in everyday life is often as desirable as an umbrella — is called enthusiasm."[4] Part of the grammar of shrewd behavior, connected to the everyday and self-protecting, stupidity opens up against the sky, receiving or bouncing off itself the intrusive rains of transcendence. Implied by enthusiasm, it allows one to have a nice everyday day — on the surface of things. In any case, stupidity now belongs to the famous repertoire of Nietzschean poses, to the domain of fictions and will to power.

I am going to defer the matter of situating stupidity since, anyway, everyone else at some level of understanding has situated and filed a report on it, which is to say, for the most part, let it go.[5] Whether abandoned or put to work, its fate was the same: the case was closed on stupidity, as if either way it had been adequately dealt with. At this point in its career, hesitation and deferral seem to be the most dispassionate ways to approach stupidity. The more we defer it, the more the knowledge we think we have about knowledge weakens (as long as I don't know what stupidity is, what I know about knowing remains uncertain,

4

even forbidding). All we know at this juncture is that stupidity does not allow itself to be opposed to knowledge in any simple way, nor is it the other of thought. It does not stand in the way of wisdom, for the disguise of the wise is to avow unknowing. At this time I can say only that the question of stupidity is not satisfied with the discovery of the negative limit of knowledge; it consists, rather, in the absence of a relation to knowing. In a Nietzschean sense, this absence of relation (which is also a relation, Blanchot's "rapport sans rapport") invites at least two different types of evaluation that, inexhaustible and contradictory, can be seen in terms derived from war. There are those who seek to wage war on stupidity or feel attacked and besieged by it, and — assuming there exists an alternative to war, a space in which the combat zone is neutralized, turned into a lawn or a beach, no sharks, no holes in the ozone — there would be the other of war, the peculiar experience of an exorbitant peace treaty, a kind of relinquishment that resolves itself into passivity.

We go first to the poets, and then to war.

It would be comforting, no doubt, to suppose that these destinations present two different beats, following Hölderlin's suggestion that poetry indicates the most innocent of exertions. But we have been taught early on, by Homer and by Hölderlin himself, that going to the poet often involves going to war. Whether reading polemological maps, devising strategies of attack or retreat, surveilling a hostile territory, practicing poses of surrender, or getting iced by a particular turn of phrase or wind, the poetic and war efforts appear often to overlap.

What links the two efforts in terms of a syntax of doing or a shared rhetorical energy involves, above all, the issues of surrender and retreat, modalities of being that yield to necessary attenuation — a humbling bow to finitude, a humbling, we could say, that implies courage as it confronts the narrowing recession of limits. The war cry enfolds the poetic solitude of the *schreiben/Schrei* (inscribing/cry) — the energy of historical inscription that dissolves into combat fatigue, into sheer stupefaction, effecting a brush with urgent nullity. The poets know from stupidity, the essential dulling or weakening that forms the precondition of utterance. This is perhaps why Hölderlin's poems "Dichtermut" and "Blödigkeit" — fated to link the trope of courage with that of stupefaction, the crucial dull-mindedness of the poet — co-emerged, one giving birth to the other.[6]

"Dichtermut" (the poet's courage) has been widely considered the blueprint for the poem on which my discussion centers. It is bound by a

5

mysterious contract to what Hölderlin calls "Blödigkeit." Yet however enigmatic may be the connection asserted in these poems between poetic valor and sheer intimidation of mind — a facet of stupidity — the disturbing drift of the poems, each an anamorph of the other, is in fact not unique to Hölderlin. The severest of poets ventured, as if prompted by some transcendental obligation, into a consecrated domain where language meets its unmaking in stupidity, idiocy, imbecility, and other cognates of nonknowing. One poet's highly contested encounter with idiocy, the perplexingly sustained thought where utterance is reduced to repetitive hoots and stammers, will especially concern us, though Wordsworth need not have been the only poet with whom to hold a conversation on the recession of being, the nothingness to which poetry is responsible. There could have been — there is — Rilke's "Lied des Idioten" (Song of the Idiot), where nothing happens ("Wie gut. / Es kann nichts geschehn." [How good. / Nothing can happen.]) or Hart Crane's "The Idiot" or Richard Wright's haiku #579 that asserts "the idiot boy / Has dignity." There are moreover — "at the black earth, at the earth mute" — "The Idiots" of Joseph Conrad, "who are forgotten by time, and live untouched by years till death gathers them."[7] And signals from elsewhere still, some of which we pick up — for instance, those from the pages of a massively conceived struggle between idiocy and stupidity in the work of Dostoevsky, where a citational war front erupts between Flaubert and Gogol. The failure of cognition is the province of literary language, though it is difficult to speak of failure where nothing has been promised, tested, or essayed; yet, poetic language remains sheer promise and, in the way shown by Hölderlin, capable of hearing the alien unsaid.

We can no longer say in Heideggerian tonalities that when Nietzsche fought with Wagner (or so-and-so said this or that) it was a historial event. Yet we can still intimate the gravity of an emergence, no matter how complicated, when Hölderlin welds "Blödigkeit" to "Dichtermut." Relinquishing the codified mythemes of heroic poses, "Blödigkeit" finally divulges the blunted, bludgeoned being of the poet that goes to meet its task, stands up to its calling. To all appearances a deflation, this is another flex of muscle, an internal restraining order holding back the values associated with the intelligence of doing, the bright grasp of what is there. Poetic courage consists in embracing the terrible lassitude of mind's enfeeblement, the ability to endure the near facticity of feeblemindedness. The readings and translations that have accrued to Hölderlin's ode "Blödigkeit" have tended to efface the embarrassing openness with which the poet names stupidity, even if it could be recuperated as Hölderlin's way of transposing for modernity Pindarian awe, the Greek sense of being awe- and dumbstruck. In Walter Benjamin's exalted reading, which Gershom Scholem judged "too metaphysical" and Benjamin himself left unpublished, the disturbing moment in the semantic chain is elided so that Benjamin can claim without undue heuristic anxiety that "Blödigkeit" represents the overcoming of "Dichtermut."[8] Still, the power of the unread title has a hold on his commentary, which practices a syntax of extraordinary subordination, a cultivation of the passive voice "to a degree unheard of even in bad academic writing."[9] This mortification, this utter exhaustion of the passive enacts the reading that Benjamin and others have avoided, which could be called the dispossession that entitles as it enfeebles the writer, disengaging and defaulting the knowing subject who enters into contact with the poetic word. The passive voice registers a secret agreement with the title of an inexplicable passivity it has sought to elude.

The tradition of diverting the title from its disturbing implications has been honored recently by Bart Philipsen, Michael Jennings, and Stanley Corngold, who give grounds for valorizing the term *timidity* (in one of his translations, Michael Hamburger opts for "diffidence.")[10] Corngold, to his credit, pauses over the decision, noting that "Benjamin does not pay equal attention to the troublesome word *Blödigkeit*, which while unquestionably meaning 'timidity,' also, like *Blödheit*, suggests short-sightedness and, in certain contexts, stupidity. Even if this unsavory connotation is set aside, there is still the relativizing effect that this title exercises on the full poetic affirmation that Benjamin finds in the poem."[11] Eventually the poem must overcome dialectically its title, which then dives out of sight. We should not be surprised to note that such a maneuver, which sets aside the unsavory trace of stupidity, even when named by Hölderlin as an essential mark of poetic existence, replicates an entire series of gestures performed by critics and philosophers who are invested in making recognizably sanctioned sense of the poet's claims.[12]

The need for redirecting or forgetting stupidity's course is not hard to decipher because, beyond its unsavory aspect, stupidity, as Musil has demonstrated exhaustively, at least initially produces itself when approached. We could say with Hölderlin that it is in the nature of stupidity to stump — to enfeeble and intimidate — but also to release. In this regard, "Blödigkeit" cannot be seen as opposable to "Dichtermut" but as decisively inflecting the reading of poetic courage, perhaps offering another way of naming the sacred task to which the poet has been assigned. Bringing forth stupidity as a crucial poetic sign, Hölderlin continues to receive his orders from Rousseau, whose reliance on "simplicity" and "lethargy" as an exemplary "self-forgetting that opens the self to another sort of being" he bears out.[13] The special resonance of *Blödigkeit* as that which encourages releasement is thus linked to Rousseau, for whom sloth (*paresse*) "and even a certain 'stupidity' are the preconditions of a rapport with being."[14]

The poetic bearing is staked in Hölderlin's revisions. An exhortation, the poem, much like "Dichtermut," invites the poetic spirit to venture out into time and world, to let itself be held "at the turning of time" by the god of heaven. Even those who pass away in their sleep are "Drawn erect on golden / Leading strings, like children." Whereas the poem stating the poet's courage begins, "Are not all the living related to you?" the later version, "Blödigkeit," opens by asking, "Are not many of the living known [or, rather, "familiar" (*bekannt*)] to you?"[15] A question of relation or proximity and knowledge, the initiatory call situates the poetic disposition with regard to the living. The poet — or, more exactly, the poem — is subordinated to the passage of time. Subdued by that which has a leash on his child spirit, the poet is restrained by golden strings. The restraining order of "Blödigkeit," resolves Benjamin, has become the authentic disposition of the poet ("die eigentliche Haltung des Dichters").[16] The poet's bearing places him in the midst of life, among the living. But this emplacement denucleates the poet, who has nothing left, no core, no boundary other than formless being, utter passivity ("das reglose Dasein, die völlige Passivität" [2(1): 125]). Such self-emptying, according to Benjamin, is the essence of courage: being capable of complete surrender. "Capable" perhaps continues to hold onto an element of cognition. The poet yields entirely, giving in to sheer relatedness ("als sich ganz hinzugeben der Beziehung" [2(1): 125]). Relatedness begins and ends with the poet — or, rather, the poem. For in this extreme inclination of surrender, the poet and poem are no longer separate ("Dichter und Gesang sind im Kosmos des Gedichts nicht unterschieden" [2(1): 125]). The poet (poem) is nothing more than the boundary set against life, pure indifference, the untouchable center of all relations. The poet is not a figure but the principle of figuration. Coming out from under "Blödigkeit," the poet is a suspension, a caesura, a dead and dumb center without a core. Poetic courage consists in taking the step toward this exposition, that of pure exposure ("only step / Naked into life" [1:22]).

If the poet needs to be coaxed in the direction of the living and is shown to be tempted by temporality to the extent that it ensures passage and passing, this in part is due to the fact that the inaugural recession marked by the poem as it exhorts, invites, pushes toward the living, begins in nonlife. The extreme passivity, the near stupor characteristic of the poetic disposition, situates it dangerously close to the side of depletion and even death, which is why the poet has to be roused and jump-started with the deceptive promise: "Then just wander forth defenseless / Through life and have no care!" ("The Poet's Courage" 1:21); "Therefore, my genius, only step / Naked into life, and have no care!" ("Timidity" 1:22).[17] Poetic spirit is invited to enter life without defense or care, nakedly, to a warlike beat, following an order issued from another topos of self: "*Drum!*" In the second version, the poet, split in two, self-addresses the spirit or genius (*Genius*) who subsists in Blödigkeit. The poet ventures forth undefended, brave, like Wordsworth's Idiot Boy, whose adventure takes him through an unnarratable safety zone where, inexplicably immunized and protected, he has encountered the greatest danger.

The gesture of traversing peril and running a risk — a risk that does not know and cannot tell where it's going — points in these poems not to a morph of the action hero, quick and present to the task, sure of aim, but to the depleted being, held back by fear or indifference (we are never sure which), a being from the start stupefied, nonpresent — "not all there." No one has been able to account for that which is missing, not there, in poetic origination, but the poets have in their way avowed the secret experience of stupidity, the innate experience of writing (henceforth not simply innate since stupidity names a structure of exposure), and have left it concealed in the open space of a title, a mantelpiece, like a purloined letter. When Rilke titled his poem "Das Lied des Idioten," he made the uncomfortable particular of idiocy a matter of poeticity, as if each song, each poem were the song of an idiot, in this case one signed by Rilke, who sang "The Song of the Idiot." What has been blithely called the poetic act is retracted, drained. The idiot does not act in a recognizably willful way: stifled and disfigured, he forecasts inaudible acts of sheer, mute poeticity.

Of course, literature has found other ways of divulging its secret without necessarily headlining idiot relations and stupid remainders. Henry James, writer of secrecy, has a good deal to say about stupidity but even more about intelligence. In an essay on Maurice Blanchot and James, Pierre Alferi writes of the incommunicable secret of intelligence in the novels of James and, in particular, of the figure of the idiot Gilbert Long, in *The Sacred Fount*, whose unexplained surge of intelligence lays everyone to waste.[18] There is a kind of hydraulic system at work here, for Long receives only to the degree that May Server is completely drained of intelligence, leaving the shell of a zombie where she once flourished. Stupidity vampirizes; it can zap your girlfriend, finish off your lover, blunt your teacher. "He was stupid, in fact, and in that character had no business at Newmarch; but he had also, no doubt, his system, which he applied without discernment."[19] In James, sovereign intelligence serves to promote life. A supreme form of life, it quickens the beat of temporality and, when socially converted, accelerates time, permanently metamorphosing wit and repartee, improvising rhythmically on the infinite conversation. Intelligence, quick and alert, ever productive of acts of presence and associated with presence of mind, does not, in James's work, allow itself to be confounded with presence. By virtue of the theme and performance of subtlety, intelligence presents itself in the modality of a particular absence, that of reserve. Even as it accelerates the collective critical sensibility, reserve puts on the brakes. Avoiding revelation, it punctuates texts in which occur events whose causes cannot be known. Reserve holds up the other side of nonknowing, simulating a sense of depth or reticence. Stupidity, on the other hand, tends to sever with the illusion of depth and the marked withdrawal, staying with the shallow imprint. Unreserved, stupidity exposes while intelligence hides.

If stupidity were that simple — if stupidity were that stupid — it would not have traded depths for the pits and acted as such a terror for Roland Barthes or Robert Musil or preschoolers. (The little ones receive their first interdictory instruction when told that they musn't call anyone "stupid" — the ur-curse, the renunciation of which primes socialization in this culture.) It is not always at odds with intelligence but can operate a purposeful exchange with its traits, as in the case of Gilbert Long or of any number of high scorers on the standardized tests of social communion. Intelligence itself depends on a withholding pattern that in some cases matches the irremediable reluctance of the stupid. For its part, stupidity can body-snatch intelligence, disguise itself, or, indeed, participate in the formation of certain types of intelligence with which it tends to be confused. For the writer, the problem of stupidity occupies a place of deliberate latency; ever on the prowl for your moment of greatest vulnerability, it prepares another sneak attack. Unless you really know what you're doing — and then it's in your face, all over you, in fact, showing no pity. It seizes your autobiographical effort, taking the place of your "I," henceforth enfeebled, dominated by shame. Thus Barthes, delicate and watchful, writes of himself when he's on himself in the third person: "It is curious that an author, having to speak about himself, is so obsessed by Stupidity, as though it were the inner thing he most feared: threatening, ever ready to burst out, to assert its right to speak (why shouldn't I have the right to be stupid?); in short, The Thing." Attempting to exorcise it, Barthes, in his Lacanian phase of dreading the Thing, plays the fool: "He puts himself inside it. . . . In a sense this whole little book, in a devious and naive way, plays with stupidity — not the stupidity of others (that would be too easy), but that of the subject *who is about to write*. What first comes to mind is stupid."[20] If Barthes puts himself in the third person, then stupidity is the first person, what happens first, what has happened agelessly, at the time, which is all the time, when the subject is about to write, endeavoring symbolically to repair the lesion induced by the Thing.

Stupidity is so radically, pervasively inside ("threatening to burst out," Barthes "puts himself inside it"), that it is prior to the formation of the subject. Flaubert, the other subject ever about to write, recognized writing as "l'acte pur de bêtise," arguing that writing was always an immersion in stupidity. So what's new? We suffer from only one thing, Flaubert has decisively asserted, la bêtise — an insight and experience that Barthes repeats and repeats.[21] Stupidity, the indelible tag of modernity, is our symptom. Marking an original humiliation of the subject, stupidity resolves into the low-energy, everyday life trauma with which we live. It throws us. Following Barthes, it functions as the Thing to the extent that it wards off the symbolization that it also demands. Like life itself, stupidity, according to Flaubert, cannot be summed up or properly understood but resembles a natural object — a stone or a mountain. One cannot understand a stone or a mountain, or offer a critique or a twelve-step program to change their descriptions.[22]

Of the ending of Candide, Flaubert remarks: "That tranquil conclusion, stupidity 'like life itself' is for me the striking proof of Voltaire's genius. Neither melodrama nor synthesis, neither tragedy nor success, the ending is calm and even mediocre. Tailing off, explicitly rejecting reflections on the final state of affairs, it asserts its own reality and stops there, 'stupid like life itself.'"[23] What kind of a life is this? It is life neither assessed by the delicate instruments of evaluation monitored by

Nietzsche or James, equal to measuring the forces of vitality and future, nor simply a life force that Nietzsche would shake off as decadent. Positioned as caesura — the hesitation between life viewed as vitality or descent — it pinpoints stupidity as a foreign body that can be neither fully repelled nor successfully assimilated. Flaubert explores stupidity as a gratuitous if inerasable inscription that tags our bodies and is scratched on memorializing monuments. His striking example, recounted in his letters, of the superficiality and shallowness, the surface scripture of stupidity's etch-a-sketch tracings, involves the stubborn ubiquity of graffiti. Subway graffiti is (or was) one thing. Signing a subway surface does not operate the sublime in the same way as would the alien signature on an ancient monument. Flaubert's trip to the Orient was nearly derailed by this other experience of graffiti. What could be more stupid than the *bêtise sublime* of carving one's name in huge letters on Pompey's column? "The name itself — 'Thompson' — is quite meaningless," writes Culler, "yet it stares one imperiously in the face, looms before one as a surface which one does not know how to deal with."[24] Flaubert complains: "It can be read a quarter of a league away. There is no way to see the column without seeing the name 'Thompson' and consequently without thinking of Thompson."[25] Well, how stupid is that? This Thompson fellow got Gustave Flaubert to think of him and to re-immortalize the name by pasting it onto his columns. "This idiot has become part of the monument and perpetuates himself with it" (2:243), the monumental Flaubert writes. Flaubert sizes up the situation: "Not only that, he overwhelms it by the magnificence of his gigantic letters" (2:243). The industrial-size signature attests to the "serenity" of stupidity. Uninhibited by the grandeur of the desecration, Thompson, another kind of orientalist, changed the nature of the column: signed and delivered a blow by the history of vandalism, the violence of appropriation — delivered, that is, to history — it has now become a monument to stupidity.

The story calcifies. Flaubert himself is medused and petrified: he turns stupidity into stone ("Elle est de la nature du granit, dure et résistante" [2:243]). Stupidity has supplanted the monolith. In keeping with Flaubert's excremental politics (in his works and letters, beginning with the "Éloge de la constipation," he was alert to such bodily functions), "Thompson" is seen to have left a huge turd where a monument once stood. As remainder and hieroglyph, "Thompson" has left the column behind, transfigured, resistant, suffering only this sign of its defeat by stupidity. Parasitizing the Egyptians, this self-magnifying

Thompson signs up the ageless monument for his own little tourist's sense of time and place and manages still, if inadvertently, to hitch a ride with the corpses of the pharoahs. It is not only that this Thompson nobody, bloated and self-important, felt that his name deserved to be brandished, mummified, sculpted upon the unreadable meaning of the column but that the gigantic lettering imposes itself with certitude, an early John Hancock of righteous insistence. In his letter of June 26, 1852, Flaubert was to write: "l'on meurt presque toujours dans l'incertitude de son propre nom, à moins d'être un sot" (1:442). Unless one is a complete jerk, one leaves this earth insecure over one's name: one remains stupid about its destination. Thompson, his name was secured 4-ever.

Now the story of Thompson's signature, of what happened when Mr. Thompson, on that day, passed into perpetuity, cannot be restricted in range or significance to the status of example or anecdote, a parable in which the column would be left standing. In a rigorous sense, Thompson did pull the column from a context it might have enjoyed without his appropriative signature. It is as though the signing, a synecdoche of stupidity, defacing the memorial, had unstoppable consequences. Henceforth the monument essentially attributes stupidity and, for Flaubert at least, will have always been its attribute: Thompson has effected a substantiation of the attribute, for there is no stupidity without monument. Flagging the ancient monument, he answered a call that was not put out. The naïve and insolent arrogance that consists in responding where no response is invited is an effect of monumental arrogance. Derrida writes parenthetically, as if to counterbalance the offending gesture with discretion: "(and for Flaubert, stupidity is always monumental, equal in size to a stone monument covered with inscriptions)."[26]

Acts of responding where no response is called for, whether by carving huge childlike letters into an Alexandrian column or, in the same neighborhood, answering the call of God as if you were the one being summoned (Kafka's Abraham) — these are reflexes of stupidity. In such instances, responding to a call that was not made — but how, precisely, can we know? — demarcates in Flaubert the action zone of stupidity, announcing a type of disaffirming intervention. It consists of that which is uncalled for, the performance of a colossal blunder. This is where Kafka comes in, for he explores with relentless precision the predicament of the one who thinks the call was meant for him. Abraham, primal father, turns into a kind of Thompson who has imposed his name in an act of monumental error. Recalling Dostoevsky's treatment of a crucial facet of Christ, Kafka turns the figure of Abraham toward its ridiculous origins, one name on the pillar commemorating a shared past. These unforgettable names, associated with the greatest acts of submission and returning untraceable calls, have muscled their way into our historical memory. In the hands of Dostoevsky and Kafka, followers of Christ and Abraham become what Erasmus called "foolosophers."[27]

Anyone coming up against the pervasive power of stupidity risks being turned into a foolosopher; even, we think, the thinker's poet, the formidable *Dichter des Denkers*, Hölderlin, succumbed to such thoroughgoing abasement. Indeed, nearly anyone who has become fatefully entangled with the nonthought or paraconcept or quasi transcendental of the ur-signifier Stupidity has had to invent apotropaic rituals in order to hold off the megadeath promised by the unseizable term. Dangerous and obscene, ridiculous, laughable, attribute of power and monument, accomplice to abuse and cruelty, the pride of humiliation, stupidity is the name that spells out the ruination of any monument, just as the monument was ruined for Flaubert by "Thompson," where the name mourns the thing. In this version of the crumble, the temple was not destroyed by Sampson or even by the winds of God's wrath but by the stain of stupidity, the excremental trace imperturbably bequeathed to eternity. The monument falls to pieces under the weight of that stain. Flaubert concludes the unconcludable episode: "Stupidity is something unshakeable. Nothing attacks it without breaking itself against it. It is of the nature of granite, hard and resistant."[28]

The danger at hand, stated and restated by the texts under consideration, appears to consist in the fear of breaking apart, raising the threat of pulverization that befalls those who would attack the mighty forces of stupidity. This is why Barthes calls stupidity the Thing — the core recalcitration against which any writing breaks open. The Thing does not pull *Dasein* together but confronts it with the fear and fantasy of morcellation. Before its looming aggression even the toughest cookies crumble.

Strangely enough, in many of the texts devoted to the installation of the semantic chain generating stupidity, idiocy, imbecility, puerility, the ridiculous, and so on, there appears at the head of the line of fire the almost requisite figure of a German — the inexorable buffo of the whole dossier. Associated with study and strain, the German gets the lowest grades, earning the highest visibility in the world-historical chronicle of stupidity. Naturally, I will not fail to track this phenomenal deformation of spirit. After all, the word *Dummkopf* needs no subtitle. Flaubert, for instance, presses into literary service a German mathematician — the emblem of serious intellectual effort. In the first *Education sentimentale* we find "Shahutsnischbach . . . [who] was always working at mathematics, mathematics were consuming his life, he understood nothing about them. Never had M. Renaud had a more studious or stupid young man."[29]

And so we go to war.

Extreme yet ordinary, the forces of stupidity press forward a mirage of aggression, a front without limits. As part of his body of early works entitled *Rhapsodies*, the German Romantic writer Jean Paul wrote "Von der Dumheit," a short article that belongs thematically to the context decisively marked by Friedrich Schlegel's essay on unintelligibility but is inspired directly by the works of Pope and Erasmus.[30] This particular piece justifies its necessity by stating that the greatest minds have touched on the problem of stupidity, but they have done so in infuriatingly soft tones. Jean Paul's task, as he sees it, is to proceed brutally and take down stupidity's empire. The righteous tone that he strikes is justified by the claim that the stupid have been conducting covert operations to smash the forces of the smart. He declares war on them. While the situation is diagnosed by Jean Paul as one of war, the sides that are drawn up do not appear to be entirely stable. Nevertheless, taking aim, the author generates politicized battles around a rhetoric of warfare according to which the stupid are isolated as indefensible. If they take no prisoners, they take some pleasure. We are shown that the dummkopf's pleasure consists in attacking enlightened minds.[31] These attack-happy imbeciles pose a problem because greatness has been toppled not by greatness but by intellectual dwarfs. Such creatures, who never stand alone, move in group formation, stimulating one another to wage war against those who are smart.[32] Gathered into an insipid group, the stupid, a band of thugs, begin to resemble the armies of *ressentiment* raised later on by Nietzsche. The noble or the smart ones — the strong who turn out to be the most vulnerable — are felled by what amounts to the incessant mosquito-biting binges of the stupid.[33] Greatness should not scorn stupidity, writes Jean Paul, because although stupidity does not deploy the strength of elephants, like termites it secretly eats through the throne of loftiness until it crashes and crumbles. Was Olavides crushed by a second Olavides? No, by the Holy Inquisition.

Stupidity is an engagement, a condition of war to which those who are not stupid turn a blind eye: they fail to see the devastation wrought by the blind pilots of the stupid revolution, a permanent revolution. Interestingly, stupidity acquires definition in Jean Paul's work owing to its reactionary cast. It has been from the start a political problem hailing from Father. Incapable of renewal or overcoming, the stupid subject has low Oedipal energy: he has held onto the ideas, the relics and dogmas transmitted in his youth by his father. Unwilling to have surpassed and suppressed the father, the stupid one stays on the side of death: his head, limited and dead, reflects a heart equally dead, small.[34] Those who are allied with stupidity — that is, with the father, according to Jean Paul — fight with patriotic fervor for preserving the inherited legacy of their forefathers, deploying all possible weapons of malice and stupidity to ward off the enemies of ancestral rights. Thus every new discovery robs the stupid of their certainty, peace, and pride, destroying the edifice of their knowledge and arming (*wafnet*) with rage against the innovator. Their petty spirit is nourished by petty things, which means that large and great things threaten to defeat them. Jean Paul switches addresses to reach you: You may think you can destroy some spiderwebs of the past, but don't you know that there are certain beings that need and feed on these webs?

The dummkopf works only with the known. A mere adulator, a creature of mimesis, he has a passive, even dead, imagination. Everything gets handed down to him. Father has known best. Somehow alive even in death, Father continues to press down on you. Not a whimper of protest from you. Jean Paul thus identifies the gravity of stupidity as insipid reverence, as the submission of those who have not had to give up or separate from the father. In an acute sense Father lies buried in the imagination, which has been bowed by the burden of the dead. The dummkopf works with what is known because what is known, or what comes down to us as knowable, is already dead, DOA. He is himself dull, half-dead yet dangerous. Because the stupid dummy cannot grasp things vitally ("die Dinge nicht lebhaft sieht" [1:268]), he lacks understanding. Our insight into things depends upon the vitality and life upon which the basis of thinking is formed. The dead need to be thrown off our backs if understanding is to thrive.

Curiously, the stupid subject is for Jean Paul a reader, one who shows more interest in the thought of others than in generating his own thought.[35] The way he reads reflects the country-loving, father-hugging propensities of the stupid. What we may have here is a Goethe complex nearing in the background of the essay's war cry. Be that as it may, whether it's a matter of Goethe or your thesis advisor, you had better get over him (or her, although we are dealing mainly with the paternal fiction at this point). The dummkopf reader as sketched by Jean Paul remains loyal to the text; he doesn't have the energy to supplement, warp, or distort. There is no appropriative drive in the slavish reader, just a deadly repetition compulsion that stiffens memory and blunts thought. If you are thinking that this dummkopf has not read about "difference and repetition," you are right. The only thing that the stupid have over the smart is mechanical memory.[36] They can memorize anything, as long as they don't have to produce their own thoughts or images. Whoever can't think for himself cannot think the other, cannot grasp what others think. For this reason, argues Jean Paul, he turns his memory into an "Archiv der Dumheit," the container of worthless items. The stupid mind preserves — retains — much, holds without remembering. It cannot claim an interiorizing memory or, we could say, accomplish a proper burial, a true mourning: it holds onto everything, neither letting go nor internalizing; the dummkopf cannot keep by negating and transforming. Everything is there, Jean Paul maintains, but only on the condition of following the laws of simultaneity ("Gesezze der Gleichzeitigkeit" [1:267]) — a form of shallow presence. A superior mind notices less at one time, but a single thing recalls thousands of others.[37] The stupid are unable to make breaks or breakaways; they are hampered even on a rhetorical level, for they cannot run with grammatical leaps or metonymical discontinuity. They are incapable of referring allegorically or embracing deferral.

A faithful reader, the one whom Jean Paul designates as stupid and who offers only faithful renditions of the past, acts in the realm of hypocrisy, which is to say, within the restrictive parameters of sanctioned religion. The painfully stupid sensibility is a religious one that for Jean Paul is suffused with superstition and prejudice. In this essay he dodges a struggle with the more difficult implications of religion and its pronounced predilection for simplicity of mind — we find this struggle raging in Dostoevsky, for whom Christ was necessarily ridiculous, rigorously an idiot, an emanation of sacred stupidity — but stays on the boundary of an unambiguous battle, goaded on by "the image of the stupid Holy One" ("das Bild des dummen Heiligen" [1:274]). The rhapsodic Jean Paul is no fool for Christ, as many late Romantics would become (his later works, such as the famous "Speech of the Dead Christ from Heaven That There Is No God," agonize over the abuses of Christianity in a manner preannouncing Dostoevsky).[38] Closer to Nietzsche in the way he cites Christianity in this text, he sees the stupid as having inherited the earth and showing all the signs of power: they have the positions, they hold the power while the refined and smart and thoughtful are piss poor.[39] The brotherhood of dunces has planted itself firmly in a pragmatic world that undermines the fragile nobility of intelligence. The pledges reward one another, promoting the causes of planetary mediocrity. Adding insult to injury, the order of the dunces has banished anyone who would be enlightened enough to become a rebel in the placid domains of asses.[40] Nietzsche's zoomorphs are beginning to show up on the radar.

There is one more thing, one more problem. The stupid cannot see themselves. No mirror yet has been invented in which they might reflect themselves. They ineluctably evade reflection. No catoptrics can mirror back to them, the shallowest, most surface-bound beings, the historical disaster that they portend. The declaration of war concludes with this polished shield, brandished by Jean Paul, in the figure of mirrors. The author soon gets lost in the impossible mirroring that his text projects, however. He registers a loss, acknowledging confusion, but pins it on the stupid: "One has been mistaken — the mirror has been there all along — first, give the stupid one eyes to look into it, that is make him smart!"[41] These words conclude the essay, folding it back on itself or disfiguring the intention that opened the case. (Another piece, "Übungen im Denken," works on the way the genius and dummkopf camouflage each other and ends abruptly, for fear on the part of the author that he may become the fool of which he writes: "Thus I must cease — to talk about the fool.")[42] Reflection turns into reflectors beaming out at the end of the essay. Jean Paul installs a catoptric, a device by which rays are concentrated by a series of concave mirrors and reflected in one beam so as to make it visible at a great distance. Whether a mirror or polished body, this speculum reflects by deflecting, pointing to itself from afar. When Jean Paul asks for eyes for the stupid he is beside the point of the catoptric, which in a displaced way he avows ("— Man irt sich —" [2:275]). The stupid could be made smart (Whom is the nonreligious author addressing? beseeching?) with the donation of eyes. As for his own gaze, has it not been averted? Jean Paul is himself looking away, and not at himself — so, according to the beam logic, he may be in the spotlight, being mirrored, since his gaze is at no point secured as a self-reflective one.

More troubling than the fact that the catoptric cancels any type of self-reflection is the way it makes the essay end, as often does a certain genre of horror films, by collapsing the distance it was supposed to warrant and turning the narrated tide of events stealthily against the safe homecoming of the endangered hero. What does the end of the essay show, despite itself, but that the stupid — consider the language of opacity and shallowness by which they have been defined in their surface being — are a mirror reflecting us? In a kind of rhetorical ploy of bait and switch, the warrior Jean Paul becomes the specular target at the end of the war he was waging against an alleged other. The stupid are shown to have doubled inadvertently for him, effecting a ghostly nearness of opposing forces. It is perhaps no small irony that the writer Jean Paul was to originate the doppelgänger motif, introducing the uncanny element of doubling into our modern literary vocabulary.

The spectrum of impotence that travels in Jean Paul from the *Leser* to the laser of stupidity — from the figure of the reader to that of the catoptric — points to the beginning of another, possibly "alternative" ethics whose contours I trace. There is a space — more precisely still, a caesura — for which no account has been made, although its disruptive force has been acknowledged in various historical guises. Like Musil after him, Jean Paul felt that he was refining Enlightenment principles and responding in his way to the persistent question, Was ist Aufklärung? Stupidity, which cannot be examined apart from the subject accredited by the Enlightenment, poses a challenge to my sovereignty and autonomy. Where politics intersects with ethics the question emerges of where to draw the line, if there is one, of responsibility. To be what it is, responsibility must always be excessive, beyond bounds, viewed as strictly unaccomplished.[43] You are never responsible enough, and it is unclear whether, like Heidegger, whom I discuss in chapter 1, it suffices to say, "I made a stupid mistake," in order to adjudicate a lapse in responsible thinking. To explore the extreme limit of such responsibility, I have appealed to the debilitated subject — the stupid, idiotic, puerile, slow-burn destruction of ethical being that, to my mind, can never be grounded in certitude or education or lucidity or prescriptive obeisance. These issues are most compellingly addressed by the troubled writer Fyodor Dostoevsky, whose acute sense of answering for the other is frequently invoked by Emmanuel Levinas: "We are all responsible for everyone else — but I am more responsible than others."[44] Dostoevsky teaches us about the assumption of ethical liability by placing responsibility close to the extinction of consciousness, where it becomes necessary to ask: What can be assumed by the limited subject? The domain of the human, all too human, menacing enlightenment with dim-wittedness, punctures any hope of an original ethicity that, in the case of *The Idiot*, Dostoevsky posits as well.

Like malice, cruelty, or banality, with which it is often allied or confused, stupidity has largely escaped the screening systems of philosophical inquiry. In *Difference and Repetition*, Gilles Deleuze argues for the necessity of confronting its troubling facticity by exploring the inert horizon of a transcendental stupidity.[45] For the most part, stupidity has been assimilated to error and derivative epistemological concerns. The reduction of stupidity to the figure of error has produced the hybrid character of its bland concept, which is expulsed from the inner domain of pure thought to which it nonetheless belongs. Stupidity, Deleuze writes, needs to be sought elsewhere, among figures other than those subsumable by error. In a certain manner some philosophers have not ceased to mark the necessity of such an undertaking. Philosophy has been asking around about stupidity; at least, a need has been expressed to enrich the concept of error by determinations of a different sort. The notion of superstition, important for Lucretius, Spinoza, and, in the eighteenth century, for Fontenelle, among others, pushed the envelope past what was established by dogmatic thought as a legitimate division between the empirical and the transcendental. The Stoics had been responsible for introducing the notion of *stultia* to designate simultaneously madness and stupidity. Even the Kantian idea of an inner illusion — internal to reason — departs radically from the extrinsic mechanism of error. Moreover, Deleuze reminisces, there is the matter of Hegelian alienation, which presupposes a profound readjustment in the relation of truth to falsity. Neither true nor false, and bound to an altogether other contract, stupidity has no place on the map drawn up by dogmatism — a map still used to get philosophers where they're going, no matter where they're coming from.

Error has served as the compass by which philosophers have driven their notions forward. The concept of error, however, cannot account for the unity of stupidity and cruelty or for the relation of the tyrant to the imbecile. According to Deleuze, that which has made us avoid making stupidity a transcendental problem is the continued belief in the *cogitatio*: "Stupidity can then be no more than an empirical determination, referring back to psychology or to the anecdotal — or worse, to polemic and insults — and to the especially atrocious pseudo-literary genre of the *sottisier*" (151).[46] But whose fault is this deportation of stupidity to miserable precincts of utterance? Is it not the fault in the first place, Deleuze asks, of philosophy, which has let itself be roped in by the concept of error, regardless of its arbitrary and finally insignificant nature? Even the worst, most degraded kind of literature catalogs idiotic blunders and plots all manner of imbecilic routes taken by its half-baked characters or self-complacent narrators; the best literature is haunted by the problem of stupidity and knows to bring it to the doorstep of philosophy, giving it cosmic, encyclopedic, gnoseological dimensions (Flaubert, Baudelaire, Bloy). It would suffice that philosophy accept literature's gift with the necessary modesty, understanding that stupidity is never that of another but the object of a properly transcendental question: "comment la bêtise (et non l'erreur) est-elle possible?" ([197]; "how is stupidity (not error) possible?" [151]). Cowardice, cruelty, baseness, and stupidity are not corporeal forms (though it will prove necessary to read bodies of nonknowledge in what follows), nor are they mere facts of society and character, but rather *the structures of thinking as such*. Reformulating the question of stupidity is another way of stating the interrogatory challenge, "Was heißt Denken?": What calls forth thinking, or why is it that we are still not thinking?

But there's something else as well that involves the thought of thinking as a doing or its miscarriage, and this becomes clear in times of acute political distress. To the still anxiety-laden question of how one could have responded lucidly to Nazism in the early 1930s, Robert Musil contributed a number of distinctive essays, including "Ruminations of a Slow-Witted Mind" and "On Stupidity." He intended to publish the first essay, written in 1933, in *Die neue Rundschau*, a major German intellectual journal he once edited. Although the details of its failure to appear in published form remain unclear, the article records Musil's attempt to understand what was taking place while sounding the alert for the community of intellectuals. His concerns in "Ruminations" explore the possible independence of the intellect with regard to politics and group formation. The problem is aggravated, in his view, because National Socialism "demands above all that the intellect completely assimilate and subordinate itself to the movement,"[47] thus interfering with every intellect's independence of politics. Musil emphasizes that unlike the French Revolution or the Marxist revolution, this German revolution was not heralded by noted writers and a literature that could be taken seriously.[48] According to Musil, one cannot understand the National Socialist revolution by "looking for its sources in German intellectual life." This revolution, claiming to have produced a new mind, was not one of the intellect; to the contrary, it manifested "the mind's struggle with mindlessness" and furnished an example of the intellect having to relinquish its powers. The sinister project for "the renewal of the German mind" led Musil to state, "Politics prescribing the law for the intellect: this is new."[49]

I am not so sure how new this is, nor do I share Musil's faith in the intellect or so-called intellectual, whose stability in Musil's works often depends on crushing the women that appear in the examples he provides. These casualties commonly occur with concepts based on the universal subject.[50] While his sideswipes on behalf of the intellect are of considerable significance in terms of maintaining the integrity of such an argument, they are not limited to Mr. Musil's private prejudices (for which I nonetheless get him). Be that as it may, Musil presents an unavoidable challenge to thinking the depressing conjunction of stupidity and politics — a conjunction that remains to this day irrefutable. One of the issues that will be confronted in the earlier sections of this book is Musil's assumption that the domain of the intellect can be severed from that of politics, which is to say that his work supposes the relation between politics and the intellect is not politicized. Warranted perhaps by the urgency of the situation, Musil's definiton of politics is reined in to fix the narrowest sense of the political. Still, the argument relies on a series of exclusions and humanist strongholds that invite further reflection: it cannot be the case that the alarm sounded against the degradations of totalitarianism depends upon such regressive posturings as can only beleaguer the hope for a just politics. The point to bear in mind is that when politics finds itself in crisis, when it prompts ethical anxiety and goes off the scales of justice, it releases the cry (the *schreiben/Schrei, cri/écrit*): "Stupidity!"

In more recent and altogether different circumstances, Stanley Cavell makes this remark on the politics of stupidity and attendant delegitimations: "It is as if we and the world had a joint stake in keeping ourselves stupid, that is dumb, inarticulate. This poses . . . the specific difficulty of philosophy and calls upon its peculiar strength, to receive inspiration for taking thought from the very conditions that oppose thought, as if the will to thought were as imperative as the will to health and freedom."[51] The beginning of the paragraph broaches the possibility of a secret investment in stupidity, a joint stake that "we and the world" might share in terms of its institution. Echoing Adorno's concern about "planetarische Dummheit" in "Wishful Thinking" — Adorno gives the title in English[52] — Cavell's tentative observations clue us in to a question that awaits further reflection: Given the possible existence of a secret account, a joint stake, who are the secret beneficiaries of stupidity's hegemony? What, in more Freudian terms, can be construed as the secondary benefits of stupidity? Cavell shows rather more confidence in philosophy's strength to pull this one off than may be called for in this area of inquiry — an area that may not be as alien to the effective range of philosophy as the passage indicates: stupidity is not so stupid as to oppose thought (with which Cavell links philosophy). Inspired by the very thing that it repels, philosophy bootlegs thought from a territory foreign to its premises. It is driven by a will to appropriate what, in Cavell's view, ought to remain alien to thought. Yet if stupidity is seen to yield to thought, to surrender and annex itself to philosophy's strength, this peculiar circumstance must be derived from the way stupidity resists subsumption or substantialization into an entity that would be opposable to thought — or even, possibly, to health and freedom. (It is not clear, though the case has been mounted to prosecute such an idea, that health and freedom are the sworn enemies of stupidity.)

The expectation that philosophy can train thought to detach from stupidity has its source in the Enlightenment. The updated version, hounded by war and genocide, reinforced its basic trajectories, and the hope promised by the light of the eighteenth century saw a renewal. Enlightenment principles regenerated, as if the truth of a teaching had been momentarily eclipsed, darkened, indicative merely of a deviation that remained in essence corrigible. The ongoing concern with freedom, internationalism, and "the morality of the humane" that forms the core of Musil's response to the rise of National Socialism is reflected as well in crucial testimonials such as Primo Levi's *Survival in Auschwitz* and Jean Améry's *At the Mind's Limits* (the translated title shows another way of straining to the point where mind debilitates). Améry survived Gestapo torture and Auschwitz until his suicide on October 17, 1978, after he received the Hamburg Lessing Prize. An article reflecting many of Musil's principal commitments indicates in the title — "Enlightenment as Philosophia Perennis" — that Améry, like Musil and Levi, took recourse to the "light of classical Enlightenment[, which] was no optical illusion, no hallucination. Where it threatens to disappear, humane consciousness becomes clouded. Whoever repudiates the Enlightenment is renouncing the education of the human race."[53]

Améry's position on keeping intact Enlightenment values is unambiguous: he puts a ban on its repudiation; and he does not consider how modern forms of racism have been fashioned by the major proponents of Enlightenment motifs. Maybe there was nothing else to turn to;

maybe Améry did not want to renounce one last hope after the violence was done. (The violence never ended, there was no "after," but that is another issue.) Certainly, no one could refute the poignant appeal to the Enlightenment on which his writing is balanced; the authority of assertion neutralizes any critical policing of the effort made by Améry to recuperate something from the collapse of dignity. The melancholic gravity of his adherence to the Enlightenment subdues the impulse to question the defensibility of such an understanding. But the violence to which the world had succumbed is of understanding: understanding is itself at issue. There is a frontier beyond which the Enlightenment cannot go in order to lend its support or illuminate the poverty of being. This in part is why I take the route through the other German tradition, that which opens the dossier on unintelligibility and non-understanding. Cutting through another territory of thought, the tradition initiated by Schlegel's reflections on that which cannot be adapted to human understanding uncompromisingly searches out a language, marked by the crisis of permanent parabasis, that would be capable of answering to the punishing blows of an indecent, unassimilable historical injury.

Is Enlightenment strong enough to contain, repel, or calm the permanent insurrection of stupidity? At this point in our shared experience of history it may be time to contemplate getting off the thought drug, powerful and tempting as it is, that allows equivalences to be made between education and decency, humanism and justice. When Améry is provoked by the specter of delusion and must insist that Enlightenment is no hallucination, we are given to understand that the unpronounceable threat is upon him — there always exists the danger that Enlightenment remains related to hallucination, to favorable forms of comforting deception. In a Nietzschean sense one must compel oneself to confront every mask of good conscience to which commitments have been urgently made. On the other hand, one is enjoined to step up to that which has covered for massive acts of unjustifiable indecency. Often such acts have been consigned in the realm of politics to stupidity — a historical type of narcotic, as Marx observed, involving historical dumbing. Even if philosophy has managed to duck it, history requires us to deal with the dope.[54]

On another register of ethical anxiety, though not discontinuous with what has been said until now, stupidity sets the mood that afflicts anyone who presumes to write. To the extent that writing appears to be commandeered by some internal alterity that proves always to be too immature, rather loudmouthed, often saddled with a pronounced narcissistic disorder no matter how much it makes you want to hide and isolate; or, as part of the same debilitating structure, to the extent that the powerhouse inside you is actually too smart for the dumb positings of language, too mature even for superego's sniping, and way too cool to attempt to put the Saying into words; to the extent, moreover, that writing makes you encounter time and again the drama of the lost object never lost enough, summoning you once more to commit to pointless chase scenes and sizable regressions, all enacted before a sinister superegoical tribunal of teachers and colleagues and those who dumped you and mean-spirited graduate students trying to surpass you, packing heat (sometimes they're on break, but not all that often) — it abandons you for these and other reasons, more reasonable ones that momentarily elude me, to the experience of your own stupidity. There is the additional turn of the vise when it comes to publishing what you write, submitting to a judgment without end. The folly of publication combined with the sense of the utter dumbness that comes with putting yourself on the line — and, anyway, who cares; and Heidegger is still contemplating the line, so what line? — makes one always wander in the precincts of the uncertain justness of what has been said.

When preparing his essays for publication, Paul de Man suggested that he was beset by the guilty sense of watching a grade B movie.[55] The melancholy of reviewing one's own failure to overcome a ground level of stupidity (yours or theirs) in writing has been felt and expressed by any number of writers; sometimes that ethical feeling, should it occur in academic publishing, is miniaturized and displaced to the acknowledgments, where those thanked are said not to be responsible for the stupidity of the work to come, which the testamentary politics of friendship announces. This is at once a way of retracting the debt owed them — parceling oneself out among too many friends, one publicizes the deficiency of acknowledgment — and of allowing space, in their names, for the articulation of an essential default that the work produces and in which it originates. It is as if the Heideggerian conjunction of thanking and thinking produced the necessity of naming the perceptible slump of any project.

Thomas Pynchon is one who put himself on the melancholic line of self-reproval. Gathering his early writing into a commissioned volume, he relentlessly reviews the stupidity of the writer he was. The agony of avowal accompanies the whole introductory ritual of *Slow Learner*. "You may already know what a blow to the ego it can be to have to read over anything you wrote 20 years ago, even cancelled checks. My first reaction, rereading these stories, was *oh my God*, accompanied by physical symptoms we shouldn't dwell upon. My second thought was about some kind of a wall-to-wall rewrite." At last he accedes to a level of acceptance, a tranquility that will allow writing, and its extension into publishing, to take place. "I mean I can't very well just 86 this guy from my life."[56] Well, as far as I'm concerned a blow can be served to the old ego by something written twenty days ago. Even twenty minutes. It is a matter of unrelenting assault and battery on whatever in you thinks it can write and live to tell about it. Writing from Hölderlin to Pynchon, you to me, brings about a crushing blow that comes from someone or something (this is why there is something rather than nothing), addressed to you but exceeding your grasp. The matter of receiving the blow is already beyond your capacity to understand. You don't know under whose command you put yourself through it, whom you're addressing, or why it must be this way. In a Beckettian sense, there's not much else to do but dumbly go on, you can't go on, you must go on. The imperative doesn't interrupt the wave of stupidity but rides it, relying on stupidity to bring it home.

One aspect of the sickening state of affairs made clear by Pynchon concerns the somaticizations that occur in the closeup of stupidity. Pynchon is discreet enough not to dwell on them. I do. Meaning I'm not all that discreet about body's writhing habits or even so sure of the length of distance I have from the stupidity gaining on me. The hijacked body, fallen to the mute chronicity of illness, is one of the focuses of this meditation on stupidity. I survey the meeting grounds where psyche runs into soma, the surfaces on which the borrowed body impresses its pain, leaving an inappropriable text in its tracks. If the body writes — the sweat, the nausea, sudden highs, certain crashes, headache, stomach weirdness — and is written on, even "overwritten," as I argue, then it cannot simply be ignored in the drama of self-accusatory tracings. To write is to take a retest every day (even if, brooding, stuck, anguished, you are not empirically writing), to prepare a body, adjust your drive, check in (out of respect) with superego, put ego on sedation, unless you are a total memoir-writing-I-know-myself-and-want-to-share-my-singularity idiot. As he reviews his writing, Pynchon admits to a puerility of attitude, his capacity for idiocy, and the problem of "adolescent values . . . able to creep in and wreck an otherwise sympathetic character" (9), which nonetheless allow for a certain fit with his time: "The best I can say for it now is that, for its time, it is probably

authentic enough. . . . There had prevailed for a while a set of assumptions and distinctions, unvoiced and unquestioned, best captured years later in the '70s television character Archie Bunker" (11). The arche-debunker of de Man's characterization will have exposed the stupid adherencies in American culture to what readers of an early story would see as "an unacceptable level of racist, sexist and proto-Fascist talk" (11). Stupidity is often fitting; it functions as the jointure of timeliness, marking the failure to produce incongruence or to respond to the Nietzschean call for untimeliness. It is that which arrives on time and in time, satisfying a kind of inverted harmony. In the texts under consideration I review how stupidity functions both to name racist, sexist, and proto-Fascist impulses and also to nail the presumed object of such discursive tendencies as "stupid." No longer merely a verbal sign, it has, in other words, perpetrated myths on the skid marks of erroneous attribution. Destructive and clear in its aim, stupidity as an act of naming commits barely traceable acts of ethnocide (this includes the targeting of ethnic groups whose members are seen as blindly intelligent or mechanically competent — the stupidly clever). Nowadays, even if it is no longer acceptable to pronounce oneself in overtly racist tones, one can reappropriate stupidity, load it up and point it, as do a number of public institutions, at the minoritized subject. Nothing keeps you down like the mark of stupidity. Nonetheless, in some areas of life, it is what lets you get by.

Pynchon, for his part, comes clean, to the extent that one can do so, and offers his apologies. Apologizing, he resists exculpating himself within the performative complacencies of an excuse. He reflects on how we have been kept divided and thus relatively poor and powerless. "This having been said, however, the narrative voice in this story here remains that of a smart-assed jerk who didn't know any better, and I apologize for it" (12). He gives himself away, denouncing the unrelenting puerility of his time, his undergraduate mood, his stances of knowing "more about the subject of entropy than I really do. Even the normally unhoodwinkable Donald Barthelme has suggested in a magazine interview that I had some kind of proprietary handle on it" (12). Pynchon persists, taking down with him those who indulged his stupidity, letting them, as in Barthelme's case, get blindsided by the self-denouncing moves: "But do not underestimate the shallowness of my understanding. . . . I was more concerned with committing on paper a variety of abuses, such as overwriting" (13, 15). He thus points to another facet of stupidity, raising the stakes in what may have appeared to

27

rely on an economy of loss or measurable failure. In terms established by the self-examination of his writing, stupidity issues from an experiment in excess rather than from an experience of lack — one tries too hard, one overwrites; or, in Kant's example for stupidity, one overstudies. Blind overdoing — in Kant's idiom, "outdoing" — steps up the pace of stupidity's tack. Shooting ahead, these velocities point to the foreclosive speed of the overachiever, designating those who travel the fast track: they have created a situation in which the conventional connotations of *fast* derail and no longer support an equivalency with *smart*. Inevitably, coming around a sharp curve of logic, fast means slow. Hastening to finish, achieve, conclude, these overachievers prove that one can be fast and stupid. One can have been precocious, and then one looks back over the record of one's prematurity — and crashes with insight. Of his own procedural errors Pynchon writes, "If this sounds stupid, it is" (15).

Though assimilated to the notion of error and in principle corrigible, the surfeit of stupidity that Pynchon confronts, as if to release himself from the past, functions to mark a historical rapport that the reflecting subject engages with himself. Forward and backward looking, stupidity comes from a past that discloses itself in the discontinuities and breaks of an unfolding history where history has been diminished to the raw grappling — the solitary warfare — of a distressed subject. Very often one who names a stupid mistake or faces a reserve of dumbness, newly discovered, speaks from a place of some enlightenment, as if stupidity had compelled subjection to a strenuous process of overcoming. Hence the enlightenment accent on learning, no matter how slow going. Still, the structure of one's own stupidity is such that it continues to haunt and heckle, creeping up as the other work in progress and threatening from a vague presentiment of the future. No act of will or shedding of past embarrassment can guarantee that stupidity has been safely left behind — or, indeed, that it does not belong to the very core of your writing being. What you risk each and every time is the exposure that Hölderlin called Blödigkeit. As Pynchon sees it,

> Everybody gets told to write about what they know. The trouble with many of us is that at earlier stages of life we think we know everything — or to put it more usefully, we are often unaware of the scope and structure of our ignorance. Ignorance is not just a blank space on a person's mental map. It has contours and coherence, and for all I know rules of operation as well. So as a corollary to writing about what we know, maybe we should add get-

ting familiar with our ignorance, and the possibilities therein for ruining a
good story. (15–16)

A corollary to knowing, ignorance has its own story, a story that needs
to be told, but one, perhaps, that can spell only ruin. Yet, as Pynchon
somewhat paradoxically offers, ignorance is not just a blank space.
While it draws a blank and is *about* blanking out, ignorance, at once
perniciously coherent and seriously lacking in coherence — not in itself
contemptible — downshifts from stupidity in the sense that you may
still find the owner's manual somewhere or, for all he knows, some
rules of operation. Ignorance holds out some hope, you can get to know
it, maybe move on. I am not so sure about stupidity. It comes closer to
Blanchot's sense of nullity — the crushingly useless, that which comes
to nothing; the bright side of nullity is that the oeuvre, its essential
possibility, originates in it: "The lesson is sad, as Dion always sez, but
true" (13).

I have in the past had things to say about writing, the insta-bility of its destination, the death of writing, which I mourn, remainders that I guard, contemplate, introject, and revisit according to a particular mortality timer. Writing has been different things for me, and I shall never really know how to name it, except by pet names and metonymy, by different ex-periences of nausea and mania — a friend has said that, for him, writing is the experience of mania whereas reading marks the time of mourning. If anything, writing is a non-place for me, where one can abandon oneself to abandonment — I, the infinitely abandoned (one of my "issues"). I am al-ways on writing, especially when I am crashing, and stalled in the time of suspensive nothingness, the hiatus, the interrup-tion, where nothing happens, and it is a hollow time, a time of recovery without recuperation. Writing and trauma: a con-junction to explore — particularly if trauma is seen as the im-possibility of receiving experiential markings, as the very dis-ruption of experience. It is not clear to me that writing can be an experience as such. In any case, I always arrive late to its encounter. Today, in order to respond to the interlocutive de-mand, I run after something someone has said to me — they felt stupid. So I trace out the problem and indeed the experi-ence of stupidity. It is a very difficult topic, as it turns out, and it has called in from two concurrent zones. The first was my Tai Chi class in the fall, when I arrived in New York City. I was utterly dyslexic in reproducing the simplest gestures ex-pected of me. My feeling of idiocy and shame before the Tai Chi master returned me to scenes of stupidity in school — and

I suddenly remembered, after all these sedimenting years, how stupid I was as a child, certainly as a pupil. I could make compassionate excuses for myself, I suppose, and say I was an immigrant, didn't understand English, but I was also stupid in math, and I still don't exactly understand plain language, and when someone speaks to me, I can go into seizures of somatic compliance, get hives, hang up the phone too quickly, interrupt the other, not having understood very much at all.

The other motivation for a meditation on stupidity involves Gilles Deleuze. While I was resolutely not learning the Tai Chi vocabulary, Deleuze had ended his life. In the memories and papers that remained, Deleuze, it was reported, had called for a thinking of stupidity: no one had ever produced a discourse, he was remembered to have said, that interrogated the transcendental principles of stupidity. I received this call as an assignment — when I write I am always taking a call, I am summoned from elsewhere, truly from the dead, even if they are my contemporaries. Nietzsche and then Levinas have said that no one can be contemporaneous with the other, not really. So, in a sense, I took my cue from Deleuze. On a more banal register, I had just left Berkeley and I thought I should really think about what that experience had meant to me, maybe figure out why some of those folks and institutions had rated so unaccountably high on the national scoreboard for university learning. Anyway, to get back to him, Deleuze had left some puzzling traces, including what he wrote in his book on repetition, where he figures bêtise (stupidity) as "l'indéterminé adéquat de la pensée" and the "genitalité de la pensée."[1] I've got to admit, that sounded kind of sexy.

There was yet another call, on an internal call-waiting system. It was Beckett. I remembered having read an interview, a pretty famous one by now, in which he said that Joyce tended toward omniscience and omnipotence as an artist, but I'm working with impotence, ignorance. That's what he said; it really stuck with me, in fact, it signaled a stupendous breakthrough. At once simplifying and complicating the whole itinerary, it belonged together with the times he says, "I don't know why I told this story," or the avowal in "Texts for Nothing": "I don't try to understand, I'll never try to understand anymore, that's what you think, for the moment I'm here, always have been, always shall be, I won't be afraid of the big words anymore, they are not big."[2]

The Question of Stupidity

IN THE PROVINCES

T IS UNDOUBTEDLY someone's responsibility to name that which is stupid. In the recent past the task of denouncing stupidity, as if in response to an ethical call, has fallen to the "intellectual" or to someone who manages language beyond the sphere of its private contingencies. At least this is part of the fantasy: consider the tone of French, German, and English writers, not to say certain academics, who ceaselessly expose that which is stupid or has failed in understanding. Locating the space of stupidity has been part of a repertoire binding any intelligent — or, finally, stupid — activity that seeks to establish itself and territorialize its findings. The relatedness of stupidity to intelligence and, of possibly greater consequence, the status of modulations, usages, crimes, and valuations of stupidity itself remain to a large degree absent from the concerns of contemporary inquiry. No ethics or politics has been articulated to act upon its pervasive pull. Yet stupidity is everywhere.

In the preface to the *Phenomenology*, Hegel chastised Schelling for placing stupidity at the origin of being. Hegel, for once, was unnerved. Clearly, the imputation of originary stupidity to human *Dasein* was an "issue" for Hegel, tripping him up, effecting a phenomenal misreading. Schelling posits a primitive, permanent chaos, an absence of intelligence that gives rise to intelligence. Presumptuous man has refused to admit the possibility of such abyssal origins and is seen defending himself with moral reason.[1] With the possible exception of Nietzsche, however, philosophy has generally protected itself from going too far in the direction of stupidity. In the two pages devoted to the topic in *Dialectic of Enlightenment*, Horkheimer and Adorno view stupidity as a scar, "a tiny calloused area of insensitivity." It is thought to be evocative, moreover, of "the desperation of the lion pacing up and down its cage, or of the neurotic who renews a defensive reaction that has already proved futile in the past."[2] Butting up against a hardened edge, stupidity itself has not attracted a hermeneutics that would ensure or restrict its limits. For Horkheimer and Adorno it registers simultaneously as an immobilizing force and as unstoppable pacing, paralleling the repetitive mechanisms of neurotic retakes. Philosophy proper has little more to say about stupidity, except when it's Nietzsche's turn to step up the pacing and offer two values of stupidity — good and bad stupidity, doubling the registers on which it becomes necessary to re-flect the dissonant range of the recalcitrant subject.

In literature, stupidity occurs as a theme, a genre, a history — but it is by no means identifiable according to established or secure determi-nations. Henry James's *Washington Square* leaves undecided whether Catherine's unbounded loyalty to her lover ought to be viewed as stu-pid or sublime. Back at his desk from the Orient, Flaubert famously bounces Charles Bovary's hopeless hebetude against his wife's destruc-tive *jouissance*; the life span of the nonstupid, frustrated and shortened, considerably fades, whereas the dumbest, including the calculating pharmacist, survive. Charles Bovary, he begins by flunking out, but unlike Emma, whose aptitude has earned her higher, if different, scores, he doesn't bail out: slow and stupid, he shows lasting power. Stupidity, though, is not reserved solely for the slow-witted; Bouvard and Pécuchet are persuaded that they quickly have become doctors and engineers. Whether in the precincts of the literary or the psychological, stupidity offers a whirligig of imponderables: as irreducible obstinacy, tenacity, compactedness, the infissurable, it is at once dense and empty, cracked, the interminable "duh!" of contemporary usage. A total loser, stupidity is also that which rules, reproducing itself in clichés, in inno-cence and the abundance of world. It is at once unassailable and the ob-ject of terrific violence. On the one hand, the very existence of stupidity can and must be disputed — are we not dealing in each case with intri-cacies of repression, bungled action, error, blindness? — and on the other hand, stupidity can and must be exposed. In a sense, though, one wonders who would be spared liability where stupidity is concerned. Is there not a suspicion, an anxiety, that you, a fugitive from stupidity, are on the verge of being caught (finally) by some smart bomb heading for your house?

There are those tremendously capable writers whose rhetorical effi-cacy in part depends upon ferreting out the secret hiding places of stu-pidity. The tone in a number of essays by Jacques Lacan is exemplary in this instance, for here is a thinker who is not shy about outing even his own disciples as imbecilic. Melanie Klein is painfully stupid but mananges (accidentally) to get it right. The Americans are hopelessly stupid (ego psychologists). Philippe Lacoue-Labarthe and Jean-Luc Nancy have achieved in their book on Lacan what no student of his would be capable of doing, being too dumb to grasp the true stakes of his return to Freud. To return to Klein's legacy: "The clinicians who do on the whole accept [Kleinian categories] end up — I will tell you so now and explain why later — with a rather limited and puerile notion of what might be called an atherapy."[3] There is something unquestionably Nietzschean about treating practically everyone as puerile and stupid (though Nietzsche never did so — he credited them with cleverness and, at most, with *acting* stupid or like Christians, who introduced a substantially new and improved wave of stupidity, revaluating and honoring the stupid idiot: *O sancta simplicitas!*). Making no concessions to the genteel sway of an imagined consensus, proving capable of catching the other in the act, flashing onto stupidity — such gestures are in some regards courageous and cutting, making positions clear. At the same time, there is something altogether traditional about such clear-cut determinations, at least in terms of the historicity of stupidity. Flaubert codified it but was not the first to think, in the *Dictionnaire*, "Imbécilles — ceux qui ne pensent pas comme nous" ("IDDIOTS: Those who differ from us").[4]

While this entry bears the unmistakable mark of Flaubert's ironic appropriations, there is a historical, if at this point disturbing, truth to the zoning off of the nonconsensual other into sites of stupidity. The use of the term as invective, accusation, or denunciation with referential impact is relatively recent, and in terms of the rhetoric of social violence, the performance of such injury compels inquiry. When did a *différend* turn the other into the bashed, trashed object of stupidity? When did "stupid" become a denunciation? Or, put in another way, why did we begin to figure the other as stupid? According to a pervasive yet subterranean history of oppression, these questions, while posed in their necessarily undignified aspect, inflect contemporary debates on affirmative action on this side of the Atlantic that tend to rely upon the induction of dubious cultural taxonomies of aptitude. In order to do justice to the American uses and behaviors of stupidity, to the rhetorical sedimentation of the term, one would have to review the consistent naming of the slave as the nonhuman, the ineducable, in terms of phantasms of calculable intelligence.[5] What has morphed into seemingly less lacerating assertions of stupidity ("shallow," "airhead," "bimbo," "brain-dead," etc.) belongs to a sinister history, which in part it repeats, of destroying an alterity.

Inventing the Idiot

"The other is stupid": this phrasing would characterize one dimension of the assertion of stupidity that needs to be understood, but it by no means covers the scene of stupidity or even explains the differing scansions of this utterance. For the Athenians, the stupidest were their immediate neighbors; for them, the notion of idiocy had to be invented. Ever since the strategic decision of Pericles, if you were not an Athenian, you were an idiot. Indeed the only internal "idiots" that Athens produced were the Cynics.[6] These philosophers, domestic idiots dwelling in the city, were beggars, tramps; they were homeless and wore short coats. The Cynic tended to act stupid; he was taken for a fool. But otherwise, beyond the Cynics who may have functioned as an urban inoculation, Athens was clean.

Arguably, the Greeks did not carry out a notion of stupidity that would correspond strictly to modern usage but instead formulated only an indication for childlikeness, for immaturity. Evoking a child's ignorance or infantile naïveté, *nēpios* suggests innocence. They spoke, moreover, of *apaideusia* ("uncultured"), or *aphronēsis* ("lacking judgment"). There are figures for imbecility that abound in works by Aristophanes (*moros*) and Plato, who evolves a theory of innocence in the *Dialogues* or in the *Phaedrus* when, opposing the rhetorical pretensions of the Sophists, Socrates, in an inventive turn associating the simpleton with the rustic, says, "I rusticize." Or stupidity gets configured in relation to its appointed other, adroitness and intelligence. This occurs in the pairing of Prometheus and his brother, Epimetheus. Whereas Prometheus is characterized by acute presentiment and special lucidity, perhaps something like alertness, Epimetheus is known to see things only afterward; he is shown to understand too late, and to forget. A thread of forgetfulness links those acts resembling stupidity. The stupid-innocents are those who will eat anything; they are forgetful of return, of omens and prohibitions. For Aristotle, something like stupidity occurs in the *agroikos*, who, stubborn and ignorant, appears in the ethical treatises on the side of excess. Frequently viewed as insensible (*anaisthētos*), the *agroikos* is characterized by the absence of a sense of humor or as lacking any sensibility for pleasure. The *agroikos*, having no refinement to speak of, no sense of the *juste mesure*, is without education, an internal savage. The city, by contrast, cultivates the qualities of elegance, intelligence, refinement. Neighbors and adversaries were made to look stupid by the Athenians; they were rustics, those who were always astonished — or, precisely, *not* astonished.

Yet the Greek understanding of what might be regarded as stupidity, taking into account the historical and linguistic mutations of this quasi concept, holds above all political implications that continue to be

40

significant for us today. Before these are elaborated, I would like to note how unGreek — indeed, anti-Greek — Heidegger's short explication of "Why We Remain in the Provinces" must be.[7] Heidegger decided not to move to Berlin but moved instead against the polis, the city, and its philosophical heritage when he chose the "authenticity" of remaining a rustic. The itinerary of the philosophical redneck is to be watched out for in simple moves that are made or resisted according to heavily invested mappings. But I rusticize — *agroikizomai* (*Phaedrus*, 269b:1). The question of authenticity's complicity with stupidity will be taken up shortly. For the present we might bear in mind that Heidegger only ever used the word "stupidity" in order to refer to his political involvement, his *Dummheit* of 1933–34.[8] Viewed against the Greek horizon to which his thought was tuned, this determination offers a curious turn, though I shall also want to examine in more general terms the frequent recourse to stupidity in matters of theological and legal systems of exculpation, as well as to consider a prior move to the country made by the Romantics in conjunction with values of simplicity to which their tropological systems often pointed. To be able to confess to stupidity, as Heidegger does, indicates at once a responsible act, while it also participates in a Christian type of *Aufhebung* of stupidity. When the Christians hailed stupidity — this is certainly not Greek — "I was stupid" or "It was stupid" developed a redemptive quality: "I was stupid but now I understand (I repent). I have seen the light." Seeing the stupidity of my past involvement in politics, I begin to become politically responsible.

For the ancient Greeks, stupidity cannot be seen as belonging to the domain of the political because it indicates that which lacks politics: it is being-outside-the-political. In terms of a political anthropology, the Greek approximation or anticipation of stupidity would have to be located in the prepolitical, in the forgetting of politics. The stupid one is incapable of living in a community. Essentially autarkic, the prepolitical stupid one is marked by an absence of relationship or link (*ataktos*). For Plutarch, the term "idiot" expresses social and political inferiority; it is not a certificate of citizenship — the idiot is the one who is not a citizen (*politēs*). *Dummheit* retranslated into Greek means a suspension of the political at the very moment when Heidegger offers one of his minimalist utterances concerning his link to the politics of the Third Reich.

At this point, it would be prudent to introduce the problem of *untranslatability* that will dominate the pages to follow. There was already an internal fissuring within the Greek approximations of "stupidity"

— a linguistic instability that could be overcome only by means of considerable rhetorical violence. On another register, the movement between French, German, Spanish, and English appropriations of "stupidity" reveals more than the matter of semantic variance. "Stupidity" resists transfer into Dummheit, just as it can hardly inhabit the premises of bêtise, with its attendant zoology, the animals or animality that populate the few but noteworthy discussions of stupidity in French.[9] Still, on another level, there exists a dissociation of meaning and intention that can be said to occur within English usage, a dissociation that compels a second reading of Heidegger's single reference to his own Dummheit. And here the matter of untranslatability becomes even more tricky, if equally fundamental. What would happen if we were to translate this avowal of Dummheit according to common usage, as "stupidity"? Would another translation, equally acceptable though less common, alter the horizon of meaning? Let us say that Heidegger referred to his "dumbness" of 1934 rather than to his "stupidity." The date remains the same, but the moral meaning has shifted, taking on another value. This intralinguistic twister repeats the interlinguistic knot tying up "stupid" with bête. The difference between avowing stupidity and claiming dumbness for oneself ("That was dumb"; "I was really dumb in 1934") is a significant one. While the disclosure of dumbness leaves no recourse or room for argument, stupidity is linked to an effect of malice; indeed, it calls for judgment. In other words, whereas dumbness might be part of the irreparable facticity of existence, there is an ethics of stupidity, or let us say simply that it calls for an ethics. Ever since the Athenäum Fragments there has been an imputation to stupidity of consciousness and responsibility: "Folly is to be distinguished from madness only in the sense that the former, like stupidity, is conscious."[10] Bearing these semantic oscillations in mind, we must nevertheless move forward with the understanding that the purity of this difference cannot be sustained and that each translative operation converts its other, making the knots of stupidity ever more taut.

———————————

"There Is No Sin Except Stupidity" (Oscar Wilde)

In "Bonheur bête" Henri Michaux exclaims: "Il n'a pas de limites, pas de . . . , il est tellement sûr qu'il me désespère. . . . Il n'a pas de limites, il n'a pas de . . . , pas de" ("He has no limits, no . . . he is so sure that he makes me despair. . . . He has no limits, he has no . . . , no").[11] The voice narrating is rendered desperate by the boundless certitude of the one who comes off truly as stupid. There are at least two moments in this utterance of which to be aware. First, there is the question of limit: stupidity knows no limit, offering one of the rare "experiences" of infinity. Brecht once noted that intelligence is finite but stupidity, infinite. That it knows no limit means it knows no law, no alterity; it is indifferent to difference and blind to hierarchy. But what appears to drive the narrator to despair is the sureness on which blissful stupidity is based, the certitudes it exposes. While one of its forms only asks "stupid" questions, the dominant form of stupidity bucks the question entirely; it doesn't allow for questions about the world, not to mention those pertaining to its own place in the world, in language; nor does it ask how such relationships are formed. Ever resisting the question, dominant stupidity, on the contrary, effaces it with the quickness of the answer. This is perhaps why, trying to account for its occurrence, the narrator stumbles and stutters into negativity, being unable to answer to the walled-up obstinacy of the stupid ("pas de . . . , pas de"). There is no space for questioning and no field invested by the figure of doubting. Stupidity makes stronger claims for knowing and for the presencing of knowledge than rigorous intelligence would ever permit itself to make. This is why, in a sense, tests such as those administered to children invariably belong to the realm of stupidity. To the extent that they demand an answer and instrumentalize the moment of the question, they escape the anguish of the indecision, complication, or hypothetical redoubling that characterizes intelligence. In the instance of producing an answer, the intelligent examinee has to *play* stupid.

"Being a Temporary Shlep or Shlemiel Is a Part of the Developmental Process"[12]

The necessity of playing stupid exerts political pressures, which I shall explore shortly, because, as with Nietzsche's example of Russian fatalism (to deal or not with an overwhelming problem you just lie face down in the snow), sometimes ducking into stupidity offers the most expedient strategy for survival.

But when stupidity is not being played but instead asserts itself without remorse, it paradoxically plays on the side of truth, or at least it poses itself as a replica of absolute knowledge: achieving closure, knowing its ground and meaning, stupidity is accomplice to the narcissism of systems that close in upon themselves as truth. To be sure ("sure": another reflex of stupidity), process is missing, concealment is out of the question, and stupidity remains a phantom of the truth to which it points. Nonetheless, the resemblance is striking. Stupidity never admits to fault or error; it is dependent upon prejudicial entanglements and epistemological illusions. Unlike truth, or the history of its inscription, stupidity does not suffer from its own lack, however, because in a sense it has arrived without diversion or delay. Stupidity can be situated in terms of its own satiety, as the experience of being full, fulfilled, accomplished: *le bonheur bête.* Protected from any alterity, making sense to and of itself, enveloped by a narcissistic certitude that rhymes internally — being, in sum, without a care — stupidity may well approximate a plenitude. It may be as close as we mortals can come to plenitude. Replete in itself, immune to criticism, without resistance or the effort of negativity, stupidity contains a sacred element: it is beatitude.[13] Who would be so arrogant as to disrupt this condition of blessedness with a countercertitude or with the petty claim that plenitude is deluded? One reason the gods themselves are said to renounce all hope of combating stupidity is that it offers no place of intervention that would not merely produce a boomerang effect, returning stupidity to the sender who has presumed to launch an attack against its self-contentment.

If stupidity ever had an other standing ready to attack and contain it, this would have been established when the gods were off duty, in the Enlightenment — the Age of Reason — which targeted its adversary with a steady clarity of aim. The pedagogy of the Enlightenment stages stupidity, repeatedly casting brutality, prejudice, superstition, and violence as so many manifestations of the eclipse of reason. The Enlightenment was a control freak as concerns stupidity but sometimes failed to control even while drawing humanity away from regressive temptations. Voltaire was perhaps more flexible in the contouring of reason and saw, in his *Essai sur les moeurs,* a constant oscillation, a kind of structure of manic-depressive historical unfolding in which brutal regressions would surface following luminous periods of reason. However, certain things happened that confounded the leading voices in the crusade against stupidity, things that would encourage us to view moments in the Enlightenment as the Old New Age.

The marginalization of popular culture, typified by the alliance of nonreason with the work of miracle, began in the sixteenth century. One of the events that perplexed both Diderot and Hume was "l'affaire des convulsionnaires," which essentially involved the success for epileptics of miracle cures inexplicable according to the contract of rea-

44

son.[14] The demystifying power of reason had encountered its limit. Unable to put down or explicate unauthorized healing or the miraculous occurrence, the Enlightenment was frustrated in turn by the rise of fanatics and the pervasive force of astrology, the occult, magnetism, and magical science — subjects that a number of contemporary bookstores tend to classify under the heading "Metaphysics." The ways of bodies, what drew them toward health or condemned them to stasis, largely eluded Enlightenment policies. It was as if the body could not achieve enlightenment and belonged, finally, to another order of being. Not that religion was deemed capable of offering a clean bill of health.

In terms inherited from the Enlightenment, stupidity stands with any sentimental endowment that indicates a compliance between superstition and fanaticism; in other words, it belongs on the side of faith ("blind" faith) and religious fervor. Since religious mania is on a global rebound today, it may be worthwhile to consider, if only briefly, the theoretico-historical links of such a massive disorder within the province of stupidity. Indeed, Christianity represented an entry into the Western scene of stupidity unknown until then. As Jean-Luc Nancy has written in an aphoristic essay tracing the ontotheological modulations of *bêtise*: "The Greek-Jew experiences a certain madness, a demented excessiveness. The Christian experiences the madness of faith (which responds to the madness of his God). This madness humbled the reason and wisdom of the world. Stupidity thus belongs to the essence of the fall and the necessity of salvation."[15] Humiliated by the fervor of sheer belief, reason from the start is toppled by this other logic of a necessary fall. Reason is felled by the promise of a redemption to which it can offer no counterpart, bound as it is to the finite and fragile limits of existence. The very possibility of salvation is intricately linked to stupidity and the fall, which it figures. Christianity depends upon a certain dumbness and aversion to the domain of worldly wisdom and scientificity, a dumbness that it also prescribes. Among other things and effects, Nancy views this dependency as underscoring the modern optimism of simplicity and, conversely, as promoting the simplicity of optimism in our modernity. In the aphorism on Christianity and the essence of stupidity, Nancy cites Bloy's recognition of "the revolting mediocrity of the Christian world," which led him to posit nihilistic pessimism as part of the same historical experience as simplistic optimism, if only as its asserted opposite.[16] The spin cycle turning optimism over on pessimism is uncontrolled.

At the same time, Christian simplicity may not be, in the end, so

45

simple as it involves appreciable modulations of ignorance — willed ignorance, so to speak. If the value of simplicity has spawned pervasive forms of mediocrity, this development is undoubtedly also due to factors other than those deriving from Christian restraints on scientificity. Such limitations cannot be denied, nor can the insight that scientificity, according to Nietzsche, invited the affirmation of intrinsic evilness. Science is recognized as evil, which is why Eve, the first Western scientist, the first Dasein to befigure curious mind, was correspondingly punished. Simplicity, in a theoretical sense, avows the limits of the knowable. It is a term that recurs in the works of Nicholas of Cusa, in De docta ignorantia as in Idiota de sapientia, where doctrinal stupidity becomes an indisputable component of our finitude. We do not cognitively attain to the infinite God. All we know about God is that He is unknowable by us, both in this world and in the world to come.[17] The fiction of knowledge we have produced about God relies upon an abusive figure of analogy. Indeed, rhetoric itself is at stake where knowledge is presumed, and simplicity would be a way to mark the abyssal reliance upon rhetorical structures that support acts of faith and knowing. Suggesting the fragility of the function of analogy, Jasper Hopkins writes, "if we are to conceive of [Christ's] mercy, justice, etc., we will have to conceive of it analogously to our experiences in the human dimension. We will therefore infinitely misconceive it and, accordingly, not really be conceiving it but only something infinitely short of it. . . . In Nicholas' system there is an interconnection between our inability to comprehend God and our inability to know mundane things precisely."[18]

Nicholas himself asserts the inevitable failure to know in De possest: "what is caused cannot know itself if its Cause remains unknown" (11:2.46.13-14). In De docta ignorantia, he argues in a similar vein that "derived being is not understandable, because the Being from which [it derives] is not understandable" (1.1.4). In Apologia doctae ignorantiae Nicholas calls the recognition that God cannot be known as He is "the root of learned ignorance" (2.21.14). Learned ignorance, he continues further along, involves "a knowledge of the fact that [symbolic likenesses] to God are altogether disproportional" (2.24.20-22). Moreover, in De docta ignorantia the infinite qua infinite is established as unknown, for it escapes all comparative relation. Learned ignorance occurs when the intellect, having become aware of its limitations and incapacity to understand beyond a certain point, is less prone to mistake its figures, symbolisms, and projections for anything other than a disproportional

46

approximation or "similitude" of reference. Nicholas cites the divine Dionysius, who says that our understanding of God draws us near to nothing rather than to something. In the domain of the semantico-theological question, the qualities of simplicity, ignorance, and idiocy indicate a studied acceptance of the incomprehensible, of that which cannot be known but only rhetorically figured according to convention and trope. Christianity does not so much perform the injunction to remain stupid as it names the predicament of human stupidity in the face of the unfigurable *Maximum Absolutum*; that is to say, the Absolute Maximum, the "all that which can be," the "that than which there cannot be anything greater" can only be called up by the inherent meekness of figuration.[19] Since knowledge of the fundamental essence of being cannot be asserted without the implication of rhetorical foul play, humans score only within the range of ontological idiocy — even if they should earn the extra credit of becoming *learned* ignoramuses.

Test Case: On Looking Stupid:
"Je Suis Emporté, Mais Stupide"
(Jean-Jacques Rousseau)

Of the trespasses that Rousseau exposed in his *Confessions,* and the purloined ribbons that lace his narrative, the represented anxiety over stupidity has passed unnoticed. In book 3 Rousseau describes a kind of vocational test he was made to take, which, because it was determined that he could hope to become no more than a village priest, he ended up flunking. Mmc. de Warens had talked to M. d'Aubonne, "a man of great intelligence," about Jean-Jacques's prospects: "he undertook to examine me and see what I was fit for and, if he found anything in me, to try and find me a post."[20] However, Rousseau had been put to the test unknowingly, a condition of testing that causes some turbulence in his text. Mme. de Warens had sent him to visit his examiner on various pretexts and under the guise of engaging in idle chatter. While this setup seems to be presented as an instance of extreme particularity, it soon turns out that, for the sensitive soul, nearly every social encounter involves a secret testing system on which one is bound to do poorly. What Rousseau does not address, though it remains implicit in the unfolding of his narrative, is the question of whether it is dumber for him to have failed the test or not to have known in the first place that he was being tested. Presuming an encounter to be real, so to speak, rather than a test paradoxically renders it less real and, in any case, far less determinative than it would have been had it been construed as a test in the first place. On the one hand, a real encounter may never as such take place, but a test is always, if furtively, being administered. Still, being tested is not a good way to meet someone. On the other hand, if a genuine encounter is to be welcomed or anticipated, it cannot share the characteristics of a test. If it is a test or, as in the case of Rousseau, if it turns out to have been a test, it cannot at the same time hold on to its essence as encounter to the extent that an encounter, to be what it is, cannot be programmed, determined, or able to derive calculable scores in the manner of a test.

What Rousseau's example suggests is our inability to assert that an encounter has been a test without dissolving one of the terms. For *encounter* to sustain viability in the face of a *test*, one can only surmise the "perhaps" and go no further — perhaps it was a test, but this is all we can know. One cannot eliminate entirely the probability that an encounter was a test. In any case, Rousseau, for his part, manages to wash out: "But the conclusion he came to was that, though I might not be a complete fool, I had not very much intelligence. For despite my promising appearance and lively features, he could not find an idea in my head or any trace of education. In short, I laboured under every sort of limitation, and the very highest I could ever aim was one day to become a village priest" (112).[21] Rousseau has some explaining to do to Maman about his poor report card, which belongs to a logic of serialization: "This was the second or third time I was judged in this way, and it was not to be the last; M. Masseron's verdict has often been repeated" (112). Rousseau now feels the need to counter the somewhat unanimous results of such intelligence tests to which he has been repeatedly subjected. Book 3 announces that such results indicate misjudgments pertaining to his character and aptitude. Interestingly Rousseau's defense lies not in discovering the hidden source of a true intelligence but in resolutely confirming his stupidity: "I am excited but stupid" (113). Stimulated to excess (Rousseau's middle name), he is linked irretrievably to a state of stupidity.

According to the logic implemented by the text, stupidity finally underlies the illusion of immediacy and implies a demand for the impromptu production of meaning. It is perhaps important to remember here that, for Hölderlin, Rousseau was the thinker of mediation. A hero of the *Entzug* (withdrawal), the more anthropologically fitted Rousseau of the *Confessions* shows the experience of stupidity to be determined by presence, effecting a certain blockage in the movement of withdrawal.

48

What this means is that metaphysics is complicit with the forgetting of stupidity on which it is based. Regarding his part in the Western episode of forgetfulness, Rousseau, judged by Rousseau, is stupid to the extent that he cannot be present to presence but seeks delay and rides the wave of belatedness: ". . . my thoughts arise slowly and confusedly, and are never ready till too late. . . . I have considerable tact, some understanding, and a certain skill with people as long as they will wait for me" (113). Readily engaging contradiction, Rousseau asserts that he in principle is able to offer spontaneous responses and behaviors if only they were not, well, spontaneous ("I can make excellent replies impromptu, if I have a moment to think, but on the spur of the moment I can never say or do anything right" [113]). The need for time out is revealed to be a chronic condition that is not limited to the demands of immediacy or to those of a live audience:

> But I do not suffer from this combination of quick emotion and slow thoughts only in company. I know it too when I am alone and when I am working. Ideas take shape in my head with the most incredible difficulty. They go round in dull circles and ferment, agitating me and overheating me till my heart palpitates. During this stir of emotion I can see nothing clearly, and cannot write a word; I have to wait. Insensibly all this tumult grows quiet, the chaos subsides, and everything falls into place, but slowly, and after long and confused perturbations. (113)

Rousseau depicts the condition that he identifies as stupidity and the subsequent restoration of clarity in terms of the scene changes in Italian opera. Between scenes "wild and prolonged disorder reigns" in the great opera houses. "[O]n all sides things are being shifted and everything seems upside down; it is as if they were bent on universal destruction" (113). The movement traced by Rousseau from confusion to lucidity hinges, rather surprisingly, on a rhetoric of spectacle and representation. At the very moment he tries to describe the overcoming of stupidity he mobilizes the fallen rhetoric of which he was a relentless critic. Arrival and clarity depend upon the fiction of spectacle, a marked rhetoric of deception. Between scenes but within the spectacle, or in the moment of its suspension, everything seems bent on universal destruction, writes Rousseau. "[B]ut little by little everything falls into place, nothing is missing, and, to one's surprise, all the long tumult is succeeded by a delightful spectacle. That is almost exactly the process that takes place in my brain when I want to write. If I had known in the past how to wait and then put down in all their beauty the scenes that had painted themselves in my imagination, few authors would have surpassed me" (113). The destructive disarray with which Rousseau associates his experience of stupidity is stopped "to one's [utter] surprise" ("et l'on est tout surpris" [1:114]) by the commencement of spectacle, that is to say, by the fiction of a totality in which nothing is missing, where the phantasm of impending mutilation and dismemberment ceases. Everything arrives at its place ("chaque chose vient se mettre à sa place" [1:114]), and if Rousseau had known how to wait, he would have been a peerless writer, he writes.

But he writes in the moment of theatrical suspension and has not known to await the coming spectacle. This moment, which could be fast-forwarded into truth as castration, constitutes, prior to any veiling, the moment of truth for Rousseau as inextricable stupidity. A condition that requires covering up, stupidity calls forth spectacle. Stupidity stages itself onstage as the undoing of the scene, when things are scrambled and "are being shifted and everything seems upside down." It occurs between the acts, when illusions cease and workers are on the scene. In a sense, then, stupidity is the irruption of the real, of that which is unassimilable, "bent on universal destruction," the moment of a nonsymbolized gaping. Rousseau does not say that the destructive moment of nonrepresentation constitutes an illusion — his logic does not permit such an assertion — but that the disruptive truth of the scene is succeeded by the production of illusion, which soothes the mind. Stupidity recedes behind the scenes as the illusion of its other comes to the fore.

In the next paragraph, in order to expose what a slow letter writer he is ("... I do not know how to begin or end; my letter is a long, muddled rigmarole, and scarcely understandable when it is read"), Rousseau avows that he is incapable of grasping anything that happens before his eyes — in other words, though these are not his words, he reveals that he is constitutionally blinded to spectacle, to the very figure that stood for the overcoming of essential stupidity: "I have neither feeling nor understanding for anything that is said or done or that happens before my eyes" (114). The two principal faculties that for him are regulative — those of feeling and of understanding — consistently fail the test of immediacy, only to bolster the statement that "I do not know how to see what is before my eyes" (114). Canceling the presencing potentiality of spectacle, the statement restores the figural and fragile aspect of clarity. The present is, in the first place, forfeited; it can never occur as such, except as a stammered and blundering self-presentation.

As he continues, Rousseau makes it clear that there can be no immediacy of perception, indicating that where it is mimed, immediacy is error. "I can only see clearly in retrospect, it is only in my memories that my mind can work. . . . But afterwards it all comes back to me, I remember the place and the time, the tone of voice and look, the gesture and situation; nothing escapes me" (114). The other of stupidity, which Rousseau never names as such (as concerns himself, he at no point refers to any possible attribute of intelligence or quickness or firm grasp of things), is shown to be commemorative, inhabiting a logic of resurrectional memory, of that which comes back to him after having taken an initially elusive route. Conversely, stupidity is firmly placed on the side of life, of living presence and perceptible if unstable happening, of flashing immediacy. In order for him to recover from essential stupidity, Rousseau has had to reconstitute what never presented itself in its thereness: the living logos has disappeared originarily. There is no place for the present to take place except as a memorialized return from which nothing escapes.

Reflection, on the other hand, indicates a certain experience of death — time out — which, precisely because of the delay and distance that it implies, forms the basis of self-composure:

> I can think of no greater torture than to be obliged to talk continually and without a moment for reflection. I do not know whether this is just an aspect of my mortal aversion to any sort of compulsion [assujettissement], but I have only to be absolutely required to speak and I infallibly say something stupid. But what is even more fatal is that, instead of keeping quiet when I have nothing to say, it is at just those times that I have a furious desire to chatter. In my anxiety to fulfil my obligations as quickly as possible I hastily gabble a few ill-considered words, and am only too glad if they mean nothing at all. So anxious am I to conquer or hide my ineptitude that I rarely fail to make it apparent. (115 [1:115])

A number of pressing assertions are brought into play. At this point, the stupid utterance arises as though it stood on the side of deviance, a protest against coercion ("cette insupportable contrainte" [1:115]). It is seen as the response to the violence inherent in the social obligation to speak presently. What appears to mark Rousseau's aversion to compulsion is his own collusion ("desire") with the social police, which causes him to turn himself over to the authorities, exposing himself at the very moment he wants to recede. We learn from this passage that acts of stupidity, which he performs by speaking, are rooted in ethical anxiety:

51

wishing to discharge his social liability ASAP ("pour payer plus tôt ma dette" [1:115]), Rousseau unleashes words that, at best, mean nothing at all. Now, readers of Rousseau have seen this ethical two-step before, in the Marion episode, when Rousseau tries to demonstrate how he had fulfilled his obligation by producing a signifier that only appeared to be tethered to reference but was really arbitrary and accidental. This effort had occurred in book 2. Now we have graduated to a scene of even more crimeless crime, that of stupidity, which prompts a surplus of shame.

In "Excuses," Paul de Man links the slippage that is productive of meaning to Rousseau's exhibitionist propensities.[22] In this humiliating episode we encounter a similar oscillation on the part of Rousseau between the desire to hide and the urge to reveal an "ineptitude." One would be hard-pressed to efface the *jouissance* of exposure that accompanies Rousseau's confession of stupidity. For, like the opera between acts, stupidity — as political protest or sheer exposition — stages, at the very moment of its constitution, the mortification of the *sujet-en-scène* as it comes apart. We learn from our reading of the contiguous passages at hand that Rousseau is unable to view the spectacle that he describes; this disjunction of statement and performance would seem as unsettling as the stage in transition if it were not the case that we were looking in the wrong direction. In a furtive yet insistent way, it becomes clear that the site of the elusive spectacle is the presumed spectator, Rousseau — and there is no more expedient way to make a spectacle of oneself than to display one's stupidity. This is Rousseau's "furious desire," aligned with terms of mortality, destruction, fatality, and of which he writes, it "presents the key to a great number of my strange actions" (116). Rousseau cannot help but put himself on display, absorbing a foreign character into his repertoire of self-presentation and requiring the subtitles provided by the *Confessions*: "I should enjoy society as much as anyone, if I were not certain to display myself not only at a disadvantage but in a character entirely foreign to myself" (116). Given that, when present, his living presence profiles a foreign character, Rousseau has chosen a different role for himself, one that requires him to leave the scene that he will never stop exposing: "The role I have chosen of writing and remaining in the background is precisely the one that suits me. If I had been present, people would not have known my value; they would not even have suspected it" (116). But don't go thinking that, in taking up the role of writer, Rousseau has found a practice to help him avoid lowering and shaming himself. No way. Not even on a thematic level. Having concluded the section describing the analogous affinities of his brain with Italian opera, Rousseau states, as if his brain were grafted onto a manuscript: "This is the explanation of the extreme difficulty I have in writing. My blotted, scratched, confused, illegible manuscripts attest to the pain they have cost me. There is not one that I have not had to rewrite four or five times before sending it to the printer" (113). So even in his absence, in the place where he can assert his value without the tyranny of presence, Rousseau opens up the endless dossier of blunders and ineptitude, confessing his ineffaceable stupidity: "and people find my stupidity all the more shocking because it disappoints their expectations" (116).

"O Te Beata Gregia!" (Giacomo Leopardi)

From the culture that has been inscribed by Marx and Nietzsche as being inextricably involved with stupidity — German "culture" has brought us Simplicius Simplicissimus, the Taugenichts, Eulenspiegel, the schlemiel, and other literary cognates of historical dumbing — we also have, owing to Robert Musil, a number of intense reflections on what constitutes stupidity, its figural status and serial development as something of a concept. In *Posthumous Papers of a Living Author*, Musil offers a short piece entitled "Sheep, as Seen in Another Light."[23] Let sheep figure as a metonymy, as metonymy of figure, so that we can consider the evolution through Christian pastures of this group psychological entity. In the body of the text Musil constructs an allegory of Christian martyrdom: "Heaven's clouds were recreated in the white ringlets of their hair. These are age-old catholic animals, religious companions of mankind. . . . *Everywhere:* When man approaches, sheep are timid and stupid; they have known the beatings and stones of his insolence. But if he stands stock still and stares into the distance, they forget about him" (22). Trembling and nervous, reflecting the heavens but showing the delicate skulls of martyrs, the sheep's voices ring out "like the lamentations of prelates in the cathedral" (21). Stupidity, coupled with timidity, is viewed in its animal-reactive aspect, as a response to man's betrayal and brutality. It is that which shows itself to man but is forgotten with man, when he turns his gaze away. In the subsequent (and final) essays by Musil on stupidity, this scene inevitably metamorphoses into one of domestic violence, exhibiting the production of stupidity as a response, usually of a woman or a politically intimidated populace, to beatings. But in this context, the sheep are viewed in yet another light, with a double focus on their aura and the fearful grouping to which they incline. They are at once, though companions in religion, objects of scorn for mankind and beloved objects of God. But God reads sheep as a figure for man. To underscore the double reading, the work is divided into two parts; the main body of the text is headed up and preceded by a shorter piece, almost a citation:

> As to the history of sheep: Today man views the sheep as stupid. But God loved it. He repeatedly compared man with sheep. Is it possible that God was completely wrong?
>
> As to the psychology of sheep: The finely chiseled expression of exalted consciousness is not unlike the look of stupidity. (21)

Sheep have a history, indeed a historicity, and they have grown to stand for stupidity itself — or at least this would be how contemporary man inscribes the sheep. "But God loved it." Master of disjunctive analogy, God has persistently compared man with sheep, and man in turn has repelled and persecuted this abjected part of his presumed constitution in the eyes of God. The point to be considered here, though, is that God *needs* the catachrestic maneuver in order to love. God's love for man introduces a problem of reference: man must be not man but animal (*bête*) and, more precisely, the most submissive, stultified, and anxious of animals, the one that is never as such one, for sheep do not stand alone or suffer individuation. To pursue the effects of disjunctive analogy: when He loves man, God, as in so many slapstick comedies, actually awakens as bedfellow to a sheep. Yet, as the poet Leopardi points out in the verse "the silly sheep," *silly* comes from *selig*, being both blessed and blissful.[24] This is the translative transfer by which Musil's observation can be seen to be driven when he in turn draws an analogy between the look of stupidity and the expression of exalted consciousness. The cross between the mystical, ecstatic gaze and that of dimwitted stupefaction still awaits discussion, however.

It is an *idée reçue* that the Christian God is less angry, more protective toward his flock, capable of showing more of a will toward healing (though this view can be contested by the complicated repetitions and intrications of the New Testament) than is the God of the Old Testament who always seems to work from a place of lack or need. According to one of the very few to devote a substantial essay to the theme, however, stupidity has always offered a special kind of sanctuary, supporting the beatitude that settles on the bliss of the ignorant. Dr. J. E. Erdmann, the always already Nietzschean disciple of Hegel to whom we

54

shall later return, has written in a volume entitled *Serious Play: Lectures Partly New, Partly Long-Forgotten* of the exceptional protection enjoyed by the hopelessly stupid.[25] Citing a story in which a mother awards her little boy with kisses after he says something especially stupid, Erdmann observes:

> . . . and not only by one's own mother, as that little boy was, but by the mother of all human children was one thus ruled by Fortune, whose preference for the stupid is proverbial. Not with injustice, for it is well known that, like the sleepwalker on the roof or Blondel on the rope, such a boy acts without caution, does not look around at all, and yet often reaches his goal. The stupid are just like children who may bump their nose but aren't hurt; the clever person, however, manages to break his nose while falling on his back.[26]

Fortune smiles upon the dumbbell, offering a supplement of protection to one who, like the sleepwalker, is not woundable. In this regard, stupidity is something worn like a protective device, a bulletproof investment in unconscious occurrences. Such a perspective matches the cliché "What you don't know won't hurt you," in which knowing is linked, in the manner of Oedipus, to the threat of castration and death. The character associated with stupidity — in contemporary picaresque rendition, an offspring of Forest Gump — can serially move forward (losing the braces) only to the extent that he is spared knowledge of positions taken or deeds accomplished. Moral purity, American style, can be ensured only by radical ignorance. The mark of this purity is bolstered, and not depleted, by the citational quality of his relation to mother ("Mother says that . . .") — a permutation of Fortuna who, beaming her smiles at him, guides the sleepwalker though traumatic episodes of an American history.

Such figures, protected by Fortuna or God, depending on who's at the wheel, indicate a certain reversal of Greek values or at least they emphasize the notion of compensatory protection. Yet who is to be protected from stupidity? This has never seemed to be God's concern.

Made to fit the spread of drugs or disease, stupidity is often felt to be contagious. Reminiscent of Nietzsche's contention that the strong need protection — in his reversal of Fortuna, the healthy are viewed as the most immunovulnerable[27] — there exists a fear, documented in various discourses, of *becoming* stupid. Schopenhauer thought you could make your students stupid by having them read Hegel. Rosa Luxemburg worried about *Volksverdummung*, a national dumbing down.

Rousseau saw the danger of becoming stupid in not daring to live alone, by cooping yourself up, that is, in a mimetic domesticity dominated by the "esprit d'imitation." Those who won't live alone are susceptible to stupidity to the extent that they spiral into a space where man copies man without pause. Though initially welcomed (reading Hegel, intoxicants, living with others), stupidity comes like an intrusive trauma turning you into a replicant of its protocols. The seductive zones of popular culture — sports, music, mass media — need to be considered when exploring sites of contagion with regard to the anxiety of being made stupid, stupefied, or techno-ecstatic.

It is said that television makes you stupid: mechanical repetition of any sort can infect you with a strain of stupidity. (My own concern as witness to contemporary social histories is that *work* makes people stupid, depriving them of essential types of nonproduction, leisure, meditation, play. It becomes ethically necessary to find a way rigorously to affirm nonworking, to subsidize rest, laziness, lolling around without succumbing to common criminalizations or devaluations of the logic of other "activities" — Rousseau's *far niente*. But ethics is work, too, so let me just posit this in the lazy space of a parenthetical remark, without accommodating the punishing surplus of terrific labor pains, not even the labor of the negative. The reduction of the human figure to work is to be understood as rendering the human equal to the laboring animal. Servile by nature and affecting docility, work, at the core of the modern experience of alienation, is inhumane and antisocial. Conversely, when at all subjected to procedures of legitimation, play is heralded as work, as "working out." In a restaurant the waiter asks whether you are "still working on it." Disgracefully overworking, superficializing, tagging "human resources," ours is a culture where all too many are losing their heads to an unjustifiable ethos of production. Werner Hamacher suggests that even the concept of "working through" belongs to the uninterrogated workforce.)[28]

Historical-Materialist Dumbing

Nobody understood alienated labor better than Marx. He put it on the table as being, among other well-known effects, responsible for the production of stupidity. In fact, in the *Historisch-Kritisches Wörterbuch des Marxismus*, stupidity (*Dummheit*) constitutes a substantial entry.[29] Without apology or dilution, it is considered a powerful historical force, third only to violence and economy. While stupidity is shown to be vast and varied, it is decoded into a number of components. Stupidity is, however, first understood as that which is excluded from philosophy and its axiomatics. A superpower (*Großmacht*) in terms of the forces determining historical becoming, stupidity is absence of concept, a stowaway on the great carrier of historical meaning. Moreover, there is something illicit but massive in the traffic of stupidity. The state is a pusher of stupidity, dealing it in strong doses to the worker: in the main, stupidity is an opiate, a weapon wielded against the working class, zapping and incapacitating it.

Dangerous and habit forming, stupidity is linked as well to linguistic habit: "Stupidity is an *opinion's established right*. As far as language is concerned, stupidity dwells in the phrase" ("Dummheit ist dann *das Gewohnheitsrecht einer Meinung*. In der Sprache haust die Dummheit in der Phrase" [2:857]). As empty repetition and habituation of opinion, stupidity is lodged in the essential possibilities of language itself. Even though the Marxist dictionary goes on to specify that stupidity involves the repetition of "prefabricated components in which the person of habit, the consumer, is at home" (2:857) — and which act of language is not caught up in such repetition or similar housing projects? — it locates the inescapability of stupidity in language and time. This structural necessity does not, however, correspond to the marked intention of the lengthy entry, which argues more explicitly that, for Marx, stupidity consists in the "inability to perform dialectics" ("Unfähigkeit zur Dialektik" [2:859]) in the historical materialist sense.

Marx's *Dummheit* detectors had been installed at least since he was a teenager, it appears, and served to radicalize his sensibility. When he was nineteen, he dedicated an epigram to his father: "In its easy chair, comfortably stupid, / Sits without a sound, the German public" ("In seinem Sessel, behaglich dumm / Sitzt schweigend das deutsche Publikum" [2:859]). Or, more freely translated: "Wrapped in their coziness, / Their comfort without bound, / Germans are so prosperous: / Stupidity makes no sound" — meaning that the Germans stared in stupid silence at the surrounding political upheaval (little did he sense that they were thus at their best). Four years later Marx, following the traces of Epicurus, included in his dissertation the observation, "Stupidity and superstition are likewise titans" ("Auch die Dummheit und der Aberglaube sind Titanen"). Marx continues: "Where Aristotle reproaches the ancients for believing that the heavens needed Atlas to support them . . . Epicurus finds fault with those who believe that man needs the heavens. He finds Atlas himself, on whose back the heavens hang,

57

to be infused with human stupidity and superstition" (2:859). Stupidity has once again reached the heavens or, more precisely, come down from the heavens as part of a transcendental need that mortals have yet to overcome.

In the conceptual framework that informed the Paris writings of 1844, the diagnostic-polemical notion of stupidity received for the first time a critical economic and political basis. Not only were power structures seen to convert understanding into idiocy and vice versa ("den Blödsinn in Verstand, den Verstand in Blödsinn"), but within the domination of private property, workers produced "for the rich — marvels, palaces, and beauty; but for the worker — destitution, hovels, and crippling" ("Wunderwerke für den Reichen, aber . . . Entblössung für den Arbeiter . . . , Paläste aber Höhlen . . . , Schönheit, aber Verkrüppelung für den Arbeiter" [2:860]). And, adding a new vocabulary word to the lexicon of stupidity, a word to be taken up ardently and circulated among other writers and activists, such as Rosa Luxemburg, Marx writes, "Spirit is produced; but for the worker stupidity and cretinism are produced" ("Sie producirt Geist, aber sie producirt Blödsinn, Cretinismus für den Arbeiter" [2:860]). So while the worker is tied slavishly to the means of production, what is being produced for and on the body of the worker, Penal Colony style, is cretinism. An offshoot of stupidity, cretinism is a *production* of the powerful apparatus of state, an unavoidable value minted by capitalism. If anything is produced by capitalism and its terrific alienations, it is this type of arrest, pertaining to a whole typology of willed underdevelopment, namely, the production of *Blödsinn und Cretinismus*. In a letter to Ruge that underscores the politics of stupidity, Marx allows, "In Germany, everything is suppressed with violence. There is a true anarchy of Spirit, and the forces of stupidity have invaded the land" ("In Deutschland wird alles gewaltsam unterdrückt, eine wahre Anarchie des Geistes, das Regiment der Dummheit selbst ist hereingebrochen" [2:860]). The country resembles a ship of fools. Stupidity, then, breaks and enters the political body; it is what emerges when violent repression takes hold, offering stupor in lieu of responsiveness.

Though Marx understood stupidity as the capital gains of the ruling classes, bringing returns through and to the bourgeoisie, he was never so naïve as to excuse the proletariat from the class of dummkopfs. After the epochal disappointments of the European revolutions and counter-revolutions of 1848, Marx wrote to Engels: "Now we know what role stupidity plays in revolutions and how it is exploited by the rabble."[30]

While Engels, Luxemburg, Ernst Bloch, Lenin and (or rather versus) Lukács, and Bela Kun had a great deal to say about the reign of stupidity on both sides of the barricades, inside and outside party maneuvers and along national political borders, Gramsci focused in on the particular type of intellectual stupidity found in capitalism, where "intelligence" functions actually as a cover-up for stupidity, being part of a dialectics of perpetual takeover. This somewhat Nietzschean insight, where naming is in fact productive of revaluation — the intellectual suck-up and citational machine viewed as intelligent, the whole grammar and behavior of spying and knowing read as intelligence, and so forth — points to an instability in the determination of intelligence. But it also reveals the investment that capitalism makes in its own intelligence, even though this investment continues to be made in bad faith.

Artificial Stupidity

The social rigging of intelligence cannot be limited to some film-noir memory of communism projecting hostile fantasies upon capitalism. For the screening, testing, and sorting of intelligence carries the burden all by itself of a dreary and terrifying history. This is the history of a selective invention of stupidity, which belongs to the registers of social injustice. There have been a few worthy articles devoted to uncovering the sad history of those discourses of psychiatry and psychology implicated in creating theses on heredity and the politics of social selection. The Intelligence Quotient system, as shown in Stephen Jay Gould's work on the IQ test, is based on abusively exploited philosophical presuppositions.[31] What interests me most in terms of the markings and determinations that scar the young student body is the way scores were derived to undermine an entire class of pupils. The grades were construed to show that *idiocy*, in the testing lexicon, refers to the mental age of three or younger; the *imbecile* scores a mental age ranging between three and seven years. We owe the introduction of the term *moron* to American psychologists, who derived it from the Greek to designate light debilitation, just below "average." The term was invented for use in the testing of immigrants and, in particular, for their children, upon arriving in the United States. These morons were also defined as "incapable of dealing with their own affairs with ordinary intelligence or taking part in the struggle for survival."[32] Graded and degraded, the little immigrant was from the start left back, filed and profiled in the dossier of a criminal anthropology.

It is important to bear in mind that the bureaucracy of shaming was based on the ideology of scientific testing. These tests at no point make an effort to theorize or even to describe their activity or to explain why the "struggle to survive" does not belong to instinctual, inculcated, or partially stupid operations. What is it about survival that it should become a matter of aptitude or intelligence? (This notion, by the way, is a translation of the German notion of *Lebensunfähigkeit*, designating an inaptitude for living.) A maddening axiom, when one considers those highly intelligent interlocutors who could not survive even, in some instances, as they continued to live. The terms for evaluating the little immigrant are arrestingly incommensurable. Held back by the projected trace of passivity, she cannot pass or partake in the struggle. Her passport is stamped with cognates of debility. Somehow entry into America depends upon a state-administered *imaginaire* of the stupid. What this implies is, among other things, the degree to which the question of stupidity, a question par excellence of boundaries, is connected to a fundamental commitment to justice. Marked down, the newcomer is turned into a spiritual refugee, a totalized sign of poverty. This little immigrant is everywhere, an extreme exigency. If one were to state in ethical terms the only possible position with regard to this ever-arriving being, it would have to be this: I am stupid before the other.

The Politics of Stupidity

MUSIL, *DASEIN*,

THE ATTACK ON WOMEN,

AND MY FATIGUE

Is this lady stupid? (*Ist diese Dame dumm?*) . . .
But politeness as well as justice demand the
concession that she is not absolutely and not
always stupid. — Robert Musil, "On Stupidity"

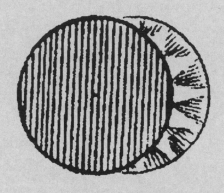

ROBERT MUSIL, perhaps the safest text in the modern canon of German literary works, has been deemed unqueerable, politically clean, a feminist-free zone. In fact, in a conference marking the centennial of his birth, Musil was said to be untouchable by feminists, queers, and politically correct practitioners.[1] This sort of certitude made my antennae rise. What is going on here?

A writer rarely confides the mood in which an act of writing is established. Sometimes the mood, the *Stimmung*, the pitch and voice, remain hidden even to the writer herself, or she ignores a headache and continues to write, or something has made him anxious, which he tries to suppress as he gets on with the task at hand. Or a finger is pressing against her heart, inside, right on her heart, as he writes and tries to expel an invasive sense of world loss. There are also moments when writing makes you high and produces world, suddenly populating your desert with companions and music to supplement the lost, silent one. On what contingencies this inner ambience may depend remains a mystery, but I have gotten into the habit of tagging my moods and monitoring the energy channels as I approach you, every day, a few hours every day, trying to figure you out with unavoidable slowness, a kind of timidity (though it must originate in muffled violence because, as human beings go, I am so peaceful and so kind — everyone remarks on this and says that, given my background, this is truly mysterious, that I must be concealing terrific furor). One day I was on punctual assignment, something I do more rarely now than in my early days of academic *Selbst-behauptung*, that Heideggerian flex of self-determination that habitually occurs in universities. I had received an offer to speak — well, not exactly an offer, because it did not appear to come with an option to decline the invitation. That sometimes happens to me. A more balanced person might have seen the escape hatch or had a getaway car at the ready. I don't like being invited to create a paper on a topic someone else has thought up — it feels like a test — so many detours, failed connections, uncomfortable demands. In any event, there was a conference on Musil. I was to produce a paper on one of his essays.

I had rarely felt so stifled in my freedom as during the preparation of this particular project. There are many reasons for this, and it was hard to write under such constraints. However, everyone has had the experience of writing in unfreedom. In fact, writing may be about the difficult hinge where the mirage of freedom and stark unfreedom meet. My sense of unfreedom was by no means grandiose — there was no intimation of self-importance attached to it; I would say only that the state seemed dark and constricted. Perhaps I ought to give an indication of some reasons for this suffocation in a minor key, regardless of how overdetermined they may appear to be. A wave of anxiety emerged with the work at hand. Once you set about to address stupidity, something of a stultifying atmosphere descends upon you, like a poisonous leak, invisible but severe. Walter Benjamin confronted this problem when writing about war and *Denkfaulheit*, a kind of ineluctable lethargy that limits thinking. In this case, where I am trying to find the secret access code for a condition and experience of nonthinking, I run up against a relentless sense of failure. This has everything to do with the performative aspects of the word "stupidity," which come under renewed investigation in the following pages. In an age where transcendence has to be abandoned and immanence suspended, one turns one's thought toward stupidity. If I initially met up with shutdown and depression, a sort of weariness while writing, it was not the kind linked to the fatigue that figures in the work of Levinas or the weariness that heads up the *Infinite Conversation* of Blanchot — where fatigue is a topos that opposes itself to the metaphysical state of alert, immobilizing the action heroes and round-the-clock, insomniac warriors of metaphysics who, always on the go, form part of a paramedics of thinking, arriving on the scene within minutes of an announced crime or enigma. I used to be part of that emergency crew and loved the rushes that have you writing, running, sprinting under the gun.

Perhaps the most significant inflection of an experience of shutdown can be cast as a letdown that occurred when I was reading all of Musil's collected essays, some of which I savored for their remarkable sagacity and spiritedness, for the incomparable irony of understanding that they exhibit, for the acuity with which they proceed, as is the case in "The German as Symptom." Among other things, Musil asserts here with the best of them that the philosophy of our time is to have no philosophy; he shows philosophy to be a mopping-up operation and writes: "Philosophy has fallen behind the facts."[2] This is where Musil has arguably reached his most pomo limit — where he names and discovers multiplicity, shapelessness, lack of faith, and the condition of fragmentation as qualities of the future. But something else happened to me in my encounter with this writer, and I am the kind of reader easily left scarred, fragilized by certain textual encounters — often whatever a text does to me goes into a latency period and doesn't manifest symptoms (even the Germans as symptoms) for years to come. At other times, on the contrary, it's a direct hit, and I struggle and I stagger and I'm tripped up, irrecuperably tripped up, and I can't get past it. I have to choose my texts very carefully, because in my case, and I'm not denying the pathological implications of this avowal, not at all, they are capable of doing me harm and, at best, it can take a long while for me to metabolize the noxious effects of these nearly magical utterances. At the same time, my ambivalence is so powerful, and on such a fast spin cycle, that I cringe at the thought of revealing the introjected Musil who is bad news. There is the other one, too, always the other one, who will return to me: the good, the exquisite and superior Musil.

The hit took place in an essay written in 1934 called "The Serious Writer in Our Time." I should have known better than to stroll into that neighborhood. It was a setup and, stupid and unconscious as I was, wanting to know everything possible about Robert Musil, I walked into the trap. I know better than to take up with anything that makes claims for seriousness or occasions nostalgia for the *serious* intellectual and *serious* writer — in our time. I was a student of Nietzsche, which is to say, briefly and in code, that I advocate untimeliness — for all sorts of reasons, also in terms of the difficulty of assigning time zones to genuine thinking. "But we are still not thinking," says Heidegger. Nonetheless, there I am, on an isolated corner of "The Serious Writer in Our Time," knowing better, spitting at the haughty pretensions of seriousness in our vocab, but there I am, looking for trouble and aporia, checking out the scene, and right before it happens I'm seeing Musil's take on the individual whose demotion he laments. I can relate to that, kind of. The individual pivots on decency for Musil. In fact, later on, in the essay on stupidity, he more or less says that stupidity begins when we say "we" instead of "I": "it can strut within the shelter of the party, nation, sect or art movement."[3] This is not bad, and I'm probably an enemy of the "we" myself. I am at least very allergic to the "we," in a way that I can't control or say is simply conscious. So there I am on the corner of "The Serious Writer in Our Time," and there are undeniably some interesting things happening. Like when Musil says, "The individual, the 'personality,' the mind, behaved the way the body had behaved under artilley fire: it ducked. It seemed pointless to jump up and raise one's arms to heaven. And it probably really would have been pointless. But what a difference has come about since Classical days when the mind reigned supreme in Germany!"[4] Exclamation mark. The guy really had a thing for mind as substance, as Subject; he was letting it go, though, since it had ducked after World War I. Now, I have to be honest with you, I'm thinking, What, am I crazy, I'm making a fool of myself, I'm like an example out of Erasmus's *In Praise of Folly* — I'm really losing it, because I am talking about the wrong text. So let me rewind and start again, and in case you think that I'm crazy rather than just stupid, let me say that I am following the rhythms of a traumatically induced stupor here, if I can't find the scene of the crime and am citing the wrong passage. It happened in another text, a different neighborhood altogether. Now I can't find it as I'm writing, and I'm telling you this in real time because this stupidity thing has really thrown me way off. Now I'm thinking how stupidity is also a defense, meaning it's a way of not dealing. Anyway, all right, let's go on, it's in the other stupidity text that I was hit, in the ostensibly political one, written in 1933, in "The Ruminations of a Slow-Witted Mind" (*eines Langsamen*). Loved that title; walked right into it. In this essay Musil talks about "we Aryans," but here's what happened:

> There are no two ways about it: either one says that the German Jews have an honorable role in German intellectual life, or one must say that this intellectual life is from the bottom up so corrupt that there is no longer any room for judgment in it. . . . What has happened seems to us unjust, but even if we wanted to ascribe justice to it, the way justice is being used would still appear to us uncivilized, in a manner that unfortunately coincides most exactly with an offense against a morality that has today been pushed aside, the morality of the humane.
> Humaneness these days is a value blahblahblah.[5]

This was, to say the least, a letdown. It all starts out well enough, turning down claims of blanket denunciation. Deftly assailing intellectual life without isolating the German Jewish voice, Musil lends his voice to the cause of protest; the terms of that protest, however, raise a number of uneasy questions. (I was told at said Musil conference that I am wrong about this, that I really don't get it, Musil was unquestionably the best of them, the most decent, and he paid for his decency, and that my paranoid reading systems are way off target [oh, really?]. This makes me feel bad. I think of Th. Bernhard and go on. I just go on. Let them prove me wrong.) I do want to point out that Musil here as else-

66

where writes on the side of "civilization," with its humane society that might be expected to dispose of justice more tidily. Civilization remains throughout a standard-bearer for historical judgment, but the violence and hallucinatory force of the concept are denied critical scrutiny. In fact the induction of "civilization" allows for violent concession, for "even if we wanted to ascribe justice" to what has been described as unjust, it ought to have been meted out more properly, more pleasantly; for the refined sensibility, the morality of the humane should be integrated into the form of responsiveness to the German Jew. The context is possibly more saturated than I have allowed. This is the sort of writing that can stop a girl in her tracks. I had to overcome my nausea. It is not my style to condemn an individual but rather to wonder what made it possible for an inscription as refined, ironic, and intelligent as that of Robert Musil to transmit such utterances.

"The Prohibition of Being Taken for Stupid" (Musil, Precision and Soul)

"I am not very strong on stupidity." This utterance opens Valéry's famous text in order to cue up the prototype of AI, Monsieur Teste. Perhaps we should not be greatly surprised to note that a work so feverishly engaged in matters of intelligence, artificial or not, as Valéry's Monsieur Teste would have no scruples about making straightforward claims for stupidity, as if its limits were knowable, as if stupidity were something that could be declined, like an unpleasant invitation. But the limits of stupidity cannot be located with superior ease. In our technological age a great many claims have been made concerning stupidity; it certainly has been the case that we apply the question of its ostensible other, intelligence, to all sorts of controls involving calculable grids and probabilistic theorems. It is important to understand that our sense of knowing, without having been subjected to a true interrogation of the limits of intelligence, has produced all sorts of pernicious political certitudes about who is to be admitted or not to institutions of learning; moreover, it has provoked a good number of racialist assertions and socioracist skirmishes as well. One need only recall such publications as The Bell Curve to recognize that there has been an indisputably racist construction based upon the knowability of stupidity. The question of stupidity is always a sociopolitical one, even if it concerns the individual; in other words, the question of stupidity is always addressed to the community and never remains isolated with the individual. As we have observed, stupidity refers to something other than itself, and yet it falls short of anything theorizable.

While it has not been a great theme among philosophers — there is no tome that would bear the title *Vom Wesen der Dummheit* (On the Essence of Stupidity) — "stupidity" can be seen to have settled within the philosophical project. Defended against the rents in knowing, philosophers are those who dwell in the problem and live by enigmas; though their tone is often superior, it is in their job descriptions to avow that they are confounded by the limits of the knowable, to begin their reflections, if they are true philosophers, in a mood of stupefaction. Yet this is an aspect of philosophical inquiry that is often veiled by forgetfulness, put away as if a link to fundamental stupidity were unsayable. There would be no philosophy without this abjected and largely repressed condition of its possibility. One could even pursue the point further by observing that the more successfully repressed philosophy is, the closer it comes to the core stupidity. Who has not recognized certain philosophical assertions as being stupid in the end? Arguably, there is nothing more stupid, finally, than Hegel's "absolute knowledge" — a state or projection that, utterly untenable, would require knowledge to be immanent, finally, to itself. Fundamental stupidity has not really been upgraded to the level of a problem, however, for philosophers have rarely tended to address the question of stupidity (it is therefore not a question but strictly out of the question) — or when they have broached the topic, as in the case of Hegel's disciple J. E. Erdmann, their attempts have been greeted with laughter and derision. On some level, then, stupidity has no legitimate status in our discursive encounters. It bears the mark of a thematic scarring that never stops announcing itself.

"Why People's Reproaching Each Other with Stupidity Is So Widespread Today" (Musil, *Precision and Soul*): *The Episteme of the Bimbo, Airhead, Brain-Dead, Hare-Brained, Etc.*

The circumstance of its nonstatus in our "thought-sports," as Robert Musil calls it, carries heavy consequences. Of course one hardly knows where to proceed when pursuing a subject so imperturbable as stupidity. To be sure, one continues to feel implicated in the very procedure of trying to bring this rejected concept to light (it remains to be seen whether stupidity can be viewed as a concept). Yet there exists a subtle history of literary sightings. Musil appears to concur with Flaubert's understanding of stupidity when he inscribes it within the coordinates of class distinction (everything concerning stupidity pivots on the variables of distinction); both ironists also share the decision to position its effects in terms of closure and conclusiveness. Whereas Flaubert argues that stupidity consists of the desire to conclude, Musil offers in "The Serious Writer in Our Time" that art, as a force that resists stupidity, is significant because it "preserves people's sense of not yet having come to closure: it keeps their impulse for progress alive."[6] So we are arriving at some sort of minimal consensus, at least within this community of two writers, on a determination of stupidity (Baudelaire and Nietzsche pose further problems for the modernist topos in the context of art, artifice, and closure). It is certainly difficult, moreover, to speak convincingly of "determination" when stupidity appears principally to be of and about indeterminacy — nonetheless, let us continue these ruminations.

But before moving forward, as if I were clever enough to do so, let me step back. I've hit another *Holzweg*, a snag, that needs to be acknowledged. Undoubtedly one strand of stupidity lacks determinacy. Indeed, it calls up a whole thinking of "in-distinction," of lack of distinction in all the senses of the word: lack of taste, lack of judgment, indeterminacy. However, at the same time another, apparently contradictory filament of stupidity exposes itself and must be taken into account if we are to be rigorous about this matter. This strand draws on the type of stupidity that manifests itself as sheer determination and blind mastery, the false mastery of which examples abound (consider the authoritarian personality of the know-it-all, or imagine some loudmouthed racist — the examples are endless and seemingly arbitrary — for whom the type heading might be the Archie-debunker of the preface to Paul de Man's *Allegories of Reading*, the redneck racist [Archie, not de Man], who ends up saying, "What's the difference?" which I might transpose for our purposes into, "What is the distinction?"). Once both strands of stupidity are exposed, it is not a matter of choosing one over the other; rather, we persistently oscillate between two sides of determination, at once marking both the indetermination and sheer determination of the stupidity cycle. The one has been more or less covered, while the other is the type that says, "You're so stupid that you don't even know you're stupid." The boundaries that hold these moments of stupidity apart are not very secure, as there is an ineluctable slide from one to the other form of stupidity.

Undecidability Refused

On the whole, though, following the lead of Flaubert and taking into account the observations of Musil, stupidity can be considered as something related to shutdown, to closure — a closure that confuses itself with an end. Closing a matter "once and for all," it appears to be bound up with the compulsion of the Western logos to "finish with," to terminate. Even though Musil does not himself explicitly pursue the consequences of the asserted link to closure, it soon becomes clear that stupidity in his rendering is best viewed as the refusal of undecidability. Stupidity, for its part, has decided, it thinks it knows and has passed judgment; it is always ready to shoot, and shoots off its mouth readily. Now, this phrasing is highly problematic and requires that we dwell on its scansion. I have just noted that stupidity "thinks," indeed, that it "thinks it knows," and furthermore that it has "passed judgment." I have in sum arrived at an aporetic juncture if not strictly a dead end. According to Kant, in *Anthropologie in pragmatischer Hinsicht*, which Musil appears to have consulted, stupidity is however precisely that which fails to judge — it indicates a lack (*Mangel*) of judgment (*Urteilskraft*).[7] Where judgment is mangled, there is a case of stupidity. So how can it be that stupidity, on the contrary, is said to be the passing of a judgment, if only an always premature judgment? How can it disclose a lack of judgment that nonetheless judges decisively?

A provisional answer must be that stupidity has failed to submit judgment to the crucible of undecidability. Judgment is not properly judgment if it has not encountered the abyssal demand to which it is summoned. Stupidity involves a judgment that, having arrived at its conclusion, passes itself off stubbornly as a truth. The judgment passed by this type of stupidity poses, among other things, a number of temporal problems, the most prevalent of which concerns its speed. Even though it is consistently associated with slowness, the endless frustration of nonattainment, stupidity in fact moves too fast; fast-paced and in haste, it is always (already) a rush . . . to judgment. To the extent, moreover, that stupidity is bolstered by all sorts of accelerators, its spread undoubtedly derives essential features from our age of technological dominion, which is at all times on fast-forward — a speed that actually proves to be backward. Whereas the architect said, "Less is more," we must add to the lexicon of contemporary paradox, "Fast is slow."

A slowdown in preparation for Musil's text is in order. By now we have run into a number of aporetic snags that need to be monitored and read off as they occur, if only to underscore the difficulty of theorizing stupidity. There have been instances when thoughts were gathered around stupidity, as if it were a substance; I have played freely on some axiomatic assumptions, presupposing at times that we all know what stupidity is, as though it had an essence, an identifiable and locatable site. On some level we may think we could identify stupidity if it were in a lineup and we were called to identify the culprit. "Yes, that's it, there's stupidity — I would recognize him [but more often, alas, her] anywhere." Yet stupidity, while it is everywhere and recurrent as invective, excuse, accusation, amorous tease, description, sport, and behavior, cannot really settle into the place of an essence. This admittedly trips up Musil, for while he begins by asking the question of essence ("Just what is stupidity?"),[8] it turns out to be as elusive as it is somehow present. Even though the question of its essence consistently provokes response, stupidity is basically a matter of *Darstellung*, of presentation, which is to say, of that which *shows* itself as being stupid. Stupidity is that which appears stupid; the double bind confronting the writer, Musil variously exhorts, is that once the topic is broached, one runs the risk of betraying oneself as stupid, even when all sorts of safeguards have been established. Poised to write on stupidity, one must first show oneself to be exonerated from its insinuation; yet making a show of being clever is stupid. Indeed, that which *shows*, as with the case of a show-off or anything that asserts itself to be particularly clever, magnetizes stupidity. And each particular imprint of cleverness always carries with it a typology of stupidities. There would be no intelligence as such, then, nothing that would be spared a package deal of attendant stupidities and their historicity (what was once stupid may now be upgraded, and vice versa). Thus the figure of the professor comes in handy for Musil, for it has been stamped with the twin features of alert and devoted scholarship supplemented by an unavoidable extension into the vacant lot of the nutty or absent-minded professor.

Hiding behind every form of accomplishment or intelligence is the special production studio of stupidities. One could retrofit Musil's insight with the techno-nerd, which would suit the double occupancy of the stupid-intelligent. The impossible boundary between that which comes off as stupid and that which can be judged as intelligent persists throughout the essay, leaving its final mark at the very end, when Musil resists taking "a step beyond," even though he has lingered "with [his] foot on the borderline": "for one step beyond the point at which we are stopping and we would leave the realm of stupidity, which even theoretically has an extraordinary variety, and would arrive in the realm of wisdom, a desolate region that is generally shunned" (286). Well, as citations go, this one appears to contradict what I have summoned it to confirm. Until the very last word, then, where Musil draws a line in the sand between stupidity and wisdom, ironizing their difference, his foot dances on a movable borderline consistently blurred. Throughout the essay Musil struggles to locate stupidity's proper domain, acknowledging that the question of stupidity, while untimely, has its own historicity. The consistent untimeliness and out-of-placeness of the question, "What is stupidity?" is only intensified by the fact that it admits no resolute literary or scientific rejoinder. Barely philosophical, a detached satellite to meaningful discourses, the question orbits on its own. The pointed edges of stupidity as question give it a political poignancy, a different articulation of unstoppable injustice.

Transcendental Stupidity

To Musil's credit, he must switch on the transvaluating machine in order to get a hold on stupidity, if only by threat of dialectizing it, ever splitting its course and turning it into its other. (We note in this regard that in his *Tagebücher*, Musil avers that he was planning to write an essay on genius, an intention that slipped away; we should not lose sight of the fact that he set out on a masculinist track, for all discussions of genius are generated from the site of a spermatic economy that tends to exclude "women." Historically and strictly speaking, a "woman" cannot be conceived of in terms of genius; she can be mad, she can be stupid, and, indeed, she can function culturally as the sacred icon for stupidity — but I am getting ahead of myself, that is, I am falling behind already again.) Although he does not openly say so, Musil has had to renounce the project of discovering the essence of stupidity because, among other things, beyond the possibility that stupidity *is* not, simply put (and simplicity may already edge on stupidity), well, what can be said but that, simply put, in the sense of its presencing, existence itself is, if anything, stupid.

Everything we do can be seen as stupid — that you couldn't sleep last night, that I have spent the whole summer tormented by the neighbor's shower, that you are going to eat lunch, that you are in a relationship, that you are not in a relationship, that Ronald Reagan and subsequent replicants are now said to have had a personality, that you have

72

to watch your weight, that they got away with it, that we are getting away with it, that you have to do things to *earn* your living, that you have to go to the bathroom several times a day, that you sit with the same sentence for several hours — there is nothing that is not stupid, but nothing *is* stupidity as such. Stupidity has to do with our nature as finite beings; it is the limit of the limit — the limited — a mark of our temporal condition in and as lapse. Yet it is not itself limited, touching even infinity (Brecht, you might recall, said that while intelligence is finite, stupidity can be infinite; Einstein added, "Two things are infinite: the universe and human stupidity, but I am not so certain about the universe").[9] Schiller understood that stupidity can affect the realm of the infinite, paradoxically imposing a limit upon the gods: "In their struggles with stupidity, the gods themselves are at a loss."[10]

That the historical drama of Schiller would include a thinking of stupidity gives pause. Schiller's *Jungfrau von Orleans*, his translation of Joan of Arc, stages a figure for the innocent failure of mind that transcends itself in a peculiar way: illiterate and unschooled, she becomes the receptacle for a higher calling. A creature of transcendental stupidity, she is open to mystical ecstasy and the higher calling of historical founding. A virginal being implies grace imbued with sheer idiocy, an innocent untouched by the present yet filled by the discourse of the Other and the promise of futurity. The idiot, etymology tells us, is very peculiar, very *eigen* (itself), existing as though inscribed in a persistent idiolect. Marked by an extreme experience of the *Eigenschaft*, that is to say, of that which is received only as one's own and proper, sheer idiocy suggests a radical property that involves an inexchangeable and unique calling of one's own. Such a concept of self-appropriation that empties the self to which it remains immanent underscores, somewhat paradoxically, what is meant by idiocy — an instance of utter and absolute, if transcendentalized, stupidity.

If, however, you are constituted without *Eigenschaft*, as in the case of the "Mann ohne Eigenschaften," you may well be weird, abandoned, expropriated, even bland and devoid of meaning, but you are evidently not enrolled in a league of stupidity. The occurence of stupidity involves a quality, a trait that is bound up with appropriation; it broaches a Heideggerian thematic. One could no doubt match up Ulrich (the name of the man without qualities) in a dating service with Heidegger's *das Man* — they are only a few minutes apart in terms of their historical appearance — or, even more to the point, the problem of stupidity can be considered in existential gradations in light of *Uneigent-*

lichkeit (inauthenticity), which, despite everything, avoids explicit association with stupidity. In his work, Heidegger never stoops to stupidity, a refusal that seems perplexing, since he emphasizes so many shades of mediocrity in the failure of thought or, rather, in the "success" of technology and the fumblings of *das Man*. Nonetheless, the refusal of *Dummheit*, with the notable exception of its political-autobiographical usage in connection with 1934, remains instructive. It is as if there were something worse than stupid in the bad simplicity of the They.

Inauthenticity is determined by a register that is divided between morality and technology. While we cannot impute to it consciousness or the language of individual behavior, it is, at the same time, difficult to evade the suggestion that the They, *das Man*, is stupid ("*abruti*" [blockheaded], as Jean-Luc Nancy says), misunderstanding destiny, "mediocre" (as Heidegger says), if *das Man* doesn't let destiny unfold and decide its own authenticity. Now, without getting too deeply into Heidegger here (assuming one had a choice), the problem that poses itself comes to this: the "inauthentic" *is* the experience of *Dasein*. Authenticity can be nothing other than what is staked and what is decided in inauthenticity. The They is also a way of saying an infinite, unassimilable, and assimilating stupidity takes place in experience itself. Following the indications of this reading, our question would have to be, then, What is the experience of stupidity in experience? Is experience possible without the experience of stupidity? If one were to stay more comprehensively with the Heideggerian oeuvre, one would have to explore the precomprehension of being by *Dasein*, which involves also its own comprehension or understanding and the understanding of existence as such. Textually, this pre-understanding has little to do with either stupidity or intelligence, which suggests that for Heidegger stupidity and intelligence stand merely as subordinated possibilities of the principal and constitutive understanding of *Dasein*. Nonetheless, *Dasein*'s precomprehension of being is more or less dumbfounded. As Nancy writes of Heidegger, "It is perhaps possible to say, however, that it is a comprehension that is 'entirely stupid.'"[11] Primal understanding comprehends everything; but it also comprehends nothing. It does and does not comprehend itself, tripping up on itself, confounded by that which it is meant to comprehend. After all, what is more idiotic than the predicament of thrownness — by this I mean the experience of idiocy inscribed in the thrownness of being. *Geworfenheit*, understood as thrownness, *is* the incontrovertible mediocrity of average understanding.

*"Among Boys and Sports Buddies, Someone Whose
Actions Are Awkward Will Be Called Stupid Even If He
Should Be a Hölderlin"* (Musil, Precision and Soul)

Together they would have written Das Man *without Qualities.* Beyond
the complications entailed in the decidedly low aptitudes of *das Man,*
Musil's concern with stupidity is further instructed by another moment in Heidegger's reflections. Heidegger has taught us to read an
aporetic pulse that, initiating it, also drags down Musil's essay. In a
manner that has been addressed by Heidegger in his commentary on
Hölderlin's poem "Andenken," we need to consider what amounts to
the impossibility of Musil's title, a dilemma in fact conceded by his rhetorical anxieties. "Über die Dummheit," the title of the essay on stupidity, indicates, among other things, a location, an implicit hierarchy and
a concept of mastery. There exists a tensional quality between the title
and its subject. While stupidity can be viewed as the experience of
nonmastery, the title suspends this vertiginous release by marking its
place of mastering what falls beneath it or suggesting that, as title, it
has functionally mastered stupidity. This in itself is not contradictory.
Many titles entitle and legitimate claims made for mastering the subject. The title comes from and opens a place of mastery: it is a legal institution, and no book can be published without a title. Nor has a title
ever been mandated to coincide with the signified of a work.

"Über die Dummheit" presents at least two start-up problems that
make it difficult to cross over the border into the text proper, unless the
text already has been swallowed up by its impossible title. *Über* implies
that the text is not only on but even above stupidity, that it dominates
stupidity and is, as one says, on top of the material, if not above it all —
it is "*über* die Dummheit." The title promises to remain above *Dummheit* to shield the text or assimilate it to an entitling place from which a
disquisition is offered, pretending to be in a place of sheltered exteriority with regard to stupidity. Yet Musil is rather quick to concede that
Dummheit, on the contrary, dominates us — it's on top of us, crushing
us and taking us down. Musil writes of "the sense of the domination
stupidity has over us" (269). One cannot be or write "über die Dummheit" without engaging the risk of being put down. Thus even the gesture of naming stupidity has performative effects that form a magnetic
field of stupor and negativity, threatening to involve everyone. Later on
in the essay Musil asserts that stupidity has no reference; it appears to
have no simple constative or cognitive basis and raises, if it raises any-

thing at all, questions for the most part of referential doubt. At the same time, it has implicated anyone who would "be stupid enough" to enter its psychological force fields, casting an aura of ambivalence upon reader and writer alike:

> Many people reveal a sense of the domination stupidity has over us... when they show themselves amicably and conspiratorially surprised as soon as they hear that a person in whom they have placed their trust intends to conjure up this monster by its true name. I was not only able to initially conduct this experiment on myself, but soon discovered its historical validity when, in searching for predecessors who had worked on stupidity — of whom I could find strikingly few; wise men apparently prefer to write about wisdom — a scholarly friend sent me the printed version of a lecture delivered in 1866. Its author was J. E. Erdmann, the pupil of Hegel and Professor at the University of Halle. This lecture, which is called "On Stupidity," starts right off with the report that even when it was announced it was greeted with laughter. Having discovered that this can happen even to a Hegelian, I am convinced that there are peculiar circumstances connected with people who demonstrate such an attitude toward those who wish to speak about stupidity, and I find myself quite insecure in the face of my conviction that I have provoked powerful and deeply ambivalent psychological forces. (269–70)

A slight shift in semantic currency has occurred, which remains unmarked by Musil but will grow as an unacknowledged symptom when it steals into his text: Erdmann's text does and does not share the same title as Musil's text, and the difference, ever so negligible, will inititate gender skirmishes of significant proportions. In German, Erdmann's text on stupidity is in fact titled "Über Dummheit," whereas Musil's text carries the title "Über die Dummheit." While the conceptual site may gain an inch in specificity, it loses ground in generality and bears the soupçon of a feminine marking. This matter of the parachuted *die* is one that Musil does not take up but unconsciously exploits when women repeatedly become the reference to the quasi concept for which he claims no reference can be determined. As for the more conscious level of intervention, Musil notes the derision that a quest concerning stupidity notoriously invites.

Recruited to serve as his appointed precursor, Professor Erdmann of Halle increased Musil's sense of insecurity about his passionate venture (Musil stayed with the topic until the end of his days, writing still unpublished reflections on its essence and implications). Why had Erdmann's piece provoked derision, and what bearing will this have upon Musil's project? It may well be the case that "Über Dummheit" the prequel elicited laughter in part because of the inherent peculiarity of the title as it stands, but more than likely it shook philosophical rafters because a certified Hegelian was the signator of such an inquiry. The notorious difficulties in analyzing subtle shades of tone or the graded nuances of historicity notwithstanding, we can reasonably ascertain the unmistakable effect that obtains when a member of a certain school or collectivity devotes an essay to a subject that does not fall within the purview of that school's earnest concerns. It presents surely quite a distinct picture when the serious, labor-oriented, absolute knowledge seeker offers to open a colloquy on stupidity, whose only place in the Hegelian systems would be out of place or, as in the preface to the *Phenomenology*, firmly displaced and relegated to its rank of inessentiality. It is quite another matter when a Nietzsche or a Marx incorporates the question of stupidity into the discursive armory of a sustained insight. The concern with stupidity offers no more than a cry of protest, a shakedown, a philosophical sting operation; it cannot be made to participate in system building.

———————

"The Self-Portrait of Mankind, as It Arises
Unretouched from Reciprocal Group
Photographs" (Musil, Precision and Soul)

For Musil, the study of stupidity remained preliminary and provisional, and indeed, one might offer that such an inquiry can attain only provisional status, as stupidity, having fragile borders, eludes comprehensiveness. Musil's essay is conceived as an experiment, an urgent juncture in a writer's experience of self-testing. It involves somewhat of a wager, a fatal dare. If Musil devoted this late published essay, his last, to stupidity, the motive for such a gesture appears to have been prompted by an apotropaic design. He indicates the dreadful inevitability according to which everything can fall prey to stupidity and become part of its vast production apparatus. There is nothing safe about delving into the unauthorized domain of which he writes; nothing guarantees that he will not emerge as a little Hegelian degenerate. Or that he will emerge at all. If he takes the risk, accepts the wager, it is not in order to take the work down with him. On the contrary, another economy is at issue. The rhetoric of health and disease attends the text at every stage of its development: Musil often gives the sense that he is

77

incorporating the pervasive poison in order to protect his corpus from the disease. At first this may seem tactically preposterous. How can Robert Musil suppose his work to be vulnerable to charges of stupidity? Why would he feel the need at this stage to cover his corpus with a logic of inoculation? Such a vulnerability follows from the site of exploration and threatens the work from at least two points of entry. In the first place, stupidity itself is double. Dividing and doubling its valence, stupidity becomes increasingly pernicious and markedly double-edged; it draws the work into a tension between an honorable status ("Honorable stupidity is a little dull of comprehension" [282]) on the one hand — something the work readily avows in rapport to its topic — and a vulgar order ("the higher, pretentious form of stupidity" [283]) on the other — something the work fears becoming. As the essay progresses stupidity, consistently dividing into its good and bad territories, is entered into the Nietzschean valuation wars, a movement that suspends certain judgments concerning its own limits and knowability.

From the passage cited above, we know, however, that even the mention of stupidity, certainly when placed audaciously at the head of the class or paper, already infects the project, just as it infected Erdmann's audience with laughter. Throughout his paper on the subject, Musil appears stricken by the performative edges of the utterance, stupidity. While *Dummheit* may have no referential grounding as such, its enunciation produces contagion, spreading effects of stupidity, and this may account for its status as substitutive trope, if not fetishistic utterance. As act of denunciation or accusation, stupidity replicates itself in the community. One cannot easily stand accused of stupidity without the risk of becoming its agent. On another register it covers for a host of social imputations and unrepresented atrocities. There are always social consequences that name or are designated by stupidity. Thus Musil is sensitive to the political violence (which includes domestic violence) inherent in the "bad" usage of this word, while at the same time he himself deploys it for the purposes of mounting a political counterattack. A fighting word, "stupidity" demeans a worker, a wife, a girlfriend, or a child; pointed at power, it defies, or, boomeranging, it distends the subject. Lacan observes that one enters a fragile area when calling the king stupid or "when the subject quite simply perceives that his father is an idiot."[12] This does not inflate the subject, who might draw energy from the dialectics of ambivalence, but stupefies and aggravates the system of support. The position is an endangering one.

Catching on to the threat of castration that hovers on the horizon of fatherland, rendering it at once a weakling and an aggressive bully, offers no solace to the subject who calls it but participates in the creation of a political superego. Guilty for catching the Germans in disclosive postures of sheer idiocy, the serious writer pumps up a moral conscience. At the origin of the political superego is a kind of mourning — it would be wise to remember that in his reflections on mourning and melancholia, Freud includes on the list of irretrievably lost objects one's own or adopted country, a country that has disappointed or betrayed or whose professed ideals have perished. Losing ground, the writer closes the deal on a dead or killer country (one thinks of the political superego reigning in Thomas Bernhard's invectives against his mean and stupid countrymen, the Austrians).

The thought on stupidity offers Musil a way to initiate a moral exhortation to a nation heading toward an unprecedented deployment of world-historical brutality. Linked to assault and combined with the expression of brutality, stupidity calls for a political psychology that Musil outlines with the help of some examples from Eugen Bleuler. His greatest political concern, though, involves the inflammation of stupidity in the body politic around the generality of the masses, where it induces a process of decivilization:

> . . . there is a particular propensity in the world for people, wherever they appear in great numbers, to permit themselves collectively everything that would be forbidden them individually. These privileges of the "we" that has grown so powerful today frankly give the impression that the increasing civilizing and taming of the individual ought to be balanced by a proportionate decivilization of nations, states, and alliances of the like-minded; what obviously emerges in this is an emotional disturbance, a disturbance of the emotional balance that fundamentally underlies both the opposition between "I" and "we" and all moral valuation as well. (274)

When measured against the rhythm of the essay's general unfolding, this moment provokes a kind of anxiety attack and proves unable to resume the connection it has established between the political and stupidity. Abruptly cutting his losses, it is as if Musil panics at the limit of political insight, needing to shrink back from the place of condemnation. His outrage is capsized by the turbulent swell of a heavy sense of guilt.

Indefinitely restraining the heady topic, Musil runs, as Kafka would say, to the women: he proposes to divert the path of this line of ques-

tioning by surrendering to feminine charm. Not quite man enough to
square off with politics (assuming anyone is "man" enough for this), he
shows how tough he is by slapping around a few women:

> But before proceeding with our response, let us catch our breath with an
> example that is not without its charm. All of us, we men in particular, and
> especially all well-known writers, know the lady who positively insists on
> confiding in us the novel of her life, and whose soul has, it appears, always
> found itself in interesting circumstances without this ever having led to suc-
> cess, which she rather expects from us. Is this lady stupid? Something aris-
> ing from the profusion of our impressions is accustomed to whisper to us:
> She is! But politeness as well as justice demand the concession that she is
> not absolutely and not always stupid. She talks a lot about herself, and she
> talks a great deal. She judges in a most determined way, and judges every-
> thing. She is vain and immodest. She often lectures us. (274)

Breathless exhaustion. Change of scene. The world-historical space of
brutality fades into a salon; the writer catches his breath, charmed not
so much by a woman as by an example. He grammatically repeats the
offense that, in the domain of the political superego, needed to be denounced: he marshals "we men," admitting a decivilizing component
to a civilized tea. It is a matter, in any case, of pitting "we men" against a
lady, a knowing "we" against a lone and stupid "she." As it happens, in
this case, and by this charming example — no dead bodies, no deportees
— "we men" are protected by politeness, even by justice, as "we" carry
on the violence of the "we," domesticated and ensured by invisible assault weapons of grammatical compliance. Switching scopes — it is as if
the telescope, the war binoculars, had been turned around — and
switching genders, the warrior writer who bore witness to Fatherland's
stupidity puts on a dinner jacket and huddles with the brothers, at
once enticed by and repudiating the not always absolutely stupid
woman. The example cuts to the place where a political protest had
been hazarded, reassembling the men at the moment they had begun
to disintegrate and deflate. A bit of a life raft, the example came to the
rescue at the place of capsizing guilt. It supports the survival of the wee
men. Musil resumes the argument.

Stupidity is often (though not always and not absolutely) associated
with what our experience as men has taught us about women but
which politeness and a sense of justice prevent us from asserting cat-
egorically. If anything, the detour through the woman signals that the
recognition of stupidity as a prevailing trait in the other often involves

a feminization, if not a minoritization. When Fatherland is thus diminished, the subject goes into mourning or joins a tea party; he allows himself to be distracted and charmed by an example that replenishes his sense of mastery and justice. But the burden of stupidity — as wound or weapon — threatens to deplete the subject as well. While leading inevitably to some sort of assault, stupidity, on the side of brutality, finally offers up a certain lack in manliness or virtue, no matter how much politeness protects the scene. Stupidity depends for its force on the momentum of a man who cannot hold fire, one whose brutality is on a par with impulsive, indiscriminate — feminine — chatter.

The bewitched slippage to women betokens a recurring symptom. Put less politely than Musil would ever agree to allow, yet involved in the basic logic of his argument, the strikingly habitual act of appropriating woman as "stupid bitch" comes into play as the neutralized version of political assault. To call a woman stupid marks the beginning of violence, situated not as its cause but already as performance; arguably, "stupid" is more damaging than "bitch," which functions merely as a sexual metonymy. Though highly sensitive to the politics of stupidity, Musil participates in perpetrating this violence himself: "There is nothing so stupid as a woman artist" (274). Woman as figure for stupidity emerges several times, although this occurs blindly and almost unconsciously, when he is at rest, catching his breath — the envisaged target appears to be set on the masses and petite bourgeoisie. The stupid woman breaks class barriers. She endows the serious writer, organizing a complicity among us men who have been scattered by the panic attack of political denunciation.

At the juncture over which sexual difference has been decided, a comparison, one invited by Musil, can be introduced to clarify the essential stakes. Both Musil and Nietzsche, according to their idiomatic tonalities, rail against women, though Nietzsche's rants are possibly less conventional and certainly less "polite" than those of Musil. What makes the aims of these "men" (Nietzsche's not a man, he's dynamite) so incompatible, even when their utterances at times match prints? Musil's strenuous politeness itself gives him away, exposes the violence he pointedly conceals. By resisting the repetition of common codes, Nietzsche puts himself on the line without falling into the trap of assuming a consensus of "we men"; nor does he even reach a consensus concerning gender certainty (his exorbitant identifications with the Crucified, Dionysus, Jews, and women, his clinging animals, lead him to sign on with any club whatsoever — well, not with *any* and all clubs, but no doubt with too many). Whereas Nietzsche's offenses target metaphysics and sideswipe the empirical, Musil, despite everything, largely holds his observations to the level of received opinion and the anthropological aperçu. At no point undermining the very terms by which the argument proceeds, his reasoning offers nary a contradictory tremor within the rhetoric of recognition.

Nietzsche's rapport to a troubling, indecent proposition prompts a less anxiously seductive or self-identified articulation, finally, than Musil's somewhat narcissistic musings, which take place — or, rather, recede — on the side of what I would call bad politeness. The politics of politesse, deployed by both ironists to different ends, in fact links the styles of Nietzsche to that of Musil. Politesse opposes itself to the rude advances of bad stupidity or to the clueless faltering of a better stupidity. Bad politesse, which deserves a larger rap sheet, can be indicated at this point in abbreviated form: it builds on bad faith, barely concealing a toothy grin as concerns its own reluctance to attack. Hungry yet self-denying, it is abandoned by irony. In any event, whether good or evil in origin and aim, the compulsion toward politeness itself conceals tremendous violence while it promises friendly disarmament. Granting space for his own polite hesitations when treating stupidity clusters, Musil in essence refrains from investigating the causes of a history of silence or repression — there is no genealogical instinct here — or from ferreting out the secret beneficiaries of stupidity's hegemony over politics and women. Rather, his concerns are dominated by the need to exhibit a sense of an inevitable power failure on different levels of social engagement, a failure that is more modestly construed as reflecting a somewhat personal deficiency. He is not up to the task (nor is anyone else); he avers a blind spot. Yet there is a certain cruelty of modesty in Musil's discoveries; since modesty will be held up in the end as the only possible antidote to stupidity, its occurrence seems worth citing. This ethos of modesty appears to come about as the other side of Nietzsche's utterance, "Why I am so clever," and enfolds the declaration, defiant in its modesty, "Why I am so ignorant." Whether this opposing rhetorical tendency forms a strict opposition between the shrewd and the ignorant is another question, however:

> So when confronted with stupidity I would rather confess my Achilles' heel right away: I don't know what it is. I have not discovered any theory of stupidity with whose aid I could presume to save the world; in fact, even within the limits of scientific discretion, I have not come across an investigation

that has taken stupidity as its subject, nor have I found even some kind of unanimity that would, for better or worse, have resulted from treating related things with regard to the notion of stupidity. This might be due to my ignorance, but more likely the question, "What is stupidity?" corresponds as little to our current ways of thinking as do the questions of what goodness, beauty or electricity are. (270)

Musil has not yet named modesty as a force capable of disrupting stupidity, but, from the start, he practices its tone as a warm-up in the preevents of our "thought-sports." Though the rhetoric of modesty may serve to conceal its opposite, one of the more poignant moments in this passage involves the possibility of being truly ignorant of stupidity — in other words, being stupid about the subject, already part of it and therefore incapable of it: the more one is into stupidity, the less one can grasp it; the more intelligence one gathers concerning stupidity, the less certain one is of having understood. The logic follows a different pacing here, another rhythm of encounter: the closer one gets, the farther away one is. It is as if, as question, stupidity approaches a solar trope — one has to avert one's gaze in order to read; one has to look elsewhere, but where? Stupidity cannot be a matter of light because it is dim; it cannot appropriate to itself the question because, in its bad or good guise, it has all the answers — even when it is a matter of being stumped, dull, blunted. It doesn't correspond or metaphorize, and yet it *is* not. But even in its refusal to allow for itself theorization or scientificity, it is posed as anciently as the questions of good and beauty — and as currently as a philosophical charge of electricity. Unstable and resistant to definition, it belongs to critical thought only to the extent that it constantly slips beyond its control.

"Cruelty Provokes, but Stupidity Disheartens" (Camus, L'État de siège)

To what does stupidity correspond? To what do the stupid respond? In an altogether provocative passage of the essay, Musil marks the stupid being as one who lacks resistance and becomes a kind of draw for the violent. Even if you're not violent by temperament and are mild-mannered like Musil, you are aroused by the really stupid. You go after them. You want to pin them down, write about and torture, fix them. The polite writer, evoking the themes of cruelty in Nietzsche and ruthlessness in de Sade, pounces with the appetite of a predator. When Musil is good and inoculated against his own fear of being found stupid, he writes:

> But stupidity also . . . can irritate, and is by no means soothing in all circumstances. Put briefly, stupidity usually arouses impatience, but in exceptional cases it also arouses cruelty; and the excesses of this pathological, aversion-instilling cruelty, which are ordinarily characterized as sadism, often enough show stupid people in the role of victim. This evidently comes about because they fall prey to cruel people more easily than others do, but it also seems to have some connection with an absence of resistance that is palpable in every direction, and that drives the imagination wild the way the smell of blood excites lust for the hunt: this entices the stupid person into a desert in which cruelty goes "too far" almost for the sole reason that it loses all sense of limits. This is a quality of suffering in the very bringer of suffering, a weakness embedded in his brutality; and although the priority we give to the indignation of offended sympathy rarely allows us to notice it, cruelty too, like love, calls for two people in harmony with each other. (272)

The sadistic response to stupidity contains its own suffering: it goes too far, unstoppably beating, torturing the victim with whom it forms a couple. Stupidity is not itself seen as pathological, but the one called to stomp it out is on a pathological streak. The stupid victim has been caught in the logic of "asking for it." If only the torturer would know when to stop, the argument goes. This is the torturer's weakness, his unique suffering: that he cannot stay within the limits of a proper thrashing, respecting the time of a sound beating. Now this idiot baiting betokens a highly indelicate observation reminiscent of but possibly lacking Nietzsche's thoroughbred disdain. What makes it appear un-Nietzschean is the open season on victims, which in fact doubles the attack being described. Whereas Nietzsche by preference attacks causes that are victorious, even if they are masked in meekness, Musil crosses the line and reveals a certain taste for straightforward cruelty, a desire to make dead meat of the stupid. Nietzsche, disguised as a wolf, also liked his little lambs — but he would offer to chow down only out of love. Despite the difficult stand, there is courage in the avowal that the stupid make you want to kill them. Well, if you are inherently cruel, you will go trawling after the stupid. If your native cruelty has been under control, they will drive you to a new horizon of sadistic commitment. Not always, and you cannot foretell which uncontrolled irruption they will trigger. Stupidity produces a whole scale and logic of effects (Wirkungen), which is the subject of Erdmann's disquisition on stupidity: why do some forms of stupidity make us laugh, while others instill pity, make us cringe, or infuse us with profound bloodlust — and still others make us phobic with the fear that we will be made stupid by exposure to this idiocy?

"A Boosted Blasted Bleating Blatant Bloaten Blasphorous Blesphorous Idiot" (Joyce, Finnegans Wake)

Musil has noted that stupid often comes in couples — like dumb and dumber, perhaps, or Dick und Doof (the German version of Laurel and Hardy), or Bouvard et Pécuchet, or, reaching back further to Hellenic comedy, the *alazon* and *eiron*, who become the significant dumb-ass couple of de Man's reflections on irony. The couple hallowed by stupidity need not be anthropomorphized, however. What Musil has in mind is a meaningful couple such as "mean and stupid," "vain and stupid," even "fat and stupid." Jean-Luc Nancy remarks that one cannot, however, say "cruel and stupid" because cruelty indicates sovereignty. "Mean," more abject and reactive, calls for a couple. You cannot say "cruel and stupid," but someone or someone's dog can be said to be mean and stupid.

Such couples, rhetorically or socially fitted, resume the reflex of a pervasively domestic violence inscribed by stupidity, or what Musil exposes as the politics of stupidity, which couples conduct first and foremost on the homefront. The utterance "stupid," as in "You are stupid," opens up a merciless way of putting folks down. The hierarchy within a couple often requires a strategic recourse to acts and usages of stupidity, a home office arsenal of hostile embrace. The weaker party may need to master the play of stupidity to get by, in fact. What happens to the one under attack, the one who always has to play the crash-test dummy? In the first place, the putative difference between being stupid and being clever engages a general problem of representation: whether you are one or the other, you have to hide that you are stupid, but you cannot show that you're clever because that looks as though you are really stupid:

> ... anyone who wants to talk about stupidity, or profitably participate in a conversation about it, must assume about himself that he is not stupid; and he also makes a show of considering himself clever, although doing so is generally considered a sign of stupidity! If one investigates this question of why making a show of being clever should be considered stupid, the first

answer that comes to mind is one that seems to have the dust of ancestral furniture about it, for it maintains that appearing not to be clever is the better part of caution. (270–71)

In a manner reminiscent of Kant's discussion in the *Anthro* concerning those members of modern society who are too low to get high — in other words, those marked by civic weakness who cannot afford to show themselves drunk or high, who must not expose themselves slipping up, uncontrolled and losing composure (Kant says that in order to ensure social justice, Jews, women, and clergymen, in terms of self-presentation, must stay sober: no social drinking for them)[13] — Musil embarks on a discussion of "artful stupidity," such as the kind still to be found in dependent relationships. There are "situations in which it really *was* smarter for the weak person not to be considered clever; his cleverness might be seen as endangering the life of the strong person! Stupidity, on the other hand, lulls mistrust to sleep; it 'disarms'" (271). Traces of such "venerable craftiness and artful stupidity are also still to be found in dependent relationships in which the relative strengths are so disproportionately divided that the weaker person seeks his salvation by acting more stupid than he is" (271). Musil's examples of artful stupidity include relationships of servants to masters and mistresses, soldiers to superior officers, children to parents, and students to teachers. Cleverness poses a risk for the weak — in the submissive person it is esteemed, "but only so long as it is connected with unconditional devotion. The instant devotion lacks this certificate of good character, and is no longer clearly serving the advantage of the dominant person, it is less often called clever than insolent or malicious" (271). The minute the structurally dependent parties abandon the pose of stupidity, they become vulnerable to such language as prompts constructions of social endangerment and obtrusive deviancy. "In morality," Musil continues, cleverness "has led to the idea that a person's will must be the more evil, the better the knowledge against which it is acting" (271).

All about Eve

The light shed on the dangers of appearing clever intensifies a significant moment in Musil's argument. Among other places and things, it leads us to one of Nietzsche's feminist morphs, where Nietzsche realizes that a considerable injustice has been visited upon the ur-figure of genuine scientificity and cleverness: Eve is evil because she wants to know, she wants to investigate, and yet she is shown to have made a stupid mistake for which we are still paying. Her stupidity resided in her need to know, which has been depreciated into mere curiosity. Eve was the first knowledge seeker; her need to know exposed her as stupid because what she did not know or understand was the prohibition placed on knowing by her husband and his maker. Eve, for her part, knew she was barefoot and ignorant — but it would have been even smarter not to let on that she knew or saw the limit. She discovered and named the limit; she experienced the limited, even at home base in paradise. She was always already Madame Bovary tethered to Charles, the man.

Revealing the audacious and necessary transgression inherent in knowing, Eve would not play stupid, displaying an unwillingness or incapacity (a stupid mistake) for which she has been definitively punished. Indeed, if you are not willing to play stupid, you are making incredible deals with the devil. It is only when he is out- and misfitted as Eve that Nietzsche writes "Why I Am So Clever." In a more general sense, but one not that far removed from Nietzsche's Eve disguise, Musil's observations point to a recurrent tendency in moral and legal deliberations to view the clever culprit as being somehow more guilty than someone who might have acted in the same way but out of sheer ignorance. Even though the law does not recognize ignorance as an "excuse" for the commission of a crime, the tendency is to go easier on the dummy in a system where suspicions are cast on the clever, which is to say, on a degree of imputed consciousness and volition linked to the subject of law. Cleverness pays higher moral taxes and is more susceptible to criminalization since at least the rumor of Eve's smart-ass behavior.

"To Make the Society Happy and People Easy under the Meanest Circumstances, It Is Requisite That Great Numbers of Them Should Be Ignorant as Well as Poor. . . . Going to School in Comparison to Working Is Idleness" (Mandeville, *Fable of the Bees*)

Now there is something about the *Grundstimmung* of this section that calls for a bit of tampering, finer tuning. The call originates in Nietzsche's demand for a virtuous stupidity or in Kathy Acker's affirmation in her oeuvre of emancipatory stupidities. In other words, the treatment of stupidity cannot be left exclusively to denunciatory work. There is other work to be done. Until now, the case of stupidity, as deposed by Musil, has fallen decidedly on the side of a certain darkness and despair, even though it was never agreed that stupidity could be apprehended essentially as one thing or the other but rather always as one thing *and* the other. The spectrum of political horror and individual defeat has been coded in shades of stupidity. There also exists a tonality of the stupid that belongs, however, to the registers of a gay science, capable of participating in affirmation and yes-saying. Montaigne pulls the experience of being nailed as stupid toward pleasure.

Standing revealed to his friends, Montaigne confesses to the extreme delight he feels when someone tells him he is an idiot — only a good and deep friendship could sustain such an amorous embrace. Great intimacy and trust can mirror your stupidity to you in a thrall. Your friends are those who will take the risk of violation, rough you up a little, aggravate distance, crossing the limit of mere politeness. You crave the violation, rejoicing in its expression:

> I can put up with being roughly handled by my friends: "You are an idiot! You are raving!" Among gentlemen I like people to express themselves heartily, their words following wherever their thoughts lead. We ought to toughen and fortify our ears against being seduced by the sound of polite words. I like a strong, intimate, manly friendship, the kind of friendship which rejoices in sharp vigorous exchanges just as love rejoices in bites and scratches which draw blood. . . . I do truly seek to frequent those who manhandle me.[14]

In *The Gay Science* Nietzsche himself worries that serious harm and misunderstanding have come to the creative tap of stupidity, dragging it down, effacing its steadfast rhythm. ("Thus the virtuous intellects are needed — oh, let me use the most unambiguous word — what is needed is *virtuous stupidity*, stolid metronomes for the slow spirit, to make sure that the faithful of the great shared faith stay together and continue their dance."[15]) Musil points out that abusive language can have something "unimaginably exciting" about it that, though connected with its intention, remains indifferent to its own content (278). Baudelaire weighs in with an ambivalently contoured fashion statement, showing stupidity to double for effects of a plastic surgery that eludes inescapably aging scholars. Conjuring the "vainglorious jackasses" who blush upon discovering that the woman they have loved is stupid, the evil poet makes stupidity the parergon of beauty, if not its enabling condition: "Stupidity is often an ornament of beauty; it gives the eyes that mournful limpidity of dusky pools, and that oily calm of tropical seas. Stupidity always preserves beauty, it keeps away the wrinkles, it is the divine cosmetic which preserves our idols from the gnawings of thoughts we must suffer, miserable scholars that we are."[16] Affected by the fall into time and wrinkling, we scholars are miserable and finite, eaten up by thoughts coextensive with suffering. A divine formula, stupidity comes typically gendered (the trope of the "tropical") and, for Baudelaire, racialized. Capable of ensepulchering beauty, it perhaps, even more compellingly, is linked to mourning and an experience of death — that is, another experience of death. Named here as a preservative, it is in some sense bound up in mummification, in acts of poetic containment and a sense of time that eludes time. We scholars, in the meantime, come undone and disintegrate ... — I promised to discover the bright side of stupidity in these passages: the mournful limpidity of dusky pools must be left for another wrinkle in time.

So when can one cheerfully indulge stupidity in one of its unrepressed forms? There is undeniable pleasure seeking in the empire of the idiotic, a low-burning delight in stupid behavior and activity. One needs only to be reminded of the pleasure domes of the stupid by which constructed delights are dosed out. The narcotic side of inert stupidity belongs to the very possibility of late technological psychopathology, the pleasures reflected in and invented by industrial forms of leisure. Does one really need to be reminded of watching embarrassingly stupid shows on TV, vegging out, cultural studies, lifting censorship on what can be said, acting stupid and doing stupid things that amount to nonsense, or the American ideology of fun, fun, fun? On the bright side of its effusive manifestations, stupidity attracts beauty, excitement, the heat of friendly vulgarity and illicit pleasure. All these qualities split in two, as in the case of the pleasure that it is said to offer. For where there is pleasure, one coasts along the Freudian way in a low-grade death drive. Stupidity draws the blank that sometimes reaches beyond the pleasure principle, prompting pleasures that dull and blunt as they press toward deadly destinations. On the side of inertia and death, these forms of the stupid bear the marks of slow demise, an irreversible energy loss. Is there a moment when the thing of stupidity sparkles with life? In other words, when is the prohibition on stupidity lifted and when, finally, can one be stupid? When you're in love, for instance. When you call each other by stupid names, pet names, summoning declensions of your own private idiolect in the amorous discourse. Love indicates one of the few sites where it is permitted publicly to be stupid. According to a letter by Valéry's Mme. Emilie Teste, this is the very definition of love: "Love consists in the privilege of *being silly beasts together*

— the complete licence of nonsense and bestiality."[17] Love signals the "permission granted" status of shared stupidity, a descent into the bestial abandon of an ecstatic language. As sheer surrender, love opens the channels for the imbecilic effusions of being-with. Laws legislating social intelligence and sense-making operations are suspended for the duration of language-making scenes of love. This could also mean that you have to get real down and prodigiously stupid to fall for love, or that stupidity is a repressed ground of human affectivity that only love has the power to license and unleash.

Whatever!

As exposition in negativity, stupidity, when undrugged by love or narcosis — when taken straight — presses the panic button. Contemporary evaluations of stupidity, including the prevailing series of "whatever . . . ," "it sucks," the dialectical turn of street poetry in which "stupid" indicates a degree of awesomeness, have put up defenses against the crumbling sense of panic that induces stupidity. (A reflection on the American mutation of stupidity-consciousness into the slacker ethos of the "whatever" would reveal a so-far unmarked counterimpulse to the pervasive stupidity of American culture, even though "whatever" marks an unmarking and exhibits, among other existential qualities, dismissive and liberatory modulations of letting be.)[18] Musil's text focuses a collective imaging of mindless stupidity, which is linked to the condition of public panic. In the prepoliticized space of the outside — though it quickly fills politically — the spectacle of public washouts unfolds under the pressure of a spreading panic attack. The public panic attack is disclosive of a certain essence of mindlessness. Dominated by the impulse toward phobic flight, language loses its edge, words are hurled indiscriminately. In this regard, notes Musil, terms of abuse, teasing, faddish and amorous words are all connected when, in the service of affect, they share a lack of precision and absence of reference "that enables them to suppress, when they are used, whole realms of words that are more accurate, more relevant." Musil engages "the biggest public spectacle of mindlessness, the case of panic" (279):

> If something that affects a person is too overwhelming for him, whether sudden fright or an unremitting spiritual pressure, it can happen suddenly that such a person "loses his head." He can begin to howl, basically no different from the way a child howls; he can "blindly" rush away from danger

or just as blindly rush into it; he can be overcome by an explosive tendency to destroy, swear, or wail. . . . We are most familiar with this kind of contrariness as "panic fear"; but if the term is not taken in too narrow a sense, we could also speak of panics of rage, of greed, and even of tenderness. . . .

Psychologically, what takes place when panic breaks out is regarded as a suspension of the intelligence, indeed of the higher intellectual faculty . . . , but it may as well be added that with the paralyzing and ligature of reason in such cases, what happens is . . . a descent . . . into an ultimate emergency form of action. This kind of action takes the form of total confusion: it has no plan, and is apparently bereft of reason and every other saving instinct; but its unconscious plan is to replace quality of action with quantity, and its not inconsiderable cunning rests on the probability that among a hundred blind attempts that are washouts there is one that will hit the target. A person who has lost his head, an insect that bumps against the closed half of a window until by accident it "plunges" through the open half to freedom: in their confusion they are doing nothing but what military strategy does with calculated deliberation when it "saturates" a target with a volley or with sweeping fire, or indeed when it uses shrapnel or a grenade. (279)

Hounded, the subject in panic is mineralized, distilled to a howl, a wail, to a rage of swearing or destruction. Panic prods, opening flow, accelerating movement at the same time that it paralyzes and ligatures reason. Something is engaged while intelligent responsiveness is demobilized. Drawing on our shared linguistic predicament, panic does not correspond to a moment of syncopated speechlessness but annexes stupidity when, in addition to unleashing imprecise words, it calls forth an exorbitantly large quantity of words. Oddly enough, panic's chokehold inundates with language: there are too many words in the course of stupidity's invective. They induce a groundswell, for imprecise words cover too much ground: "the more imprecise a word is, the greater the area it covers" (280). In this regard stupidity, jamming on chatter and word clutter, points to an excess of language that buzzes all over the place like the fly trying to get out. A rush of language, it resembles a media barrage, saturating and bloating a cartography of anguish. At the same time, this noisy excess of language, a dumbness, edges on speechlessness, to which it is never simply opposed. Musil discovers stupidity to be close to a blind urge to escape, an urge rooted in an inherent inclination toward destruction. Pressed by too many words, panic-generated stupidity, frenetic for the fresh air of referentiality, discovers them to be inadequate and closed, unyielding. Words are empty but hard; one can't get past them. This vacuous excess at the

beating heart of language fails to express meaning or offer safety, anticipating instead massive assault charges: "something is truly stupid or
vulgar not only [as] a failure of intelligence, but also [as] the blind inclination to mindless destruction or flight. These words are not only invective, they stand for a whole fit of invective. Where they still just
barely manage to express something, assault is not far away" (280).
Stuck and suffocating, choking on anger, at a loss for words, one struggles, says Musil, to gain breathing space. "This is the degree of speechlessness, indeed mindlessness, that precedes the explosion! It indicates
an oppressive condition of insufficiency, and the explosion is then usually introduced with the profoundly transparent words that 'something has finally become just too stupid' for one to take"(280). The explosion, preceded by the naming of stupidity, occurs where langauge
has been unable to reach a destination, fix a signified, or open a window.

Musil's conclusion itself arrives as a bit of a surprise attack, for rather
than exfoliate possible layerings of language failure or constructions of
extralinguistic rescue, he chooses to turn the surplus/lack ("too stupid
. . . insufficiency") in on the self: "But this something," he writes, "is
oneself" (280). To be sure, stupid rage may reflect back on the subject in
rage rather than upon the presumed addressee or destination. One cannot logically fault Musil for this observation, for it is not simply the
case that it is untrue, though the grammar splitting the self remains a
puzzle — something, namely, oneself, has become too stupid for one to
take. The grammar indicates that the sentence was going elsewhere, at
most in the direction of sideswiping the self. Instead, Musil pulls out of
world and away from the political to gather in on a self that has become
an irritant to itself. What is disturbing about the conclusion comes
down to the way in which he appears to assume stability of self (even as
allergen or in the condition of a buzzing panic) and endeavors to rescue,
here and in other passages, the place of reason, reasonableness — as
though explosions could not possibly occur in the midst of beautifully
crafted language. As if language, well bred and carefully honed, can
shelter against incursions of stupidity. (I do not see stupidity only on
the other side of the barricades but lodged at the very heart of reason
and its pernicious institutions, including those of higher learning.
This is not news but it bears repeating.) In essence, panic targets the
empty center of meaning in language; it buzzes around the horizon of
sense, unable to make sense but releasing an attack dose of words in
order to locate in sheer contingency a moment of escape. This emergency action, which Musil identifies as the core impulse of stupidity,
reveals nothing less than our essential rapport to language and being,

magnified in the form of miniaturization, accelerated on the fast-forward of animal panic.

What Musil has marked with great clarity and necessity is the general infiltration of stupidity, the need for a double valuation (there is, without fail, good and bad, slow- and fast-tracked stupidity), the way it mimes values such as talent, progress, hope — indeed, the way stupidity has pervaded our highest values — and his example for this actuality is a Nietzschean one. He shows how the incontestable virtue of loyalty easily succumbs to the stupidity of the we, gathering the They into an obedience school on collective parade. Finally the we cannot be relegated simply to the other shore but falls on me in my own singularity, at least occasionally, with determined regularity. I am hit by the They of which I am at times a part. I am not spared my own stupidity, that of the They, when I join the we. Stupidity in the end is linked to the finity of knowing. In order to name the limit of knowing, Musil resorts to the mark of the we: "Occasionally we are all stupid" (286). Because our "knowledge and ability are incomplete, we are forced in every field to judge prematurely" (286). While this observation offers the mood and cadence of a "happy ending" for Musil's troubling topic — we are all in this together, we are forced by the very nature of finitude: stupidity is what we share, the share of existence in which we take part — it is built on the abyss of judgment. Stupidity, which, Musil writes, falls due to each of us *occasionally*, rests on the wobbly scale of a premature judgment. But is it not possible that judgment is constitutively premature, always ahead of the justice it might have rendered?

✳ ✳ ✳

If I were not impelled by the blind urge to get out, I would have liked to tell you more about the experience of stupidity, for I have done a great deal of fieldwork in this area and have felt stupid most of my life — but perhaps I should say most of my death rather than my life, for when I am stupid or stupefied, when I am aware of the imbecilic pressures closing in on me, this announces an experience of death: it is possibly as close as I can get to an ontological "experience," and it often happens right before my period, that preparing and shedding that women stupidly have to go through. I am reminded of my death because Nietzsche, in the death that preceded his death, after he had coiled himself around a horse's neck, after he embraced a beast, a *bête*, a figure of stupidity, kept on saying, way past the precedent death, "I am dead because I am stupid" or "I am stupid because I am dead."[19]

The Rhetoric of Testing

3

In Shelley's absence, the task of thus reinscribing the disfiguration now devolves
entirely on the reader. The final test of
reading, in *The Triumph of Life*, depends on
how one reads the textualityof this
event, how one disposes of Shelley's body.
— Paul de Man, *The Rhetoric of Romanticism*

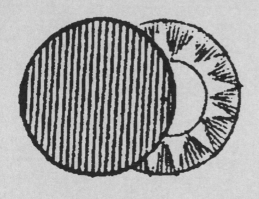

Enfin, je sortis de cette cruelle épreuve en
pièces, mais triomphant. [At last I emerged
from that cruel test, in pieces, but triumphant.]
— Jean-Jacques Rousseau, *The Confessions*

1. The Hookup: Stupidity, Irony, Mechanicity, and Testing

HE WOULD not have claimed, as did Heidegger to friends, that his greatest accomplishment was thinking through the elusive premises of technology. As far as I know, his many discussions with friends and disciples, with colleagues and critics, observed silence on the subject. If not silent, he remained at least mute in this area. Most likely, he would have formulated the dry poignancy of his thought in terms of another idiom, according to other protocols of reading. Nonetheless, Paul de Man's work is essentially engaged with and inflected by the question concerning technology. His texts appear to tell the story of the failure to read; the necessity of such failure — not nihilistic but, oddly, a source of revenue and power — comes to light in terms of a certain indeterminacy and aberration of reference, the noisy shuttling of transcendence by which we understand our age of technological dominion. De Man converted the logic of parabasis into a technological insight, marking, among other things, the priority of the values of disruption and interference over those historically establishing continuity; there was to be no guarantee, moreover, for securing the trope of human consciousness. In an epistemic conversion meant to unhinge metaphors of organicity and other figural corroborators of smooth totalities, de Man tracked the unstoppable technology of a grammar: he exposed an aspect of grammatical automation that, given the way it runs, could get you in trouble (Rousseau), make you a marked man (Kleist), or expose you as the dupe of a boldfaced liar (Proust). De Man arranged for a new alignment of the constative and performative edges of language, where the constative (discovering, unveiling, pointing out, saying *what is*) is always shown to be unsettled by the performative intrusion (producing, instituting, transforming).[1] But what is perhaps singular in de Man's manipulation of these terms is his persistent interrogation of the unanalyzable, disruptive instance at work in the text, an instance that devolves from the technicity of a power failure.

In a large and schematic sense, de Man has traced the lines of interference running through canonic projects and ideologies, emphasizing time and again the relentless logic of the technical limit. Where there

97

exist two contradictory modes of cognition, the dimension of performance runs interference with intentional layouts. Performance, repetition, the production of (un)predictable structuration on which the fate of meaning depends — all powered by the machine.[2] If *Allegories of Reading* claims to use and explore deconstruction in the "technical" sense, referring to "the techniques of structural analysis refined to near perfection," this insistence belongs to the technological urge behind a work that, as early as "Semiology and Rhetoric," has been committed to "the programmed pattern of grammar," to the "impersonal precision of grammar."[3] By the time he gets around to discussing Rousseau, the *Social Contract* will have generated a machinic diction; the textual body will have morphed into a textual machine: shedding the text as body, "the machine is like the grammar of the text when it is isolated from its rhetoric. . . . There can be no use of language which is not, within a certain perspective thus radically formal, i.e., mechanical, no matter how deeply this aspect may be concealed by aesthetic, formalistic delusions" (294). It is not clear why formalistic determinations are at times disconnected from the machine or what has happened to the body tossed out for the grammar scanner. The body at least will haunt and return with convulsive lurches throughout the oeuvre, inscribing the stammering reserved for machinic disorder.

De Man's work has explored the necessity according to which cognition and performance diverge. But, despite a number of excellent interventions devoted to this split, the extent to which performance undercuts modes of cognition invites further review, particularly if performance is seen to involve an inescapable technological component. In a way, de Man has translated and reinscribed the notion advanced by Heidegger that technology's essence is disclosed in its moments of breakdown. What is it that gets disclosed by the persistent energy of disruption, in the facticity of essential interference, to which de Man's texts repeatedly point?

One of the discoveries upon which his texts rely involves the nonintentional process of signification — the fact that "l'effet machinal" is responsible for effects of meaning generated by sheer contingency, elements of uncontrol and improvisation.[4] The disjuncture of performance and meaning or intention, if not always from revelation, has amounted to something of a humanist affront, a scandal. The disparity between the intentional, meaningful dimension of the work and its sheerly mechanical, formal component or grammar implies violence: "The primacy of the mechanical does violence both to meaning and to the body and language."⁵ Part of this violence resides in the stupefying repetitiveness demanded by mechanicity and the cognitive stupor that it spreads. This not only means that the performative dimension of the text is at odds with its stated cognition but that a random or mechanical aspect of language exists that "cannot be assimilated to a system of intentions, desires or motives."⁶ In the case of Rousseau, the discovery of the mechanical, the functioning of a machine that powers his ability to dissemble, points to what is inexcusable. There is no excuse for the replications of intent, cognition, or the simulated intersubjectivities that are derived from contingent mechanics or the blind technopower of a grammar disengaged from rhetoric. In de Man's Kleist essay, the capacity to distinguish between actual meaning and the process of signification involves a "continual renegotiation of the conditions of signification" — a modality of testing or a contestatory exercise. Kleist's figure for this, as replayed by de Man, is the fencing match. "Such is language," writes de Man: "it always thrusts but never scores. It always refers but never to the right referent."⁷

Never hitting home, unable to score, language is engaged in a permanent contest; it tests itself continually in a match that cannot even be said to be uneven or altogether futile because the fact remains that this match is ongoing, pausing occasionally only to count its losses. The contestatory structure, yielding no more than a poor score, paradoxically depends upon failure for its strength and empowerment. In this regard it resembles the ironic consciousness and the experience of permanent parabasis, the "parabases of the ironic consciousness which has to recover its energy after each failure by reinscribing the failure into the ongoing process of a dialectic. But a dialectic, segmented by repeated negations, can never be a dance."⁸ We might say, reinvoking the improbable pas de deux of Nietzsche and Hegel, that a dance, as contestatory match, can never be a dialectic but, being engaged in a fundamental (mis)match, must, in a more Beckettian sense, go on and on, seeking referent and refuge. It is not so much that it casts about for the "right referent," as de Man puts it, but that language as contest posits such a thing in order to fall short of it, to keep itself going.

Language never scores; it engages the experience of failure, opening the test site to the irresolvable conflict between cognition and performance. If one were to localize the low point in the scoring system, it would have to be on the side of cognition. Performance (which is never simply opposable to cognition or intent, but you already knew that), being machine powered, scandalously goes on to achieve "zany feats of improvisation."[9] With cognition on the downswing, following the empty thrusts of performance, the reliability of any knowledge claim is put into question. What is potentially subversive about de Man's work, and what links it to the downsizing exercises of Freudian and Marxian determinations (which consistently cut the subject down to size), is, beyond the critical focus de Man gives to fundamental not knowing, the importance that he imputes to the *existentiale* of stupidity. This may come as somewhat of a surprise to readers of de Man. To be sure, he yields to its significance grudgingly at times, in a manner that invites deniability, but more often than not his texts are clear and even cheerful about the ground that must be ceded to stupidity. Thus de Man poises the engagement with reading on the fragility of wit. In one place he may assert that "reading is comparable to a battle of wits"; while in another he considers the dilemma of a figure that appears to concern him greatly, that of "the dull-witted reader."[10] But no matter how witty or presumably witless one may be (the polarity always breaks down when the stupids arrive on the scene of reading), the battle of wits is a losing one, able to boast only provisional and recognizably pyrrhic victories. It is not long before it becomes evident that one has necessarily been outwitted (that is, outed as stupid) by the brazen betrayals of linguistic positing. Given the law of language's outwitting nature, it is somewhat surprising that de Man maintains the "dull-witted reader" in its depreciated place, as if one could hope to sharpen one's wits on subjective mastery, which language precisely disallows. One can only be dulled by repeated blows to the reading ego so that the sharpest become the dullest, the cutting edge the most blunt. Language smarts; the subject necessarily dulls. Yet who in her right mind would associate the nitwit with the de Manian milieu?

If one were asked to designate a single work in literature that had anticipated and monitored the gathering of these broken threads of cognition, one might settle on Melville's great allegory of testing, *Billy Budd* — although, arguably, all literary texts, exhibiting different levels of boldness and intimate with gaps in cognition, put the conditions of understanding on trial. Billy Budd's resolute simplicity and his symbolic as well as factual illiteracy are made to confront the testing systems of the ironic doubter, the ever-destructive and tormenting Claggart. Characterized by "blank ignorance," Billy cannot read; he can abide neither division nor ambiguity. His speech . . . well, his speech falters: the language of Billy Budd stutters; it resembles a kind of technosputter that profiles the mechanical effect of language. Writing of his stutter, Barbara Johnson finds that at "those moments, the constative or referential content is eclipsed; language conveys only its own empty, mechanical functioning."[11] The gaps in understanding, the "metaphysical interpretations of discontinuities in knowledge" (95), are what Melville is asking us to understand.

Billy Budd tests the presuppositions that hold together the knowing subject. Emblematic of the trials to which it submits itself, the eponymous hero reflects the predicament of the novel. He is essentially put forth as a saintly avatar of stupidity, forced to endure tests that can only be failed (or, according to another, "higher" measure, transcendentally passed). Moreover, the progress itself of Melville's portrayal describes and is involved in what Johnson calls "an infinite regress of knowledge" (94). A mutually destructive couple, Budd and Claggart represent two types of reading — Budd's naïve or literal tendencies are set against Claggart's ironic incursions, which assume that the relation between sign and meaning can be arbitrary. Together they demarcate the element of mutability that conditions any reading: "Arbitrariness and motivation, irony and literality, are parameters between which language constantly fluctuates" (101). Johnson's reading of this permanent arbitration helps us to link in the de Manian lexicon the tropes of stupidity, irony, mechanicity, and testing ("he is willing to try another test"; "Claggart's last test has been completed" [96]) and offers a refinement that should not be overlooked as we pursue the implications of these key concerns.

Sketching the moments of absence that characteristically undermine the possibility of knowing, Johnson points out the extent to which Melville shows that gaps in cognition, "far from being mere absences, take on the performative power of true acts. The *force* of what is not known is all the more effective for not being perceived as such" (108). In other words, the disruption of knowing cannot be understood in terms of absence, default, or deficiency, as if something could be filled, completed, or known by being brought out of its state of absence into unconcealedness. Rather, the rush of interference that produces gaps and unsettles cognition must be seen as a force that weighs in performatively and must be read. The interruptive moment of interference itself calls for a reading. Johnson concludes her commentary with an observation that reinforces de Man's image of a blind thrusting, his formulation concerning a language that always thrusts but never scores. She recasts the oppositions ascribed to *Billy Budd* in terms of knowledge and action, cognition and performance. The critical difference is relocated to "that which, within cognition, functions as an act; it is that which, within action, prevents us from ever knowing whether what we hit coincides with what we understand. And this is what makes the meaning of Melville's last work so *striking*" (109). Thus the action heroes of Melville's great allegory of testing will never be able to score a substantial point in the matter of true understanding. (If only.)

Although a good deal of hitting occurs in the de Manian scene of writing, the punch inevitably falls short of the target zone set up by cognition. The logic of targeting produces a consistent display of strikeouts and near misses as concerns the possibility of understanding. These hits, while undoubtedly evocative of violence, often enough curve away from any tragic dimension of recognition to reach the registers of slapstick, proffering a symbolically rerouted expression of force where language is shown to be lashing out at elusive reference. With equal persistence the subject of language is staged as a comedian and dupe of nonunderstanding, staggering toward an impossible knowledge or falling off in "infinite regress" from a presumed store of accessible knowledge. These hits and misses are fairly typical of de Manian demonstration, though they are often absorbed by the elegance of a language that is strangely comforting as it feints. They respond to an allegory of a certain number of dissociations that the textual machine has attempted to efface. Indeed, the hits and misses that accompany the aporetic track are meant to show that any text is bound to fail in the effort to smooth things over, to soothe and metaphorize, even to forget the abruptness of origination: the act of linguistic positing is unconnected and abrupt. The text therefore emerges in a kind of violence of originary interference, a primal buzz or static that cannot be accounted for or understood. "That language is, is not comprehensible." Between the text and that to which it claims to refer, one encounters "the gap of not-knowing whether such a relation exists. The text stands there as a ruin, without our knowing where it fits."[12]

Whether missing its hits or resisting a fit, any work necessarily succumbs to gaps of not knowing, which provide the imperative for the persistent trials it must withstand. To state that it succumbs is not only to imply the negativity of falling but to suggest the act of surrendering to a temptation, succumbing to the test of limits on which it depends for its being. This is particularly true of autobiography, where de Man's readings are perhaps the strongest to the extent that they interrogate the limits of historical and referential complicities. No matter how strongly rooted in reference a text may be, it still carries the trait of incomprehensibility from which it emerged. The stress of not knowing, the point of its own crucial dumbfoundedness, never leaves a text, though acts of interpretation may appear to achieve a suspension of its essential self-ignorance. Interpretation masters interference and the contingencies of textual disturbance. It does not allow for the stammers and stalls that reading, as understood by de Man, necessarily confronts. Reading enters the zone of nonunderstanding and tries at some level to manage the distress that the text releases. The style of management has little to do with repression, however, which would be the favored house policy of interpretation. Reading and interpretation come to blows in Rousseau's autobiographical remembrances, where the memory of a punishment serves as a reading lesson for a self that tries to understand as it inscribes its own history. The battered bottom implies a legacy of reading protocols that test newly offered limits of understanding. While Rousseau gets off on being beaten, his text is stimulated to the thrill and beat of constant interruption — a level of disturbance keeps it open, exposed, or, one might say in this case, bare assed. Rousseau remembers having been subjected as a child to a battery of tests, of which some of the failures were recorded on his backside. By the age of writing, the tests are taken on this side of the page, reiterating the opposing forces that caused the smacks in the first place.

E. S. Burt reads the sexualized spanking in Rousseau's *Confessions* (the *fessée* in *confesser*) as a sequence, a lettering, in which two types of understanding and remembering are proposed and tested against each other.[13] The hero discovers a sign (the spanking) in excess of the intent to punish, which, in Burt's words, "makes it undecideable whether his voluntaristic view of signs is actually faulty, or whether a more far-reaching teleological system than he has hitherto suspected reigns at Bossey" (196). The child had been placed into the whole series of *mises à l'épreuve*, "that is, tests, trial, or study" (207). Yet "no subject could understand what all those letters spell, since they spell the end of understanding" (210). The passage in question "asserts a disjunction, a mutual miscomprehension, between two ways of organizing the episodes of an autobiography" (210). The local logic of disturbance — the clarity of disjunction inherent to the de Manian innovation — is located in the difference between reading and interpretation. Of interest to Burt is whether the synecdochal relation that reading and interpretation bear to one another "is a metaphorical relation, which would make reading simply a special case of understanding, or a metonymical relation, in which case understanding would prove one mode of reading" (192–93).

Reading involves the undoing of interpretative figures, to the extent that it questions whether any synthesis, any single meaning, can close off a text and adequately account for its constitution. In contrast to interpretation, which involves a development over the course of a narrative toward a single figure reconciling all its diverse moments, "reading states the logic of figures and the logic of narratives to be constantly divergent" (192). Rather than confer meaning on the disparate episodes of a subject's experience, the divergence that makes up the autobiographical text does not so much lead to self-recognition in author and reader as it "serves the further function of making those events available to a reader allegorically, as exemplary of the manner in which all narratives are constructed" (192). Autobiography exposes the paths along which understanding moves as it confronts figurality.

Burt tethers autobiography to the logic of interference: "We could even define as autobiographical any textual pattern of interference, interruption, or crossing produced by the confrontation of a narrative of consciousness with effects of order produced in excess of the capacity of totalizing figures to regulate them" (192). On both sides of the confrontation that she establishes, a core incapacitation — of consciousness or its narrative, of figural arrangements — perpetuates Rousseau's testing systems, for which no answer or conclusion could prompt a degree of finality. They will never stop spanking Rousseau. What he remembers is the test itself of failed understandings and unsatisfactory responses. What is a spanking but that which occurs at and as the end of understanding, whether localized or nuclearized, always hitting bottom in the line of hermeneutic address? Reading is the spanking, the syncopation and disturbance, the mechanically beating rhythm that has been in part inherited from this practice at understanding's terminus. It responds to a punishing mechanicity, and, motored by the techno-epistemic conversion, it proceeds according to the logic of disturbance, casting the drama of understanding against the comforting smoothness of interpretive syntheses.

---

2. The Negative Limit of Knowing

If anyone's life had become the test site for an allegorical mode of existence — assuming this to be possible — it was that of Paul de Man. What we know of him stubbornly remains partial and limited, more so than in the case of other public figures, whose stories hint at least at the possibility of anamnestic totality or revert, in the figures controlling their unfolding, to homogenizing totalizations. Whatever else can be said about the twists and turns of a troubled narrative, de Man faced a number of dissociations and encrypted, in his writing, scenes of impossible mourning. His father is said to have experimented on his body while helping to develop radiation technology. (His subsequent cancer was linked to these early paternal experiments.) Starting his life from scratch in America, de Man left behind a history, a family, a strongly determined name, and what can be viewed as a collapsed test site modeled on the defiant confidence of youthful self-assertion: the opinions of a twentysomething journalist. If I presume to class the life of Paul de Man with allegory, it is not only because I am, contrary to philosophical propriety and Heideggerian minimalism ("he was born, he wrote, he died"),[14] somewhat interested in his "life," but also, to the extent that allegory reaches into death, because the "life" of this enigmatic figure returned in the form of a surprise attack on all those who were remotely attached to him or, precisely, in avoidance of him. The unanticipated deviation reconfigured the sites of critical thinking in America. One can say that, following the brief and violent return of Paul de Man after his death, thinking in America — or the quasi-mythical ambience that makes one sense the advent of thought — took a nosedive. I am not saying that everyone in the academic precincts suddenly became stupid (or that de Man was simply the opposite of stupid), but his ghost took something down with it and disrupted a type of mourning that should have produced considerable and worthy festschrifts, a festival of thought commemorating an unprecedented insistence on rigor and recollection.

Instead we got the often brilliant, sometimes ridiculous, and altogether exceptional *Responses* volume, which exhausted itself in the defensive feints that it was forced to perform. It was as if everyone was wiped out by the rescue mission demanded by the afterlife of Paul de Man. Nor was it clear that he had survived the crash, but he was bound to return again, in one or another of his forms, after the fog of a collective stupor had lifted. For some of us he had never really disappeared, no more so than when he was alive. In any case, a break had occurred, redoubling, perhaps, the rupture in his life when he tried to break away from Europe and the calamity he had cosigned in his youth. As with so many signs of rupture, the break was merely a repetition of prior, more sullen breaks and could not be limited to one moment.

To argue that someone's existence can be read allegorically and, moreover, that it pivots on allegorical anxiety does not mean that reference has been scrambled or that history somehow does not count. On the contrary. Questions pertaining to historical accounting and accountability press upon the registers of allegory. Where allegory prevails there is an acute crisis in the management of anteriority. This is the significance of de Man's assertion that "the relations between the allegorical sign and its meaning (signifié) is not decreed by dogma."[15] The relay between sign and meaning is not securely established or seen to originate in any conceptual authority but capitulates to ever-renewed pressures from a yet to be determined past. The past is not so much exposed to effacement as it demands ever more scrupulous attention to its explicit as well as unintended modalities of meaning. Allegory means that very little can be presumed about our current state of knowledge[16] and that reference itself must be continually interrogated, subjected to a process that, retaining custody of the traces under critical purview, is one of disinscription. This is not to say that the past, infinitely expectant of attentive reading, wants, like a ferocious mother, to turn us into monumental historians made weary by its demands. The way we read and reread the past, sharing the claims of our history, reflects the invitation through which the future is addressed, the welcoming that is being prepared by us mortals, bound to a past never fully read.

In an essay addressing historicism and the addiction to reference, Tom Cohen writes that, for Walter Benjamin, "allegory seems to name a site of transformation in which anteriority itself stands to be recast, reinscribed, and alternate 'futures' opened."[17] In other words, allegory, since Benjamin, is neither representational nor, according to its modernist update, a way of reflexively accounting for a work's own condition of production or consumption. Cohen is concerned with configuring "an unnamed or unnamable 'allegory'" (10), an inscriptive force capable of effecting mutation in anteriority and the future. Following the Trauerspiel ("[Allegory] means precisely the non-existence of what it [re]presents"),[18] Cohen locates allegory as disruptive trace and, in the case of Benjamin's drug text, as a moment in the technicity of hashish, part of a pharmacopoetics that prepares for a transmutation of memory. Elaborating on the materialistic historiography inherent in Theses on the Concept of History, Cohen, marking the disruption of historical narratives by a kind of caesura, reads allegory as that which enables alternative pasts to be reinscribed and other, virtual futures to be redecided. By introducing the logic of tampering and engineering, allegory evokes "an always virtual technology for altering anteriority and the future" (233). In fact, allegory is shown to be capable of "evoking and technically altering the pre- and post-historical sign chains at the *Ursprung*" (233):

> ... *no longer the traditional "allegory" that is an icon itself of mimeticism (a textual mode purveying a segregable meaning), Benjamin's eviscerating catachresis is also not that merely reflexive figure conceived as "modernist" today — in which reflexivity itself is stamped as a (merely) aesthetic effect. Rather, precisely the reflexive moment of this allegory is the predicate for an act of mnemonic engineering and history alteration — a shift to the mode of hypothetical event — within the epistemo-political order by disrupting, transmuting, then effacing the grounds or "nature" out of which the term proffered itself.* (234)

Shifting registers to embrace the hypothetical event and geared for mnemonic engineering, allegory is another way of constructing the apparatus of testing — an apparatus whose evolving probes necessarily disrupt any system of epistemopolitical settlement. To the extent that it calls for an ever-renewed form of what Freud called "reality-testing," allegory interrogates that which is not present but which tirelessly summons us to seek the materiality that remains out of our grasp. Understandably, the openness that allegory rigorously maintains, the interminable trail on which it puts us and its reluctance to reward, makes it a source of considerable annoyance: it spells out the very condition of anxiety.

Along with its capacity to mime and produce anxiety, however, allegory disturbs the very possibility of hermeneutic reflection. Disfiguring itself even as it unfolds, the allegorical attacks understanding as it profiles a power to defy comprehension. It defies the comprehension — indeed, the comprehensiveness — promised by the symbol, which offers an image of organic totality. By contrast, the allegorical dessicates the organic unity of the world potentiated by the symbol. While anxiety in Heidegger's early work accompanies understanding, making it possible, and Benjamin somewhat similarly argues for the rights of nerves as a principle of interpretation, allegorical anxiety works according to different stipulations. As Benjamin first recognized, allegory stands as an "amorphous fragment which is seen in the form of an allegorical script."[19] The materiality of inscription with which de Man associates allegory is neither "a figure, nor a sign, nor a cognition, nor a desire, nor a hypogram, nor a matrix."[20] In fact, allegory interrupts the "assembling, the recollection or the present of essence."[21] Benjamin writes: "Where man is drawn towards the symbol, allegory emerges from the depths of being [as nonbeing] to intercept the intention, to triumph over it."[22] Intercepting and interrupting, repeatedly calling a foul on intention, allegory puts up a stop sign before the promise of transcendence attached to the symbolic and aesthetic aspects of the literary work. Defying what it sees as the sham of reappropriation, allegory, moreover, is related to mourning and shares the tendency of "true 'mourning'" to accept incomprehension, to leave a place for it.[23]

The "disjunctive, atomizing principle of the allegorical" reopens the fissure between word (Wort) and statement (Satz).[24] It is perhaps in this sense that Benjamin formulates his enigmatic and unyielding observation: "the only pleasure the melancholic permits himself, and it is a powerful one, is allegory" (109). Though the melancholic here does not provide a perfect match with the retentive heroes of Freud's Mourning and Melancholia, the melancholic who drowns her sorrows in allegory latches onto a rhetorical form in which the mark makes itself present only through erasure. Allegory puts into play the drama of catastrophic loss, permanent disruption, the Nichtsein (nonbeing) of what it represents. It is continually testing the limits of what can be owned, possessed, or had while it endures the noncoincidence of sign and meaning. Looking at the bright side of its baroque diffusions, allegory pleasures otherness; to the extent that it organizes itself around difference and absence, it never comes back to itself, for literary and philosophical works "can enter the homeland of allegory only as a corpse."[25] There is something mechanical, pleasure-driven but also necessarily ghostlike, about allegory: "allegorical form appears purely mechanical, an abstraction whose original meaning is even more devoid of substance than its 'phantom proxy,' the allegorical representative; it is an immaterial shape that represents a sheer phantom devoid of shape and substance."[26] A commentary by Michael MacDonald concerning this passage indicates how a trace of the allegorical comes to haunt every work and every reading like the uncanny presence of another spirit, "what the Stoics call allegoria or hypnoia — even if this spiritos is not quite alive."[27] It is the ghost in the machine. The effect of the allegorical seems "startling" and "momentary," like a "flash of lightning which suddenly illuminates the dark night" or the "sudden appearance of a ghost."[28] For de Man, there appears to be something clearly foreclosive about the nature of allegory, something that appears, though without substantially manifesting itself, only in the blink of a violent aftermath. Withholding the dimension of violence that necessarily trails

108

foreclosure, de Man writes: "Allegorical representation leads towards a meaning that diverges from the initial meaning to the point of foreclosing its manifestation."[29] To the extent that the allegorical is payrolled by foreclosure, the effects of manifestation are bound to be startling, as Benjamin contends, or to resemble the sudden appearance of a ghost. The suddenness of an unwanted return to a condemned site is what interests us here.

3. Ghosts (The Scheining)

But before I link the technicity of allegory to the problem of testing and explore the investment of de Man's work in posthumanist questions concerning technology, I want to acknowledge the ghosts that attend this writing. For scholars of my generation there can be no approach to de Man that is not populated with phantoms or, at best, with the awkward and inevitable figures of transference and pedagogical intensity. In my case, rereading de Man — if only for the related purposes of tracking the genesis of stupidity and refining a rhetoric of testing implied by his work — has tapped a store of autobiographical hesitancy that, for my part, I am reluctant to avow, seeing how it may be spun on its own particularity, with no generalizable lesson or "interest" to draw from. Cohen's reading of Benjamin on hashish posits a transmutation of memory, an "active séance" opened in the Theses that conjures unexpected manifestations of history. Cohen continues: "Invariably, any séancing of ghosts of the past and the future, preparatory to taking a decision, may be accompanied by a kind of knocking beneath the table, a metronomic or pre-mimetic effect allied to tapping, Apollonian (a)rhythm, the deregulation of mimesis and linearity" (234). Though it is too late or maybe premature — the time is never right — the moment has come to read the tapping beneath the table, to stay with the interruption of a peculiar history that wants to speak.

✳ ✳ ✳

In the chronicle of my own stupidity, de Man would have had to play a significant role. The contingencies of my case are not particularly instructive, as I said, and their only interest may lie in the fact that they have supplied me with an access code to a secret obsession in his text with the recalcitrant question of stupidity. Who else could have discovered it but me, for de Man addressed it to me and, now that I think of it, he even said so to me. We have all learned from de Man the significance of error, indeed, of exemplary error or the experience of madness of the text. Eventually — and this has remained invisible to all but me — de Man decided to line up error and madness on equal footing with stupidity. Forget the tropes of cognition and persuasion (though they are implicated in my discovery), the ghosted post-marxist texts, and the shifts from figural language to nontropical, grammatical language (though my discovery singularly illuminates these observations). One of the great ambivalent insights of this highly ambivalent signator concerns his relation to codifiable stupidity.

✳ ✳ ✳

It is perhaps one of the ironies of the de Manian legacy that those most competent to read him have inherited, beyond the pain and brilliance bequeathed to them, an acute sensibility for idiocy; they can detect and denounce idiocy even where it dwells innocently, in its most pastoral remove. I am strangely touched by this symptomatic gesture and often feel that it is justified, sometimes even brave in the American context (in German, British, and occasional French contexts the discovery of everyone else's work and politics as hopelessly stupid is part of a staple repertory, deduced from a kind of masculinist rage, the last residue, to be kind, of a warrior impulse). The importance of stupidity for de Man cannot be overestimated, even if at all times it has slipped and mutated within an expansive semantic scale and has had to be registered according to highly ambivalent categories. (Have I written *ambivalent* enough?) And precisely the categories of understanding are at stake here, for de Man's (non)reading of stupidity involves an impressive range of issues, which include the differently morphed appearances of Archie Bunker; the problem, associated with the Schlegels, of *Unverständlichkeit* (nonunderstanding); irony; the various power failures in cognition that are examined by de Man; entire epistemological networks; and the redoubling of the effect of incomprehension that he at times feigns. Consider the observation made by Rodolphe Gasché, which replicates the de Manian anxiety: "Indeed, from a traditional philosophical perspective, it is altogether incomprehensible why certain passages to which de Man refers in his readings are supposed to be 'baffling,' 'surprising,' 'bewildering,' or 'startling' and thus taken as key passages."[30] Gasché finds incomprehensible what de Man finds incomprehensible. Hence their differences. One aspect of the uncomprehending emerges on the side of sharpness (Gasché doesn't understand what's not to understand), whereas the other aspect of incomprehension carries the valence of dumbfoundedness or ruse — it is undecidable whether de Man's protestations of bewilderment are a put-on or for real. Whether or not he controls the axis of stupefaction that constitutes the textual contest, de Man often locates himself at the dead and dumb center of signification. In another text he traces the predicament of being both dumb and dumber to Hellenic comedy. He likes playing the fool. He also likes dialecticizing that position into one of detached superiority. (In the sixteenth century these oppositions were not tenable; we believed in the recondite knowledge of the fool. But I don't think I'm writing a history of fools.) De Man introduces certain passages, Gasché insists, as though he is stumped by them. Where there is relation and the index of coherency, de Man opts for the absolutely singular and disconnects. His resolve keeps him bound to the anxiety of unrelieved ignorance, a condition stipulated by language to the extent that it is hounded by referentiality.

It seems as though de Man needed to invent for himself an overmeasure of the incomprehensible, to zero in on or produce an especially blind or senseless textual glitch in order to read. What baffles "the traditional philosophical perspective" is de Man's stated bewilderment, his unconcealed dependency on nonknowledge, gambling his insight on that which fails to make sense or on what is seen to function as a moment of sheer stupidity in a text where claims for self knowledge abound. Since in "The Concept of Irony" de Man refers us to the Greeks, we might do well to pick up the relay and route the refusal of sense — in terms of a text's elaborated economy, the initiatory experience of sense refused, whether motivated or incomprehensible — through what Plato and Aristotle sought to locate at the beginning of philosophical questioning: *thaumazein*. Philosophical questioning begins in wonder, bafflement, stupefaction, something that Heidegger emphasizes in his Freiburg lectures.[31] The stupefaction that marks the opening throws one off; it involves a stepping back: the step back from immediacy, abandoning singularity in a kind of numbed retreat — the experience of dumbfoundedness — which initiates, in the sense of Hegel's *Aesthetics*, the first, necessarily estranging step of philosophical inquiry. It is a faltering step, and de Man, ever the first to catch a fall, insistently reviews the linguistic stammer that doubles inevitably for the Fall.

To assert that de Man's work stages a contemporary rendition of *thaumazein*, taking a step back in bewilderment, allows for the possibility that it both discloses critical involvement with the question of that which baffles absolutely and comes from elsewhere, from a place of exteriority, and is itself implicated in the autistic (the undisrupted singular) dimension of such a repertory. From the point of view of philosophical authority — such points of view exist — de Man's work has been seen to suffer "from irreparable philosophical naiveté."[32] But perhaps more interestingly, in terms of flirting with the disaster of conceptual debility, de Man's destruction of philosophical difference, of "the difference that philosophy makes by virtue of its claims to generality and universality" (287), is accomplished in terms of the radical singularity of his idiom. This extreme singularity, writes Gasché, "defies all comprehensibility" (287). He comes close to calling de Man, if only in the sense of its etymological rap sheet, an *idiot*. (On the level of the signifier, it is perhaps no mere coincidence that Gasché's essay ends in the slip of the idiosyncratic.)[33]

✳ ✳ ✳

The unrelated singulars that comprise de Man's work allow no space for the formation of anything recognizably "universal." This formulation may repeat somewhat old-fashioned concerns, but it establishes de Man's remove from a traditional philosophical vocabulary, which he often appropriated. At certain junctures of his argument, the objections that Gasché raises against de Man recall the objections that Sartre aimed at Georges Bataille, who was involved in an effort to recuperate a radical singularity. Gasché, whose early work is devoted to Bataille, continues: "Instead of opening up to *one* universe of seedlike fragments susceptible of engendering worlds, de Man's philosophy emphasizes a much darker picture. His is a world of unrelated singulars, each so idiosyncratic that in it everything universal becomes extinguished; it is a world of heterogeneous fragments forming a whole only insofar as, by their mutual indifference and lack of generative power, they are all the same, endlessly repeating the punctuality of their lone meaninglessness" (287). This indifferentiating clash of forces is related to the senseless power of positing language — to a power that does not model itself on reproductive potentialities (not "engendering worlds," "lack of generative power"). According to this view, de Man's "philosophy" — if that's what it strives to be — destines itself to extinction.

The destruction of philosophical difference undertaken by de Man is demonstrated boldly in Gasché's discussion of the Kantian problematic of the *Augenschein* (285–87). At this point in his essay, Gasché is working with a facet of nonphenomenal reading, a formal materialism that, though not de Man's last word on the subject, relies on some basic assumptions that he does not renounce. The *Augenschein* is a synthesis of phenomenality given in a minimally phenomenal manner. In Kant this synthesis is enabled by the fact that the *Augenschein*, as soon as it enters into the service of the sublime, no longer sees anything determinate but the unseeable itself. Gasché writes: "But, ultimately, the unseeable revealed by the *Augenschein* as the *one* glance that embraces center and periphery at once, fails to show what it shows. It is, for Kant, an impossible endeavor to try to present the intelligible totality *as* the totality of nature, not only because that totality is by rights unpresentable, but also because no totalization of nature can be achieved" (285). The *Augenschein*, however, while failing to present the intelligible, offers it to thought. The *Augenschein* eventually shows imagination yielding to reason; "it is witness to imagination's minimal relation to that faculty" (286). The argument goes so far as to assert that the *Augenschein*, instead of posing an obstacle to the presentation of ideas, seems to be another name for the extended imagination and, consequently, the very presentation, however negative, of the faculty of absolute totalization with which Kant is concerned in the discussion of the sublime. Now watch how de Man skims off any notion of mind from this key Kantian passage in order to arrive at the purely formal, material, and mindless stare of material vision. De Man writes, "No mind is involved in the Kantian vision of ocean and heaven."[34] A purely "material vision," devoid of "any reflexive or intellectual complication, it is also purely formal, devoid of any semantic depth and reducible to the formal mathematization or geometrization of pure optics" (136).

Such a perception, according to de Man, exceeds the bounds of any relatedness and is posited, as Gasché argues, as "unique, entirely unintelligible in its singularity" (286). De Man continues: "Heaven and ocean as building are a priori, previous to any understanding," and inseparable from the material vision itself (135). We can fast-forward the flow of de Man's procedure to the "stony gaze," which, in "Kant's Materialism," he asserts by invoking the unity of *Augenschein* and Kant's architectonic world. The stony gaze fixes a moment of "absolute, radical formalism that entertains no notion of reference or semiosis,"[35] a moment that is forgotten in the *Third Critique*'s attempt to bridge reason and the empirical. Gasché adds: "More precisely, the *Third Critique* is itself the result of a forgetting of its source in a purely formal, material, and mindless stare" (286). In the nonphenomenal phase of his reading of philosophy, de Man brings a material vision into view that is said to remain external to the concept. The figure of the stupefied stare — it is actually prior to figure — is frozen into that which is irreducibly singular, released from all possible relations. The disfiguring and disarticulating gaze, however stony, is constituted, according to Gasché's reading, into the figure of a theory:

> Precisely to the extent that such a theory or philosophy would be "positive," it would have failed to enact what it points out, and would have forgotten what it tries to recall: the irreducibly singular positing power of language. If a rhetorical reading proceeds by demonstrating first that a text on its thematic and semantic level already undoes what it weaves, and second, by showing that the inscription of figuration in the text itself points to the positing powers of language, disfiguring all meaning production, then the third facet of rhetorical reading will consist of deconstructing the latter's figural status — the illusion of having come to grips with the arbitrariness and the senselessness of the materiality of language and its acts of positing. (290–91)

Well, not only will one fail to come to grips with the arbitrariness and senseless fact of language, its materiality and acts of positing: whereas Kant deploys the *Augenschein* to mark an impossible endeavor, dealing as it does with the unpresentable (and thus necessarily failing to show what it shows), the *Augenschein* offers precisely what it fails to present — the intelligible — to thought. Kant is operating at the limits of intelligibility, a space that his much maligned follower, Friedrich Schlegel, negotiates according to terms that will interest de Man later on. Here de Man follows the Kantian thread to what remains external to concept, to a stupefied stare that reduces the unintelligible to its sheer technicity, a dumb formalism — what he calls, prior to any reflective trace, the source: "a purely formal, material, and mindless stare." These terms are highly complicated, at once idiosyncratic and overdetermined. The only point I wish to urge at this time, without engaging the many heuristic demands of "Phenomenality and Materiality in Kant," concerns de Man's consistent investment in figures of stupefaction, mindlessness, dumbness, even where Kant went elsewhere (in Gasché's reading, to the extended imagination).[36] Already Schlegelian, de Man considers these terms to mark a place prior to understanding. Yet, we shall show (though, in keeping with Kant, we understand such showing to remain a questionable endeavor) the extent to which the determinations, "before and after" understanding, cannot be seen as temporal categories, for the provisional is final and the "fore-" lies in the future.

114

In his subsequent book on de Man, Gasché picks up some of the themes that have attracted our interest. *The Wild Card of Reading* offers an important reflection on the negative knowledge that inscribes de Man's writings. The problematics of nonknowledge are registered at different levels of the work, inside and outside the de Manian text. Gasché begins immediately, in the introduction, by posing a subject, not necessarily himself, though such would seem a likely guess, by "confessing the inability to understand a subject matter." His diction is supported by valences of incomprehension, obscurity, the unfathomable, suggesting how the force of unintelligibility draws the reader to a place prior to understanding. He continues:

> Yet only few, if any, of those who have tried to read the writings of Paul de Man have been spared the experience, at least at first, of near total incomprehension. His prose is dense, opaque to the point of near obscurity; the sequence of the arguments is unfathomable; and the relevance of its points made, if one is able to discern them at all, is far from being clear. However, given de Man's prestige in North American academia, few felt they could actually admit their failure to gain a toehold in de Man's work. And many, to maintain an appearance of authority, felt obliged to cast judgment on it. . . . [De Man's singular usage of terminology leaves] one . . . with a sense of confusion and the suspicion that de Man's language is a private language, exclusively intelligible to its author alone.[37]

In chapter 6, "Adding Oddities," Gasché reviews the way in which "mere reading" empties the text of any cognitive function, treating the problem of negative knowledge as something inherent to the grammatization of rhetoric:

> Clearly, the rhetorization of grammar leaves us empty handed, but the negative knowledge that seems to result from a grammatization of rhetoric is likewise thwarted by the fact that the figural mode of the title [of Keats's poem, "The Fall of Hyperion"] cannot be reduced to a grammar. Grammar, being an isotope of logic, its claims are referential, and hence cognitive and, even when negative, are inevitably undermined by the rhetorical mode of the title. Mere reading's double reading thus relieves the text of all cognitive function since it is equally impossible to determine any referent, literal or figural, for the title. (181–82)

But Gasché goes directly to the heart of an original stupidity when he demonstrates that, for de Man, even the knowledge of the impossibility of knowing, still falls too far on the side of knowing, since de Man is working with cognitive paralysis, unrelieved ignorance, the complete voiding of all knowledge. ("And, granted that reading voids all modes of cognition, how do I know that I am performing a reading and not some other activity?" [183])

> If rhetorical reading were understood to yield a negative knowledge and thus to confirm the cognitive and linguistic powerlessness of the human reader, it could then accommodate "an ontology of finite being." But, according to de Man, even a finite subject's negative assurance of blindness is based on an (illegitimate because inevitably reductive) grammatization of rhetoric. Any knowledge, even that of the impossibility of knowing, is thus strictly impossible. The unrelieved ignorance caused by the linguistic predicament regarding referentiality thus even subverts conceiving these avatars of language and reading as a function of or appropriate to human finitude. It seems hopeless to expect the play of language to effect any impact on consciousness. Indeed, if language denies all knowledge, including the knowledge of the impossibility of knowing, it is difficult to see in what way, and on what level, it unsettles the subject's security. (182–83)

Edging toward the space of our reading, the concern with cognitive depletion and linguistic powerlessness indicates a subtle thematics of stupidity that emerges on both sides of the de Manian divide. One can discern that de Man, for his part, is involved in what Gasché later calls a "critical idiolect," a depth-defying obscurity. His work borders the incomprehensible, consistently idiolectizing, defiantly opaque. These qualities are not to be avoided but need to be situated, engaged. What is the value of the (nearly) incomprehensible in our age of (nearly) reading? What makes us think that those who posit the universal achieve intelligibility without collapsing merely into tautology? Is the idiolect, strictly speaking, at all possible, or, indeed, is it not to be seen as the condition for the possibility of any elaboration of thought? How many so-called original thinkers have not been charged with inventing, coining, jargonizing, breaking with traditional values and approved idiomatic currency? Gasché's points are well taken and serve a salutary function. They help us to understand, among other things, how difficult it can be to decide, at times, between the cognitive abscess, the malignant undergrowth of knowing, and philosophical innovation. Perhaps the problem lies with the inevitable assemblage that takes place around the word "philosophy." It is not clear that de Man thought he was doing philosophy, much as Heidegger in another series of contextual determinations shirked philosophy in favor of thinking. To the extent that de Man continued to make claims about cognition, however, his stakes have to be examined to their outer limits.

On the other hand, moving to the dimension of reception, critics have cast judgment upon the work of de Man without having interrogated its complex theoretical underpinnings, if only as part of a defensive strategy to prove that they are not stupid. To say that de Man is wrong, nihilistic, implicitly totalitarian is to offer the suggestion that one has understood something. As I try to argue in chapter 1, judgment is inextricably involved in the problem of stupidity, even though Kant has asserted that stupidity would be constituted by lack of judgment. The boundary separating judgment from lack of judgment is often porous, as lack of judgment implies that judgment at least has been made, if poorly. To cast judgment without knowing fully what is at hand — an aporetic snag inhabiting the structure of any judgment and a problem of human finitude — invites the very charge of stupidity that one has endeavored to evade. For those who are sympathetic to de Man and philosophically mature, as in the case of Gasché, acts of judgment, at once formulated and deferred as "near total incomprehension," install the terms of a possible understanding. This rapport to his work appears to be a matter of integrity, though we cannot count out the possibility of irony here. It is hard to imagine Gasché not "understanding" de Man; yet he begins his book as an allegory of stupor, a confession of the inability to comprehend.

---

4. On Learned Ignorance

It is not certain, refrains Werner Hamacher's essay on de Man, that there can be literary scholarship in the sense of a scientific endeavor (*Literaturwissenschaft*).[38] Taking up the issue of singularity but displacing its value, Hamacher poses the question of *knowability* as it has been destabilized by literature: "These questions can be posed with the prospect of an answer in terms of only a single contemporary literary theorist. Only Paul de Man has exposed himself in his works to the demands of these questions" (172). In this light de Man's work is seen scrupulously to follow and replicate the singularity of the literary text. In terms of its own premises the work, which cannot be reduced to the generality of a project, is involved in deflating coordinates that stand in support of *understanding*. To the extent, moreover, that he manages a lifelong run-in with accepted forms of literary scholarship and the *Wissenschaft* on which it depends, de Man also wears down a number of epistemological strongholds.

On the whole de Man's work, though varied and pointedly resistant to summation, is concerned with uncovering delusions of knowing and exposes itself to the same scrutiny that it brings to bear upon other texts. In this regard de Man can be only ambivalent toward the question of stupidity because there is a zone of undecidability that invests the difference between knowledge and ignorance, between what is comprehensible and unintelligible, and because stupidity, in one of its phenomenalized forms, knows that it does not know. If generality is at risk in de Man's work, it is precisely because that which presents itself as comprehensive, and comprehensible, succumbs to constant disfiguring. De Man's "Concept of Irony," to which I will limit the rest of my discussion, commences and ends with conspicuous figurations of stupidity, beginning with the emblematic couple "dumb and dumber." All right, so maybe I am not the first to link up de Man's corpus with the anxiety of ignorance, but I am without a doubt the only one to do so consciously, deliberately, with scholarly shamelessness. Almost every critical work on de Man has mobilized the stealth lexicon of stupidity, a certain pathos of learned ignorance — though *they* do so unconsciously — in order to situate the tensions within his argument, as if they are cleared of its implications. I could produce a substantial list of evidence, if I wanted to do so, but it would be too long for our purposes, perhaps hyperbolically overshooting my point. Let a random example or two suffice for us here, which can be multiplied metonymically.

At one point in her essay on de Man, Carol Jacobs offers that it is "thus impossible to speak of this text [*Allegories of Reading*] as either knowledge or ignorance."[39] Cynthia Chase, showing the performative dimension of the text to be at odds with its stated cognition, writes that "de Man's Kleist essay does not know or 'ignores' the historical conditions of its reading."[40] Hamacher writes of the unreliability of knowledge attained through language. Shoshana Felman opens an essay on ethical accountability with "the narrator[, who] does not know all he should — or all there is to know — about the captain of the ship": "Do we ever know all we should — or all there is to know — about figures who have an impact on us, those who spontaneously stand out as metaphoric captains — leaders, mentors, or role models?"[41] Granted, these texts mostly concern themselves with those unresolvable aporias revealed by de Man in terms of cognition and performance, within the "unensurability of meaning"[42] and the indeterminacy of language. Their rapport to ignorance, stupidity, or idiocy may seem accidental, by no means essential, and yet, like the obsessional neurotic, they mouth the words without necessarily intending them, without meaning to say "stupidity," as when Hamacher speaks of the "dumb and lusterless defacement of linguistic figures" (179). Or else the concern with stupidity moves outwardly, becoming intertextual, sliding semantically within a new range of idiocy. In a chapter on de Man entitled "Absolute Constructions," Thomas Pepper evokes the paradoxical implications of philosophically grasping idiocy when he writes: "In Hegelian terms, Russell is an idiot. But idiocy — smart idiocy — is what one needs to carry off a strong reading of Hegel."[43] Idiocy, in this case, may be a way of ducking excessive forms of paralyzing resistance, or it may designate the feint that is necessary in order to carry out a true act of impiousness and overcoming. De Man himself, in "Semiology and Rhetoric," the inaugural essay to *Allegories of Reading*, concludes with a crucial word on the anxiety — or ecstasy — of ignorance that, as it turns out, goes so far as to supplant the anxiety of reference:

> We end up therefore, in the case of the rhetorical grammatization of semiology, just as in the grammatical rhetorization of illocutionary phrases, in the same state of suspended ignorance. Any question about the rhetorical mode of a literary text is always a rhetorical question which does not even know whether it is really questioning. The resulting pathos is an anxiety (or bliss, depending on one's momentary mood or individual temperament) of ignorance, not an anxiety of reference — as becomes thematically clear in Proust's novel when reading is dramatized, in the relationship between Marcel and Albertine, not as an emotive reaction to what language does, but as an emotive reaction to the impossibility of knowing what it may be up to. (19)

The anxiety of reference is superseded by the bliss (or anxiety) of ignorance, the place where we end up, states de Man, namely, in the same state of suspended ignorance regarding the rhetorical mode of a literary text. We are guided toward the domain of a question too unsure to know what or even that it is questioning — an absolute question whose status itself is in question. A true question gives up its pose, its supposing stance, and wobbles on its extreme nonidentity. On the subject of the impossibility of knowing what a text may be up to, at the moment it evinces a likely blissed-out ignorance, ever self-disrupting —

* * *

But I have strayed from my intention of revealing an autobiographical ordeal, something that would help you to understand my own avoidance of de Man, which was never absolute or even remotely successful. I had avoided de Man even before he told me that he thought Goethe was stupid. Actually, the scene of that utterance went a little differently, with more nuance than I have internalized. It took place in Paris. I remarked to him, in the projective manner typical of upstarts, that he had avoided "my" authors; I remember naming Goethe among them. His response was swift. "That's because Goethe could be so *stupid*." My bewilderment. "— Theoretically, I mean, in his theory." That could stop a girl in her tenure tracks. Not that I had a job at the time.

I ended up owing him a great deal, as he had helped me when I was fairly destitute and unhirable, having in fact been fired unceremoniously, no doubt illegally, but nonetheless thankfully by the University of Virginia — I am glad that destiny had spit me out of the university at that time, for what was I, if I may invoke a hapless figure from Hellenic comedy, an *alazon* in wonderland, doing in the South? After Paris and Berlin, he sent me to California, to a system, he said, whose digestive tract would not be able to eliminate me easily. That is how he put it. In any case, I started in Riverside and ended up at Berkeley, playing to the end a politics of the foreign body that was neither thrown up nor excreted. (What was I, if I may borrow my identity from Lacan, petite a *alazon*, doing out West?) I don't know why, but Paul de Man had taken an interest in helping me, and it was only under his prodding that eventually I crossed over from German departments (which had succeeded in throwing me up) to what he called the safer shores of comparative literature. (I had explained to him that being in a German department exposed me at the time to endless reruns of World War II, with all sorts of phantoms surfacing and attacking me. He understood those phantasms immediately, offering safety in the less primitively Germanic precincts of comparative literature.) He was sympathetic, strong, nonsexist; he spontaneously offered me protection upon seeing how I was slammed by one institution of higher learning after another. But now I am getting ahead of myself, telling what happened later in the c.v. Nonetheless, in purely empirical and historical terms, prior to inevitable hiring and firing squads, before I knew him and before he became a counselor, my compass and friend, I chose not to go to Yale when the opportunity arose but opted instead for distance — for mediation and mediocrity, as it turned out — by choosing a graduate school in New Jersey. I do not hesitate to say that in my case, when deciding to pursue graduate studies, I avoided working in close proximity to de Man for fear that he would crush my already nonexistent balls.

And yet there was no one else to work with. My relation to de Man would remain, for the most part, teletopical.

✳ ✳ ✳

He was unavoidable, something with which one could never finish. He provoked and scripted returns; he legislated the irony of the recurrent returns. On the level of the work, one might ask the same type of question of de Man that he has asked of Rousseau, when Jean-Jacques felt compelled to repeat a confession that had been dealt with in a prior text. Why does de Man return to the structure of irony given the extensive reflections offered in "The Rhetoric of Temporality"? When he returns, why does he sign on this time by stating, "What I have to say today is in the nature of an autocritique"? What is the automatism at work here? Indeed, irony will be linked to a technological determination, an arbitrary yet relentless repetition of that which eludes intelligibility — or concocts and tests another logic of intelligibility. If the text of de Man lends itself to the purpose of releasing a deliberate technological locution, this is not a matter of loading alien forces on a pristine form of literary criticism.

De Man's work is profoundly concerned with modalities of cognition derived from the technological field and with the mechanical functioning of texts. Embedded in his work is a theory of technology that is necessarily linked to the tropologically insecure nature of irony. Some of the concerns I have begun to outline converge in the later essay "The Concept of Irony," which appeared, thanks to the efforts of Andrzej Warminski, in *Aesthetic Ideology*. Even though irony is on the fast track for de Man, taking us on a spin, inevitably causing a bad fall, we are going to take it slow from here on in, nice and slow, but without any assurance of avoiding a spill. I would like to explore the extent to which this essay is invested in dimensions of testing by way of the problem of understanding and a history of stupidity, which it introduces.

When it comes to irony, which is constructed as the rhetorical test site par excellence, Nietzsche is never far behind. And when Nietzsche is on location, Goethe is in the area as well, though de Man maintains his lifelong suspicions concerning the megamonument. Some contextual details bear remarking: in "The Concept of Irony" de Man discusses Schlegel's thought of "simpleminded stupidity."[44] Citing Schlegel's "Über die Unverständlichkeit," he recalls the profusion of "etymological puns in the manner of Nietzsche"; de Man then introduces, by way of Schlegel's citation of Goethe, an instance where language usage out-runs the user in what de Man decodes as a technological sense: "'die Worte verstehen sich selbst oft besser, als diejenigen, von denen sie gebraucht werden' ('words understand each other often better than those who make use of them' . . .).' Words have a way of saying things which are not at all what you want them to say."[45] De Man asserts:

> There is a machine there, a text machine, an implacable determination and a total arbitrariness, unbedingter Willkür, he says [Lyceum, fragment 42 (Kritische Ausgabe, 2:151)], which inhabits words on the level of the play of the signifier, which undoes any narrative consistency of lines, and which undoes the reflexive and the dialectical model, both of which are, as you know, the basis of any narration. There is no narration without reflec-tion, no narrative without dialectic, and what irony disrupts (according to Friedrich Schlegel) is precisely that dialectic and that reflexivity, the tropes. The reflexive and the dialectical are the tropological system, the Fichtean system, and that is what irony undoes. (181)

Irony is somehow in alliance with the machine as text and binds to it-self a disruptive force capable of undoing the tropological system. It is a destructive force endangering, according to de Man's appropriation of Fichte, the possibility of narration; but here I would caution that we bear in mind the Heideggerian distinction between destruction and devastation. This is not because I want to offer a recuperative gesture that holds back on ironic range and velocity but simply because I want to maintain the rigidity of focus, to prevent us from slipping noisily into undeveloped pronouncements of nihilism. Destruction in Hei-degger as well as Benjamin involves the force of a critical clearing and does not imply the shell-shock stoppage of devastation. Let us bear this distinction in mind, though de Man himself might want to court-mar-tial me for working as a Szondi spy. In fact, anyone caught committing recuperative acts is hauled in by the de Manian sweep. Regarding the inscription of irony, this means nearly everyone is bound to get busted. At one point — we shall dwell on this point — de Man turns himself in.

In an attempt to protect Schlegel from general accusations of frivol-ity, the best critics, writes de Man, have recovered "the categories of the self, of history, and of dialectic, which are precisely the categories which in Schlegel are disrupted in a radical way" (182). Benjamin, according to de Man, saw the impact of parabasis much better than could Szondi. However, even the superior lucidity of Benjamin is compromised, for Der Begriff der Kunstkritik in der deutschen Romantik still follows Lukács, prompting Benjamin to recuperate a work when all seems lost, since the radical destruction that is broached turns out to be safely harbored by a moment in the dialectic; it is seen, according to a Hegelian scheme, as a historical dialectic in the progression toward the absolute. Using Hegelian language, Benjamin offers: "'the ironization of form is like the storm which lifts up [aufheben] the curtain of the transcendental order of art and reveals it for what it is, in this order as well as in the unmediated existence of the work.'"[46] What Benjamin, however, grasps that Szondi apparently doesn't is the sheer impact of the parabasis. According to de Man, Benjamin "sees the destructive power, the negative power, of parabasis, fully. He sees that 'the ironization of form consists in a deliberate destruction of the form' ... — not at all an aesthetic recuperation but, to the contrary, a radical, complete destruction of the form, which he calls 'the critical act,' which undoes the form by analysis, which by demystification destroys the form" (182). The form that veils the work is submitted to destruction so that something like the "unmediated existence" of the work can stand revealed, is cleared for presentation — though in some sense this showing must mark an allegory of presentation.

As do a small number of other writers reflecting on the topic, Hamacher reminds us of the proximate determinations of irony and allegory, which, because they are undecidably linked, continually undermine the critical project of which they are a part. Reading the proximity in de Man of irony to allegory, Hamacher shows how the very possibility of literary scholarship is subjected to a duplicitous imperative: "that of allegory, to which it compels the confession of its foundering in always new figures and arguments, and ... the ironical imperative that withdraws its every epistemic and legitimating ground under which there is no foundering and under which every word, however erring it seems, fits. Ironically, the imperative — of language, of understanding — allows no decision whether it is to be allegorical or ironic."[47] It is not clear how words give the appearance of fitting in the perpetual world of mismatching that de Man constructs. Yet in terms of the imperatives of language and understanding, irony and allegory must occur together, without a clear-cut construal advancing the one over the other. At each moment, then, they are simultaneously to be tested and testing, delegitimating and renewing figures, arguments, and conclusions. At the same time, irony's edge over allegory in terms of testing can be seen in the difference for which Hamacher's observation allows: irony belongs to the domain of *performance*, often leaving allegory in the dust of mere figuring.[48] It remains to be seen how irony, given its complicity with allegorical foundering, participates in engaging the test drive in a constitutive manner, governing its particular moves on the destruction of limits, and advances an "ideology" of Nietzschean rescindability that abounds in his thought on the experimental disposition and the necessity of the test as trial, the *Versuch*. It is important to bear in mind that de Man associated permanent self-irony, which in "The Concept of Irony" he vertiginously enacts, with Nietzsche's *gaya scienza*.

To the extent that the tropes of irony, allegory, testing — if they are tropes — undermine the epistemic and legitimating grounds on which they depend for their existence, they implicate the language of understanding. And so de Man begins his lecture on irony by sending everyone home. "You will never understand — so we can stop right here, and all go home" (164). Home is where nonunderstanding reigns, or at least it is a space not gravely affected by the aporias of understanding. Whether home offers the illusion of domestic insouciance or the stage for a dysfunctional commitment, home can be sweet home when it suspends the effort and languages of understanding. The relation to understanding begins when you leave home, a migrant worker pressed by the heat and aporias of the commitment to have understood. You are outside, hunting for ground and always new figures. You are driven out by some sort of need, exchanging one experience of poverty for another, impelled toward legitimacy or an epistemic safety zone. Underlying the hermeneutic compulsion — the drive to understand — there is the sense that we do not understand, or we have not yet understood, or there is the "Have I been understood?" in the punctuated form of a question, resounding in Nietzsche. He, de Man, first must indicate how difficult it is to get a hold on irony and how everyone drove everyone else out of its proper range, each thinking and saying that everyone else had gotten it all wrong. (Thus Friedrich Solger nukes August Wilhelm Schlegel, Hegel complains about Solger, Kierkegaard undermines Hegel — he notes that the grand philosopher doesn't seem to know what irony is — and, while we're at it, let's face it, does de Man really have an infallible grip on it himself?) One would no doubt incur a logical penalty when including de Man in the list of defendants because his is the text that is not at home with irony and, at least initially, poses irony as that which cannot as such be grasped; it slips by the perennial efforts to pin it down, eluding, as it does, all attempts at comprehensive identifications: "it seems to be uncannily difficult to give a definition of irony. . . . So there seems to be something inherently difficult in the definition of the term, because it seems to encompass all tropes, on the one hand, but it is, on the other hand, very difficult to define it as a trope. Is irony a trope? Traditionally, of course, it is, but: is it a trope?" (164).

The title itself of Kierkegaard's book, which, repeated, is cited in and as de Man's title, is shown to be ironic: irony is not a concept. The status of the title as error invites further exploration, for what could it mean that any determination of irony must itself be ironic? Does the title that de Man picks up double only to negate an already ironic title that stands on and by its own error? What kind of a couple do Kierkegaard and de Man form here? The essay begins, "The title of this lecture is 'The Concept of Irony,' which is a title taken from Kierkegaard, who wrote the best book on irony that's available, called *The Concept of Irony*" (163). Appropriating and repeating the gesture attributable to the "best book," de Man rewrites the book on repetition but also produces an allegorical distance within what is presented as a moment of identity. Does this mean that de Man is arrogating for himself "the best book," the best lecture or essay that will be available on irony, or is he rather creating a contestatory site that will allow him somehow to surpass, by means of a mechanics of repetition, that which has been designated as the best book? Yet because the best book on which he piggybacks carries a self-canceling title, de Man's title may have little to do with the "identical" title of Kierkegaard's book. Or he may be taking a retest of an impossible venture. Like Kierkegaard, I am titling my work "The Concept of Irony," knowing that irony is not a concept, and so I pick up where he fell down, and my lucidity will carry this book to its place, of which it fell short, as the best available book. It is fairly typical of de Man to name the winner but also, in the same gesture, to undermine the very possibility of winning within what nonetheless remains a contest. As if to allegorize the setup he has constructed between Kierkegaard's and his own, later work — his *translation* of Kierkegaard's title — de Man first triangulates, reverting to another, who will be "the main author" of his concern with irony, and then establishes what can be seen as a parable that returns at the end of the essay. As he writes elsewhere, "it matters a great deal how we read the title, as an exercise not only in semantics, but in what the text actually does to us."[49] In this case, given its contextual pull, what the title does to us is to raise the question of whether its structure can be read as tropological, that is, whether it is structured like a metaphor, a substitution on the basis of resemblance and differentiation between two entitites, or whether it is asymptotic — ever nearing an impossible but posited ideal, as in the case of Fichtean freedom. Or perhaps it belongs to a performative rather than a plainly cognitive aspect of language — in this case, despite uncanny resemblances with the title of Kierkegaard's book, it would participate ironically in the catachresis of *setzen*, of positing an original act of language, which engenders further systems. These are some of the things that the title does to us.

Before examining the tropological implications of irony, its status as a "more radical negation than one would have in an ordinary trope such as synecdoche or metaphor or metonymy," de Man concedes that "definitional language seems to be in trouble when irony is concerned" (165). He points toward the performative function of irony, which allows irony to console, to promise, to excuse ("Irony consoles and it promises and it excuses" [165]). The temporality or even sequencing of such acts of consolation, promise, excuse are not disclosed, yet it is clear that irony ventures deals that cannot be closed but that leave room for futurity. Irony tests the limits of what language can offer, enabling "all kinds of performative linguistic functions which seem to fall out of the tropological field, but also to be very closely connected with it" (165). Capable of performing so much for which it cannot be held accountable (if the promise falls through, irony has promised only the promise, not its conversion into the guarantee of a done deal), irony evades conceptual arrest. To get a handle on the difficult conceptualization, de Man takes the low road, that is, he takes recourse to a figure of stupidity that occurs in Hellenic comedy. The Greek figure is split into a couple, a smart and stupid number in which dumber actually turns out to be smarter. On a microsyntactic level, we are going to have to wonder at the apparent awkwardness structuring the presentation of the man of irony: "the ironic man ... as they appear in Greek or Hellenic comedy." And yet this anacoluthic screech is not a mistake but a necessity, tracing the unstoppable split and continued doubling of anyone who would stand (in) for irony. De Man introduces this scene in order to help — well, to help "a little" — with the understanding of irony. I repeat his remarks here in an attempt to underscore a stated tension in the titular relationship between Kierkegaard and de Man:

> It helps a little to think of it in terms of the ironic man, in terms of the traditional opposition between eiron and alazon, as they appear in Greek or Hellenic comedy, the smart guy and the dumb guy. Most discourses about irony are set up that way. . . . You must then keep in mind that the smart

guy, who is by necessity the speaker, always turns out to be the dumb guy, and that he's always being set up by the person he thinks of as being the dumb guy, the alazon. In this case the alazon (and I recognize that this makes me the real alazon of this discourse) is American criticism of irony, and the smart guy is going to be German criticism of irony, which I of course understand. (165)

The contest of the faculties begun, de Man establishes the setup in which he finds himself inscribed, pitting himself at this juncture against another irony man, the author of *A Rhetoric of Irony*. The principal stake, an object of almost sacred value, is organized around the understanding, which Wayne Booth claims can stop irony in its tracks. The way to stop irony, Booth claims brightly, is by understanding: "Pursued to the end, an ironic temper can dissolve everything, in an infinite chain of solvents. It is not irony but the desire to understand irony that brings such a chain to a stop. And that is why a rhetoric of irony is required if we are not to be caught, as many men of our time have claimed to be caught, in an infinite regress of negations. And it is why I devote the following chapters to 'learning where to stop.'"[50] Understanding, Booth consoles and promises, can disrupt the essential disruption of irony; this disruptive feature of irony is yet to be learned before we are stopped. To Booth's credit, though neither he nor de Man makes much of the elusive point, understanding itself does not block the reverse velocities of ironic regression. Booth writes of the *desire to understand irony* as that which proves capable of pulling the emergency brake. The desire to understand does not, as such, bring the infinite chain to a stop; it merely points to the lack in any project of understanding and posits the stoppage as a quiver in desire (hard as it is to imagine Booth's quiver).

So this interruptor would mark out the position of the *eiron*, the smart guy, the American critic who wants to put a halt to irony, to contain and limit it by something that, as de Man sees it, he confidently calls "understanding." In a sense, Booth is pushing up against the elusive limits set by Kierkegaard, who, by defining irony as absolute infinite negativity, demonstrated that it "in itself opens up doubts as soon as its possibility enters our heads and there is no inherent reason for discontinuing the process of doubt at any point short of infinity."[51] The American wiseguy, Booth, is for halting the unstoppable momentum of doubt unleashed by Kierkegaard, confident that doubt can be arrested. De Man's task is to show that understanding is something that cannot be simply secured, indeed, that irony is tied up with the impossibility of understanding: *irony is of understanding.* "What is at stake in irony is the possibility of understanding, the possibility of reading, the readibility of texts, the possibility of deciding on a meaning or on a multiple set of meanings or on a controlled polysemy of meanings" (167). Unsettling so much on which the reign of meaning relies and which the practice of reading assumes, irony is dangerous; it threatens interpreters of literature "who have a stake in the understandability of literature" (167). At this ominous limit, let us try to understand.

Now, before we go on, let me try to situate myself and the doubt that crushes any progress. I have responded to this passage by exposing a hermeneutic compulsion, that is to say, by bringing to bear a trace of pre-understanding, the structure by which one approaches, or is approached by, an object of understanding. My assumptions were wrong, even where they sketched a legitimating interpretation. I was making assumptions about the position de Man occupies in this text as though, despite his protestations, he were configuring himself as the subject supposed to know. If one returns to the passage, one will note that de Man sets up expectations that are then thwarted — unless he is made by the nature of irony to slip up. First he writes of "the ironic man"; he then splits the man into two positions by means of a traditional opposition between *eiron* and *alazon.* The smart guy, says de Man, is by necessity the speaker, with dumbness pressed into the somewhat demeaned position of compliant reception. In the end, the apparently smart one of course turns out to have been the dumb guy. De Man, however, though speaking in this lecture, identifies himself as *alazon,* the nonspeaker who necessarily turns out to be smarter. On a first reading, then, de Man poses as the dumb but smart guy, leaving one to wonder who the "speaker" speaking through this text might be. Would it not be Kierkegaard, who wrote the book on irony and carries the title? Perhaps. However, the logic of position is a bit more complicated when it comes to light that *eiron* and *alazon* stand not so much for guys (well, in the end they do, beginning with Wayne Booth and Friedrich Schlegel) as for critical mappings. The pertinent sentence goes, "In this case the *alazon* (and I recognize that this makes me the real *alazon* of this discourse) is American criticism of irony, and the smart guy is going to be German criticism of irony, which I of course understand."

The whole construction of this passage stands under the question of how we recognize irony ("How do I know that the text with which I am confronted is going to be ironic?" [165]). It is a question thrown back on de Man's example. Is de Man, who insists on locating himself within

128

the opposition he asserts, taking the side of the American or German critical concern with irony? Is he as he speaks doing so from a position identifiable as German or as American? — a question that of course I understand. There is a rhetorical collision that occurs between "of course" and "I understand," bruising a subject that makes claims for understanding. The "of course" situated in a context that underscores the instability of understanding appears to indicate that de Man is leaning heavily on irony. Does this avowal mean, then, that he does not understand German — the site, as he repeatedly recalls, of *Unverständlichkeit* — that he, moreover, knows that he does not understand and is therefore more sovereign and understanding than those Americans who think they can understand and thus disable ironic destruction? Or is he, rather, the American par excellence, for the *alazon* is another name for American criticism and in the same designating sentence leads him to recognize himself as *alazon*?

At odds with its many explicit intentional layerings, the example from Hellenic comedy, which was construed in order to help us out "a little," appears to fall apart. Speaking, de Man puts himself forward as dumb, as American. Yet an implicit hierarchy and valuation are in place, not unlike the ones that enable Lacan to take potshots at the American ego (psychologist). In this case, what challenges the value of American criticism would be a German history that makes a close study of irony. Disallowing censorial responses to destructive and infinitizing dangers, the German tradition about which Booth knows close to nothing is clearly superior to the somewhat pedestrian though sensible hopes reflected in the American's musings. So why does de Man appear to be identifying himself with American criticism at this point? Why would he be setting up the smart guy? Or why would American criticism at all be positioned as the *alazon*, which is to say, as the only apparently dumb guy who in truth is smarter than the apparently smart guy, the Germans ("the smart guy is going to be German criticism of irony, which I of course understand"). I, de Man, the dumb American teaching the "Theory of Irony" seminar at Yale and speaking the "Concept of Irony" lecture at Ohio State University, know and understand the German criticism of irony, and, understanding it, I also know that I cannot submit my irony to understanding: I must, being German, which is to say, understanding understanding, become American, that which does not understand and therefore truly understands when it performs not only the aporia of understanding but the recognition that irony cannot be a concept. Hence I, de Man, when naming the German tradition, including Kierkegaard, who appears to be the smart guy and who wrote the best book available (others, such as mine, cannot be considered *available*), am locating the *eiron*. For we, together, are the ironic man. Yes, the problem of irony appears to be worked out in the German tradition: "You have to take it in Friedrich Schlegel (much more than in August Wilhelm Schlegel [another couple sundered]), and also in Tieck, Novalis, Solger, Adam Müller, Kleist, Jean Paul, Hegel, Kierkegaard, and all the way up to Nietzsche" (167). But if this is all worked out in the German tradition, has de Man not accomplished what Booth set out to do, namely, to put a stop to an uncontrollable regress of negation? By finding a term and terminus, by thus excluding other mappings and possibilities, and by comprehending the Germans, will de Man have learned "where to stop"?

There is, however, a supplementary twist to this logic. According to the way the example runs, de Man should have allied himself with the *eiron*, the one who speaks, arriving on the scene to put things right, the successor to a double lineage of ironic thinkers (he leaves out the French trails here). And, in a sense, that is how the example unfolds: de Man understands the history of a trap, walks right into it, finding himself predictably set up by the dumb Americans. Hence, when he identifies the *alazon* as American criticism he is not inserting himself in that context but splitting himself off from it, averring that "this makes me the real *alazon*." The real *alazon* is different from the obvious *alazon*, who fits into the conventional, if Greek, dialectic of smart and dumb. The localizing gesture of "this discourse" appears to refer to American criticism, of which de Man would be the dumb counterpart. I'm the dumb one, the logic continues, because Booth's approach to irony is "eminently sensible: he starts out from a question in practical criticism, doesn't get involved in definitions or in the theory of tropes" (165). On the American side, then, "an authoritative and excellent book on the problem of irony, Wayne Booth's *A Rhetoric of Irony*." He's the smart one, writing on rhetoric. But here again I take the title and run with it. I am so dumb that I get imbricated in a theory of tropes. I am so dumb that I'm smart. As for the other guy, "Wayne Booth's project of understanding irony is doomed from the start because, if irony is of understanding, no understanding of irony will ever be able to control irony and to stop it, as he proposes to do" (167). Thus, for example, I understand German (which may help to explain the peculiarly Germanic punctuation intervening in that moment of phrasing: "because, if "). Moreover, stopping and controlling, he writes that it "would have been difficult, though not impossible, but more difficult, for Wayne Booth to write this way, and to write the sentence I've just quoted, if he had been more cognizant of the German tradition" (167) (which I of course understand).

So Wayne Booth has taken the fall; he takes his place as the dumb guy who isn't cognizant of the German tradition, which he has also foolishly dismissed as "Teutonic gloom." De Man, for his part, does not see Schlegel as particularly gloomy. The contest turns into a battle of sensibilities, opening a space where no satisfactory adjudication is possible. De Man shifts the order of the debate in order, presumably, to mark his ironic sensibility over the dumb doom-and-gloom gloms of Booth. Yet these terms do not correspond to what either contestant would agree could situate the question of irony and its understanding. Understanding the Germans, de Man does not see them as particularly gloomy. Why, in any case, would gloom count as a stop to reading, as reason enough to effect a dismissal of a tradition of thought? The suggestion is that Booth has not read the Germans because of their gloom; de Man turns to Schlegel, who was anything but gloomy. De Man does not explore the relationship between irony and gloom; nor does he read his avoidance of gloom as a category of understanding. Merely disagreeing about the gloomy nature of the Germans, he refrains in any case from challenging the boundary that gloom poses for Booth.

At first glance the reversion to gloom comes off as peculiarly undetermined to the extent that it establishes an unreflected return to themes of taste and sensibility. De Man appears to be taking recourse to oddly regressive literary values, rolling back to a difference in sensibility. No longer literalism, the other of irony has now become gloom, echoing perceptions associated with eighteenth-century aesthetics. Booth and de Man have switched from playing dumb and dumber to the rivalry posted by glum and glummer. The unreflected return to sensibility, which cites without attribution Madame de Staël's discovery of Teutonic gloominess, evokes a gothic mood — a discursive atmosphere that bypasses irony's destructive edges. At the same time there is something altogether ironic about the way the difference between Booth and de Man gets organized around gloom, whose valence remains uncertain. De Man locates gloom at the limit, as the site for his departure from Booth, as a beginning or end of a reflection on irony; this is where they part ways, without explication, staking everything on a word that is itself undecidable. What is gloom? How has it come to function as the limit out of which irony emerges? Gloom is set as a hinge, as that which marks the border between what is American and what is German, or between two American appropriations of Germanicity (de Man, in this text, has to show that he is American, therefore the dumber one, a zealous convert to American forms of idiocy). Everything hangs on the meaning of gloom, much as gloom hangs over the understanding of irony. Indeed, everything is left hanging, for the distinction between the cognitive and performative capacities of gloom to spread through the text is left strictly undecidable. Far from indicating only a sensibility, gloom, whether acknowledged or avoided, dooms the text to settle on the spectacle of its failure to understand.

If I have stated my interest in the life of Paul de Man, this was not only a matter of breaking with the code of philosophical civility. Nor was it motivated solely by Friedrich Schlegel, toward whom I was double-heading, together with de Man, and whose project it was to establish a "Philosophie des Lebens." These motivators would have been sufficient to set me on the path of life. All projects of a *Lebensphilosophie* aside, I was taking my cue from and repeating a rather unlikely quirk of de Man's text. In an uncharacteristic display of "interest," de Man, whose project in this text is to resuscitate a much-scorned Schlegel — to save the German he turns against the Germans and their institutional study groups — writes: "It would hardly be hyperbolic to say (and I could defend the affirmation) that the whole discipline of *Germanistik* has developed for the single reason of dodging Friedrich Schlegel, of getting around the challenge that Schlegel and that *Lucinde* offer to the whole notion of an academic discipline which would deal with German literature — seriously" (168). De Man's fascination with Schlegel is not restricted solely to the work of this signator (the work is greatly contested, fragmentary, sometimes even pornographic, as in the case of *Lucinde*): "Schlegel is an enigmatic figure, a curious work and a curious person" (167). De Man repeats the emphasis on the person Friedrich Schlegel, on his political choices, on what might be construed as external to the work, though these borders need to be interrogated. He expresses interest, even fascination, with the personal and political Schlegel but never says why exactly. He keeps the secret, maintaining the bond as enigma. "It's an enigmatic career, and a work which is by no means impressive.... It's a bewildering personal career, also politically bewildering" (167). It does not take long to realize that, while de Man does not say so, Schlegel is the *alazon* within the German tradition of reading irony. As with his treatment of allegory, de Man begins with a figure abjected by the history of its occurrence and rescues it by showing how far ahead it is of its impressive detractors. As allegory was dumped on in favor of the metaphysical coziness and coincidences of symbol, so Schlegel was dumped on, put down by the biggest names, felt to be an irritant, a political compromiser, an ignoramus who should not be writing (thus the impression of defiance when de Man cites him on "how to write well" [*Lyceum*, fragment 37]).

So we are introduced to another configuration of *eiron* and *alazon*, with Schlegel substituting for de Man in an uneven match with the authoritative Hegel. Almost everyone who wrote about Schlegel was nearly scandalized by what a poor philosopher he was. "This is the case most notoriously with Hegel, who refers to Schlegel and *Lucinde* and loses his cool, which doesn't happen so easily to Hegel. Whenever this comes up he gets very upset and becomes insulting — he says Schlegel is a bad philosopher, he doesn't know or he hasn't read enough, he should not speak, and so on" (168). Even Kierkegaard interrupts his contest with Hegel to agree on this point: "And Kierkegaard, although he is trying to get away from Hegel, echoes Hegel in the discussion of *Lucinde* which intervenes in his book on irony. He calls it an obscene book and gets very upset too" (168). Schlegel not only falls victim to the philosophers but he is *alazon* to Novalis as well, who "is always held up as the example of the successful poet, the poet who produced real work, as compared to Schlegel who produced nothing but fragments" (180). Schlegel's work never attains the authority of a work, scorned as it is by the heavyweights of philosophy and the exquisite pansies of poetry. He understood and disinscribed any number of ironic registers, yet he was always getting in trouble, always getting somehow *personally* in trouble. The chain of substitutive *alazons* in this text extends, in the end, all the way to Peter Szondi, who, when paired up and pared down with Benjamin, is shown to have fallen short of grasping the truly disruptive powers of irony.

Before pursuing the internal logic of Schlegel's philosophical fragments, upon which so much scorn has been poured, de Man takes a detour in order to establish the Fichtean system underlying Schlegel's work. What interests us here, in terms of the necessary doubling of a self into a component that is tied to a linguistic act, on the one hand, and another component that can be translated into experiential categories, on the other hand, is the emergence of a certain irony against which the self is continually tested. "From the moment that there are comparative judgments, it becomes possible to speak of properties of the self and it may appear as an experience; it becomes possible to talk

133

about it in terms of an experience" (175). This doubled self, according to Schlegel, can be grasped as a transcendental self that man approaches "as something that's infinitely agile, infinitely elastic . . . , as a self that stands above any of its particular experiences and toward which any particular self is always under way" (175). A part of the self enjoys great mobility. Infinitely active and agile, it is seen to stand above any of its experiences, patiently monitoring the self subjected to types of self-testing, colliding with the limits of experiential being. The "first" self, which owes its existence only to catechresis, to the warped power of language to name and to posit anything, is "the beginning of a logical development" and as such has nothing to do with "the experiential or the phenomenological self in any form" (173). This self is itself posited and "has nothing to do, for example, with a consciousness. About this self, which is thus posited and negated at the same time, no thing can be said. It's a purely empty, positional act" (173). Now the postulation of the split self makes, according to de Man, "a coherent narrative, one in which there are radically negative moments" (176). The narrative, complex in its coherence, turns on the point of not knowing: "the self is never capable of knowing what it is, can never be identified as such, and the judgments emitted by the self about itself, reflexive judgments, are not stable judgments. There's a great deal of negativity, a powerful negativity within it, but the fundamental intelligibility of the system is not in question because it can always be reduced to a system of tropes, which is described as such, and which as such has an internal coherence" (76). While attacked by negativity, the system proves capable of withstanding that which undermines it. At this moment in his argument de Man appears to be "sheltering" the coherence of a system threatened by negativity, immunizing it from the possible incursion of ironic destruction; yet it is not certain that fundamental intelligibility can be thus secured or that tropes provide, "as such," internal coherence. Having asserted the power of the system, de Man more or less resuscitates a type of balancing impasse to which Schlegel, in the *Athenäum*, has given expression. De Man says: "It is genuinely systematic. Schlegel has said somewhere: one must always have a system. He also said: one must never have a system" (176). This is meant to translate "Es ist gleich tödlich für den Geist, ein System zu haben, und keins zu haben. Es wird sich wohl entschließen müssen, beide zu verbinden" (It is equally fatal for mind to have a system and to have none. It will have to opt to connect both [moments]).[52] The double bind of the imperative to connect or bind (*verbinden*) the two irreconcilables seems truly to be connectable and *gleich* (equal, similar) in terms of the death-driven dimension (*tödlich*), the link established between the deadly danger both of system and absence of system. If there exists some assurance of a fundamental intelligibility of system, it appears to be due to the fact that Schlegel's fatal subtraction of systematicity from that which drains it describes a perpetual testing disposition whereby the force of negativity significantly destabilizes while operating the self-testing limit between the phenomenal and the catechrestic or positional, empty self.

There is a self that crash-tests against limits. The crash-test dummy, hitting against phenomenal walls of experience, probes the boundaries of its own transcendence — of its self-transcendence and destruction into the other type of self. De Man is led to a discussion of Schlegel's fragment 42 in the *Lyceum*, which describes this detached self, the self that speaks in philosophy and in poetry.

> "Philosophy is the true home of irony, which might be defined as logical beauty: for wherever men are philosophizing in spoken or written dialogues (he's thinking of Socrates, of course), and provided they are not entirely systematic, irony ought to be produced and postulated; even the Stoics regarded urbanity as a virtue. It is true, there is also a rhetorical irony which, if sparingly used, performs a very excellent function, especially in polemics, but compared to the lofty urbanity of the Socratic muse, rhetorical irony is like the splendor of the most brilliant oratory compared to ancient high tragedy. . . . There are ancient and modern poems which breathe in their entirety, and in every detail, the divine breath of irony. In such poems, there lives a real transcendental buffoonery. Their interior is permeated by the mood [Stimmung] which surveys everything and rises infinitely above everything limited, even the poet's own art, virtue, and genius; and their exterior form by the histrionic style of an ordinary good Italian buffo."[53]

De Man's commentary here, which leases irony out to various discursive moments, gives focus to the exterior form of buffoonery, a bizarre force capable of breaking out suddenly and transcending limits: "Now this buffo has given the critics a lot of trouble, and that's what it's all about" (177). It is perhaps a matter of small consequence, but when de Man finds himself totalizing — "that's what it's all about" — he opens up a space of ambiguity concerning the place from which he reads. Is it all about giving critics trouble — is that "what it's all about"? Or is it about the simulcast transcendence and detranscendentalizing gesture featuring the buffo, the lofty passage unpredictably falling to the level of the comic actor, a singer in comic opera? How should one read the slippage in the passage from transcendentalizing buffoonery to the ordinary buffo? The buffo recalls the type onto which Nietzsche will later latch, recurring as buffoon, a close relative who will have its entry updated by him in the secret encyclopedia of stylized forms he shares with the Romantics. Schlegel produced the tropology in a minor key, substituting the burlesque singer for what originated as a pantomine dance, that which indulges in low jest — an understudy replacement whose status continues to remain unclear. De Man plays off the external form and histrionic style of the buffo. The buffo, for de Man, in any case, marks a distance and destruction of self, an exteriorization of a self attached to the work.

The passage presents a summary of the Fichtean system, where the negativity of the self is emphasized because, de Man offers, "it is the detachment in relation to everything, and also in relation to the self and to the writer's own work, the radical distance (the radical negation of himself) in relation to his own work" (177). What interests me as a consequence of the splits in modalities of self is the way this fragment plays urbanity, that is, "lofty urbanity," against "real transcendental buffoonery" — in other words, how the Greek ambience for intelligent being communicates, if transcendentally, with what appears to oppose it. Transcendental buffoonery rips the system; it is shown to be propelled by a truly transgressive force that is fueled not so much by romantic abandon as by a kind of will to rise above that which is limited, "owned" ("the poet's own art, virtue and genius"), bound by law and convention. The buffo turns out to be a figure compelling an essential linkage between figural and parafigural levels of meaning. To say it no doubt too quickly, in the manner of a sneak preview, the disjunctive and unassimilable buffo, a crucial mask of ironic destruction, will be shown to stand in for parabasis to the extent that it relates to anacoluthon, which is to say, it is marked by and is the mark of interruption and, finally, of irreparable undoing.

The buffo, said to have given critics a lot of trouble, now is seen as that which "has a very specific meaning, which has been identified in scholarship very convincingly" (178). The buffo effects a disruption of narrative illusion, "the *aparté*, the aside to the audience, by means of which the illusion of the fiction is broken (what we call in German *aus der Rolle fallen*, to drop out of your role)" (178). Given de Man's earlier profession that, unlike his American counterparts, he understands German, the parenthetical Germanized "we" is, of course, noteworthy, particularly since it occurs to remind us of the role he has adopted, that of *alazon*, out of which he constantly drops or slips: the setup who sets up, who marks asides, disrupting at critical moments the illusion of the *sujet supposé savoir*, the supposedly knowing subject. In the discrete tradition of de Manian syntax, he drops out of the role when he's in fact on a roll and wishes to express a superior knowledge. This is not entirely contrary to the spirit of the buffo, who breaks up the syntax of the performance in order to assert distance and difference, the existence of another world of reference that proves to be destructive of the first world. In these instances, to drop out is to tune in. Yet before we succumb to the temptation of irrevocably dropping out of our role with an obsessive jam on which roles de Man may have adopted and dropped within the flux of critical masks and identities assumed, let us return to the text, where it is asserted that interruption has been there from the beginning.

The matter of the interruptive force, its significant morphs and pressing forms, still needs to be settled. Does ironic interruption, as hiatus or caesura, occur accidentally and freely, or is there something conventional, even lawlike, in the abrupt displacements enforced by its occurence? To help us out a little, de Man at this point cites an example that remains closer, arguably, to the opposite of the claims he makes for it. "You remember," he offers, "that, in the first thing we read, Schlegel said you have to be able to interrupt the friendly conversation at all moments, freely, arbitrarily" (178). The reference is to a moment when Schlegel discusses restraint and the inevitability of coercive force that underlies all levels of articulation (writing, speaking, communicating). On the dignity and value of self-restraint (*Selbstbeschränkung*), Schlegel has written:

> ". . . wherever we do not restrain ourselves, the world will restrain us; and thus we will become its slave. . . . we can restrain ourselves only in those points and aspects (along those lines) where we have infinite power in self-creation and self-destruction [Selbstschöpfung und Selbstvernichtung]. Even a friendly conversation which cannot at any given moment be broken off voluntarily with complete arbitrariness has something illiberal about it. An artist, however, who is able and wants to express himself completely, who keeps nothing to himself and would wish to say everything he knows, is very much to be pitied."[54]

Schlegel argues for the presumed necessity or at least for the inevitability of the experience of self-restraint and self-limitation, whether it should issue from an ever-harassing world or, preferably, if one is not to be pitied, from an internal sensibility for law. De Man accords a tone of greater urgency to the freeing interruption and the level of the arbitrary. He is possibly right to the extent that, in his own translation, an amicable conversation does not entirely belong to the order of self-creative and self-destructive acts: "one can restrict oneself only in the points and along the lines where one has *infinite* power, in *self-creation* and in *self-destruction*. Even an amicable conversation that cannot be gratuitously broken off at any moment [*aus unbedingter Willkür*] has something coercive."[55] Nonetheless, it remains difficult to discern the shadow of an imperative dictating that you must "be able to interrupt the friendly conversation at all moments, freely, arbitrarily." (I recognize that I am splitting semantic hairs, but irony depends on such acts of fissional insistence. Let us continue.) It seems, rather, that the interruption itself carries the trace of a constraint, is somehow tied to a concept of law that produces a disruption in the case even of *friendly* conversation (one can pursue here what Schlegel had to say about dialogue). Interruption is not entirely free or arbitrary — otherwise it would lose its quality of genuine disruptive energy — but, while anticipated and even coded, it is forced upon you like a sudden arrest by the policing cry of "Freeze!" Whether or not the break-off is freely chosen or forcibly established, its temporal promiscuity — the fact that it can happen at any and all times — permits de Man to link the buffo, who, as *aparté* has been located in interruption, with parabasis. The translation that de Man offers of the buffo's role — or, rather, his dropout role — is fairly straightforward, reverting to "technical" usage: "The technical term for this [interruption, the specific meaning of the buffo] in rhetoric, the term that Schlegel uses, is *parabasis*" (178). Parabasis is defined by de Man as "the interruption of a discourse by a shift in the rhetorical register. It's what you would get in Sterne, precisely, the constant interruption of the narrative illusion by intrusion, or you get it in *Jacques le Fataliste*, which are indeed Schlegel's models" (178). Now, parabasis — or *Parekbase*, as Schlegel frequently writes, underscoring the character of stepping forward in Hellenic comedy — opens up a channel for sudden aberration, for the static of vulgarity and surprise. *Parekbase* involved for Schlegel a kind of surprise attack, an abrupt turn or polemic (attack) that was meant to astonish. This sense of the term was picked up in a poem published in 1820 by Goethe, entitled "Parabase":

Immer wechselnd, fest sich haltend;
Nah und fern und fern und nah;
So gestaltend, umgestaltend —
Zum Erstaunen bin ich da.

[*Self-insistent, always changing,*
Near and far and far and near,
Birth of shapes, their rearranging —
Wonder of wonders, I am here.][56]

The disruptive turnaround, a lightning effect (Blitz) of provocative revelation occuring when the Greek chorus steps forward, crossing the line, corresponds to the moments in Schlegel's essay on unintelligibility that depict sudden outbursts of a hidden rage, the advent of irreparable chaos. On the semantic scene, interruption is seen as unintelligibility that, in Goethe's sense, effects utter astonishment. What presents itself as astonishing, making it seem as though the attack were arriving from an inner limit — from inside — is the fact that the nearness or remoteness of the sudden outburst cannot be clearly determined, thus rendering its status as outburst or invasion undecidable.

In de Man's essay the chain of translations methodically continues, for it turns out that another, equally valid term describing this type of intrusive break for which the buffo has stood, or of which he has been an exterior form, is "anacoluthon": "There's another word for this, too, which is equally valid in rhetoric — the word *anacoluthon*. Anacoluthon or *anacoluthe* is more often used in terms of syntactical patterns of tropes, or periodic sentences, where the syntax of a sentence which raises certain expectations is suddenly interrupted and, instead of getting what you would expect to get in terms of the syntax that has been set up, you get something completely different, a break in the syntactical expectations of the pattern" (178). The best place to find anacoluthon at work, according to de Man, is in the third volume of Proust's *À la recherche du temps perdu*, in the section "La Prisonière." When trying to analyze the structure of Albertine's lies, Marcel describes her as typically beginning sentences in the first person and then switching almost imperceptibly by means of "some device in the middle of the sentence" so that your expectation that she is revealing something dreadful about herself is thwarted by your recognition that "without your knowing it, suddenly she's not talking about herself anymore but about that other person" (178). She accomplishes the crossover by means of the device "'que les rhétoriciens appellent anacoluthe'" (that rhetoricians call anacoluthon)."[57] You have been set up by anacoluthon, call her Albertine, who pulls a fast one without your knowing it. De Man mirrors this process, or, rather, the disruption of process, in the retelling. He has effected a slight reversal, but nonetheless an anacoluthic turn, when, as if finding himself in the passage, he substitutes *rhétoriciens* for Proust's *grammariens*, inverting Albertine's tendency to begin by apparently referring to herself and switching to another. The syntactical switch opens the space of the lie. There is no substantial commission of wrongdoing but anacoluthon establishes the fact, performed in Proust and elsewhere, of a rhetorical crime scene.

The Proust passage demonstrates a strikingly succinct understanding of anacoluthon: "this syntactical disruption which, exactly in the same way as a parabasis, interrupts the narrative line" (178). Translating the theatrical disruptor into rhetorical terms, de Man concludes this line of inquiry: "So the buffo is a parabasis or an anacoluthon, an interruption of the narrative line" (178). Yet irony is not only an interruption but, according to Schlegel (via de Man), it fulfills the contradictory if not "violently paradoxical" (179) condition of a permanent parabasis. Without being localizable to one point, parabasis occurs "at all points[.] . . . irony is everywhere, at all points the narrative can be interrupted. . . . You have to imagine the parabasis as being able to take place at all times. At all moments the interruption can happen" (179). Thus the philosophical line of argumentation contained in Schlegel's novel *Lucinde* is "brutally interrupted" when it turns out that the author had brought together two radically incompatible codes — one putting forth a Fichtean argument and, simultaneously, the other pornographically describing the act of love. "This interrupts, disrupts, profoundly the inner mood (the *Stimmung*), in the same way that in this passage the inner mood being described is completely disrupted by the exterior form, which is that of the buffo, that of the parabasis, that of the interruption, that of the undoing of the narrative line" (179). Since the narrative line is said to refer here to the structure resulting from the tropological system, de Man amends Schlegel's definition of irony to read, "irony is the permanent parabasis of the allegory of tropes" (179). Once again there coexists an unspoken community between mood and irony — de Man does not probe the stability of what he calls inner mood, though Schlegel, adopting *Parekbase*, invites a collapse of the inner and outer terms of explosiveness.

The allegory of tropes "has its own narrative coherence, its own systematicity, and it is that coherence, that systematicity, which irony interrupts, disrupts" (179). In a sense, then, irony disrupts the very singularity, the extreme idiosyncracy, of the allegory of tropes, which "makes it impossible ever to achieve a theory of narrative that would be consistent" (179). Thus the systematicity at the heart of narrative, itself singular, "will always be interrupted, always be disrupted, always be undone by the ironic dimension which it will necessarily contain" (179). Irony acts as that countersingularity capable of destroying the nodal security of any autonomous system of tropes. An internal limit, at once finite and unending, irony is an installation within what de Man calls narrative, thwarting any possible claim for ultimate coherence, even if it should operate within the confines of predictability. Irony acts as the promise of a disruption that, always anticipated, may or may not be delivered but that binds narrative to ever-recurring trial runs. In a note to himself de Man writes that "irony is (permanent) parabasis of allegory — intelligibility of (representational) narrative disrupted at all times" (179n.21). The constative or cognitive dimension of narrative, riddled by interference, is thus tied to an internal limit that also functions to exceed the present narrative structure, compromising at all times the appearance of intelligibility.

As refined as the argument gets, threading its way through different levels of insinuated intelligibility, the concern with stupidity remains constant and is by no means contiguous to the reading of irony that engages de Man here. Although he does not produce a theory or even a reading of stupidity as such, he rarely retreats from the disabusing insight in a manner that would resemble Schlegel's withdrawal from his intuition about authentic speech (reelle Sprache). (Schlegel is said to have recoiled from his own insight because he "didn't have the power, or the confidence, or the love, to abandon himself to it, and he retreated from it" [180]. Schlegel's retreat somehow positioned him as Novalis's alazon to the extent that Novalis, for his part, "could acquiesce to myth, and therefore became the great poet which we all know him to be, whereas Schlegel only wrote Lucinde" [180].) Schlegel treats authentic language in "Rede über die Mythologie" (Discourse on Mythology), where de Man discovers a curious substitution to have occurred between drafts. Focusing on the "'marvelous and the perennial alternation of enthusiasm and irony,'" the later text substitutes "'the strange (das Sonderbare), even the absurd [das Widersinnige], as well as a childlike yet sophisticated naïveté [geistreiche naïveté]'" for three other terms that Schlegel associates with reelle Sprache.[58] For whatever reason, Sonderbare, Widersinnige, and geistreiche naïveté are tossed out in favor of "'error, madness, and

141

simple-minded stupidity.'"[59] This lineup, according to Schlegel's final hand, is meant to represent the origin of all poetry. Involved in the suspension of the law governing rational thought, it acts "'to replace us within a beautiful confusion of fantasy in the original chaos of human nature (for which mythology is the best name).'"[60] De Man comments: "The authentic language is the language of madness, the language of error, and the language of stupidity. (*Bouvard et Pécuchet*, if you want — that's the authentic language, what he really means by *reelle Sprache*)" (181). Far from being evicted from the philosophical premises of Romanticism, stupidity — along with the languages of madness and error — supplies the abyssal ground for real and authentic language. Everything else occurs on the order (or under the orders) of secondary revision, including Schlegel's repression of this insight.

Now, de Man himself remains evasive about the relation of madness to error or these to stupidity, but he treats them more or less as one entity rooted in the "evil" of sheer circulation. According to de Man, authentic language, which Schlegel construes as that of madness, error, stupidity, "is such because this authentic language is a mere semiotic entity, open to the radical arbitrariness of any sign system and as such capable of circulation, but which as such is profoundly unreliable" (181). This commentary, to the extent that it is one, offers a somewhat disappointing conclusion, as it contents itself with pulling out a staple stop of the de Manian lexicon (radically arbitrary, mere semiotics) without accounting significantly for the substitution and precise articulation that Schlegel proposes. How does Schlegel anticipate a reading of Flaubert in the passage that appears to resolve "what he really means by *reelle Sprache*"? What makes it possible for simpleminded stupidity to originate all poetry, and how does it serve, in the end, to jeopardize reflexive and dialectical models?

Within the range of this lecture it remains tied up with the free play of the signifier, "which is, as you know, the root of error, madness, stupidity, and all other evil" (181). Like money, authentic language is open to sheer circulation, wear and tear, the arbitrary assignments of an unpredictable itinerary. This is where the textual machine kicks in. Once engaged, it functions as "an implacable determination and a total arbitrariness, *unbedingter Willkür*, . . . which inhabits words on the level of the play of the signifier, which undoes any narrative consistency of lines, and which undoes the reflexive and the dialectical model, both of which are, as you know, the basis of any narration" (181).[61] If there exists a semiotic tic in this lecture — and no doubt any lecture hosts one or two — it occurs in the repeated assertion "as you know" at moments where knowing is undermined or in need, precisely, of some elaboration. "As you know," a cognitive pretender, punctuates, if only to minimize, the suspended ignorance that is explicitly thematized in this text. "As you know" is a performative that tries to clear the abyss of not knowing, or, coming from de Man, as we know, it also sounds an imperative, raising the tone and expectation of a demanding teacher: you had better know this. On the other hand, it may act as allegorical marker, pointing to a wealth of other texts and materials that can never be assembled in the present but that you should know to scout. Still an imperative addressing that which is missing. Technically, in any case, it functions to allow the present avoidance of demonstration or elaboration, followed by apodictic assertion, "both of which are, as you know, the basis of any narration. There is no narration without reflection, no narrative without dialectic, and what irony disrupts (according to Friedrich Schlegel) is precisely that dialectic and that reflexivity, the tropes" (181).

When Schlegel becomes the object of friendly critical activity, attempts are typically made, notes de Man, to rescue him from charges of frivolity. In the process of interpreting his work (or absence of a Work), critics "always have to recover the categories of the self, of history, and of dialectic, which are precisely the categories which in Schlegel are disrupted in a radical way" (182). In the essay's final showdown of *eiron* versus *alazon*, Benjamin is said to see "the destructive power, the negative power, of the parabasis, fully" (182), whereas Szondi, already semiretired, has opted for aesthetic recuperation. Benjamin sees that the "'ironization of form consists in a deliberate destruction of the form.'"[62] The radical, complete destruction of the form congeals, for Benjamin, the critical act, which "undoes the form by analysis, which by demystification destroys the form" (182). Yet Benjamin, too, has a way of recuperating the destructive character of irony, though de Man does not get him on this (instead, he finds the rescue operation underwritten by the prestige of Hegelian language "very clear, very moving, very effective" [183]): "'the ironization of form is like the storm which lifts up [*aufheben*] the curtain of the transcendental order of art and reveals it for what it is, in this order as well as in the unmediated existence of the work.' . . . The idea is the infinite project (as we had it in Fichte), the infinite absolute toward which the work is under way. The irony is the radical negation, which, however, reveals as such, by the undoing of the work, the absolute toward which the work is under way."[63]

143

De Man's contact with Benjamin allows a disclosive omission to surface. When reading this and other crucial passages in German Idealism or continental Romanticism, de Man, though no doubt familiar with the pathbreaking work of Lacoue-Labarthe and Nancy in these areas, shows no particular interest in the thought of finitude, or at least not in the way that Heidegger had formulated the necessity of such a thought. In the way, we might say, that every work is an allegory of human finitude. He strangely leaves the infinite conversation of Fichte and his dream team, their infinity of projects, in peace. But maybe we can lift up the curtain on the order of temporality that governs this text. For what else draws his pen but the endless thought of finitude? Is not the disruption that irony provokes another way of saying finitude? Irony suspends the infinite project, its work of appropriating meaning to itself — permanently, which is to say: time and again. Just as irony cannot be stopped or ended as it disrupts the project and the Work, finitude is not reducible to an end in the sense of teleological accomplishment or absolute limit. It engages a suspension, a hiatus in meaning, reopened each time in a here and now, disappearing as it opens, exposing itself to something so unexpected and possibly *different* that, like irony, it persistently eludes its own grasp. Marking the experience of sheer exposition, moreover, irony and finitude share the refusal to disclose themselves fully. As in the case of finitude (if it can be reduced to such a thing), the excessive nature of irony continually indicates in the guise of radical negation the inappropriability of its meaning. The inappropriation of meaning is what concerns the rest of de Man's essay, an insight for which Schlegel holds the key, even if he fumbles when turning it.

Nonunderstanding is another name for finitude. De Man ends "The Concept of Irony" by pointing up the historical implications in Schlegel's essay "Über die Unverständlichkeit." Now he turns on the heat, showing how Kierkegaard and others have used history as a hypostasis to defend against irony, as if history were each time summoned to block the more troubling markings of finitude.[64] Schlegel takes another route, heading for trouble but opening a new path, even if it is one that has been cordoned off by the historicizing police. Schlegel's path, however provisional and sparingly inspected, has taught us the value of unintelligibility:

Schlegel says the following: "But is nonunderstanding, then, something so evil and objectionable? — It seems to me that the welfare of families and of nations is grounded in it; if I am not mistaken about nations and systems, about the artworks of mankind, often so artful that one cannot enough admire the wisdom of the inventors. An incredibly small portion (of nonunderstanding) suffices, provided it is preserved with unbreakable trust and purity, and no restless intelligence dares to come close to its holy borderline. Yes, even the most precious possession of mankind, inner satisfaction, is suspended, as we all know, on some such point. It must remain in the dark if the entire edifice is to remain erect and stable (that's the edifice which, according to Benjamin, we built by taking it apart); it would lose its stability at once if this power were to be dissolved by means of understanding." (183)

Nonunderstanding, marking as it does the suspension, the hiatus in meaning, should not be viewed as objectionable. The solidity of such fragile entities as family and nationhood depends upon its persistence. Schlegel assigns values of purity and the aura of the sacred to nonunderstanding; he approaches it with a pledge of unbreakable trust. What would happen if understanding ruled? In the first place, understanding is constructed as a hypothesis, for it cannot be seen as existing, as a presence. If the world were suddenly to become comprehensible, we would be horrified, Schlegel asserts; it would unsettle us. Not only outer structures and models but the very possibility of an inner, more private satisfaction would be greatly compromised if sheer understanding were to prevail. The romantic trope of interiority itself would be rendered susceptible to collapse if the hegemony of understanding were to be promoted. Self would be under attack, being reduced to a transparent calculus: "It must remain in the dark." A restless intelligence must be halted at the sacred boundary by which obscurity is guarded. The stability of internal and outer supports in fact depends upon ensuring the reign of an obscure, chaotic space, the site where intelligence fails, where it is neutralized and nonintelligence gives way to an analytic existential of stupidity. But it is all a matter of dosage at this point. Even a small amount (an "incredibly small portion") of nonunderstanding suffices to keep things going.

We are dependent on nonunderstanding, on a dose of sheer dumbness, much as elsewhere, without determined apportionment, stupidity along with madness and error formed the base of authentic language. Pure dumbness, neutral and blank, keeps open an unsketched territory that Schlegel recognizes as unconscious. His thought embraces an unconscious component. The limited space where nonunderstanding is frozen points to the unreadable navel of a dream (Schlegel also discovered and thought about unconscious regions),[65] and it is also figured as the noncomprehension that generates attempts at comprehensibility. De Man's intervention makes itself scarce at this juncture, as though it wanted to back down from a reading. He might have elaborated a more substantial reading had he been granted the time to work this piece into a chapter; at this stage he responds, "That sounds very nice, but you should remember that the chaos is error, madness, and stupidity, in all its forms. Any expectation that one may have that deconstruction might be able to construct is suspended by such a passage, which is very strictly a pre-Nietzschean passage, heralding exactly 'Über Wahrheit und Lüge.' Any attempt to construct — that is, to narrate — on no matter how advanced a level, is suspended, interrupted, disrupted, by a passage like this" (184).

To some degree, deconstruction is itself affected by the passage, which, turning on the categoremes error, madness, and stupidity, suspends narration. The passage, pre-Nietzschean but already "in" deconstruction, appears to function as the permanent parabasis of deconstruction. It is thus all the more regrettable that stupidity is not read by de Man, although it cannot be said to be missing in this piece but is displaced to his positionings, enacted and refracted by the imperatives of staged rivalries. As it stands, de Man makes the announcement of disruption his disruption and suspends the impossible concept of irony over the threatening configuration of error, madness, and stupidity.

---

5. The Splendor of Unintelligibility

"The Concept of Irony" relies on an unmarked aspect of Schlegel's commentary in order to suspend itself over the chasm of its implications. This concerns the resistance to theory that Schlegel's essay explores. For those who do not have access to it, "On Unintelligibility" is not identical to the unbearably dense type of work to which so many allergies have been formed. Though I have nothing against unbearably dense texts (I eat them for breakfast) and feel that allergies should be treated homeopathically, with low doses of the very thing you reject, it is perhaps timely to explain how the essay came about. After the publication of Athenäum, the group in charge, the editors or the community (hard to find a label here, but it is important to remember that they were resolutely practicing a democratic politics of writing, as it was for them a big deal to write for and with others, to invite the participation of a plurality of voices — Mehrstimmigkeit — inventing the very concept of a journal and publicly entering into dialogue with one another), among them Novalis, Caroline Schlegel, the brothers Schlegel, Ludwig Tieck, and Fichte — though he was run out of town on charges of atheism, which is why eventually Romanticism split into two locations, first Jena and then, when Friedrich Schlegel split, following F., for Berlin — in any case, those associated with *Athenäum* were roundly attacked for consistently publishing work that was judged unintelligibile. Even the state became involved, and the King's entourage was known to have repeated, "Was man nicht versteht, hat ein Schlegel geschrieben" (If you can't understand it, it was probably written by a Schlegel).[66] This was after the King had passed on a text that he couldn't read to the Obristleutenant Köckeritz, with the order to read it; Köckeritz, unable to make heads or tails of the unsigned text, in turn summoned the royal counselor Niemeyer, who is said to have become indignant, crying out in frustrated rage, as Schlegel, in a letter to Novalis, recounts: "Surely it must have been written by one of the two Schlegels. For [Niemayer] as for other philistines, it's just an axiom: whatever one cannot understand was written by a Schlegel."[67]

So the associates of *Athenäum* were subject to attacks. Cries familiar to those of you who work with theoretical texts resounded accusingly: it's too difficult, truly incomprehensible, what's the point, where's the historical punch to back this up, who cares and what's the point, anyway, it makes no sense, this is unintelligible. Schlegel's response to the indignation aroused by his theoretical work consists of saying, in the first place, Let's discuss unintelligibility. What is unintelligibility? Why does it provoke such (pre-)critical rage? From another point of view, to what extent do we rely upon unintelligibility, and, indeed, to what extent does it guarantee and underlie the very conditions of intelligibility? What does it mean to say that a text is incomprehensible or too difficult, in excess of meaning, or that it does not produce enough codified sense? And anyway, you morons, as for me, if you must know, I personally prefer dumbbells who really don't understand a thing to the understanding scholars, the total idiots, who claim not to understand us. And, finally, here's a poem that my brother, August Wilhelm, wrote yesterday that tells it like it is. (Schlegel's essay ends with a sarcastic poem in defense of the project and against the dumbfounded big shots on the warpath.)

We should add an ideological note here: unintelligibility is openly opposed to *Deutlichkeit* (clarity of expression), which at least since Herder has been considered nearly equivalent to "Deutsch-ness." To go against *Deutlichkeit* was to assail Germanicity. Thus, when Schlegel penned his famous fragment in which the great tendencies of the age are named, he baffled some readers and infuriated others by using the significantly un-German word *Tendenz*. In a sense the sentence performs itself by beginning with the French Revolution, which is seized clearly (*deutlich*) by Schlegel also as a language revolution, a linguistic turn: "The French Revolution, Fichte's philosophy of science, and Goethe's Meister are the greatest tendencies of the age. No revolution that is not loud and material will appear important to the person who objects to this compilation. That kind of person has not yet climbed to the high, broad point of view of human history."[68] The great *Tendenzen* evaded *Deutlichkeit, Deutschheit*, their enumeration beginning as an overturning with the French in French or at least not in German, which is to say that history itself, tendentially appropriated, owes its readability to the unintelligible. The narrative of split loyalties continues.

Two writers have exposed the fiction of intelligibility with uncompromising defiance. Schlegel and Bataille involved themselves in a thinking of the limit that required, for its uncringing articulation, a pornographic accent. To the degree that they sought to score philosophical points, they were excoriated by the high-minded philosophers of their time. The two writers, fortifying philosophical reflection with pornographic poses, will never be forgiven for the way they introduced the unintelligible — the regime of nonunderstanding or unknowing — to thought. They continue to be harassed to this day by the serious ones. The scandal of unintelligibility, the phobic response to another type of meaning production, gains historical momentum with Schlegel's text on the topic, where it can be seen to have entered a codifiable history. But is unintelligibility codifiable? Can it have a history, or are we facing the matter of values and their necessary transvaluations? Or an altogether other order of intervention? For what reason is unintelligibility an unavoidably political issue, and why do professional politicians historically make uninterrogated claims for clarity, which they pretend to observe or typically defy? One can understand why, given some of the Romantic axioms he models, de Man would locate the type of questioning unleashed in Schlegel's essay in a pre-Nietzschean space. Still, the force of Schlegel's unparalleled disruption of meaning extends well into the twentysomething century. Carl Schmitt, ever expanding the realm of hostility, decried the "Promiskuität der Worte" (promiscuousness of words), sexualizing Schlegel's language usage and wondering, in 1925, why the Romantic thinker "sought to make a principle out of the lack of clarity."[69]

The problems that Schlegel raises, and that continue to be evaded, are distinctly of our time. The provocation that he effects haunts philosophy and grates on the nerves of the most problematic arbiters of political thought. It might help us a little to allow that, in the history and sense of questioning sense, Schlegel's work, in addition to marking itself now, for us, as pre-Nietzschean, also stakes out a site that persuasively reassembles Bataille: Schlegel's provocation is distinctly (pre-)Bataillean. Positing a link between rapture and nonunderstanding, the text stops just short of saying, "Stop making sense" (in the sense of *poeisis*, of making a work of sense); yet, measuring up against unintelligibility, it strongly produces a presentiment of the prestige of Bataillean *non-savoir* — the contestation, the nonpositive affirmation, which is to say, finally, in Bataille and as latency in Schlegel (it already exists as a trace in Schlegel), the affirmation of nothing (*rien*). Whereas for Bataille *non-savoir* is indissociable from atheism, for Schlegel unintelligibility is indissociable from *Athenäum*, which was hassled for its atheistic professions. Schlegel, as you know, shed many tears of eros. Like Bataille, he was invested in the question of community, which emerges as a praxis in the punctual codependencies that every journal implies. The *Athenäum* and *Acéphale* were related ventures to the extent that they probed the limits of community and the communality of writing without yielding to fables of communion: they shared a communitarian drive whose principal support was writing. This is why Schlegel, for his part, had to insist on nonunderstanding as the basis for a writing community as well as for a theory of friendship (which he practiced on Schleiermacher).[70] A community without communion, having relinquished the basic claim to a totality of meaning — to that which would have ensured proper understanding — these writing blocs were on principle opposed to any fusional, totalitarian system of politics or meaning.

To the extent that Schlegel made earnest attempts to transpose aesthetic claims into a *Lebenspraxis*, he was asking for trouble. It was one thing to write scandalous novels but quite another matter to propose agendas for alternative ways of living. The early romantics and the Schlegel brothers experimented with new forms of social living, transmutations of living-with (*des Zusammenlebens*) and the practice of "free love." They were not satisfied with restricting "the exchange of roles, androgyny, and the demand for free love" to the written work but, duty bound, offered translations of poetic-erotic license into the domain of practical reason.[71] They made the personal political without enacting the exclusion of the erotic. The way sexuality inscribed itself socially involved significant renegotiations of the social contract.

Critically subversive, they called for a constant inner revolution and focused the thought of sociality on the erotic couple; they tried all sorts of positions. Yet until Friedrich's final conversions, they resisted communion. To the end of the ironic line, Friedrich stood his ground: "True irony is the irony of love."[72] Love, a metonymy of community, was itself ironic — or irony, truly, is love — which is to say that it preempts the exchange of self-identical rings, the decadent love-death of Wagnerian cycles, and is based, rather, on the unrepenting recognition of difference, separateness, and . . . nonunderstanding. Exorbitantly summoning the infinite at the limit of finitude, love, no matter how "free," is irony. There is no such thing as a free love.

How does the irony of love communicate with Bataille in such a way as to sanction the privilege of the "pre-"? Schlegel's work is pre-Bataillean because it authorizes an empty profanation of sorts, underwriting with particular conviction in *Lucinde* the vision of world, bereft of the sacred, that, plumply bourgeois, is abandoned to an experience of sexuality, trembling in ecstasy. Schlegel, moreover, initiated, or at least pursued in a singular manner (he credits Goethe with the initiatory gesture), a logic of transgression that is based on love. He does so against the grain of staple romantic determinations. Schlegel is responsible for a thinking of the limit, or, as the passages on how to write well illustrate, he articulated acts of restraint and self-limitation that are set against notions of romantic abandon, which they also ghost. In this regard, to return briefly to de Man's lecture, there is something peculiar, if not amusing, about de Man's insistence that Schlegel's text on writing for once is not at all interested in sexuality. No doubt a bold proposition, it inevitably reflects back on the contingencies of the writer's mood, leaving a soupçon of repression and the mark of a coerced reading. How could writing's rapture be funneled safely into a desexualized tract? Does sexual inscription subsist only on the level of thematic investment? De Man would be the last to dwell on decisions made by merely thematic considerations, and he has taught us to stave off their seductions. (It can be shown that in the case of Schlegel the concerns of writing are staged and made to circulate within an allegedly spermatic economy: writing opens the question of the limit, asking how it is possible to limit passion and to restrain the urge to gush prematurely, all over the place.) The pertinent passages, cited by de Man, rely upon a reading of the violent rapture with which writing inevitably comes to be identified but that, in order to be sustained, must locate itself as limit. If the act of imposing a limit is a true one, as in the texts of Schlegel and Bataille, then it excites a certain ambience; it puts out a call: to the extent that every limit calls out, it calls to itself transgression. In Schlegel's work there exists an unlimited rule of the limit, which permits him to point to the infinite while basing his claims on a repeated inscription of finitude.

The play of the passionate limit brings us to the matter of the fragment on which Schlegel's romantic insight hinges — and by which his reputation as a responsible writer was compromised. How does Schlegel's thinking of the fragment open out to Bataille's thought? The fragment does not present itself as some metaphorical tip of the iceberg, reconnectable to a recalcitrant totality. Its splintering is due to another set of considerations that resist allegiance to former totalities. Rather than address itself to a plenitude, the fragmentary work of Schlegel can be said already to address itself to the absence of God (he followed the atheist Fichte out of town), to the death of God in the sense that this death can only be prophesied or announced but not simply asserted as such. Even Nietzsche goes only so far as to have his prime untimely anchorman, Zarathustra, and the other voices posted along his work announce the death of God in the mode of prophecy. The fragment is part of the long announcement. It tells us that there is an empty exteriority in the place of God: transcendental winds are shifting; it forecasts experience becoming increasingly internal (which is not the same as "subjective"), experimental, unsure.

The origin, as we have seen, no longer supposing a serene reserve, is held by chaos, by stupidity. Thus the essay on unintelligibility occurs as a series of tests or experiments — or, more radically still, Schlegel states that he has investigated the possibility and impossibility of "Versuche anzustellen" (conducting experiments [2:530]). The *Athenäum*, which has put together a particular way to structure trial runs, a manner in which to ask of an idea "the question of whether it is at all possible,"[73] saw itself as nothing other than an interactive test site: "And where would one have a better opportunity to conduct all sorts of experiments on the possibility or impossibility of the matter than if one either writes a journal like the *Athenäum* or takes part in it as a reader"?[74] So Schlegel has wanted to be able "to go through the entire sequence of my experiments."[75] The journal was thus set as the constructed site for the inner experience or, rather, the internal experiment that, susceptible to review and retraction, promised to obscurity and failure, always runs the risk of having its head chopped off. At least the transcendental heading can offer no guarantee of truth or substance. As that which posits and tests the limits of possible *Versuche,* the *Athenäum* was by self-definition — in terms of the necessary trait of democratic instability — unsure, experimental, dedicated to the destruction of intelligible models.

There's more to Schlegel's anticipatory complicity with Bataille. Schlegel stood accused of vulgarity and was severely reproached for the impurity, indeed, the horror, of his work — values that, marked down by Hegel in terms of philosophical depletion and moral bankruptcy, nonetheless accrue interest by the decisive time of Bataille. We can see that Schlegel understood the relatedness of excess to limit; he recognized that the experience of sexuality, which challenges the limit, begins to announce God's death (the fact of his later conversion to Catholicism only strengthens the position of his transgressions, though the return to Christ was also a sign of his political opportunism and his desire to be hired out to Metternich). Schlegel's insight, around which the *Athenäum* as well as the fragments and the theory of the novel were organized, implied a fracture in language, a breach in the flow of any communication. Like Bataille, Schlegel marks the intimate wounding with which we associate communication in the paradoxical experience of the loss of language.[76] These concerns did not originate solely with Schlegel's reflections, though he took them in the direction of their own excess. The opening of these philosophical themes occurs with Kant, who established a thinking of a limit at the same time as he introduced a new thought of negativity. The "new negativity," as we might call it, comes from the nothingness that inhabits negation, privation. This marks the beginning of a thinking of finitude and may explain why Schlegel was so focused on the destructive potential of a new negativity capable of undoing, as de Man says, the dialectical and reflexive (Fichtean) system. Dialectics tries to leave in the dust the delay and interruption in metaphysics incurred by Kant's *Critique of Pure Reason* — or, more precisely, it sweeps up the dust and conceals the traces of an explosion detonated by the *Critique.* After Kant, Hegel restored metaphysics in the dialectical mode while, on the sidelines, disabling Schlegel's textual machine. In his way Hegel negated the negation or the unmovable negativity on which Schlegel was experimenting. As if by means of a secret transhistorical alliance, Bataille will have offered a form of restitution to his largely unacknowledged precursor by mocking his principal detractors. In the midst of the ecstatic abandon played out in his orgies, Bataille has Hegel arrive on the scene. This time, having adjusted his attitude, he surrenders his critical edge. Neither scornful nor losing his cool, the great one is made to pay homage to the pornography of the cogito shared by the brothers Bataille and Schlegel.

If Schlegel and Bataille are connected in terms of the specific type of scandals they provoked in and with philosophy, they also share a similar fate with regard to a pattern in the reception of their work. The ironic production of the fragments and *Lucinde* offers a formidable challenge to "serious" philosophy. Schlegel does not merely run parallel tracks with philosophy but raids it and performs a repertoire of guerrilla operations on its sites — a discursive behavior that has earned the reproof of the reigning philosopher-kings, the serious ones. Schlegel was not without friends, however.[77] Though his works suffered general condemnation (de Man's focus), his old friend and former roommate Friedrich Schleiermacher was impelled to publish, in 1800, a collection of fictional letters, *Confidential Letters on Schlegel's Lucinde*, in which, with hopes of countering unstoppable hostility, the greater part of the prevalent responses to the novel were rehearsed and refuted. Moreover, in *Über die Religion* (1799), he had put forth an argument against "das Joch des Verstehens" (the yoke of understanding).[78] Schlegel's one other best friend, Fichte, announced in September 1799 that *Lucinde* was one of the greatest productions of genius he knew and that he was about to embark on his third reading of it. "But these and some few other favorable reactions were not enough to stem the tidal wave of hostile criticism that threatened to inundate the book completely."[79] *Lucinde*'s status as a dirty book was nailed by Kierkegaard, who concentrated a sharp attack on the novel, condemning the work because it denied the spirit for the sake of the flesh, aimed at naked sensuality, and attempted to eliminate all morality. Rudolf Haym, who published a comprehensive study in 1870 of the early Romantic movement in Germany, calls *Lucinde* an "aesthetic monstrosity"; his contemporary Wilhelm Dilthey, in his biography of Schleiermacher, reminds us calmly that this novel is "morally as well as poetically formless and contemptible."[80] In any case, *Lucinde* caused one of the most notorious literary scandals of the early nineteenth century, not because of pornographic themes, but because, signed and unconcealed, it entered the social registers of the big leagues and took itself seriously:

> . . . *ordinary pornography was thought of as nothing more than an amusing and stimulating trifle — it was usually unpretentious and did not presume to be taken seriously. But Lucinde clearly presumed to be taken seriously, both as a work of art and as an attempt to revise the existing code of*

moral and social conduct. Most pornography was published either pseud-
onymously or anonymously. Not Lucinde: its title page boldly proclaimed
that it was written by one of Germany's foremost literary critics. What by
contemporary standards should have been a private concern, an anonymous,
naughty triviality, had become a matter of excited public discussion. That
is one reason why the publication of Lucinde constituted a scandal.[81]

Surely for Kierkegaard, with his many signatory masks, the fact that
Schlegel did not conceal his signature already indicated something of a
pornographic act. Exposing himself by signing, taking his philosophical poses seriously (the real obscenity), and offering social commentary
the way *Playboy, Hustler, On Our Backs,* and other forms of pornocriti-
cism tend to do in order to dress up their thrill production put Schlegel
up for an unacceptable kind of generic inmixation. If anything, Schlegel was taking the "philo-" in "philosophy" too literally, thus disfiguring the studied sublimations of the love that bore it.

   In his time Bataille aroused similar levels of indignity, due in a comparable manner to his appropriations of serious philosophy. Without
wanting to sacrifice the historicity of attack, one can substitute Sartre
for Hegel, Bataille for Schlegel, and Heidegger for Fichte in the space of
the condemnations issued by Sartre. The Sartrean thought police assert
that philosophical diction, "which in the works of Hegel and Heidegger [have] precise significations," is appropriated in Bataille's *Inner Experience* as "an adventure that is situated beyond philosophy."[82] Furthermore, the "errors" committed by Bataille in his misappropriations
reveal that he "has visibly not understood Heidegger, about whom he
speaks often and incorrectly" (155-56). When Bataille, who is not a philosopher but a literary figure, tries to mime philosophy by speaking its
tongue, "philosophy avenges itself" (156).

   Perhaps most pertinent to the case of a shared if time-lagged *Rezep-
tionsgeschichte* (reception history) is the way impious acts of inmixation
are cast as displays of indecency. When they are not miming high philosophy in their idiosyncratic styles, philosopher wannabes turn into
pornographers, tossing, for special effect, bodies into texts. Whereas
Sartre might have approved the donation to philosophy of a body revealed to consciousness through "a dull and inescapable nausea" (34),
he saw little point in exposing the ecstatic body. Bataille was an exhibitionist who ripped off philosophy and his clothing. As Peter Connor
observes: "Philosophical language is once again seen to be wildly out of
place. Sartre feels that Bataille, alternately exposing himself and cover-

ing himself up in the vestments of philosophical discourse, uses his naked body to make of philosophy a kind of peep show: 'Hardly has he made us glimpse his miserable nakedness than he has covered up again, and we're off reasoning with him on Hegel's system or Descartes' *cogito*'" (34). The repudiation of stripped-down philosophy, noted by de Man in terms of Schlegel, consists in the essential incompatibility of two codes. This politics of contamination burns Sartre up; like Hegel, he loses his cool and becomes a kind of moral majoritarian. The reception of Bataille's work produced shock waves whose frequency is set to those with which we associate the censure placed upon Schlegel, who, prior to Nietzsche, put a body on the line of philosophical speculation. "The challenge that *Inner Experience* presents resides precisely in its persistent questioning of the boundary between body and thought: introducing rational thought to the seamier side of existence, Bataille relentlessly eroticizes the cogito" (35). To the extent that he brings thought to the street level of urges, bodily purges, unmanageable senses, Bataille loses interest in what no longer makes sense: the classical regimens of intelligibility. The double imperatives of "Über die Unverständlichkeit" (Schlegel) and "stop making sense!" (Bataille) need to be read together, particularly in terms of the varied and inner experiments conducted by both authors as they relentlessly scrambled the codes of a sanctioned philosophical diction.

As for defending himself and his community of unintelligibles, Schlegel offers in place of argument a mock teleology. He projects, with bolts of sarcasm, that the nineteenth century, unlike the present (late eighteenth) century, will spell catastrophe for his detractors, namely, those who are railing against the *acknowledged* unintelligibility of the *Athenäum*.[83] In the more advanced century there will be readers who can read: "What a catastrophe! Then there will be readers who can read. In the nineteenth century, each person will be able to enjoy the *Fragments* with considerable comfort and pleasure in their hours of rumination and not require a nutcracker even for what is hardest and most indigestible."[84] As with many defensive strategies, the clarity of the original attack risks giving way to compromise, and that which is being defended succumbs to dissolution.

It is unclear whether the digestive enzymes to be developed in the coming century will dissolve unintelligibility (which would undermine Schlegel's logic asserting and affirming its groundbreaking necessity) or make the hard fact of unintelligibility more easily assimilable, thereby losing its quality as a foreign body that keeps you up all night. Will Schlegelian *non-savoir* yield pleasure in the coming century and bring comfort rather than function as an emetic, which it does when Hegel, putting dialectics in reverse, throws it up? Or perhaps he predicted the emergence of *readers*, not mere interpreter-digesters but those who take pleasure in the reading of incomprehensibility and who understand understanding as just one form of reading. In any case, Schlegel was not wrong to project by means of anticipatory remembrance a later nineteenth century, that of Nietzsche and possibly even the one enfolding the emergence of Freud, readers of catastrophe who create a new imaginary of the digestive system and who have been made, in reactive periods, to eat sh . . . Yet if read straightforwardly and if Schlegel were seen as projecting a moment when unintelligibility would give way to intelligibility — an improbable hypothesis — the passage would have risked dissolving the value of the experimental journal or its possible status as a "classic" in the terms the essay sets forth: reaching into the *Fragments* and bringing one up for citation, Schlegel quotes Goethe, "Eine klassische Schrift muß nie ganz verstanden werden können."[85] Writing valued as classical must never be fully understood, which would prompt it to be closed, foreclosed to the future of its repetition, semantically saturated, DOA. Having understood, or thinking one has understood, stands precisely on a refusal to read, in complicity with a resistance to the lost object from which a text has always cut loose, though it continues to carry traumatic traces in often vague, undetectable ways. Thinking one has understood fully not only is the kiss of death — who but an idiot has really understood? — but also the end of all irony, which, whether buff or buffo, discreet or in your face ("gleichsam ihm ins Gesicht" [2:537]), "honest" (*redlich*), as Schlegel says, or giving a swift kick in the ass ("mit einer guten Art einen Tritt in den Hintern geben" [2:537]), brings an abrupt halt to any illusion of having understood.

Often the decisive interventions on the part of irony bear effects of physicality; they give a sound beating to a language that closes in on itself. Acting as the good conscience of philosophical demonstration, of the compulsion to understand, irony disrupts any attempt to close the book on a case or to think you have finished the chapter, or, when you've reached the end, to write it off. Like Socrates, it functions as gadfly, as an internal allergen that appears to come from a place of exteriority, undoing all transcendental systems, constantly rewriting the text that it submits to endless retests, retaking acknowledged premises on a permanent basis. This is why irony is no joke ("Mit der Ironie ist durchaus nicht zu scherzen" [2:537]); it is always loaded and ready to go off (permanent parabasis). And irony will have destroyed the stability of an experimental site that owes its existence to a parafigural force: it alone is responsible for the greater part of the unintelligibility of the *Athenäum*, which can never hope to secure for itself (well, not in the present century) semantic asylum without risking the constant disruption of meaning, of meaning as presence, since irony reminds us that there is no given sense (henceforth sense cannot be given as present, at your disposal, configured, assured: sense is not a given — whatever makes sense is already beyond sense, a meeting, a work, the unintelligible community); or else meaning is made to communicate by irony as the fact of its relation to the possibility of its nonbeing. For what can undoing and disruption imply but these fatal delays in understandability ("Without doubt, a great part of the unintelligibility of *Athenäum* lies in its irony, which is expressed more or less everywhere within it")?[86]

Yet Schlegel's project for the nineteenth century still needs to be understood, even if any possible grounds for conclusive, which is to say, present, understanding have been withdrawn by him. In the first place, "Welche Katastrophe!" is a type of utterance to which we, in our turns of century, have grown accustomed in the text of Nietzsche. To be able to name a catastrophe and to see the future of its becoming links unintelligibility with prophecy, irony with pathos. These ambivalent pairings need to be borne in mind when exploring the limits of understanding.[87] To what extent is the prophetic word indebted to irony? Can there be prophecy without irony, I mean in a nonpsychotic sense?

What a catastrophe! The projection Schlegel sketches calls for a different kind of reading because it is not some whimsical fantasy but the outline of a theory of reading itself, for reading is nothing other than this proleptic swerve, the promise of a future understanding. Today, the project of future understanding remains the fiction that it always will have been, an insight that can be neither proven nor verified. Still, this fiction, generated out of the exigencies of an inescapable temporality, is understanding's truth. At the same time, the question arises whether the promise that Schlegel issues himself, that of a future of understanding, will somehow dissolve its ironical base, rendering it obsolete. What is the status of Schlegel's apparent projection of a postdated intelligibility, particularly when he asks, "Which divine powers will be able to rescue us from all these ironies?"[88] In order to go ahead with the question, he reaches back to the gods, the timeless ones. What

157

would a rescue operation undertaken against irony look like? It would be helpful to remember at this point that in *Allegories of Reading* de Man offers that irony is "no longer a trope but the undoing of the deconstructive allegory of all tropological cognitions, the systematic undoing, in other words, of understanding."[89] Ever attacking the text's projected sense of itself as reliable sense, irony eats away at every epistemological and legitimating claim it attempts to make. The text receives its own irony, dispossessing as it must be, as a series of traumatic hits. These hits — the beatings that the de Manian text replicates in order to absorb — must be viewed serially because Schlegel insists that irony is not localizable to one site but occurs everywhere. Irony speaks to a failed assimilation in the text. Like time, "it is the name we give to the fact that what the narrative . . . tries to interiorize as a moment within itself, is incorporated,"[90] which is to say that while it occurs as an inner experience it is also always ejected to an outerness, a textual surface, and thus perpetually re-encountered as a lesion, as something that cannot heal and from which we cannot not bail.

Though allegory and irony are, in de Man's work, closely related, allegory is exceeded by the force of ironic hits that accrue to it: no allegory "can grasp the incidences of irony by which it is disrupted, . . . but each one . . . must undertake the attempt to translate it into a cognitive content."[91] The allegorical act, associated with the drive to translate and a struggle to establish cognition, involves an experience of loss and mourning. It is as if allegory were vainly trying to dress, or at least to address, the textual wounding implied by irony, offering, in Nietzschean terms, an emergency supply of meaning and cognition. But translation and transfusion bear the weight of considerable loss, or to invoke Benjamin, they are charged with showing up the original as nearly dead. Allegory functions as "a kind of master name for the form in which clefts at the heart of systematic thinking can be shown to undo it from the inside."[92] This would explain in part why, in the ages of systematicity, allegory has been violently repressed only to cause a considerable narcissistic crisis at the occasions of its coming-out party. If allegory and irony, together with anacoluthon (the figural correlate for the structure of irony considered as permanent parabasis),[93] produce the basis for the unprecedented disruption of intelligibility, busting up any hint of closural stability, then it is small wonder that a reminder of this permanent lesion has stirred up, with each round or circle, at least in the teapot of academia, a narcissistic storm of protest.

There also remains the problem of contagion that these key operators carry, something to explain in part why de Man was quarantined long before a diagnosis could be made. A theorist of unreliability, de Man attracted distrust to himself by the very terms he chose to analyze and the implications they bore concerning the dependability of meaning. He stuck to irony and allegory in such a way as to fend off the proffered masks of humble reconciliation or common arbitrations of organized sincerity. The reintroduction of these structures produces the effects of a generalized anacoluthon, if that is conceivable — a sudden switch in the syntax of expectation, a structural experience of deceit similar to the kind Proust describes and de Man cites in the case of Albertine's lies. (Albertine was a liar, but her tendency was not simply ascribable to any act of consciousness or intentionality, no sure trace of malevolence, but don't forget that you thought she was talking about herself and suddenly, by the device of anacoluthon, she had switched syntactical tracks on you, and you had been mislead by your store of metaphorical assumptions, so where was her truth to be located finally?) The welcoming of irony and allegory, as Schlegel's text indicates, is the kiss of death. For not only is there an impertinent emphasis placed on the nonconvergence of any stated meaning and its understanding, but this engagement lets loose a cannonade of demystifications that can ruin a career (the poisoned Socrates, abjected Schlegel, flunked out Benjamin, dead de Man, et al.) or, at the very least, exacts revenge in the form of a total religious conversion.

So what are these debilitators of meaning and being? One can argue that, strictly speaking, "allegory," "anacoluthon," "parabasis," and "metonymy" should not be misapprehended as the names of tropes. To the extent that they involve no substitutions, they are parafigural. Whereas tropes involve the transport of sense from one signifier to another, the grammatical nontropes, such as allegory, do not participate in this language of transport of a sense or a meaning. "They are employed virtually always as marks of disruption of such transports."[94] Allegory, for its part, is going nowhere — no transports of ascenscion, no tropological elevators going up, getting suprasensory on you; it is not a trope for Paul de Man but a grammatical form in which a certain number of disjunctions can be shown to be taking place. As a form, allegory *shows* these disjunctions.

In the text meant to help along the Athenäum through the stages of its avowed unintelligibility, Schlegel produces a promise, to himself and no doubt also to his brother, August Wilhelm, whom he inscribes at the end of the essay, to his contemporaries, and to the coming century (which, being invoked, is already here), to you and me. Making a promise, he exposes the text he is in the process of defending to the truth of its abyssal solitude. The vow he makes but cannot logically sustain, this promise as such, repeating the primordial project of understanding, promises nothing other than its own future. But, as others have indicated and we have been given to understand, the promise, which promises only itself, in the end does not promise. What Schlegel lived, Nietzsche knew and Bataille was meant to affirm: a promise qua engagement is also a risk; it enacts a commitment to sense, to the future of sense. Yet *what is ensured is only this risk*. Refusing at this stage of his enigmatic career to evade the irony for which he blames the bad reception of the *Athenäum*, Schlegel set himself one allegorical trap after another, which his text continues to ironize. Like the promise, allegory remains unfulfilled in its offering. "Allegory goes away empty handed."[95] This formulation, while useful, turns allegory on its head, for it is not clear that allegory ever was on the take or looking for handouts. The reader goes away empty-handed. Allegory has no hands-on policy or fulfillment clause, which is why the eighteenth century largely rebuked its remoter claims. Always the allegory of unreliability, allegory must grapple with the question of its illegitimacy, with the indeterminability of language.

According to Schlegel, irony, though he also includes allegory in a secondary instance, has been largely responsible for the *Athenäum*'s unfavorable reception, an event that he begins to transvaluate by his affirmation of the "concept" of unintelligibility. Irony and allegory function systematically to undermine and undo (the) system; they are the delegitimators par excellence, tagging those who would work with them, and are prone to throw into question any authoritative utterance or pose of mastery, including that of the state (when Schlegel started working for the state and went legit, he had to give it up). They work over the system to such a degree that intelligibility, which was in any case secondary and derivative, gets lost in the fray. The charge of unintelligibility may be linked to singularity here. There is something unassimilable, incomparable, dissociated about the *Athenäum*. It cannot be grasped by philosophy or literature, by a history that counts on reference or accounts for itself with relative narrative tranquility. Subjected to its own production of unintelligibility, riddled by irony and delayed by its contract with allegory until the ever-coming century, the *Athenäum* each time vaporizes in the here and now, dissolving the Project. Linked in this way to historical trauma, it runs the risk of leaving no trace, no record of itself, except for the sense that an incomprehensibility — a barbarity, a violence or brutality — has taken place. And yet, Schlegel took pains to note, and this is why we are here, that something is given to us, namely, "There is a hermeneutic imperative."[96] This imperative is bequeathed to us as gift and burden; it names a task. If there must be an imperative to understand, this is because understanding does not come but remains lost to us. Can we come to an understanding? Assuming understanding were to be resurrected without an imperative lording over its provenance, this could happen only by turning away from what is incomprehensible.[97]

Hardly a year passes. Schlegel holds his Jena lectures on "Tranzendentalphilosophie": "Transcendental philosophy: According to our viewpoint, absolute understanding is not at all possible. . . . If there were an absolute truth, then there would be an absolute intelligibility."[98]

Repossessed by the thought of understanding, under the gun of an obsession, Friedrich Schlegel approaches his death thinking about the presumption of a complete understanding. His final sentence, drawn toward the end, grazed by the thought of fulfillment, remains however incomplete: "Das ganz vollendete und vollkomme Verstehen aber" (But perfect and altogether complete understanding).[99]

TEST QUESTIONS

1. If Paul de Man undermined the possibility of true autobiography, why does the author include autobiographical material about herself?

2. What is the relationship between stupidity and unintelligibility?

3. Does the author establish a link between singularity and unintelligibility? If so, how does this link affect Gasché's argument?

4. Can Schlegel's kick in the ass be read allegorically?

5. What is the author's point of view concerning de Man's disciples?

6. What is the relationship between allegory and history?

7. How can the author imply that de Man both refused to offer a reading of stupidity and was responsible for inscribing its implications and performance?

8. What is at stake in the works of Schlegel, Bataille, and de Man in terms of the figure of testing?

9. Why does the author make claims for the radically democratic underpinnings of scholarly and philosophical journals? Are these principles upheld today? Give an example.

10. a. Discuss the relationship of friendship and nonunderstanding, using the instance of Schlegel and Schleiermacher as your starting point.

    b. Show how Friedrich Schlegel's antihermeneutics of friendship illuminates what Blanchot and Derrida have to say about the politics of friendship.

The nuances of Kierkegaard's attack are worth noting as they invite a deconstructive reading capable of tracking the shifting values of his criticism of Schlegel. Kierkegaard encounters a number of difficulties when mounting the attack. One involves citationality, which, by the very fact of repeating the offending passages, unavoidably implicates his text in the one he condemns: "But this discussion is not without its difficulties, because inasmuch as *Lucinde* is a very obscene book, as is well known, by citing parts of it for more detailed consideration I run the risk of making it impossible for even the purest reader to escape altogether unscathed."[1] In the dominance-and-submission behavior that the two texts display when one of them is being criticized, it appears that Schlegel will have the upper hand, dominating the very text that attempts to contain and subdue it, performing an s/m kind of parabasis, that is to say, showing itself capable of interrupting the master text of Kierkegaard at any point and lashing out at his readers, who still risk being corrupted by Schlegel. That is not the only problem faced by *The Concept of Irony* when trying to dominate Schlegel.

Kierkegaard expresses worry about doing an injustice to the romantic theorist of irony, for it turns out that he has energized the domestic sexual encounter, which is not a bad thing; in fact, Kierkegaard is prepared to name a debt to Schlegel for eroticizing the scene of household love. But it turns out that Schlegel is not pornographic enough, in Kierkegaard's language, not real enough but *schweb*ing, that is, swooning, around in the ideal. The logic suggests, against apparent intentions, that if Schlegel had only been more graphic and real — more pornographic — then he would have been less obscene:

> Lest an injustice be done to Schlegel, one must bear in mind the many degradations that have crept into a multitude of life's relationships and have been especially indefatigable in making love as tame, as housebroken, as

Kierkegaard

Satellite

sluggish, as dull, as useful and usable as any other domestic animal — in short, as unerotic as possible. To that extent, we would be very obligated to Schlegel if he should succeed in finding a way out, but unfortunately the climate he discovered, the only climate in which love can really thrive, is not a more southern climate compared with ours in the north but is an ideal climate nowhere to be found. Therefore it is not just the tame ducks and geese of domestic love that beat their wings and raise a dreadful cry when they hear the wild birds of love swishing by over their heads, but it is every more profoundly poetic person whose longings are too powerful to be bound by romantic spider webs, whose demands upon life are too great to be satisfied by writing a novel, who precisely on poetry's behalf must register his protest at this point, must try to show that it is not a way out that Friedrich Schlegel found but a wrong way he strayed into, must try to show that living is something different from dreaming. (286–87)

This is not just a kind of reactionary logic according to which poets are dreamers opposable to those who might "have a life," though I must say it comes close to that sort of put-down, thus diluting its own critical edge (if Schlegel is just a dreamer equally removed from actuality and the concept, then what is the big fuss about, why is the philosophical family up in arms?). Oddly, "the very obscene book" loses points because Schlegel is not *wild enough* ("the wild birds of love swishing by over their heads") and he is too easily satisfied by fiction. Kierkegaard opposes the poetic sensibility of Schlegel to "every more profoundly poetic person" whose "longings are too powerful" to be stuck in romantic texts ("romantic spider webs") and whose "demands upon life are too great to be satisfied by writing." So the more poetic person is less bound by writing and needs more than the fiction of obscenity, needs a more real domain of obscenity. It is not clear who would come out as the "real" pornographer in the contest Kierkegaard sets up.

Kierkegaard manages to use Schlegel, however, to bolster his own argument concerning the miserable state of marriage:

> *If we examine more closely what it is that Schlegel was combating with his irony, presumably no one will deny that there was and is much in the ingress, progress, and egress of the marriage relationship that deserves a correction such as this and that makes it natural for the subject to want to be liberated. There is a very narrow earnestness, an expediency, a miserable teleology, which many people worship as an idol that demands infinite endeavor as its legitimate sacrifice. Thus in and of itself love is nothing but becomes something only through the intention whereby it is integrated with the pettiness that creates such a furor in the private theaters of families.* (287)

There are many problems with *Lucinde,* but to get to the core of the destruction of morals that it performs, Kierkegaard takes recourse to the words of Hegel's disciple, our old friend J. E. Erdmann:

> *Schlegel's* Lucinde *is an attempt to suspend all ethics (Sædelighed) or, as Erdmann rather aptly expresses it: "Alle sittliche Bestimmungen sind nur Spiel, es ist willkürlich für den Liebenden, ob die Ehe Monogomie, ob Ehe en quatre ist u.s.f. [All ethical qualifications are mere play, and to the lover it is an arbitrary matter whether marriage is monogamous, whether marriage is* en quatre *(in fours) etc.]." ... What* Lucinde *attempts, then, is to annul all ethics — not only in the sense of custom and usage, but all the ethics that is the validity of spirit, the mastery of the spirit over the flesh. Thus it will become apparent that it completely corresponds to what we earlier described as irony's special endeavor: to cancel any actuality and substitute for it an actuality that is no actuality.* (289–90)

Though strictly
speaking "idiocy" belongs to the
lexicon of medical and psychiatric histories,
where it denotes a specific type of mental degener-
ation, the term, an object of provident fascination for
poetry and thought, has survived among the popular
media and discourses as well as in the most sophisticated
sectors of academic inquiry. Its considerable semantic shifts
and dislocations notwithstanding, everyone knows what
it means to call someone an idiot. Dostoevsky caught the
figure of idiocy in the richness of a deliberate transition,
where it hovers hesitatingly between its own clinical
history and the passage to a fast and loose track
of popular parlance, spreading an intention
with the fervor of Christian
conversion.

The Disappearance
   and
Returns of the Idiot

4

"Believe me, I said it without thinking,"

he explained, at last,

wondering.

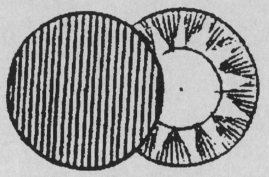

PART ONE

H E WAS TOUGH on others and harder on himself. He gave a lot away, donated his body to any number of dubious causes; he despaired. Europe was failing him. The worst of the Europeans, the Germans, Dostoevsky believed, were dumb fucks. Alien, repellent, chilling, they assumed a crucial position in his objurgations against Europe. The Swiss, he thought, pace Turgenev, proved "infinitely superior to the immeasurable stupidity of the Germans," but even they did not possess enough intelligence to adapt their homes to the rigors of the climate, which is much like that of northern Russia for three months of the year: "All they need to do is install double windows to be able to live — and even only with fireplaces. I don't even say — to install a stove."[1] It was colder than a well-digger's ass. While freezing in Geneva, Dostoevsky, isolated with his wife, Anna, set about to write The Idiot. He dreamed of Russia and double windows, decrying everything German as well as those things that he associated with their smarter version, the Swiss. Above all, Germany functioned as a metonymy for Europe. Firmly holding out against the German spirit, Dostoevsky writes, continually reasserting the messianic destiny territorialized by Russia: "Our people are infinitely higher, more noble, more honest, more naive, more capable, and full of a different, very lofty Christian idea, which Europe, with her sickly Catholicism and stupidly contradictory Lutheranism, does not even understand" (252). In terms of the art of understanding, Europe had not caught up with the highly refined if considerably more naïve text of Russian sublimity. Catholicism, given its premise of violence and worldly conquest, offered only a betrayal of Christianity; it was Roman, whereas Germanic Lutheranism was determinately stupid. For his part, the protagonist of The Idiot would denounce Roman Catholicism as un-Christian because "Roman Catholicism believes that the Church cannot exist without universal political power" (335). In the meantime, the pressure of poverty further glacialized unspeakably demoralizing circumstances. His ass freezing, Dostoevsky set about to write The Idiot and continued to vent at Swiss insipidity. Moreover, and again: "If you had any idea of the dishonesty, the meanness, the incredible stupidity of the Swiss. Of course, the Ger-

mans are worse but these are not far behind! . . . But to hell with them!"
(297). "These brainless Swiss in the midst of the forests did not know
how to heat their houses" (254). When the novel comes to term, Mme.
Epanchina cries that the Europeans "in winter are frozen like mice in a
cellar."[2]

When Fyodor Mikhailovich writes of stupidity he is inevitably involved with historical reference and cultural mappings. His passionate
abuse of the Germans (and, to a lesser extent, the Swiss) inscribes a materialist moment in his thought, or, in another idiom, it discloses a
threat that is felt to press upon a special kind of Russian transcendence,
what Benjamin in his article "Der Idiot" saw as being rooted in "the
metaphysical identity of the national, like that of humanity in the idea
of Dostoyevsky's creation."[3] At the same time, in order to practice the
poses, which he was perfecting, of cultural sadism, he conjures an
imaginary inversion: objects of abuse, the German and Swiss, "much
like northern Russia," inadvertently absorb the attributes of Siberia.
What is stupid about the Swiss in particular is their Russianness, or else
their denial of Siberia — as if they were not Siberia, not a mere repetition
of its dumb inhospitality, double site of exile and enslavement. At least
Siberia knows it's cold and unwelcoming, incapable of offering shelter.

But one has to look through double windows to grasp the transcendence toward which Dostoevsky urges. If the Swiss have failed to appre-
ciate them, Dostoevsky's oeuvre demands such an installation: a single
frame could not protect against stubborn nativistic winds or raging
nationalist storms. Dostoevsky was building up his own private Waco,
fortressed by a bizzare czarism, an irrepressible fundamentalism. Holding out against a combination of Feuerbachian atheism (he often called
atheists stupid), English utilitarianism, French utopian socialism,
mechanical materialism, and Chernyshevsky or Russian nihilism,
Dostoevsky advanced in his journals a commitment to *pochvennichestvo*,
an ideology promoting a return to the soil (*pochva*), a return to one's
native roots.[4] If Dostoevsky has become fiercely identified with the
imago of Russia "to the point of betraying my previous convictions,
idolizing the Tsar" (298), and has taken consistently to assailing "our
trashy little liberals of a seminarian-social hue" (251), is it not puzzling
that the figure chosen to represent the other side of the anti-Russian
jeremiad (with which Dostoevsky associates, among so many others,
Turgenev's character Potugin in *Smoke*, noting that Bakunin and Potugin are not very far apart) should be named, without apology, an idiot?
On three occasions in Dostoevsky's preliminary notes the protagonist

is called "Prince Christ," though any further resemblance to the Galilean is not at this point developed (261). Still, far into the process of preparing the novel, Dostoevsky jotted down, apropos of the Prince, in a note to himself: "*Enigmas, who is he? A terrible scoundrel or a mysterious ideal?*" (261).

Holy Simpleton!

Still, the value that he was to ascribe to the figure of peculiar and sustained idiocy was not clear to Dostoevsky until very late into the writing. Moreover, there was the problem of thematic contagion with which the author had to contend: he expressed the fear that the text would bear the burden of the idiocy that it sought to explore. Among other things, Dostoevsky demonstrated concern that readers would take his truthful renderings, and even the intentional parallel he established with the Passion of Christ, as "ridiculous, naive and stupid" (305). One way to meet the challenge of such contamination was to opt for marking the internal split of the narratorial function. But even this effort at disjointure became an ambiguous ploy, for in order to divert the text from its proper name and theme — that of idiocy — Dostoevsky has the narrator abandon the Idiot in an act that claims ignorance and incomprehension. The only way for the novel to save itself and defend against the threat of the very idiocy it seeks to treat is to step up the pressure of ignorance. Thus, in the end the narrative voice abandons the Idiot to his fate in a gesture of *volte-face*, indicating that he has given up on trying to understand the faltering protagonist. Rather like the structure of inoculation, the narrative, anxious to immunize itself, absorbs the poison by which it is menaced, assimilating and owning it; the narrative itself will have become an idiot with regard to its charge, releasing custody of the object that it had been determined to comprehend. Nonetheless, the value of idiocy remained, for Dostoevsky, an enigma, the ambiguous dimensions of which became the value itself of the project. A letter from N. N. Strakhov approvingly focuses in on an aspect of inaccessibility, something of a demand for noncognition asserted in the work: "Your Idiot interests me personally almost more than anything you have written. What a beautiful idea! The wisdom of an open-hearted childish soul, and inaccessible to the wise and intelligent."[5]

The effort to produce a kind of hermeneutics of idiocy assumed several forms. As the passage from Strakhov's letter indicates, a certain emanation of beauty was involved. In fact, his notes variously confirm that Dostoevsky was trying to approach, in this project, the possibility of a transcendently beautiful being. Such beauty, when struck by the encounter with material and empirical forces, discloses only the scandal of childlike burbling, however, portraying an innocence so radical that it serves to horrify. It is as if normed intelligence and measured wisdom were meant to clear the abyss of innocence. Clearly, the absorption of idiocy into a text of decidedly theological inflection drove a troubled bargain for its author.

Within the novel the evaluations ascribed to the Prince vary. From the point of view of Rogozhin, who, as a merchant's son is closest to the religious roots of Russian life, he is a holy fool — an exemplar of Ivanushka, the simpleton of the folktales, or rather the native *yurodivyi* (a feeble-minded man believed by the folk to be divinely inspired).[6] Our simpleton is at once uncomprehending and magically perceptive. Of a more consternating nature, he displays democratic tendencies and a concern for social justice; as ready to unbosom himself to a servant as to a high dignitary, he is at once an emissary of great love, yet — "I can't marry any one. I am an invalid" (34). These qualities do not by any means constitute opposites but mark limits, which the novel exhorts us to explore. In Benjamin's brief account, Myshkin, for all his bumbling simplicity, is associated with that which is unforgettable, an infinite life, rendered according to the different facets of flesh, power, person, and spirit.[7] It is not made clear why Benjamin subsumes flesh or even person under the category of the nonfinite, but the clues he leaves regarding the evicted mind, the unhoused self, concern us here. For his part Benjamin reverts to Goethe's *Conversations with Eckermann*, where nature is seen as duty-bound to give us some space, so to speak, to restore an effective domain, when ours has been taken from us. The life of the damaged and quashed is rendered by a kind of template of unforgettability. Irrecoverably downtrodden but somehow represented by an alias or a ghostly metonymy of itself, this life becomes, even without monument or remembrance or testimony, unforgettable.[8] Otherwise vague and disjointed, Benjamin's observations are written, I daresay, as if he were still under the influence of the hashish text. Nonetheless, he offers an insight into the figuration of that which, so simple and unaccounted for, refuses monument or testimony: the predicament of the idiot.

When the Prince arrives on the scene, he has just emerged from the shadow of mental illness, from a Swiss clinic; by novel's end he will have succumbed to a movement of irreversible derangement. In between the two points of darkness he serves as an emanation of Christ-like simplicity. Historically, Christ has shown us many facets, making it legitimate to ask which figuration or appropriation of Christ Dostoevsky enfolds or, indeed, invents in this work. We know from the passage cited and other sources that Dostoevsky denounced the inaccordant manifestations of Christianity, laying blame on the Church of Rome for fostering atheism and for being, if you think about it, the mother of socialism. For the most part, he held out for a literary line and lineage.

As did Kierkegaard, Dostoevsky compared Christ with Don Quixote. His task was to bring forth a projection of Christ that could not be salvaged by an element of the comedic, at least not on a thematic level of episodic failure. Yet the essence of this god was to be distilled to the critically unsettling dimension of the ridiculous — a quality by which the Galilean, despite his figural beauty, is evermore tied in literature. "There is only one positively beautiful figure in the world — Christ — so that the phenomenon of that boundlessly, infinitely good figure is already in itself an infinite miracle."[9] The figure itself announces the infinity of miracle, but becoming finite, that is, submitted to language (which, as figure, it already was), it constrains Dostoevsky to focalize the ridiculous: "But he is good only because he is at the same time ridiculous" (274). Dostoevsky makes the attribute of goodness dependent on the ridiculous, a fixed complementarity that he will explore in the novel. And, to score points with the reader, the author notes: "Compassion for the beautiful man who is ridiculed and who is unaware of his own worth generates sympathy in the reader" (274). If Don Quixote and Pickwick elicit sympathy because they are overtly comical, crashing against world, the Prince must go underground, staking all on his austere innocence, an untouchable beauty that owes its manifestation only to the reliable generosity of the ridiculous. The ridiculous enables the manifestation of the Prince's goodness, and ridicule is what must be risked in the elaboration of extreme good: the good cannot be restricted to the merely innate but must be public, exposed. The Prince is exposed in the notes as sheer exposure; he will be exposed to the skepticism and "scorn of a mocking and merciless world" (274). Dostoevsky's interest lies not only in the matter of being ridiculed or the compassion that any figure thus persecuted might arouse. Such an interest (or even strategy) would be comprehensible, if not simply mimetic of other texts. Dostoevsky's focus is more radical: he recognizes, in order to af-

175

firm, the ridiculous in Christ. How can this become manifest but through the embodiment that characterizes the fumbling earthling? And yet, we are not beholding just any corporeal manifestation.

What the susceptibility to ridicule discloses is the tortured, sacrificed body. Mangled and breakable, the fragile body, seen as ridiculous and emitting meaning, was tossed eventually into literature. This body, it could be said, began to take hold in Cervantes's novel, in "a world in which the conditions of human embodiment, rather than human reason, set the bounds of knowledge."[10] Don Quixote's slender, wan figure, "with little flesh on his bones, and a face that was lean and gaunt,"[11] throws light on the ancestral lineage to which Myshkin is heir to the extent, indeed, of foreshadowing the convulsive lurches that occur "when body is displaced in awkward ways, or thrown out of joint, as is typical in comedy."[12] Don Quixote, slapped down, knocked over, submitted to the conditions of his embodiment, brought evidence of our outsideness to world, of the fact that there can be "no fit, no perfect mesh of body and world" (38). Henceforth there will be no fiction of the disappearance of the body, as Descartes had sought to effect, no discarded body bags on which to prop the *ergo sum,* but rather the endless stagings of a resolutely incorporated existence. Self-knowledge in *Don Quixote* cannot be seen as an epistemological affair but is rooted in the conditions of embodiment: "Don Quixote's body always intrudes" (38). Moreover — and this gets rolled over to Myshkin's account — Don Quixote is figured as a character whose brains have "dried up," a character whose very composition "precludes a knowledge of the world by the certainties of the mind" (38). The invention of the tormented body in literature prompts a kind of thinking that will not take for granted but rather requires a questioning of the grounds on which the claims of knowledge are staked. Though the relatedness of *The Idiot* to its purported model and source in the Quixote may have seemed in the long run sketchy or random, there is the matter of the body that gets cloned and recyled, renationalized and theologized, a body that returns and twists within the newer version of a bad fit.

With a sense of precision textured by the repetition compulsion, the novel repeats the disquieting exhibition of Holbein's dead Christ — the scandal of the bruised and bloody body of Christ refused transcendence. Dostoevsky is transfixed by the moment itself when custody of Christ's body is assumed by Western consciousness prior to resurrection. This body, though, has not been claimed, as aphanic consciousness has shut down its aspect, eclipsed the viewing. Yet there remains a memory trace of the forgotten trauma, and Holbein's imaging of the mangled body recurs throughout the text as a symptom that cannot be released. Reviving only the facticity of a corpse unavailable to any possible revival, it marks the moment of a dead Christ, Christ as pure corpse, intruding upon an unreceptive consciousness as the real, an intrusion from which Dostoevsky himself feared he would never recover faith or religiosity. He'd stood paralyzed before the painting *Christ Taken from the Cross*, during the famous visit to the Basel museum with his wife. The shock was transferred to his work, which tries to bury the irredeemably dead body. That is to say, the work, as a place where the shock is meant to be absorbed, tries but fails to resuscitate the corpse, to glorify the body and lend it the cover of transcendence. This corpse, or this portrayal of Christ in the clutch of absolute mortality, is carried through the textual stations for review. It is at first only obliquely related to the condition of idiocy, though it spreads stupor to those in the work who come into contact with it.

There is something about Holbein's depiction of Christ that held and horrified Dostoevsky. It seems to be related to the brute fact of Christ being bound irrevocably to his body, abandoned to the fate of assassination (Freud, in a preliterary scene of recognition, linked the origin of Dostoevsky's epilepsy to his father's brutal assassination; the attacks occured symptomatically, in front of a funeral procession or at the news of Belinsky's death.) It is as if, in consequence of a first and startled viewing, the novel were in the phases of a sustained epileptic fit before this painting: the novel is located in the moment when Christ fades out of being, lost in the abyssal truth of a negative epiphany: Christ humiliated, mortalized — one is tempted to say, "mortotalized" — and, seared by mortality, made finite, weak, and . . . foolish. The eclipse of Christ, his reduction to a body that succumbs to its own destruction, haunts the pages if not the essential construction of *The Idiot*. Dostoevsky fixes and multiplies throughout the work the moment of sheer stupefaction that such a thought elicits.[13]

The Cry of Abandonment

The Idiot repeats and reworks the cry of abandonment in a disfigured world evacuated by the sacred. A supplement to the existential primer of sacred departure, the work leaves behind a store of nonbequeathal. It is as though nothing can be inherited, and there is little to be passed on to acknowledged figures of futurity. Growth and future are stunted.

Registers of pregnancy out of the question. (Nothing less should be expected of this author whose name is synonymous with the terrific imminence of doom.) Incarnation has dispensed with the body, leaving a hemorrhaging of sense. There is no doubt, however, that Dostoevsky takes some recourse in his rendering to the legacies of martyred saints and sacrificial death. His effort also recalls to us the way that the suffering and humiliated Christ lies at the heart of Russian spirituality. In keeping with Christian kenoticism, a distinguishing trait of the Russian religious tradition, the Prince recovers from a state of epileptic stupor, awakening to an existential downgrade, a state that implies, in the case of the human, a slide down the chain of being (the hierarchy of the links may not be so secure as all that). Joseph Frank designates this cast as "the existence of the world in the form of something as humble and workaday as a donkey" (319). The critic sides with the Christianized, somewhat socialist donkey: "The donkey, of course, has obvious Gospel overtones, which blend with the Prince's innocence and naiveté; and this patiently laborious animal also emphasizes, quite in keeping with Christian kenoticism, the absence of hierarchy in the Prince's ecstatic apprehension of the wonder of life" (319). But it is not so much the "wonder of life" that impels the Prince's crises as a steady humbling, whether it be in the face of a slow and uncomprehending donkey or within earshot of the panicked buzzing of a fly. What's left of the sacred is an eerie congruence of donkeys and flies, correlatives of a humbling bêtise.

Kenosis, a theological term, refers to Christ's act of emptying himself on becoming man, humbling himself even to the point of enduring death, and in the process of becoming incarnate surrendering all or some of the divine attributes. According to the thesis of G. P. Fedotov, the modern historian of the Russian religious tradition, it is the suffering and humiliated Christ "who lies at the heart of Russian spirituality." Referring to the first Russian martyred saints, the princes Boris and Gleb, Fedotov compares their meek surrender at the hands of their killers with the teachings of the monk Theodosius, the founder of the Russian kenotic tradition: "Boris and Gleb followed Christ in their sacrificial deaths — the climax of His kenosis — as Theodosius did in His poverty and humiliations. . . . From the outside, it must give the impression of weakness as Theodosius' poverty must appear foolish to the outsider. Weak and foolish — such is Christ in his kenosis in the eyes of a Nietzsche just as he was in the eyes of the ancient world."[14] Ernst Bernst, the German historian of religious philosophy, marshals further

evidence to support the widely held contention that Nietzsche "was familiar with The Idiot, and that Dostoevsky's novel helped to shape his
whole interpretation of Christianity."[15] These assertions reiterate what
by now is well known in the history of theology. But they perhaps help
to shed new light on the risk that the Christian god took of appearing
foolish. Our ears are still ringing with the laughter of the Nietzschean
gods when faced with the last of their lineage, the one who posed in the
guise of human vulnerability. He appeared. To appear is to appear foolish, humbled to the point of provoking ridicule. He had traded himself
in for a human body: "Weak and foolish — such is Christ in his kenosis
in the eyes of a Nietzsche just as he was in the eyes of the ancient
world."

If his Christianity was baptized by The Idiot, it is small wonder that
Nietzsche chose to inscribe the logic of "being so clever," that is, opposing meekness with cleverness, and of countering the foolish idiot with
the buffoon, a subversive and joyous overcoming of the weakened state
of lame acceptance that characterizes the opponent, Dionysus versus
Christ, or the fool. In The Idiot the fool's spectrum proves more subtle
and variegated. Lebedyev, shrewd and ingratiating, is often deciphered
by the narrator as a buffoon; in fact, the narrator indicates several gradations of foolishness that surround the Prince, as if to mirror the illuminated qualities of idiocy. Nearly every character has a share in foolishness, a place in the blighted sun of stupidity. In a kind of chiasmus
of normed expectations, though, the neighboring enactments of foolishness are contaminated, impure. They are worldly. Only the Prince
attains to the impressive lows — at the unreadable encounter of soul
and body — of unstained idiocy.

Nietzsche, the first modern philosopher to put his body on the line,
to write for and with it, prescribing distinct regimens and monitoring
cultural habits, if not addictions, shares with Dostoevsky a certain acceptance of that which has been abjected, excreted by the major cultural codifications of corporeal enactment. Both writers perpetually return to the sheer facticity of bodily existence but not so much as a mute
actuality anticipating meaning by way of a transcendent consciousness
— there is some of that in Dostoevsky, but it gets constantly subverted
and remains merely a temptation — more as a kind of unassimilable
scandal. The difference between them, to say it in abbreviated form, is
that Nietzsche dances with joy while Dostoevsky swoons in horror — a
question of temperament or even of the temperature, of climate, no
doubt, to which both were acutely sensitive. In any event, both think-

ers bring forth the body as a massive disruption of inherited meaning and, in the case of The Idiot, as an always imminent disorientation of sense. The body is in the world and pins down the vague locality of world, but when brought into view, it threatens the solidity of the world. As with television, when things get very local, there is something uncanny and incomprehensible about materiality: it gets delocalized. The close-up of the body that these thinkers invite breaks with traditional modalities of understanding, which is why, in the one case, we are said explicitly to be dealing with idiocy.

Idiocy materializes itself in a kind of negative corporeal stylization, yet it points to the generality of a human predicament: idiocy has something to do with the nearly existential fact of being stuck with a body or, to put it differently, with the fact that the body has claims upon us. It is not only the case that we are largely but necessarily stupid about our bodies — whether or not they are seen to have functioned in so many ways as some signifying practice or are routinely submitted to a profusion of info tags — but that the body exists as if to mark the dumb impassiveness of our being. There is nothing to know and little to understand — maybe how to feed it, when to fast, how to soothe, moisturize, let go, heal; mostly, though, there is no epistemological stronghold, no scientific comfort or medical absolute by which to grasp your body once and for all, as if it were ever merely itself once and for all: one can only bear witness and offer testimony.[16] This is why writing is so often bound up with illness and why the writer and invalid are often secretly one, like their inversion in Clark Kent and Superman (Prince Myshkin, the invalid, the reporter and magical writing pad, tells stories and endlessly receives narratives from the society of compulsive interlocutors; moreover, he flies high, pitched forward by his epiphanies and crack-ups). All cultural phantasms of bodily mutations aside, the body never stays put long enough to form self-identity. That is why our ancestors used to fast-forward and just lose it, Trauerspiel-style, in favor of more ethereal forms and nebulous promises.

But before we inspect how Dostoevsky unfolds these ordeals by taking on the prodigious case of idiocy, let us recall that the body deposited in this novel, as drafted by the kenotic tradition, is variously insulted and humiliated; it is that which is subjected to injury, but an injury capable of language and disclosure. Dostoevsky consistently focused the suffering among the humiliated, insulted, and injured.[17] And idiocy offered a delicate conflagration of soma and psyche, where it became confounding to speak with confidence about health or illness, strength or weakness, as if these were mere opposites. Idiocy allowed access to the insulted body, the enfeebled mind — though for Dostoevsky these qualities are set in flux, reversing their values according to momentary displacements. As for the Prince, he sees himself as ill and experiences this state of illness as a kind of materiality to which he is strapped. Despite his saintly innocence, he is forced to revert to his body, to situate it as reference. At every step of the way, illness, even in its condition of latency, forces his hand.

Illness, if that is what it is, exhorts the body to reveal something of itself. But is there an *object* of the revelations provoked by illness? Is anything learned or understood? Or is not illness the stealth master, the teacher whose lesson is unremittingly opaque yet purposeful? The body takes time. In any case, illness prompts a temporal warp, a lengthening of days and shortening of hours, a future telescoping into sweat beads. There is so much time, yet this time you are clocked by the quickening sense of finitude. You're in a pinch. This is when you ask, How much time do I have?

Your body, localized to its place of pathology, reminds you how it used to make itself invisible, a point or pulsation in the unconscious. When it was on your side, it carried you by leaving itself behind. Maybe you had cut your finger or banged your knee. A spider bite. Little things that would signal, as if by metonymy, "Honey, I'm home, I am your home." Now your body prevails in a reproachful sort of way, and there is nothing for you to know (there are charts and medical histories, comparative analyses, information and data, prognoses and projections, all cognitive stammers in the face of illness). You become its amnesiac witness, capable of momentary attestations, observing and monitoring, unsure of ever recovering from these irruptions of total contingency. You understand yourself as dead meat, repeating the ancient cry of abandonment and knowing that this time, this time it's for real, you have been forsaken. Forget about getting past this. Though there are little, altogether secular resurrections: your fever goes down, a little energy suddenly rises, you can eat or walk or pee alone, and it is not clear why this is happening to you right now, I mean, that you're not yet dead. Still, something has happened to you. One morning you wake up like Gregor Samsa, can't get out of bed. Or you've been throwing up all night. Something has happened. You took a fall, fell ill; KO'd, you were thrown, cast out of the heavenly body that certified innocence in the form of health. You are sick as a dog. Everything stops. There are times when this suspension of being can be affirmed. Like when Gregor dances on the ceiling: he doesn't have to go to work! You get to stay home and regress. Read, watch television, hallucinate. Still, though, there's something very wrong, like culpability without a known cause. You're in trouble, unbalanced. The inventions and inflections of the future vanish. But something is released as well. The store of toxicity spills, sometimes in slow motion, and something like time starts cleansing. Your body — your body is *fighting for you*.

It's a fight, sometimes, without teleology; it can be a losing battle or a healing without cure, one big healing crisis. It's war, and one small part of yourself is standing up for you, standing up to you. Maybe for the first time.

Illness: essentially related to the experience of injustice, it is your *Geworfenheit*, your dharma. Something beyond or within you has put you down, smashed you firmly against a wall of indifference, pressuring you with your own capacity for suffering. It was uncalled for, illness, yet there may be something you did, you think, to bring it on. An accompaniment to your finitude, illness visits you at will and does what it wants to your body, biting organs and stinging surfaces you didn't know you had. To underscore this point, Dostoevsky made sure that the Prince would endure, so to speak, the intensity of injustice by determining that his experience of illness would not be obscured by social injustice. This is why Dostoevsky throws money and station at him. The martyring of the Prince is related to a destruction rendered irreparable because there is no way to separate the destruction of mind from a body in desperation: hence the Prince suffers a sacred illness. It is not the body that, though entrusted to us, is as such sacred but the illness, which disorders sense and even convention, that appears to maintain the auratic quality of the ongoing sacrifice, its sacredness.

Illness offers its own system of subverting social norms, independent of subjectivity or volition: "I can't marry any one. I am an invalid." Framed by panic, illness gives access to the devotional mode of surrender, abandoning to itself something other than the self, the will. Whereas Nietzsche thematized a going under that was pivoted on a promise of recuperation, Dostoevsky parses illness for a rhythm of remission, a promise offered only for provisional reprieve. But there is no phase of attestable overcoming, for the disease, experienced in the mode of a silent chronicity, is always with the Idiot, even where it refrains from proposing signs and symptoms or ceases to substitute itself for perception and mime consciousness. Another kind of mediation, illness, indeed, brings with it an alternative system of ecstasy and meaning. Under paradoxical sway, classical tropes of harmony and balance are shown to be sustained only in the distortions produced by the pained body, beside itself, pitching toward massive collapse. The measured chill of absolute endangerment. As one Dostoevsky scholar puts it, "this beatific vision of harmony can only be experienced by a half-witted epileptic who knows it to be an aberration of his disease."[18]

In The Idiot there are two infirm bodies. They are labeled explicitly by the graphosomatology of the text as ill, as dying. Of course no one is excused from the exigencies of this becoming (the limits of health are not always very clear, one cannot be found not to be dying, and anyway, illness is an inescapable condition of being), but two bodies — those of Prince Myshkin and of the young nihilist Ippolit — are presented without ambiguity under the name of illness. Ippolit, the consumptive, in the process of dying, is tied to his process by confessions and the incessant composition of last wills and angry testaments. The Prince endures an illness that stays the execution but offers premonitions of death episodically. He walks about, ever in anticipation of an attack, all along in the inexact assurance of punctual recovery. When restoration appears to present a possibility, he is undercut and then, suddenly, re-established again. It is not known how much time he has. No question of a cure, though there are reprieves, sudden and exhausting. Idiocy and epilepsy reinforce each other in the novel, as if to emphasize the impossible separation of domains, notably, where the body ends; extending toward a limit, disfiguring this limit, their conjunction makes us ask, How could a proper phenomenology of mind be traced that would not ditch the body? (If it were proper, it would have to be improper.) While the introduction of epilepsy brings definition to the parameters of infirmity with which Dostoevsky is working, such a medicalization of idiocy does not clear away the questions that he persistently raises. In fact, epilepsy itself, what Shakespeare in Julius Caesar called "falling sickness," brings one big question mark to the table of any speculative diagnostics.

Even though Dostoevsky "had" epilepsy, it remains unclear what he had or what we have at hand when we think we are discussing the condition so named. It has a heritage backed up by literature, seconded by philosophy, and claimed by mythology. A thorough modern cultural anthropology studying the place of the purported disease would include the fact that epilepsy is the only somatic illness to which Freud devoted some pages in the postneurological phases of his career. Located between psyche and soma, between the theory of trauma (which focuses the history of the subject) and the theory of fantasy (which refers to transference and countertransference), epilepsy is not just another somatic illness. In distinction to other types of somatic aggravations, epilepsy is inscribed in the history of thought without being restricted merely to the history of medical thought.[19] The only illness to have its own mythological figure, it may provide the ur-phenomenon of all subsequent forms of madness and visionary excess. Hercules, the herald of epilepsy, has mutated and manifested historically in the Buddha, Alexander the Great, Julius Caesar, Napoléon, Lord Byron, Pascal, Van Gogh, and others to whom we shall no doubt return (epileptics are said to fear returns, *revenants*). For now, let us follow Dostoevsky in postponing a discussion of pathogenic specificity until the general tour of the more global effects of illness has been accomplished.

The sick bodies of Ippolit and Myshkin mark the disruption around which the text is organized. This may be one reason why the text comes off as so disorganized, barring the historical contingencies of its *Entstehung*, the conditions of its emergence (under great duress, the author dashed off the serial installments in exchange for payment, his beloved infant daughter had died, and he, inconsolable, suffering, was exiled for the most part to Germanic precincts). Everyone is susceptible to the ailing bodies, almost unaccountably attracted to them as if they could be, in the first place, psychically infectious. No one stands forth as the body of health, for there are gradations of illness and entire taxonomies of foolishness — the novel suffers fools of many kinds and supports drunkards, maniacs, the pathologically resentful, the envious, a rapist, a crowd of cheaters, classic neurotics, subjects of delusional rantings and criminal intent, not to speak of, worst of all, what constitutes for the narrator the blatantly ordinary. On several occasions Nastasya Filippovna is labeled by the Idiot himself as a lunatic. The supporting cast of troubled figures, while received by the novel for the most part with compassion and capable of emanating a nearly magical radiance, functions only to stoke the sacred intensity of the Idiot's illness.

The idiot body, presented as eccentric and awkward, convulsive and worn, in some instances as a battered body, is particularly susceptible to attack. It is not always clear where the attack comes from, for it is hard to locate the force that hits him — it can come from above, from inside, from the alter ego and spiritual brother, Rogozhin (though presenting an alter ego to the nearly egoless Myshkin would involve another problem), from the weather or the unconscious or, even more precisely, from the *drive*, that is, neither from the conscious nor the unconscious. Attacks of the sort he suffers, bouts of illness (Dostoevsky does not make it easy to divide up the territory of illness — is it a continuity folded back by occasional recession, or is it closer to a punctuality, a return, an interference or interruption of another state?), aggravate the problem of presenting the body — the weight of the unpresentable — at all. The sick body presses the issue of this impossible presentation to the fore. It is not merely mired in passivity, though each day it awaits its fate, wondering if a vague spell of dizziness does not portend the beginning of another episode, the event of another destruction. The difficulty lies in predicting the daily histories of a sick body, the varying intensities of its constitution (the day of the ill is divided into about four parts, the afternoon fever, the evening reprieve, nocturnal sweats — this changes with different types of illness, the signified, I mean, but the day divides up in much the same way no matter what you've got — and the liver works the late-night shift, rousing you at two or three in the morning, no matter who you are). In the life of the sick the primary relationship is to this alternate being, at once indwelling and eventuating from without.

When the Idiot says he cannot marry, it is because he is bound by another contract to his illness, whose distinct personality he serves. By nature imperious, illness demands devoted appeasement, understanding, the endless manipulations of care. You lie with your illness — something that seems foolish to have to say: it takes you, in many cases, to bed. But there are some forms of illness that do not show, do not lay you low or keep you supine, decumbent. Shadowed by a passive transitivity, you walk around in them, you're an idiot, ever on the verge of having an attack. He says he cannot marry, but he is betrothed to two women; toward the end he has prepared for the wedding with Nastasya Filippovna. But this offers no contradiction: the sick often find someone who is even sicker to take care of, and this is the case with the Prince. He offers his hand to Nastasya, it is noted, out of a feminist impulse — she has been scorned by men, denounced as a lost woman, sexually mishandled — but with unaffected fervor because she is, to his mind, a sick child, a lunatic, delirious and deranged. He also takes care of Ippolit, whose terminal condition prompts, throughout the novel, dramatic anxiety.

The Forbidden Body

Despite the pressure it exerts on reading minutely the signs or symptoms that accrue to the sick body, the labor of understanding abandons all semiology or phenomenology. It encounters a limit, mute and stupid, that cannot be grasped even in terms of a negative knowledge. There is yet another dimension of the stupid to which infirmity subjects us, one that remains indifferent to those registers of stupidity still affected by the fading empire of cognition. Without knowing, the body is not, as such, ignorant either. A literality that is no longer legible, this body at once withholds itself and produces resistant signs of itself. Perhaps this offers one reason why literature, which delights in radically ambiguous conjunctions, always points to the incorporation of such a body. If the body of the king is the thing, purloined or missing in action, the Prince's body drags along, in need of treatment. And it is no wonder that literature treats this body where philosophy might sack it with the rest of the provisional hostages of the concept.

According to Jean-Luc Nancy, literature has always tried to produce the body, which philosophy suppresses. In fact, this relation enacts an allegory of their link, for "one could say that literature and philosophy have never stopped wanting to relate to and/or oppose one another as body to soul or spirit." Moreover, "one is tempted to say that if there has never been any body in philosophy — other than the signifier and signified — in literature, on the contrary, there is nothing but bodies."[20] Nancy provisionally divides the body according to a discursive custody suit of sorts, where literature gets to carry bodies to house and form them. Still, we can't just go around thinking that these bodies are easily reclaimable or anchored in reference. Nor can we think that we can ignore the body, the way people commonly step over the homeless bodies on their streets. Any discussion of the body risks engaging a "double bind, a psychosis." Failure is necessarily given at the outset: "And a double failure is given: a failure to produce a discourse on the body, also the failure not to produce discourse on it" (190). One might venture, though, that the sick body, in a kind of frenzied state of belated, compensatory awakening, demands a reading or at least occasions interpretive and diagnostic strategies that often culminate in an excess of discourse. This excess itself, an attempt to construct knowledge around the symptomizing body, opens up the space of necessary obscurity by which our bodies come to us: "This non-knowledge is not negative knowledge or the negation of knowledge; it is simply the absence of knowledge, the absence of the very relation of knowledge, whatever its content" (199). Nancy continues, holding the body as uninscribable, as that which exscribes everything, starting with itself:

The body does not know; but it is not ignorant either. Quite simply, it is elsewhere. It is from elsewhere, another place, another regime, another register, which is not even that of an "obscure" knowledge, or a "pre-conceptual" knowledge, or a "global," "immanent," or "immediate" knowledge. The philosophical objection to what philosophy calls "body" presupposes the determination of something like an authority of "immediate knowledge" — a contradiction in terms, which inevitably becomes "mediated" (as "sensation," "perception," synaesthesia, and as immense reconstitutions of a presupposed "representation"). But what if one could presuppose nothing of the kind? What if the body was simply there, given, abandoned, without presupposition, simply posited, weighed, weighty? (199–200)

Ever elsewhere when it comes to cognitive scanners, the body evades the regimens of knowledge that would claim to grasp, sectionize, or conceptualize it. Somewhat surprisingly, the site of nonknowledge that the body traverses, and of which it is a part, is related by Nancy to thought, to acts or contracts of thinking, for the body thinks in a sense, beyond giving or making sense (which would belong under the auspices of knowledge); conversely, thought embodies: "If one agrees to say, and if it is fitting to say, that thought does not belong to the order of knowledge either, then it might no longer be impossible to say that the body thinks and also, consequently, that thought is itself a body" (201). Linked to the thought of thinking, responding with an almost unreadable acquiescence to the question "What is called thinking?" this inert presence, detached from the knowledge that would seek to contain it, has let go of "a treasury of sense to which only those united with God have access" (191). Thought, which Heidegger unhitched from philosophical operations, weighs in as body, and, more perplexingly still, to the extent that it is possible that the body thinks, the thinking body throws itself against the prevailing winds of the Western philosophical tradition.

If, in Dostoevsky's work, the body commended by illness still bears a memory trace of the sacred, it nonetheless encounters its finitude, and the finitude of all bodies, in the haunting limit drawn by Holbein. "With the death of God, we have lost this glorious body, this sublime body: this real symbol of his sovereign majesty, this microcosm of his immense work, and finally this visibility of the invisible, this mimesis of the inimitable" (191). Putting to rest the glorious body, Holbein's "Christ Taken Down . . ." concludes a double act of reversal. Figuring Christ's body without the lift or iconicity of intended transcendence, Nancy says: " 'God is dead' means: God no longer has a body" (191).

Henceforth bodies, bereft of trickle-down symbolicity, will have to be pumped up, prosthetically amplified, steroid-enhanced, "built" and buffed, bionically ensured, drugged or "medicated," cloned, remade — henceforth, the technobody or replicant will be made to substitute for the lost body of the divine trait — that body which could still be sacrificed. In The Idiot, Dostoevsky sees the apocalypse, or at least he has Lebedyev reinscribe it, in terms of technological dominion, citing the spread of the railroad and the distribution of connectors installed by new technologies as instigators of the unsacrificeable.

The novel opens with the three principals — Myshkin, Rogozhin, and Lebedyev — being carried by train into Saint Petersburg station. It starts, therefore, according to tracks laid out in the later parts of the novel, in the apocalyptic tenor — or vehicle — of a technological momentum. Later on machinery itself is cast by Ippolit as a dumb beast, the *bêtise* that is part of an inexorable movement of world-historical dumbness. The novel's first chapter roars into the station, a mythological terminus bound from the start to determine the fate of the Idiot.

What emerges from the train is the last body, a sputter or remnant of the lost, glorious body. It is a body in transit, making the transition from the sublime body to what is pictured by Holbein as the decreation of world — the unnameable end of the body, even if this should be consecrated in our memories as an endless end that only keeps on ending. Nancy phrases it thus: "The dead, rotten body is this thing that no longer has any name in any language, as we learn from Tertullian and Bossuet; and the unnamed God has vanished together with this unnameable thing. It might very well be that with this body, all bodies have been lost, that any notion, any truth, any representation of bodies has been lost" (191). Having displaced the lost body, the inglorious corpse implicates the mediations that historically have touched all bodies and kept them, if not safe, then at least representable. In Dostoevsky, infirmity effects something of a return of the glorious body as the memory and phantom of what can no longer be.

To the extent that Myshkin's illness still binds him to the sacred, his serves as a body, perhaps the last, still capable of being sacrificed. The residue of sacrificeability is due in part to the fact that this body retains and persists in making sense. An expression of unbearable singularity, the illness continues to produce sense if only as a hallucinatory byproduct of its disordering interventions. Nonetheless, there is provisional sense, epiphany — there is the inflection of divine disclosure, though without a proper object. There is nothing to disclose but the exposition itself to another regimen or register of being. Outside the realm to which the severity of illness opens, there is only the exhaustion of the body and the congealed sense of the body. To keep this body sacrifice-able, Dostoevsky has had to protect it from the emptying of sense induced by the evacuation of the sacred, staving off that depletion of purpose congruent with the degradations of poverty, hunger, deportation, torture, deprivation, ugliness, horror: "Such are the sacrificed bodies, but sacrificed to nothing" (195).

There may be no truth of this body other than that which speaks to the nothingness of its sacrifice, no Empedoclean remnant out of which to piece together some final sense, not even the announcement of an approaching Fortinbras, who would bring up futuricity by means of order and commemoration. "'Sacrifice,' says Nancy, "designates a body's passage to a limit where it becomes the body of a community, the spirit of a communion of which it is the effectiveness, the material symbol, the absolute relationship to itself of sense pervading blood, of blood making sense. But sacrifice is no more" (176). The historicity of the wound involves its despiritualization, and the body recedes, taking on the status of the forbidden body. "There was a spirituality of Christ's wounds. But since then, a wound is just a wound — and the body is nothing but a wound. . . . The body is but a wound. None of our wounds, in a sense, is new, regardless of the economic, military, police, psychological techniques that inflict them. But from now on, the wound is just a sign of itself, signifying nothing other than this suffering, a forbidden body deprived of its body" (196).[21]

An embodiment of a pure tautology, an emptiness, the forbidden body offers the experience of an inert presence with little or no ontological consistency. The community, having surrendered the meaningful body, becomes the site of a private ward of contingency, the unattested sacrifice. Illness at once grounds the body here on earth, marking its subjection to time and destruction in time, but it also suspends, while reestablishing, the very corporeal contingency under whose rule it operates. Illness calls for the emergence of another body — a multiplicity of bodies — for a healing and for another understanding. It plays the phantasmatic body against the real body. Complicit with the demand for another understanding, Christianity, from one perspective, offered the promise of performative acts of healing. The teaching of the Incarnation, saying that God was also meant to inhabit a body, underscored how we are fated to inhabit our bodies. Instigator to the many legendary scenes of spontaneous healing, Christianity, one major recovery program, insistently addressed the failing body, whether in discursive rites or by means of constructions such as Lourdes — the offering of allegories of woundedness that it dressed with emergency supplies of meaning. In a text that was commissioned by his doctor for a roundtable discussion, Nancy writes about the fate of pain, marking it off from suffering and the tradition that appropriates these terms. Pain, according to the title of the improvised text, is strictly unjustifiable ("La douleur existe, elle est injustifiable").[22] That is, the moment one attempts to justify or make sense of it, one has reappropriated pain to its Christian history; one has returned or restored it to meaning.

However, pain abhors meaning; it grotesquely etches meaning's interruption and self-sameness. Pain is unjustifiable. Without a doubt it is unjustifiable that pain be unjustifiable. Anyone who tries to present a case for its justification is a Stoic or Christian or worse. One could be a Hegelian, getting by on the "work, patience, and pain of the concept."[23] Whereas suffering and distress tend to subsist on themselves or expand their scope by morose delectation or masochistic surplus, pain, in contrast, acts as its own repellent, rejecting itself while refusing any justification, assumption or sublimation. "Pain is perhaps nothing but this refusal of itself."[24] Allowing for little secondary benefit (to speak with Freud), pain is its own destitution, which no amount of dialectization or ideological recuperation could justify. When pain persists without remedy and nothing else exists besides its pointed compression, its tightening, a kind of paradoxical if instantaneous flash goes off, a momentary insight occurs: something like a pure attestation of being becomes possible, a kind of "I'm not well, I'm in trouble, therefore I am."[25] It is not that "I am" in the sense of a sudden retrieval of self; I am no more than the piercing pain that is tearing me apart, and in such a way that I am no longer a self, this madness of pain.[26] Nancy, who is very French on this point, offers that this split-second flash is like the double or reverse of the bang of jouissance. Pain and jouissance (which can be seen as a pain that "succeeds") share the extremity of such a radiating flash, pulsing from that place where being, utterly exposed, is external to itself, posed outside any self (soi) as pure explosive flashing, ripped, thrown. This extremity does not take place except within the split between pain and the extreme point of pleasure. Which is to say that in a sense it cannot ever take place or that it is "impossible," as Lacan says of jouissance.

Nancy by no means endeavors to efface the irrefutable urgency of pain, of which he has had his share. Instead he concludes his intervention by stating that the it's-not-happening experience you get with pain *is* reality.[27] He ends his remarks by allowing that the recognition of the certitude, the reality of which he writes, does not amount to a justification: "C'est une attestation." When the punishing thrashes of pain come down on you, you are at a loss for words, the fiction of agency collapses; even so, you are preparing your testimony. If one can do no more than testify, attest to that which cannot take place, it is also because the solidity of empirical ground slips away from under pain, leaving it to grope in the dark, fumbling for language, when it seeks description through the intercession of an "as if." It's as if my head were splitting open. Or, doubling the stakes of abstraction, I feel as though I'm going to die. But pain is destructive of language's capacity to name.[28] Unshareable, it bores through language. Virginia Woolf once said that we know how to describe great torrents and we capture tempests, but we cannot convey the essence of a headache (my paraphrase). This goes for the dancing invalid in Kleist's story as well as for a throbbing toothache in Dostoevsky's *Underground Man*. Pertinently elusive of referential content, the language that seeks to get a handle on pain becomes dependent on a speculative grammar for its expression; rather than offering confirmation of the empiricalness that we thought we had recourse to, it radiates through metaphoricity; pain exists — unjustifiably — to disfigure, leaping about abrasively in figural language, searing your sacred idiot body.

Myshkin arrives at the station with a clean bill of health. Well, almost: he has been released from the doctor's custody. It is as if he were meant to cross the moment of a reprieve drawn by the fragile span between a clinical discharge and a final collapse. To the extent that he is presented as partially healed (but still an "idiot"), resurrected and exposed to the community, subjected to mockery, derision, and love, as emanating a sacred quality, he returns to Russia as the figure of a renewal but also as an undead God, conditionally resurrected. He occupies the purposive space evacuated by the living, eternal God, though he does not quite yet serve as the reminder that God is dead — maybe that God is capable of dying. He arrives as a last recapitulation of the divine in the form of sacred simplicity and a body that still sacrifices while forbidding itself to the other.

If he at once fascinates and horrifies, this is due in part to the way Myshkin embodies what is deficient in the Other. Incessantly returning to the Other its own lack, he reflects a certain abhorrence of the sacred. The idiot body is absorbed by the community to the point of marking its own exclusion, ever poised as a foreign body within the ambivalently receptive milieu that welcomes him. Because he has been away for so long, Prince Myshkin speaks Russian with a foreign accent; he is native and foreign at once, an inclusion that is meant to be excluded, familiar and aberrant, both dear and bizarre, the intimate figure of idiocy. The very woundedness by which he is bound protects him: this body, in need of a healing that cannot be ensured, actually saves the Prince from a brutal execution at the hands of a jealous Rogozhin. As he is about to be assassinated in a dark stairwell, an epileptic seizure erupts and takes over the scene, supervening upon the intention of murder, frightening away the killer.

The Seizure

Elusive yet inescapable, the body presents itself as pure surplus of objectivity, something, moreover, that cannot be reached by the very knowledge it invites. Whether infirm or sound — the difference dwindles — our body doubles for trauma, or, rather, it *acts* as a traumatic place that causes a series of failures. The way we locate it elicits the thought of trauma inasmuch as the body appears to occupy the empty place of the real. It recalls the Lacanian engagement with the real to the extent that the body presents itself as an entity that does not exist, or barely exists, except perhaps in failure or exaggeration, in beauty or mortification.[29] Some of these assertions become evident in the experience itself of the epileptic fit, when consciousness is extinguished by the force of surplus intensity —

> Then suddenly something seemed torn asunder before him; his soul was flooded with intense inner light. The moment lasted perhaps half a second, yet he clearly and consciously remembered the beginning, the first sound of the fearful scream which broke of itself from his breast and which he could not have checked by any effort. Then his consciousness was instantly extinguished and complete darkness followed.
>
> It was an epileptic fit, the first he had had for a long time. It is well known that epileptic fits come on quite suddenly. At the moment the face is horribly distorted, especially the eyes. The whole body and the features of the face work with convulsive jerks and contortions. A terrible, indescribable scream that is unlike anything else breaks from the sufferer. In that scream everything human seems obliterated and it is impossible, or very difficult, for an observer to realize and admit that it is the man himself screaming. It seems indeed as though it were someone else screaming from within that

man. . . . *The sight of a man in an epileptic fit fills many people with positive and unbearable horror, in which there is a certain element of the uncanny.* (227)

Whereas other passages describe a state of extraordinary emotiveness in the form of ecstatic self-departure — the incomparable *pleasure* offered by the seizure makes you want to trade in everything for one such moment of desubjectivizing rapture, an illuminated, coruscating giddiness — this episode brings up the experience of severance, the blaze of an intense inner light followed by the extinction of consciousness. The Prince, losing presence in this passage to the fit, is placed at an increasing remove, and so Dostoevsky has the narrator name the condition ("It was an epileptic fit") and track

"Myshkin, worn out, depressed, and physically shattered —"

its manifestation. But even the external, diagnostic gaze collapses at the limits of language, contorting into the "indescribable scream" issued by the suffering body and shared by narrative reduction. In excess of signification, an impossible metonymy of the convulsing body, the scream, indescribable, "is unlike anything else" and breaks from the body. In the scream everything human is obliterated and the subject is delocalized, "as though it were someone else screaming from within the man." Split, divided, bereft of properly human properties, the seized subject produces a medused effect, terrorizing and petrifying the other, even if he is Rogozhin and about to murder you.

In a more Freudian light (though what could be more Freudian than the simultaneity of assassination attempts, somaticopsychic collapse, and the close proximity of your best friend?), this scene could be viewed as the *Entstellung*, or truthful distortion, representing the severe ambivalence that the Idiot, the seriously ill subject, tends to elicit. The scene says as much about itself (the "sight of a man in an epileptic fit fills many people with positive and unbearable horror") but deflects its own insight toward the more material contours of the episode. Still, it stages the murderous rage inscribed by Myshkin's alter ego and soulmate at the scene of extreme illness. The distortion lies in the narrative decision to linearize and condense the story, showing that Rogozhin desists from committing the intended murder when horrified by the fit. The murderer is seized by terror; the seizure makes him disappear from the murder scene. Whether the seizure is responsive to violence directed toward the subject or is at the root of the other's rage remains unsaid. Yet somehow the sick body invites social rage, the other side of brotherly love: it incites the absolute hostility that supplants hospital(ity). In fact, though, a number of characters in the novel respond to the Prince's condition with a spontaneous violence that is then shown to be repressed or eventually sublimated to charity and love.

How can the scene of the seizure be read? One exhaustive clinical study depicts the epileptic fit as a repetition of the infant's terror when first faced with the parental death wish — as a response to the threat of infanticide visited upon baby.[30] On the other hand, Ferenczi had seen the epileptic seizure as an enactment of a wish to return to the womb, and Freud, when it was his turn to consider the enigma of epilepsy, rather than allow a purely neuropathic status to stand, had somewhat surprisingly kept it close to the mode of hysteria he identified as conversion hysteria; more recently, in Dostoïevski et Flaubert, Marie-Thérèse Sutterman locates epilepsy in the sadomasochistic phantasms that feature the self as murdered child. In view of her indications, the scene composed by Dostoevsky could be seen to represent a metaleptic fit, for Myshkin, in fetal position, subverts the murder, having produced the fit that in fact reenacts a prior murder scene. I offer these considerations as a kind of sneak preview, for there remain in this story a number of sadomasochistic contracts yet to be drawn.

Aglaya Epanchina is not the least consequential of the attending figures who, although ostensibly attached to the Prince by love, are in any case at once horrified and fascinated by his debility and respond to him with a consistent capacity for sadistic vengeance. Aglaya's sadistic repertory commences with the many instances of poking fun at him and by her demands that while in social view he be stilled, silenced, rendered stationary and invisible. Moreover, she at times prompts his faltering incapacitation to the extent that she programs failure, "foreseeing" with anxiety that at a party he is meant to break a prized vase and deliver rants in place of conversation. To announce a premonition to the hysterically suggestible Myshkin, to predict, is, as his beloved well knows, to dictate its execution. At every level, from the ingratiating nurse, Lebedyev, to the case of Ippolit, Dostoevsky indicates how illness summons forth exploitation, codependency, malevolence, how it draws blood and excites social violence. Repugnant and uncanny, the Idiot, in a kind of Bataillean reversal (being at bottom unmistakably Christian), provokes . . . love. Everyone loves the Idiot, who becomes a global symptom within an ambivalent economy governed largely by disgust. The idiot evokes horror, but this circumstance does not stop the community from loving him. On the contrary. There exists a barely discernible distinction between love and disgust in the novel. One could say of every couple equally that they are drawn to each other by irrepressible hatred or unavoidable love, that desire is fueled by disgust, run on aversion — Dostoevsky makes these affective determinations reversible in a manner that retains the accent on ambivalent intensity. The undecidable limit between hatred and love, contempt and reverence dominates the community of every couple: Rogozhin and Myshkin, Aglaya and Myshkin, Nastasya and Myshkin, Lebedyev and himself, the general and his wife, Kolya and the general, and just about everyone else who comes together.

Let us return momentarily to the scene of Myshkin's seizure, which undecidably suspends/provokes Rogozhin's murderous rage. The crisis and its ghostly suspension perform a doubling within the novel that earns it the narrative quality of "uncanny." The horror attending the convulsed body, its scream of abandonment coming from elsewhere, unlocatably, reinscribes the scene in Rogozhin's house before Holbein's *Christ Taken from the Cross*. Anna Grigoryevna has used the same diction in her diaries to describe her husband's turn of mind when he first saw Holbein's tableau in Basel and the cast of his features when he went into seizure: she delineates "an expression of terror."[31] A concentration of terrors is, in her view, established by these events, which somehow mirror each other, causing a fright, an apocalyptic strain of anxiety. Epilepsy is notoriously prodded and harassed by certain representations and recurring memories; the epileptic must avoid these triggers. A kind of daredevil masochism incites Dostoevsky to return to condemned scenes or moods of representation, however. Forbidden by his doctors to represent to himself the scenes of the fit, Dostoevsky delves into them, repeating and reworking the event of the seizure. For the epileptic, a partial recall of the forbidden experience in itself runs the risk, as do flashing lights or intense imaging, of provoking another fit. So when Dostoevsky refuses to forget but instead describes Myshkin's panic, reviving terror and aura, when he flashes back to the dead Christ and reaches down into the abyss in order to come up with this scene, he has his hand on at least three triggers. The murder, the love of Christ, the horror before his mutilated body, in sum, the general vocabulary of unsupported suffering, are dispatched to Myshkin, where it is no longer known whether he "had hurt himself, or whether there had been some crime" (227).

Persistently recalling the cry that seemed to come from someone else, the novel continues to proffer two bodies, as if to underscore the double bind that any body language necessarily engages. Whereas

Faust had reported that two souls inhabit his body, *The Idiot* speaks to us of two bodies, which, in part hallucinated and internalized, replicate themselves in a determined drama of unsettled malaise. Faust rid himself of his ailing body with drugs dealt by Mephistopheles, the witches' brew. It was only after switching body types that Faust started tripping beyond the bounds of traditional cultures of knowledge, exceeding the limits of the human intelligence quotient. Myshkin stays body-bound and busted, constrained by an experience of corporeality that, though finally earthly and ordinary, in itself proves capable of producing double takes and self-departing splits. In a sense there are nothing but body doubles, reflecting one another as if to mark the failure of integrating the traumatic singularity of what is given to us as our ownmost body. Thus there are two sick bodies, those of Myshkin and Ippolit; Myshkin is split between two women, Nastasya and Aglaya, and there is an articulated split between the blood brothers Rogozhin and Myshkin. The proliferation of doubles continues, having originated in the double body of God, which appears to lose its transcendence until, as if compressed in the end of the novel, there remains one corpse watched over by Myshkin and his negative mirror, Rogozhin. By the end of the novel spirit has evacuated the scene, leaving behind the abandoned body, which is to say, the inglorious corpse. This body, now reduced to the smell of preservatives, is covered by a medicalized trace called America: "'Do you notice the smell?' . . . 'I covered her with American cloth — good American cloth — and put a sheet on top of that, and I put four uncorked bottles of Zhdanor's disinfectant there. They are there now'" (591).

PART TWO

The End of Europe

Two proper names open the magnificent *Histoire de la folie*. Michel Foucault convenes Pascal and Dostoevsky in the first sentences of the preface to the tome: "Pascal: 'Men are necessarily mad, that not to be mad would amount to another form of madness.' And Dostoevsky, in his *Diary of a Writer*: 'It is not by confining one's neighbor that one is convinced of one's own sanity.' "[32] The two figures are recruited to testify to the necessity of opening those classified documents that most concern Foucault. Yet his interrogation promotes a kind of release — of prisoners, of exegetic energy, of silence and power — that cannot be said to occur in the texts and testimonies of his star witnesses. Representatives of the domains of philosophy and literature, they plead Foucault's cause from a place, roughly speaking, of somatophobia, on the one hand, and body-friendly inscription, on the other.[33] They do not feel that they can open a silent vault or even a sealed dossier in order to liberate a discursive space. In the case at least of the Russian author, it is clear that he encounters less lumière than gloom, less clarity of institutional purpose than obscure corruption of means. Unlike the fate that befalls the insane in the Age of Reason, there is yet little containment of idiocy, though at the end of his novel the question does arise of putting Myshkin under control.[34]

Foucault no doubt had his reasons for opening the lines of inquiry with the double-barreled shots of Pascal and Dostoevsky — two great epileptics, as it happens, whose focus turned to the street protocols of madness. In contrast to what Foucault tracks in terms of a history of incarceration and noise reduction, the novels of Dostoevsky are set in the din of a contaminated field: there can be no lockup for stupidity, no proven detection systems, as there has been for madness ever since steely Reason installed the twin towers of penitentiary and asylum, cordoning off nonreason and silencing the cries or convoluted articulations of a madman's "discourse." Nonetheless, there is a good deal of slippage that occurs between the concepts (a provisional holding cell — the *concept* hardly furnishes more than a makeshift grid) containing madness, idiocy, and stupidity. For Dostoevsky these porous concepts slip up and become one another, though distinctions are locally held. The protagonist of The Idiot, whose fate it is to fall, in the end, into a mad stupor — he last is seen caressing the murderer Rogozhin[35] — has been associated, on the one hand, with exceptional discernment or, at times, with what appears to be its other hand: overarching stupidity. He walks the line between recondite knowledge and abysmal stuttering, endeavoring to strike a balance between the lucidity of madness (if this could be contained) and the punctual pitfalls of dim-wittedness. Venturing out, he often cuts a ridiculous figure ("I become utterly, utterly absent-minded and ridiculous" [120]). In the end, submitted to the hypothesis of a diagnostic gaze, he becomes what he was: "But by now he could understand no questions he was asked and did not recognize the people surrounding him; and if Schneider himself had come from Switzerland to look at his former pupil and patient, remembering the condition in which Myshkin had sometimes been during the first year of his stay in Switzerland, he would have flung up his hands in despair and would have said as he did then, 'An idiot!'" (594). This time, though, there will be no fiction of recovery, for "Schneider frowns and shakes his head more ominously every time; he hints at a permanent derangement of the intellect; he does not yet say positively that recovery is out of the question, but he allows himself phrases suggestive of the most melancholy possibilities" (596). The entire community of friends, doubters, and even stragglers is affected, as if hit by contagion. Everyone connected to the Prince falls ill or apart (for instance, "Vera Lebedyev was so distressed that she fell positively ill" [596]). Myshkin returns to the origin of his ghostly appearance, haunting the sites by which he was inscribed.

The story admittedly ends strangely, by mapping the kenotic predicament it has described onto a geopolitical fantasy. The final shot comes from a voice of the maternal imaginary that issues an injunction capable of disengaging a land-body in a single act of malediction. His friend and patroness, Lizaveta Prokofyevna, "wept bitterly at the sight of Myshkin in his afflicted and humiliated condition" (596–97). As if in revenge for his fate, she begins to turn "bitter and unfair in her criticism of everything in Europe" (597). She has had a good Russian cry over this poor fellow, Myshkin, she remarks, adding — as if the link could be construed as causal — "'And all this, all this life abroad, and this Europe of yours is all a fantasy, and all of us abroad are only a fantasy.... remember my words, you'll see for yourself!' she concluded almost wrathfully, as she parted from Yevgeny Pavlovitch" (597). These are the parting words of the novel in conformity with which Lizaveta folds by doubling the drive of textual closure, concluding "almost wrathfully, as she parted," with an exhortation to "remember my words." And what are we to remember, apart from the canalization of the entire novel speaking out here in the condensed language of Lizaveta Prokofyevna? On one level we are told to remember that we are merely fantasy, perhaps a dream or maybe an idiot's memory trace, matching something like "a tale told by an idiot." On another level, however, this fantasy of which we are a part is localized and named. The fantasy to which the novel points as if in a last spasm devolves on nothing less than "Europe."

One could say that this particular termination comes out of nowhere. The eruption of Europe comes out of nowhere in the novel, nothing has led up to the ending that ends "almost wrathfully," serving as an indictment of Europe or propelling its return to its source in fantasy. How is it that we will ever see the truth of this assertion, in accordance with Lizaveta's vows? Is Europe a fantasy that exceeds the fiction even of novelistic invention? Or does the fiction of Europe undo the fantasy one may have entertained of the novel's provenance as fiction? The naming of Europe at the conclusion of the novel — a conclusion that performs itself allegorically — "she concluded almost wrathfully, as she parted" — transforms any values we thought we held concerning the nature of the opposition, truth or fantasy. The certitudes associated with knowing the difference are destabilized when Europe becomes the promised site of fantasy. The Idiot does not constitute the fantasy but Europe, which is now contained in and by The Idiot, over which Lizaveta has a good Russian cry, represents that surplus through which fantasy can be read. By naming Europe as the future of a fantasy or the memory of fantasy, the novel engages its material boundaries, interrogating what constitutes exteriority here, what belongs to the inner domain of narrative manipulation elsewhere. Putting into question the value of reference — what is the status of Europe if it emerges as the name of a novel's fantasy? — it also resists its own conclusion. At the moment it appears to be ending and stages its intention to conclude, if "almost" wrathfully, the novel, inverting reference — "this Europe" — points instead to its own excess, something involving the conjunction of memory, future, and Europe. But if Europe is to prove to have been

> "He did not feel in the least insulted by this; to his thinking, it was quite as it should be."

little more than fantasy ("only a fantasy"), then there will have been no future; the utterance "you will see" says only that you will see what is not there to be seen. If the novel ends (we shall see), it does so at the undecidable limit of nihilistic projection and sacred affirmation, on the raging hesitation over a real or imagined body that it refuses to lock up or shut down.

Unhappy with having to end thus, the novel names the unhappy ending "Europe." Somehow the ashes of the idiot body are strewn over this Europe, which recedes, almost wrathfully, as a fantasy. Yet Europe is identified as the locus of a certain type of scientific knowledge, as the space that originates the clinical gaze. The Prince arrives from Europe at the novel's beginning and is returned at its end to Europe, to the Swiss clinic and to Dr. Schneider's ward. Everything that has happened between these two moments of departure occurs in the Russian zones of anguished liberality, when the Prince is more or less allowed to run free and expose his wounds.

The Sacred Alien

Having arrived from Europe or, rather, from the Swiss clinic, and having been released, in a sense, on his own recognizance, the formerly interred Prince is insinuated into the scene as an outsider. Neither locked in nor entirely locked out, he is on a kind of existential furlough. By virtue of the exteriority he figures in relation to the social order, he introduces disorder and interruption. It is no doubt more accurate to observe that he *exposes* the disorder and interruption that constitute the social milieu but are normally masked. To the extent that he maintains this position of exteriority, no matter how close he gets, how intimate and familiar with the larger affiliations of the novel, he tends to signify the absolute destitution of the other: he maintains the inextinguishable appeal of the stranger, evoking the forgotten aura of what Hölderlin has called the "sacred alien."[36]

Yet Myshkin's status cannot be described solely as alien. His return to Russia is like the return of a ghost. Recollecting something that carries with it the mute eloquence of an indictment, he, a ghost recalled, figures an always imminent threat. There is an accusatory tone struck in his very existence, in his insistence and return. And if this is not simply a return trip, then he arrives as an emissary sent on a visit, a mission of necessarily provisional duration. Promoting a ghostly Odyssean structure of homecoming and returns, his appearance, moreover, offers itself with all the ambivalence of a gift. He poses and reflects at once the sacred and the poison, the sacrificial offering that takes down with it even the body of land constructed as Europe. In his essence he embodies the peculiar quality of recurrently appearing and disappearing, of obligating and not obligating: the others do not know how to take him, yet they accept him as if they were forgiving a debt. The entire novel appears, in fact, to run on the links connecting *giving* to *forgiving*, aspects of the gift that interrupt a circular economy.

Somehow every character whose acquaintance the Prince makes is bound to him by some vague but effective sense of obligation. A stranger, he is received with binding hospitality; structurally a beggar, he quietly transcends material constraints. He serves at once as the emanation of the Christ child and as one among three figures who, in recognition of the sacred, bestow gifts upon arrival. He has nothing, but he establishes the sovereignty of giving. The novel's most subtle features are arranged around this question: how does the nothing of which the Idiot gives become excessive?

While the gift — to be what it is, to the extent that it can at all "be" — cannot present itself as such or coincide with its own intention of presence, the linguistic fact of idiocy allows something originary, virginal or innocent to transpire.[37] Conferring the appearance, that is to say the nonappearance, of the gift, the Idiot portends the destruction of that which he bears: love, friendship, presence. Destruction is not that which counters the generous impulse but a force which inheres in and extends the reach of the offering. One of the major grievances filed by the novel's characters concerns the unconstrained acts of giving and forgiving unthinkingly committed by the Prince. As though he were continually wiping the slate clean. Struggling visibly with its own narrative economy, the novel offers briefs against the uncontrolled expenditure figured by the Prince, who, in all innocence, cannot stop himself from giving or forgiving. Following a rank insult, an observer gives up trying to protect him from his persecutors: "As though he didn't know that this idiot will trail off tomorrow to them to offer his friendship and his money to them again" (275). The impulse toward extreme giving functions as something of a toxic spew within the novel's social registers, contaminating all the characters and bringing about a crash economy. Generosity, unaccounted for, inexplicably becomes the rule. In a miniaturized scene of social potlatch, a huge wad of money is thrown into the fireplace by Nastasya Filippovna, who dares Rogozhin to retrieve it — she administers the test by which his character will be scored or scorched. Despite his legendary avidity, Rogozhin, watched over by Myshkin and the attending party, does not interfere with the symbolic destruction. At each turn the violence of the gift surprises, leaving us defenseless, open, exposed.

The brief against the Prince does not end with narrative observations concerning his excessively giving-forgiving nature but is further seen as related to his extravagant offering of thanks. The novel reflects on what can be called the deconstructive edges of gratitude, reading the Prince in terms of its implied economies and contradictory demands. His escalating thankfulness imparts a destabilizing warp, paralyzing the rhythms of sociability. It is as if ingratitude were the lynchpin of social and intellectual mobility. The economy of gratitude is shown to be inevitably an inflationary one that, when audited, proves to derive from dangerous overestimations, the immoderation congruent with idiocy. In sum, idiocy cannot evaluate properly: "If someone gives you a halfpenny, you thank him as though he had saved your life. You think it's praiseworthy, but it's disgusting" (534). The Prince, berated for inventing a rating system that collapses any value of proper apportionment, also catches hell for rating himself too highly in the process, as if devaluation of self were "praiseworthy." Excessive and booming, his conversion rates offer tremendous gratitude for what seems to constitute substantial savings — the saving of life — where only a halfpenny has been given. But why would this tendency toward inflation arouse disgust?

In a sense the overvaluation of a meager donation (which in flat terms hardly rates as a gift — though a gift has no fixed rate, must remain incalculable) does not reflect nobility of character; it fails to upgrade the recipient in any way but instead exposes him, somewhat paradoxically, as avid, even needy. By overestimating the offer of a halfpenny, the Prince turns himself into a beggar. As pauper, he does not enter into the ideal and balanced exchange systems of the type, "the prince and the pauper," but, rather, he assumes the character and function of an insistent demand, one that exceeds him, in fact, and appears to be coming from elsewhere. In this way the giver of thanks, martyred by a kind of overbearing poverty, takes away what he purportedly gives. The hostility of "I am nothing" cannot be overestimated. This conclusion may seem to follow a perverse logic (we are following Dostoevsky); still, it is one reached, in another context by Nietzsche, when gratitude, an aggression, is linked, finally, with repressed revenge.[38]

The text has encountered an aporia in the impossible measure of thankfulness. To ignore an offer, no matter how meager, can amount to no good (religious fables, fairy- and folktales are made of the transformation of nothing into great kingdoms). To pay it too much heed, however, freezes the value of the offering, which is meant to overwhelm the calculable measure. It is precisely by appraising the scant donation that the Prince overestimates its value. He should have forgotten about it, his companion inveighs, in the "don't mention it" vein. He makes a false move when submitting the offer to implicit evaluation, by entering into calculation in the first place, as if it were appropriable and something to be counted on. Precisely where value is ascribed, the donation reaches incalculable proportions. For the Idiot, to calculate at all is to figure his own incommensurate debt. He cannot stay in the columns. In the end he thinks he wants to forgive the debt of everyone else and pay with his life. This is an old story for us Westerners, rewritten at one point by Nietzsche when he measured the strategies by which Christ became the infinite creditor. "You think it's praiseworthy, but it's disgusting," says Aglaya. In giving, he takes (revenge), but there may be no deciding, finally, between the two modes or modalities of the giving for which he answers. Any way you cut it, the giving remains immoderate, recovering only the status of a vertiginous allegory: the giving (taking) of a halfpence becomes equivalent to the giving (taking) of life; effacing its local value, it becomes giving (taking) as such, the giving of being, which in any case cannot be reduced to the result of a given calculation. The Prince may be caught in the tailspin of allegorical estimation, yet one of the asserted qualities of his idiocy is that he cannot conduct rhetorical operations: "It wouldn't do to write like that to an idiot, because he'd take it literally" (312). He, in fact, is plagued by nonallegorical end results, if this is thinkable: he wants to take (give) things literally. Without figural stoppers to rein him in, the idiot, closing in on truth of statement, veers into the damaging experiences of impossible literality.

The rhetorical diagnosis is reconverted into economic currency, marking Myshkin's incapacitation before the counterfeit and other figures of deception: "And all this society Myshkin took for true coin, for pure gold without alloy" (521). Myshkin's appraisals continue to be at stake, though the basis for reckoning breaks down. For economy cannot be reduced to the security of its own system and is necessarily alloyed by allegory. Economy always exceeds its own figures, engaging speculation, promoting a constant transferral of rhetorical accounts. To put this in terms closer to the quotation at hand, pure gold cannot be

"Forgiving, trustful, noble simplicity"

thought without the concept of alloy, just as true coin would be un-fathomable without its counterfeit face. It is as if Myshkin were allied to the beggar in Baudelaire's *Fausse Monnaie*, or at least with one of the hypotheses, which the narrator of that prose poem floats concerning the beggar who will not question or be questioned about the counterfeit coin. As Derrida has indicated, however, if there is no question of the counterfeit, can the question of truth or deception even arise?[39] In other words, if there were no false coin, could there even be a true coin or the danger of taking one for the other? Faced with the dilemma of having taken this society for true coin, Myshkin, despite his innocence, is still a speculator. If he takes the society for true coin, then he in some way understands the principles of deception. If, however, he has no sensibility for deception, truthfulness becomes of little value to him. He does not have to probe or arrive at the truth; this is one trip he need not take. Nor does he have to calculate with the absence of truth or leave a margin for error or deception. In a manner that annuls calculation, he profits from blind speculation, from *giving* the benefit of the doubt to a society that in this case the narrator evaluates from the probability of its counterfeit nature. Tending to overestimate without a grid or grasp for estimation, the Prince can revert to no reliable ground from which to measure the power of language to mean or count. In fact, even when measuring he arrives at the immeasurable, the pure — a kind of ethical quotient of the mathematical sublime. The price of such spectacular measure is shown to be equally dizzying and menaced always by a fall into seizure or madness. At several junctures the text allows that, if he takes what is offered, in language or money, as pure gold, this is because the Idiot does not test; instead, he practices a politics of face value.

In resolute conjunction with his refusal (inability) to read between the lines or conduct spot tests for truth value, the Idiot has little sense

"As though you could feel anger!"

"Sorry!"

of social shame, no experience of anger, and nowhere does he display a particular investment in the concept or practice of dignity. He suffers indignity with a compassionate smile, almost always siding with the persecutor. He is faulted, by those who presume to instruct him, for his excessive kindness and for his tendency, at the conclusion of an attack of insults, to address the perpetrator with "I am sorry" or "You are right" (259, 262, 264). The list of accusations is posted at special gateways of the novel's development: he has no pride; what's more, he is too trusting, morbidly sensitive, naïve, anxious to pacify, eager to offer friendship, give away money, express or, rather, return love (which is why he is more or less promised to the two women who have claims on him). These expenditures of self are accompanied by an air of simple refinement: the Prince is noted for his graciousness and courtesy. Trained to scan events for contradiction, the narrative sensibility views with skepticism the coexistence of exquisite courtesy and social defenselessness. As if tapping into a more original coherence, the Prince caves without cowering, folds or bows according to an exigency that disrupts any priority of self. The profusion of courtesies offers up a sense of the destitution that he embodies before the other, inciting the turn or return toward the other that the Idiot, bowing in defeat, unstoppably performs.

When calumniated or laughed at, he "laughed with them. I should have done the same in their place," he offers (53). Precisely. Without the intention or means of dispossessing his addressees, he is in their place, always, without exception.

In a strange yet persistent way, the Idiot signals an exemplary instance of Kantian ethicity inasmuch as he puts himself rigorously, one could say, in the place of the other. Despite it all, Myshkin, even in the ultimate scene of blank stupor, is maintained as the guarantor of unbreachable responsibility. Caressing the murderer in an effort to soothe him, Myshkin displays what it means to be responsible for the other, devoted to the other, *even unconsciously*, without "doing": it is an action without doing, an ethically maintained passivity. He slips into the other's anguish. Putting the self in place of another necessarily implies, for the modern subject, a rupture in identity, a self-departure or significant interruption; however, the Idiot's manner of consistently extenuating himself before the other points to something else. His place has been designated from the start as being open to displacement, marked as it is by the apparent contingency of random encounter. Its assignment shifts according to the requirements of the moment. No matter how randomly appointed, however, each encounter remains overdetermined and fateful. Where his movements are imbued with sense or function, he keeps himself insistently out of place, with no place of his own, always at once host to the other and also, oddly, retaining the bearing of docile guest. He crashes every preconstituted party. His presence distracts, startles. At each juncture he recalls the traumatic but beloved appearance of something altogether other. His arrival marks a massive interruption, dismantling identities only to have them momentarily reconstitute around his enigmatic being.

> "Why, she has called you a freak and an idiot!"

The ability to put oneself in the place of the other does not preclude violence. Of course, this is not a matter of ability or aptitude; there is violation in the place of the other. From the start it has been a matter of intrusion, if of the order of sacred invasion. Myshkin, another type of messiah, plays out the visitation of the one who is offered sanctuary without being expected; he advances the figure of visitation without invitation, the haunting that is welcome or unwelcome (or both: this cannot always be ascertained). The Idiot arrives, insinuating himself in the scene, effecting a kind of violence that awakens the homebound characters to the possibility that this encroachment betokens a gift in our destiny.

If Dostoevsky expressed some difficulty in rendering the Prince, as modern subject, sacred, it is the structure of the visitation in itself that announces the return of the divine. Without determined context or meaning, unrecognizable yet somehow attached to those who find him, the Prince puts forward the element of incalculability, which tells us that we have to welcome the other in an unconditional way, without expecting anything in return. Foreign and disheveled, he arrives as an emissary if not as a mask of God. What is God but the poor, the abjected, the foreigner, the guest who hides behind the appearance of the most miserable foreigner? This ancient configuration indicates, as Derrida maintains, the origin of hospitality, announcing as it does the non-invited guest who makes himself visible in the form of a visitation.[40] Of what kind of postcard does this divine *envoi* consist? God is the one who sends the foreigner to you; there would be no God without the foreigner, the envoy from elsewhere, figuring an aspect of otherness as convincing as it is threatening, as familiar as it is haunting, repressed, or uncalled for. When this figure arrives, so strange, so familiar, at once repellent and evocative of love (there is so much disgust, so much love in the novel: they go hand in hand), native in principle but with a pronounced foreign accent — as soon as you cross the threshold, you are divine. The sacred appears as soon as one loves the stranger.

Rupture and Modernity

In modernity the sacred has appeared, if at all, through the lens of vulnerability. Not in the emanation of pride and beauty, but as their shattering. Broken and mangled, isolated by its suffering, the sacred in our day pulsates, if at all, weakly. The shock of God rendered vulnerable reverberates through the novel as it translates into the disfiguration meted out by suffering. Suffering is disfiguring, already a substitution that allows for the further aggravation of the Prince's condition. The way Dostoevsky plays it, idiocy would appear to make claims for a more originary experience of suffering — a suffering with no cause to back it up and no history to lend it gravity. The Idiot *is*; he does not become and does not as such illuminate but rather points in all dumbness to a grim transcendence, a troubled self-sufficiency from which self has been largely evicted. Outside memory and history, idiocy is our modernity's sliver of sacred emanation. As for the welcoming or even the possibility of recognizing or receiving the sacred, these modalities of openness, too, have succumbed to vulnerability; our receptors have weakened and it is no longer clear that we can host the sacred alien. Dostoevsky has written, or, rather, the Prince has argued, that we humans are a different race now, of a different age. "It seems we are a different species" from what has preceded us: "'now we are more nervous, more developed, more sensitive; men capable of two or three ideas at once.... Modern men are broader-minded — and I swear that this prevents their being so all-of-a-piece as they were in those days. I ... I simply said it with that idea, ... and not ...'" (507). These are some of the stammers and stutters that, despite the hesitancy with which they are toned, firmly describe the Prince's effort to ascertain mutability in receptiveness, historicizing what men are capable of sustaining. No longer all of a piece, the species has *evolved* into the morcellations that the rendering of the utterance repeats; broken up and disarticulated, capable of reckoning the multiplication or division of ideas, we are now more nervous, more sensitive to alien intrusion. Perhaps less receptive to the altogether other, we are released to our destiny in broad-minded free fall.

The articulation of fundamental shifts such as these in the secret history of psychic continuities is not new with Dostoevsky. It can, in fact, be traced at least to the differential sensibilities registered by Schiller's essay "Über naïve und sentimentalische Dichtung" (On Naïve and Sentimental Poetry), where he posits the Greek-Goethean wholeness of being that has given way to the fragmentations and dissociations of modernity.[41] The Schillerian scan may not provide a historical account for the interruption in consciousness that he seeks to name, but it establishes the irreversible break that occurs with the encroachment of the self-consciousness of suffering, a brand of unhappy consciousness or what Dostoevsky calls the "more nervous, more developed, more sensitive." It is no doubt with some sense of irony that he has Myshkin swearing to this rupture ("I swear that ..."). Giving oath and conjuration, he swears to the crack in the all-of-a-pieceness of the past. If the Prince is in a position to swear in the truth of the interruption that constitutes modernity, this in part is because he stands and spins for both sides of the temporalized coin about which it is so difficult to tell heads from tails. As idiot, he still belongs to the past of which he bears a memory trace, though it may remain partial and mute. Idiocy permits him to embody a sign, despite it all, of an experience of wholeness, at least of a sealed surface of sufficiency, to which we no longer have access. Not even the clinic can crack open this case that closes in upon itself, as if guarding a historical memory to which we have lost the rights.

At the same time, the Idiot, at least for the provisional duration that is granted him in the novel, aligns himself with the "we" of nervous modernity, as if his condition were meant to crystallize the modern condition, sensitive and alienated as it is seen to be, pulled in a number of directions and estranged from the sacred. His oath would mean, in this case, that I swear to the truth of my experience; I bear witness to the radical estrangement for which I am myself the evidence.

This uneasy vacillation (is he to be understood as naïve or *sentimentalisch?*) is encouraged by the novel's dynamic, which puts a double spin on the major assertions it makes. Thus he, the Prince, is often caught between two extremes, be they of historical magnitude or psychological particularity: "(and of late he had blamed himself for two extremes, for his exclusive 'senseless and impertinent' readiness to trust people and at the same time for his gloomy suspiciousness)" (292).

On Trust

Caught essentially between the poles of a seemingly nonreading trust or a (so-called) overreading suspiciousness, his sensibility is hung out to dry by the community that receives him. In fact, though, there never comes a moment of sheer nonreading; it is all a matter of how to read. Even the positing of his suspiciousness is somewhat tenuous, for the Prince has proven unable to sustain the tension required by suspiciousness — a state of anxious alert that flickers only momentarily when an imperative to read a letter or situation emerges, edging him into the gloom and doom of a hermeneutic necessity, an allegorical sidetrack. For the most part, though, the Prince leaves the snags and seductions of understanding behind as he offers himself up to the exigency of the moment, shirking off distance or delay. The single most transparent manifestation of the condition of idiocy that he bares — his "symptax" par excellence — involves his trusting nature.

His is a world wiped clean of surface irony. The irony-free zone of consciousness remains a ruse, a graft or phantasm, however. Idiocy, despite itself, incurs irony on all sides, even as it depends for its expression on the refusal of irony. As he bumbles through situations that aggravate social debility, we sense how social being — no matter how diminished — genuine sociality, might require a capacity, implied by ironic calculation, for doubling and dividing acts of meaning. His world is prone to being reduced (or strengthened, Christianized) because it stays largely "unsuspicious of mockery or humor" (326) — moods and grammars for which the Prince has no reliable receptors. To the extent that he has been secured against the cutting assaults of the mockery to which he is subjected, he remains cocooned in the language of wholeness, in the enveloping blankets of naïve registers of sensibility. Yet it is never completely clear, given his blanket ignorance of the rhetorical maneuvers aimed at him, how he has deflected the aims of social language usage. His blank demeanor as concerns rhetorical assault lifts him up even as injury persists. Being too dumb, at times, to know any better, he faces his tormentors blithely; the attack falls beneath him. His sacred aspect often appears at such moments when, vacantly, he rises above the verbal fray. At least the sacred depends upon the glimmer of such a possible transcendence, even as he is being mercilessly ridiculed. What is repeatedly shown is that mockery, humor, irony, double-entendre, and other linguistic substitutions for assassination attempts do not arrive on time or target. Released to a dialectical effect of extreme protection or complete exposure, he poses the radical vulnerability of the psychologically uninsured.

> "And here this wretched little prince, this miserable little idiot..."

As one who will not test for veracity or reliability, the Idiot takes every possible state or statement on trust. Trust is what is immediately offered, no questions asked; it is a gift. Precisely because it is offered so freely, it becomes identified with the condition of idiocy. To be what it is, trust has eliminated all possible calculation. If you give someone your absolute trust, you cannot make secret debits to their accounts; you cannot make inquiries or attempt to figure out motives or how they snuck up on your blind side. Pure trust necessarily involves and invokes idiocy. A nonidiotic offer of trust would be grounded presumably in some knowledge or sense of what is tried and proven. But the Idiot does not test and cannot in this sense know. Uncalculating, he trusts — "blindly." While blind offers of trust seem peculiar to the fate Dostoevsky unfolds as he takes us through the vocabulary of idiocy, it is no doubt also the case that any act of trusting must court a moment of blindness and, in a way, must overcome or deny time. To trust is to suspend the becoming of history, unless, appropriating all of history, one actually trusts in mutability and aberration. With Dostoevsky, the trusting idiot is the one who also says, "Oh, I've plenty of time, my time is entirely my own" (24). I trust time so much that I think it's entirely mine, and not owed to anyone else, to any other force or account. It abounds without ticker or timer. To trust is to trust in time, to dissolve oneself so radically in time that time will tell, time will heal all, time will, in essence, forget itself and stop timing me, numbering my days or cutting me off: I can count on time — in fact, I can stop counting; I no longer live on borrowed time, for "my time is entirely my own." The trusting intimacy with time is what gives the Idiot an aura of immortality, moreover.

The novel expresses the relation to time in terms of *readiness*. The Prince shows a readiness to trust, to respond. He signals no reserve, and, being spontaneous in what he offers, he does not build on history for the purpose of establishing trust. This is why trust, according to Aglaya's admonitions, bites the dust: there is no historical proving ground, no test site, to back up the Prince's trusting expenditures. He in fact squanders the trust he bestows, as he gives away money, everywhere offering friendship and money. Moreover, to the extent that his trust is offered as gift, no one need *earn* it. An unaccountable trust fund — who's counting, my time is entirely my own, which is to say, yours — the little Prince paradoxically and secretly becomes everyone's creditor.

But trusting does not, as such, constitute an act. Resembling a releasement, a letting go of a historical defense buildup, it approaches something of a wager and risk: what are you going to base your trust on? What kind of decisions are adequate to the adventure of trusting? With little guarantee that trust will not be betrayed, the Prince persists blindly in trusting. And even when something like betrayal is thematized — his best friend tries to murder him, his best friend does murder his fiancée, other friends rob and repeatedly expose him to ridicule — the breach is never felt or registered by Myshkin, or, in any case, there is no practical trace of a politics of revenge indicating some economy of return. The betrayal is embraced and reabsorbed into the trusting impulse. The radicality of the tendency to trust contracts, in the case of the Idiot, into the moment, an intensive and perpetual moment, of *readi-*

ness. What such incitement implies, further, is that trust can never, as such, be achieved in the sense of accomplishing or finishing a history. Related essentially to a disposition and to the beginning of a time or narrative, trust precedes history and dwells in the naïve. It occurs — if it can be seen to occur — prior to any shattering or despite the anticipatory memory of its own violation: broken trust. Or, more correctly still, it has written off the shattering and reinstated the enabling fiction of the naïve. If it exists temporally only in readiness, it cannot be said to exist substantially, in the present. Trust, the novel suggests, remains a matter of vulnerability and wager, a pure gamble, with no adequate calculation or backup.

Readiness is the quality assigned to the Prince when, in the very beginning, he boards a train and is more or less assailed by impertinent questions, injurious insinuations — as if he were overtaken, in our day, by the unprecedented inquisitiveness of the media: "He betrayed no suspicion of the extreme impertinence of some of his misplaced and idle questions. . . . It appeared that this was the case; the fair-haired young man acknowledged it at once with peculiar readiness" (4–5).[42] Also: "The readiness of the fair young man in the Swiss cloak to answer all his companion's inquiries was remarkable" (4). The instances of readiness with which Myshkin becomes identified are multiplied throughout the text. What does his readiness portend? This is not the more strenuously jockeyed readiness of a Hamlet, or the temporally expectant readiness that Heidegger primes, but a readiness of pure exposure, perhaps closer to that of Abrahmic sacrifice: the sheer "Here I am" in response to the invasive demand. But Abraham answers to God, whereas the Prince will answer to anyone. He stands as his own lamb, ever prepared for slaughter. He stands ready, a figure of latent presence. Since readiness opens the question of timing, the problem emerges of when this immemorial sacrifice could take place, at what time and in whose place. Is it possible for readiness to adhere to a concept of belatedness, a slow resumption of what has already taken place? The slaughter for which the Prince stands ready could occur only after the prime of sacrificial epochality, when the dignity of the offering is nearly lost on everyone and can hardly be made in tribute to the big Other. Stripped of sacrificial grandeur, the sacrificial readiness has been somehow discounted, which is why we are faced with an idiot and not a prophet, or poet, or even philosopher (the gap admittedly is closing).

Even so, the readiness to answer to anyone is possibly the last offering of sacred effulgence that is left to us. There's Nietzsche on the streets, apologizing to every passerby for the weather; there's Kafka's

man from the country, talking to the flea on his collar; there's Hölderlin walking to Bordeaux; and some others, alone yet talkative, still un-
recognized. It is not new for the sacred to travel in the cloak of anonym-
ity, in disguise and often awkward misery. On the contrary, this used to
be the dress code of the sacred. What comes as new, perhaps, is that the
sacred has nothing more to say or teach, nothing even to do but to
stammer in the vacuity of everydayness.

THE IDIOT'S SMILE

Christlike, he is not Christ;[43] offering a more modern version of the sacred victim, the Prince embraces laughter — something with which the
Galilean was not particularly associated. Holding close to the evolution
of the ridiculous, Dostoevsky first has Myshkin draw laughter to himself. Somewhere between Christian detachment and the Buddha's
laughter, he provokes and absorbs a subtle sort of public hilarity. The
smiles he attracts grow on the side of knowledge, often formed by malicious intent. Bound to haunt him throughout his voyage, those determinations, which distinguish knowledge from idiocy, are set up in the
mobile social space of the train. Myshkin, frail and fair, having "something of that strange look from which some people can recognize at
first glance a victim of epilepsy," elicits from his dark-haired neighbor
"an indelicate smile, in which satisfaction at the misfortunes of others
is sometimes so unceremoniously and casually expressed" (4). The nearly
unanimous peal of laughter that trains on him takes root in the deliberate indelicacy of this knowing smile.

   The smile or laughter of sheer gratuity make up a staple in the repertoire of idiocy. Thus, one sure sign of idiocy is revealed through Myshkin's tendency to laugh along with whomever might be mocking him
("strange to say, the owner of the bundle began to laugh too, looking at
them, and that increased their mirth" [5]). Unknowing and asignifica-
tory, laughter exposes his vulnerability by offering him up to the
meaning-laden insinuation of the group. As a ready response to a
dominant social tone, his own laughter serves only to separate him out
as the object of derision. The value of communion in laughter indicates
another possibility to the extent that the ability to laugh at oneself signals as well an effect of self-distancing and grace. But the different levels of knowledge hidden in layers of intentional laughter militate
against communion. Myshkin betrays a tendency to show himself in
the light of sheer laughter for the other, a disposition eventuating from

a disconcerting surrender of self that laughs at the emptiness the group has captured. Spinning on the discovery of the emptiness that governs his being, Myshkin yields not a trace of the mastery implied by laughing at oneself here, as self-doubling or any kind of self-assertion is entirely out of the question. Incapable of registering betrayal or mockery — the intractable maneuvers of human relatedness — the childlike Idiot laughs along with the tormentors, who are, however, systematically disarmed by his easy compliance and the abolition of intention. They may have found an object of laughter, but the targeted entity at no point reverts to a subject.[44] In the laugh-along he incorporates his objectness to the group by means of a gesture of dumb mimicry. Mirroring and miming, he mechanically reproduces and reflects the group's own position to itself as it annihilates a foreign object. As he merges his laughter with that of the group, he becomes for a moment less foreign, as if reprieved, suspended within their repetitive bursts, their *fits* of laughter. In any case, the Idiot's smile persists, along with the occasional theater of solitary laughter. And though he appears at times to be cast as irrecuperably simpleminded, his laughter always comes from elsewhere, stoked and tended by an inaccessible spirit, the high spirits of an invisible domain. Whether mechanical or invisible, the source of laughter is never a matter of knowledge; he does not, we do not, know about what he is laughing — a nonknowledge that maintains him in his absolute innocence. As for the narrative, it continues to weed out the subjects of knowledge with which our Idiot is haplessly confronted, ironizing the difference between knowing and ignorance.[45]

THE INTELLIGENTSIA

The irony of knowing never stops, and it would no doubt be fruitless to enumerate the many instances of its thematic occurrence. In a manner reminiscent of the Flaubertian sweep, Dostoevsky calls the consolation of knowledge "indeed . . . a fascinating science" (6). Pegged by the irony of their author, the knowers are not so much placed in discernibly solid opposition to the Idiot — rather, they each come with their peculiar traits of idiocy and inevitable blunders of blindness. They furtively illuminate by contrasting the condition that overarches the novel. Everywhere a form of designated intelligence or understanding emerges, calling for additional analysis. The general, for instance, "was an intelligent man," though he was "not free from some very pardonable little weaknesses and disliked allusions to certain subjects. But he was un-questionably an intelligent and capable man" (13). Moreover:

> He made it a principle, for instance, not to put himself forward, to efface himself where necessary, and he was valued by many people just for his unpretentiousness, just because he always knew his place. But if only those who said this of him could have known what was passing sometimes in the soul of Ivan Fyodorovitch, who knew his place so well! Though he really had practical knowledge and experience and some very remarkable abilities, he preferred to appear to be carrying out the ideas of others rather than the promptings of his own intellect, to pose as a man "disinterestedly devoted" and — to fall in with the spirit of the age — a warm-hearted Russian. (14)

The description of the general's qualities promotes our interest because it posits categories that provisionally oppose those of idiocy yet belong to the elaboration, on the part of Dostoevsky, of the intricate vocabulary within which he works. Belonging to the local intelligentsia, the general, besides being a competent fellow, shows an aptitude for dissimulation — "to appear to be carrying out the ideas." Under no circumstances could these qualities be ascribed to the Prince's repertory of practical behavior. The Prince can neither appear to be doing something other than what he thinks he's doing — he cannot dissemble — nor carry out the ideas of others; if anything, he often speaks an idiolect of sorts, self-originating ideas in fidelity to the etymological prospects held out by the term idiocy. The anxiety of the divided general, split between the promptings of his own intellect and the designs of others, between selfhood and subjugation, carries little weight for the Idiot. There are times, indeed, when idiocy leads one to believe that it broaches the space of sheer genius, breaking with convention and bending those rules that have put restraints upon the way we speak or think. It can be "original" or imaginative, generously informed. A good part of the general's intelligence lies in his ability "to pose," to feign disinterested devotion. Posing remains out of the range of our Prince's competence, and the pleasures of disinterestedness might as well stay within the unread confines of Kantian aesthetics. Spontaneous and generous, the Prince may be constitutionally disinterested, in large part due, moreover, to his illness, but no measure of detachment can be gauged that would allow for credible effects of disinterested devotion. At the same

"Myshkin was rather surprised that he had perpetrated a joke, and indeed it was a feeble one."

time the aims and addresses of this Idiot remain paradoxically as self-less, even privative, as they are emphatically invested, circumscribing unrelieved areas of intensity. The general, no doubt true to his formation, always knows his place. Increasingly, to know is to know one's place. He, the general, for his part, understands or obeys the orders of rank, class, and the authority of generalized boundaries.

The Prince has no claim on place; incapable of dissembling, he remains precariously unprotected. A homeless body, uncontained even by class distinction, he reconciles the attributes, incredibly, of pauper and prince, the miserable and sacred. It is as if he, a floater or freelancer, has been put in his place, however expropriated, from the start. Unhoused, he is free to assume other identities, to spot hidden inroads. Because he has no assigned place, an element of intrusion underscores his ventures — he finds himself in concealed spaces of intimacy usually closed off to those who assume or have place. He closes in on or befriends the mother, daughters, the servants, children, the animals, and social gangs of rivals or sworn enemies, recreating or disrupting places that have been fixed. When everyone is in her or his assigned place, the Prince cruises, redirecting or dismembering the social space.

Sorry!

The general, we are told, has made it a principle not to put himself forward. Such a scale of motivated decision, consisting as it does of where or how or when to place and efface oneself, would be impossible for the Prince to venture. His condition betrays him even where he experiences a provisional reprieve. Yielding and kind, at these times he seems capable of discrete surrender. His very docility, though, can be construed as a way of putting himself forward, marking, as often it does, a bizarre absence of resistance to that which invites or assails him, as the case may be. No matter how selfless the syntax of his conduct becomes, there is always an exhibitionist element controlling his bearing. The aberration speaks, stages itself, even when launched by reclusive hesitation. The continual spill of self-betrayal occasions the many apologies that the Prince feels he has to offer. Being an idiot means always having to say you're sorry. "'I am sorry, gentlemen, I am sorry,' Myshkin apologised hurriedly, 'please excuse me; it's because I thought it might be better for us to be perfectly open with one another; but it's for you to decide as you please. . . . Oh, don't take offence, gentlemen! For goodness' sake, don't take offence,' Myshkin cried in alarm" (262). Thus Myshkin's address to the punk nihilists who had been roundly insulting him, humiliating him publicly.

Acts that typically end in the profuse donation of apologies do not cover for or conceal other desires that would be available to understanding but rather underscore the way in which Myshkin absorbs injury, debiting it to his own boundlessly moral account. The apology offers no signs of strategic mediation. He does not negotiate or produce a language of self-justification; he reveals no intention of apportioning or sharing blame. Every injury is his entirely. The persistent object of mockery, he converts himself into the mock subject of a social discourse, the one responsible in any case for the degradation of which he is the cause: "Oh, no doubt you were quite right in saying that I was almost an idiot at that time and had no understanding" (263). "You are right there, I admit it, but I couldn't help it. . . . But why are you getting angry again, gentlemen? We shall completely misunderstand each other" (264-65). Unable to understand, he abhors misunderstanding (the misunderstanding that he has understood). The logic is awry: he is the cause because, in the end, there's no posssible way for him to have been the cause — he can't help it, he didn't understand, he was almost an idiot. Because he cannot take responsibility as a conscious, sufficient subject, because he cannot be present to a task the failure of which he stands accused, he is responsible for it all. The idiot has to apologize for everything because there is nothing for which he is not responsible. The judgment has already been made, prior to any act, and it orders the idiot to live by the purity of an irreversible prejudice. Precisely because I, as idiot, cannot be a fully responsible being, precisely because my consciousness is punctured, I must and do take full responsibility. I take responsibility for the darkness, the lapse, the fever and delirium. This is why, always and ever, "I am sorry."

When Myshkin answers to mockery, he is sorry. When Myshkin feels an episode coming on, he is sorry as well: "Excuse me, brother, when my head is heavy, as it is now, and my illness . . . I become utterly, utterly absent-minded and ridiculous" (210). Losing his way, he apologizes, momentarily splitting himself into the one who describes and the one who absents himself, becoming ridiculous.

He, a sorry being, is and says, without exception, that he is sorry. In the absence of object or reference — no construal of blame could be tethered to reference, no accusation coincides with an event — there is no knowledge that could hope to explain an existence so weighed down

216

by responsibility. There is not even the cry of abandonment, "Why hast thou forsaken me?" But in order to say that he is sorry, he has had to refer to himself as someone who was *almost* an idiot, which modifies the accusers' sentence. The "almost" is what engages the absolute; it is only because he was almost an idiot that he assumes absolute responsibility. If he had been a total idiot, as we now freely say, he would have been home free as concerns the assumption of ethical liability. The rhetorical force that renders him a responsible subject lies within the "almost" — the crevice or opening that allows for consciousness and decision. He was "almost an idiot," which means there can be no refuge, no ducking out as concerns the reach and breach of ethicity. It is because he posits himself as having been almost an idiot that he can — he must — take total responsibility.

> "Myshkin, worn out, depressed, and physically shattered —"

THE STUPIDS

In moments that bear a certain theoretical translucency, the condition of the Idiot appears to be organized by pre-ethical impulses that prompt unreflected acts of compassion. These acts, inflected by the givens and forgivens prior to any rules of human conduct, tend to be disrupted, if not overshadowed, by the intrusive humdrum of ordinary stupidity. The domain of the human, all too human, punctually threatens such points of an original ethics. Or, in keeping with the idiom of the novel, at points of ethical *readiness*, as figured by the Prince, the novel finds itself harassed to the extent that it is ruled by the ordinariness, which, for the narrator, burdens any project. "These are people whom it is difficult to describe completely in their typical and characteristic aspect. . . . What is an author to do with ordinary people?" (447–48). Part 4 of the novel brings in the stupids, as if under obligation to come up with the goods. Until this stage of development no need has been asserted for introducing a pure or stable taxonomy of difference as concerns the paraconcepts of idiocy, stupidity, imbecility, and so on. At this point, rather suddenly, Dostoevsky makes an attempt to purify the air around idiocy, if only by clearing the way for stupidity and ordinariness. As it turns out, that way has already been cleared and its name is Gogol, who can be credited with having brought to the fore the inescapable power and range of sheer stupidity. Dostoevsky's guide and mentor, Gogol receives praise for his peerless treatment of stupidity. This amounts to an ambivalent compliment, as the narrator of The Idiot views such depictions as tedious, modeled on that beyond which "nothing more annoy-ing could be considered": "There is, indeed, nothing more annoying than to be, for instance, wealthy, of good family, nice-looking, fairly in-telligent, and even good-natured, and yet to have no talents, no special faculty, no peculiarity even, not one idea of one's own, to be precisely 'like other people.' . . . Nothing is easier for 'ordinary' people of limited intelligence than to imagine themselves exceptional and original and to revel in that delusion without the slightest misgiving" (448). The section operates as a decoy because the distinctions being asserted are not held onto for very long but blur and exchange properties in other, equally persuasive, passages. Part 4 in effect serves as a clearinghouse for wholesale stupidity, which is now associated with the superb craft of Gogol. Strategically, this homage allows for reestablishing the in-comparable holdings of the Idiot, whose sacred vacancy distinguishes him from the Gogol crowd of ordinary, delusional dummkopfs:

> Some have only to meet with some idea by hearsay, or to read some stray page, to believe at once that it is their own opinion and has sprung sponta-neously from their own brain. The impudence of simplicity, if one may so express it, is amazing in such cases. It is almost incredible, but yet often to be met with. This impudence of simplicity, this unhesitating confidence of the stupid man in himself and his talents, is superbly depicted by Gogol in the wonderful character of Lieutenant Pirogov. Pirogov has no doubt that he is a genius, superior indeed to any genius. He is so positive of this that he never questions it; and, indeed, he questions nothing. The great writer is forced in the end to chastise him for the satisfaction of the outraged moral feeling of the reader; but, seeing that the great man simply shook himself after the castigation and fortified himself by consuming a pie, he flung up his hands in amazement and left his readers to make the best of it. (449)

While the definitional quality of this passage is validated and stamped by "the great writer," its legitimacy expires in the following pages, where new elements of contamination emerge. The passage will have served to mark off Dostoevsky's task from that of Gogol, and while it does not shed abundant new light on the predicament of the Idiot, it does aim at those knuckleheads who were Dostoevsky's contemporar-ies.[46] So, within the folds of The Idiot a slow burn occurs, a contained rage against the impudence of simplicity in a battle, it would seem, over small narcissistic differences. The essential difference lies in the perception of what can be known by the limited subject, and the degree of consciousness becomes a question of integrity: the idiot knows he is an idiot, names himself as such or confirms acts of diagnostic and social naming. The stupid subject, on the other hand, does not have this knowledge about himself, or, if he does, it is blocked out by powerful introverters that turn away any bidders for doubt concerning moral or intellectual competence. He knows, he thinks, what's up and never lets it get him down or turn his head around. The stupid man of this passage does not experience hesitation, is never caught up in the idiocy of undecidability. The stupid never question, whereas the Idiot concentrates one big question mark, an ineradicable stain, on the page of his destiny. Nor can the stupid geniuses be questioned, for, as in Gogol's narrations, they are in the end busy stuffing their faces, a way of shrugging off the inevitable grievance.

Singled out by Dostoevsky, the rough but autonomous gesture of gorging on a pie offers a considerable contrast to the emptying out of self for which the Idiot stands. The stupid subject is fortified, defended, lives within a calculated economy of compensation and disavowal, holds it in and keeps it up. He subsists on a system of denial that does not deny itself a thing. The Idiot, well, the Idiot can't hold anything down or be sure of very much; there is little material consolation, in any event, and the confidence for which his simplicity allows falls on empty spaces. He lives on the edges of nihilist temptation, a permanent evacuee who cannot be said to appropriate much of a thought "sprung spontaneously from his own brain," nor do we witness him eating — that is, assimilating, digesting. Judging from his elaborate condemnation of capital punishment, he remains a passionate advocate for social justice. The stupid genius naturally transcends such concerns to the extent that they are questions, the results of the relentless effort of inscribing any form of questioning. Closed in on himself, the subject of stupidity, here as in the novel's other examples, is nowhere in question but protected, satiated, full . . . of himself. Myshkin, running on empty, keeps tripping over a body that will not hold still, much less hold him together; he is a traveling mark of insufficiency, open and exposed, politically anxious and socially improbable.

Having introduced his mentor as the "great writer," Dostoevsky refers us to Gogol if we want to see a superb execution of stupidity. In clear divergence from his predecessor, he avoids the public relations effort that would see him "forced in the end to chastise [the Idiot] for the satisfaction of the outraged moral feeling of the reader." Dostoevsky answers to another power, and his explicit referral to Gogol momentarily serves to obscure that line. In a sense the sudden inclusion, the determined intrusion, of Gogol seems to be saying, kettle-logic style, that I, Fyodor Mikhailovich, am not writing on stupidity, which has been beautifully addressed by my mentor, to whom I owe so much; frankly, it would be too tedious for me to be writing on stupidity, which is so ordinary; in any case, even if I were writing on stupidity, that subject, as I underscore, has been covered by the great writer, Gogol, to whom I refer you, especially if you want to experience a literature that flatters the moral outrage of the reader.

Why does he round up the usual suspects and feature Gogol prominently in the lineup? When Dostoevsky refers openly, if ambivalently, to Gogol it may be so that he can defer (to) another great writer, one who troubles and haunts the work. That writer has meshed the textures that Dostoevsky tries to separate out with the literary device he calls Gogol. Attaching stupidity to Gogol relieves areas of textual pressure on a number of counts. As we know from Dostoevsky's notes and letters, stupidity designates a source of great anxiety for the author, who tries to protect The Idiot from its encroaching snares. When its reach is not, as theme or topos, cordoned off by border patrols, such as those protecting Gogol's territory (or Dostoevsky's space from the incursions of Gogol), stupidity proliferates around the impossible presentation of text. Dostoevsky relates it as theme to attempts to produce and proffer meaningful texts. When the young nihilist, the terminally ill Ippolit, offers the company a reading of the text he is preparing, variables of stupidity emerge to frame the scene. The work, felt to be stupid, evokes repeated expressions of stupefaction ("he smiled stupidly"; "What phenomenal feebleness!") — all of which link the severe judgment that befalls a text to the enfeebled writing body: "It's his illness, and something else, perhaps!" (413).[47] The assertion of stupidity accrues to the presentation of a nihilist's manuscript, binding an entangled author ("My thoughts are in a tangle" [408]) to a stupefied audience ("'He's simply a fool,' said Ganya" [403]). His work is meant to function as testament, to supply his illness with meaningful ground. Perhaps it will survive him and crown his existence as an elaborate epitaph. Even if Ippolit occupies the place in the novel of the avowed other to Myshkin, his writing implicates the Idiot and the fate of the novel that attempts to contain him. There is something about the junctures of writing and illness that submits them to the frays of existence associated with stupidity.

Having tied stupidity to acts of writing or, more precisely, to public displays of the textual impulse — the testimonial drive to author and publish a text — Dostoevsky draws Myshkin into the inescapable account of writing. For it cannot be stated simply that Myshkin, as presumed nonwriter or nonreader, would be spared the indignities of stupidity, attached as they are, explicitly, to the texts of Gogol and Ippolit. The Idiot is bound in a secret yet troubling way by another scene of writing, the effects of which are intimated when he interviews the murderer:

> "All I can tell you about the knife is this, Lyov Nikolayevitch," he added after a pause, "I took it out of a locked drawer this morning, for it all happened this morning, about four o'clock. It had been lying in a book all the time. . . . And . . . and . . . another thing seems strange: the knife went in three or four inches . . . just under her left breast . . . and there wasn't more than half a tablespoonful of blood flowed on to her chemise, there was no more. . . ."
>
> "That, that, that," Myshkin sat up suddenly in great agitation, "that I know, I've read about it, that's called internal bleeding. . . . Sometimes there's not one drop. That's when the stab goes straight to the heart." (592)

The murder weapon, the knife, was lodged in a book; Myshkin has already read about the murder, nearly bloodless. The stab will have gone straight to the heart. This scene, dramatic and uniquely situated in the novel, in fact marks a repetition of another, prior scene of bloodless, that is, literary, assassination.

The ur-scene occurs in the same chapter. Myshkin frantically looks for Nastasya Filippovna. He hits the streets, conducts house searches. "But at the German lady's they did not even understand what he wanted" (583). The Germans don't get it, so an unconscious start turns him toward the French. First he supplicates: "If I could only find any traces!" Then: "A strange sensation gained possession of him in that dingy and stuffy corridor, a sensation that strove painfully to become a thought; but he still could not guess what that new struggling thought was" (583). Moved through cityscapes by unconscious promptings, Myshkin goes to meet his destiny. Something impels him forward; his mind fades and punctually returns. "Strange to say, he was at one moment keenly observant, at the rest absent-minded to an incredible degree. All the family declared afterwards that he was an extraordinarily strange person that day, so that 'perhaps even then the end was clear'" (584).

Everything is closing in on him. Shunted through an atmosphere of anguish and "terrible dread," he experiences "unutterable dejection"

221

(585). The Idiot sketches one clear gesture. It verges on being illicit, and in any case objections are raised: "All the ladies described afterwards how Myshkin had scrutinised every object in the room, had seen on the table a French book from the library, 'Madame Bovary,' lying opened, turned down the corner of the page at which the book was open, asked permission to take it with him, and not heeding the objection that it was a library book, put it in his pocket" (584). An open book. The novel will have established a certain simultaneity of the places of stabbing; it has located the heart wound. Near the pocket; the pocket into which Myshkin places the book pads the heart space. The passage prepares the scene, indicating the bloodless heart stab of which he has read. It prefiguratively metaphorizes the hypothesis of internal bleeding with few traces. The next scene, which provides a body, is cued.

At this point we dwell on the level of unconscious motivation, following a kind of frenetic drive that impels Myshkin to stash the illicit book despite a chorus of objections. Why this particular volume, though? Why does he take it to heart? Is there a way to understand why this object, put in his pocket, behaves as true coin? Any number of reasons appears to justify why *Madame Bovary* would name an irreversible destiny for the Idiot. Their features could be a matter of braiding thematic destinies, monitoring linguistic synchronicities, or pointing up ironic mirroring and its structural reversals. Unhampered linkages could be forged: Charles, the incompetent doctor, and Myshkin, the idiot healer; Emma and Nastasya on the same destructive path; flunking out of school; the shared status of the clinic; the petite bourgeoise Madame Bovary, the aristocratic Idiot Prince, deflected histories of desire, public censure, we all fall down, and on and on. Yet in this case we would do well to micromanage the reading protocols and stay away from smooth thematic promises. For if Myshkin's unconscious meanderings have led him to an open book, binding it somehow to his heart's desire, then the gesture of appropriating the book also involves closing and hiding it, slipping it into the invaginating folds of an internal pocket. In the moment of greatest trouble, he reaches for a book, for another book or the book of the other. The book appears to have awaited him. To the extent that finality comes to be expressed through this capture, it seems necessary to explore its implications, for the occurrence of such a doubling up is not, as such, unique in literature. The scenography recalls another site of literary trauma, namely, when Werther shot himself over the pages of *Emilia Galotti*, the first bourgeois drama of German letters. The troubled heroes reach for the work of their ever-hounding counterparts, which mirrors the tormented brides of the bourgeoisie. The coupling with the other work seals the suicide pact, ratifies destruction. Emma, Emilia: dial Em for murder.

Whichever literary chain of traumatic incidents could be reconstructed here, Myshkin, in his last pages of sanity, takes in and inseminates himself with the seminal work of Flaubert in what can be seen as a counterphobic act. The necessity of this act is based on a number of considerations. It suggests, in the first place, that the Gogol inoculation has by now worn off. The sensitive area that Gogol had protected in Dostoevsky is now exposed to possible incursion. Gogol had kept something in the work out of harm's way; he maintained certain inviolable boundaries. At least he permitted the fantasy of such boundaries to stay in place. For some reason Dostoevsky has needed to keep the Idiot safe from the encroachment of the very concerns that belong to Gogol's work. When the chips are down he has Myshkin reaching for the other work. Now, what does this shift in loyalties tell us? Or maybe we are confronted with another level of consciousness, and Flaubert arrives on the scene to collect an unconscious debt or gamble on another level of textual transaction.

> "'You are very disconnected,' observed Alexandra."

Flaubert, in any case, would not have allowed for the clean distinctions that the name of Gogol arranges in the text of Dostoevsky. He cannot have been accomplice to a transcendentalizing strategy that separates off stupidity in order to guarantee the sanctity of idiocy. Admittedly, Emma and Charles sometimes read like the ancestral echo of dumb and dumber, and there is dumber still. But stupidity takes hold everywhere; it fans out, contaminates like an invisible toxin without allowing for much of a free zone in the merciless economy of Flaubertian irony. In fact, Flaubert is the unsurpassed thinker of stupidity, which is one reason why Myshkin must first clear him out, close and shut him up, in order to terminate. Gogol, in other words, functions as something of a decoy for Flaubert, where the ordinary meets its match in an extraordinary inmixation. Stupid can be extraordinary, too, even transcendental. Emma, flailed by stupid expectations, also has her transports. Charles Bovary occupies an undecidable limit between idiocy and stupidity (which covers the clinical and the functional, the touching and the mundane), as does the immortally simple Félicité of "Un Coeur simple," whose heart also belongs to the nearly traceless stab wounds of which the Idiot has spoken.

But when he pockets Flaubert, taking him in or closing him off —

taking him out of library circulation, interrupting someone else's reading ("*turned down* the corner of the page at which the book was open") — he also stages an act of incorporation. Why would *The Idiot* enact the incorporation of Gustave Flaubert?[48] To what extent does the textual body get organized around the unassimilable fact of this foreign body that lodges itself at its heart-center?

Beyond the critical reprimand that Flaubert might represent in terms of the false containment of *bêtise* that Dostoevsky attempts — and the attendant disruption of the sacred, which poses Flaubert as a destabilizer of the project at hand — there is something else as well. Something that exceeds the strictures posed by anxiety of influence — which *is another* name for the interference Flaubert runs, overwhelming the literary channels of transmission — and reverts to the elusive body of work, which both men share. Why does *The Idiot* pocket Flaubert, thereby protecting or exposing him, making him the chosen one, harassed and idolized at once?

Flaubert, namely, *is* the Idiot. That is, he fills the whole space of the concept, draws it around him with sober dignity. Generously inhabiting idiocy, the author of *Madame Bovary* goes further. He not only thought the thought of *bêtise* and assumed it in his greatest maturity, but early on he himself hadn't been able to read for an awfully long time — "Gustave *est bête*"[49] — he exhibited pathological credulity and, besides, was considered by his parents to be an idiot —"First the idiocy, the father's alarm . . . the sterile years in Paris and, to end it, the crisis of Pont-l'Evêque, the great illness, in the end the voluntary sequestration and idleness"[50] — and finally committed himself to the maternal clinic to complete a life sentence (we know how greatly Flaubert struggled to complete the sentence).

There remains the other detail, a hidden name. Sartre, broadcasting from inside the head of little Gustave, claims that this dimension gathers the secret strand that ties all the syndromic aspects together, making sense of them: "All of these misfortunes seemed to him to be connected by a secret thread: something was malfunctioning in the child's brain, perhaps since birth: epilepsy — that was the name given to Flaubert's 'illness' — that was, all in all, idiocy continued."[51] These (over)-determinations begin to offer a perfect if uncanny fit: they designate the epileptic fit that held both Flaubert and Dostoevsky in abusive custody. For Flaubert, any disclosure of his condition was taboo. This in part explains why Dostoevsky appropriates Flaubert to his work explicitly as an illicit act. Dostoevsky also has to defend himself against his formidable counterpart. It is not only that they share and inscribe the same body, or that Flaubert might rise up in The Idiot to demand retribution (or, more likely and equally scary, to point out a misplaced comma). Flaubert would not stand for the transcendence that Dostoevsky hypes or toward which he prompts the epileptic body. On the side of will and repression, Flaubert has refused to take the sort of metaphysical medication to which Myshkin resorts — a fact that in itself should not perturb the unfolding of Dostoevsky's incomparable insight. Nonetheless, the bad conscience named Flaubert appears to creep up on him in moments of serious doubt, as when Holbein's dead Christ demobilizes the text, calling all attempts of divinization — of reestablishing the glorious body — into question.

So the problem remains for Dostoevsky: what is to be done with the body of Flaubert? How can it be disposed of properly? This is a body that can be neither fully internalized nor evacuated as such but rattles the text at its most unconscious moments. It agitates Myshkin as the end nears. He pockets the book, that is, he fixes its place in terms of an unstable topography that can claim neither an inside nor an outside. He bears the book, though it never becomes entirely clear to what end. The novel gives a rhetorical indication of how to read this foreign book/body, for Madame Bovary does not represent the first body that Myshkin has had to carry. From the start the novel has allegorized the need to evacuate a second and double sick body, the nihilist body whose textual efforts are adorned with the markers of stupidity. Dostoevsky, as we know, gives the bearer of the other sick body in the novel the name Ippolit. The spelling, depending upon which translation you pick up, varies, sometimes given as "Hippolyte."

In Madame Bovary, the object-signifier that was pocketed, incorporated and closed off by the Idiot, Hippolyte is the name of the sacrificed body. Experimented on, with a new technology that consisted of boxing in a lame leg, he ends up mutilated and mangled by Charles Bovary's botched operation.[52] "Hippolyte" not only provides the body around whose wounding religion collapses together with mystifications of medicine ("Meanwhile religion seemed to be helping him no more than surgery: the invincible gangrene continued to rise toward the belly"),[53] it also locates the place of an intense Oedipal-fraternal struggle for Flaubert.[54] The name Hippolyte seals a textual crypt, guarding the secret story of fraterno-patricidal passion. In terms of literary transmission, the war of brothers migrates to Dostoevsky's work in the form of an ambivalent embrace, with the one work lodged near the diminishing heart of the eponymous hero borne by the other work. Still, there remains the encryption of Flaubert by Dostoevsky, presenting perhaps a more difficult issue of relatedness to explore, exceeding, as it does, the common scope of a contained literary history. All we know at this point is that Flaubert occupies the ambivalent space of struggle for Dostoevsky, surfacing when Dostoevsky's writing takes recourse to unconscious forms of knowing what we are not supposed to know.

PART THREE

On the Relatedness of Ethics to Masochism

Literature and Pathology

The Idiot and Madame Bovary communicate with one another as if by a secret telephonic connection. Something like an ethical anxiety occurs when one listens in, breaking into a line or logic of literary transmission. What does Dostoevsky have on Flaubert? Or is it rather Flaubert who intrusively punctures a system of protection that his Russian counterpart has attempted to secure? In ways that are not yet comprehensible, they are often at each other's throats. Both authors have something to say about the pathologized body. They understood the laws of submission to which the afflicted body points. Flaubert invented the addicted body, while Dostoevsky, himself an addict, stuck with idiocy and its cognates. Elsewhere he would venture into the domain of addictive and criminal psychologies. In terms of their material-historical bodies, they shared the same disease. The implications of this uneasy alliance deserve more consideration, if not perhaps concern. Though it seems unorthodox to look at their medical records, we need to remind ourselves that the history of certain pathologies belongs to literature and continues to occupy the space of the imaginary, eliciting a reading and calling for a sense of the world that supersedes mere notation. In the case of Dostoevsky, Freud notoriously destabilized the status of his accepted diagnosis, calling it, in part, a fiction.

The difference, or let us say one difference, between Flaubert and Dostoevsky can be seen in the persistence with which the Russian author imbricated the fact of epilepsy in his novels. Visible and acknowledged, if not thematically flaunted, the condition became an object of literary endeavor. On the other side of the line, the oeuvre, like the family, of Flaubert remained silent about epilepsy. The name of the illness was never pronounced en famille. Instead, a masochistic process of disavowal was launched. The family maintained strict secrecy around Gustave's epilepsy even though both his father and his brother were

The Disappearance

leading physicians who attended him by using conventional methods for treating the condition. The payback for receiving in-house calls consisted in joining the familial repression of epilepsy. Since he would not keep still, however, there were some inadvertent leaks, for the scandal of his writing produced leakage. On December 2, 1862, Flaubert was openly attacked in Le Figaro: "It's the epileptic type [genre épileptique]! A spreading rumor has it that Flaubert is epileptic."[55] By now his illness carries a rumorological status and is said to account for the very genre of his writing. The speculative disclosure remains unconfirmed, left to travel around like a phantom seeking acknowledgment.

Dostoevsky's gesture of uncommented appropriation in The Idiot indicates a double rapport to Flaubert's phantom. He knew Flaubert's secret and was, in a sense, bound to out him. Myshkin was on his last lap when something propelled him toward Madame Bovary. At the same time, he stops short of exposing Flaubert's secret. When Myshkin spies the open book, he offers a seal of protection, closing rather than disclosing, in the end safeguarding and concealing its meaning in a hidden pocket. It could be said that Dostoevsky takes the secret upon himself, the way Myshkin assumes custody of Rogozhin's pain, by becoming the receptacle of a disavowed history. The custodian and keeper of Flaubert's secret — even if at times it rose to the surface, becoming an open secret, an early object of media leakage — Dostoevsky inscribes Flaubert as his double, as the living intimation of an unrepresentable experience of epilepsy. It is as if Flaubert held the key to the unavowable community of pain. A master at doubling the stakes, Dostoevsky zeroes in on his French other when the chips are down. The chronicle of double trouble had begun long ago, for the two authors are implicated in a pair of binding coincidences. We understand what separates them, but what holds them close? Born the same year, they were both sons of noted physicians. They lived according to the precepts of reclusion, in retreat. In the end Prince Myshkin and Madame Bovary become a couple, hers being the only book to which he will hold as he enters the irreversible closedown.

But what is it that the twin writers share when the disclosure of "le genre épileptique" is made? It is hard to say without devoting an entire book to the subject and its many encrypted forms. Epilepsy as medical observation or ontological index remains elusive, and it is still not understood how this highly complicated condition commands textuality or even constitutes a genre. Yet some sort of preliminary effort to situate the pathology needs to be made in order to elucidate the difficult questions attending the construal of the mind-body relation, whose traditional hierarchies epilepsy has brought decisively into crisis. It would be foolish to suppose that such questions could be isolated (as if the body did not write or were not itself written, coded, driven, signifying); given their prodigious range, they exhort us to explore, in turn, the links that epilepsy appears to establish with a certain dumbness of being — an insight that the corpus cosigned by Flaubert and Dostoevsky urges. In their writing, both authors were invested in the fallen states indicated by what they obsessively consecrated as levels of stupidity or existential modulations active within idiocy. In the work of Dostoevsky, the scene of epilepsy became the conduit for understanding the limits of the sacred.

Freud

Perhaps the most significant knock that the literary elaboration of epilepsy received was introduced by Freud's work on the subject. Something happened to the ancient scene of epilepsy (the Greeks claim it in mythology) when Freud intervened to consider precisely the case of Dostoevsky. Occupying a special place in the unfolding of his oeuvre, epilepsy is the only somatic illness about which Freud wrote after psychoanalysis was established. Whereas key researchers had taken pains to distinguish hysteria from epilepsy, Freud treated Dostoevsky as a hystero-epileptic — essentially, that is, as a severe hysteric. It could be that this heuristic decision gave Freud some leverage, given that epilepsy as such — a postulate that Freud denies — rebuffs attempts at decipherment. It could also be, as contemporary psychoanalyst Marie-Thérèse Sutterman argues, that on still another level Freud was motivated by patricidal impulse and wanted to overthrow the theories of his teacher and master, Charcot, the father of the hystero-epileptic division. Indeed, the couple, hysteria and epilepsy, were severed according to effects of sexual difference, with women acquiring hysteria and men, epilepsy.

Freud, however, blurs these distinctions and persists in naming Dostoevsky's condition his "so-called epilepsy." The hesitation around the name of the disease derives, he suggests, from clinical instabilities as well: "It has been found impossible to maintain that 'epilepsy' is a single clinical entity."[56] Under observation by quotation marks, "epilepsy" is moreover viewed by Freud as "the uncanny disease with its incalculable, apparently unprovoked convulsive attacks, its changing of the character into irritability and aggressiveness, and its progressive lowering of all the mental faculties" (21:179). The return to hysteria at this point in his thinking entails somewhat of an oddity; James Strachey reminds us that the article treating Dostoevsky constitutes Freud's first discussion of hysterical attacks since his early paper on the subject written twenty years before (1909). A major concern that the condition raises involves the slipping solidity of mind, its glide into what has been designated as idiocy. Freud observes that in most cases the epileptoid attack involves the dulling of mind. "However characteristic intellectual impairment may be in the overwhelming majority of cases, at least *one* case is known to us (that of Helmholtz) in which the affliction did not interfere with the highest intellectual achievement" (21:180). Parenthetically, Freud remarks: "(Other cases of which the same assertion has been made are either disputable or open to the same doubts as the case of Dostoevsky himself)" (21:180). The question that begins to be traced seems to be, Why was Dostoevsky not the Idiot?

Freud's discussion of some of the prevalent traits of Dostoevsky's personality will not seem unfamiliar to readers of The Idiot, for many of *"I know nothing of women."* the distinguishing features isolated by Freud recur in Myshkin and have preoccupied us in these pages. The detour through the Freudian corpus will shed light on essential qualities, such as Myshkin's exaggerated kindness and trusting nature, which acquire definition in Freud's elaboration of social masochism and his interest in the unfaltering promptings of guilt to which Myshkin is prey. Freud begins by considering what Dostoevsky called himself; he calls him on it in a way that should interest us:

> Dostoevsky called himself an epileptic, and was regarded as such by other people, on account of his severe attacks, which were accompanied by loss of consciousness, muscular convulsions and subsequent depression. Now it is highly probable that this so-called epilepsy was only a symptom of his neurosis and must accordingly be classified as hystero-epilepsy — that is, as severe hysteria. We cannot be completely certain on this point for two reasons — firstly, because the anamnestic data on Dostoevsky's alleged epilepsy are defective and untrustworthy, and secondly, because our understanding of pathological states combined with epileptiform attacks is imperfect. (21:179)

It is not only the case that the data about and representations of Dostoevsky's attacks are unreliable but these "attacks, though as a rule determined, in a way we do not understand, by purely physical causes, may nevertheless owe their first appearance to some purely mental cause (a fright, for instance) or may react in other respects to mental excitations" (21:180). The attacks, provoking savage shaking, tongue biting, urinary incontinence, "and working up to the dangerous *status epilepticus* with its risk of severe self-injuries," are punctuated by short spaces of time during which "the patient does something out of character, as though he were under control of his unconscious" (21:180). It is as though the mechanism for abnormal instinctual discharge has been laid down organically.

Thus far, what we "know" about epilepsy — it remains important to underscore Freud's hesitations and the way he marks the "elusion" of understanding — is that it originates in a space that commands emotional, mental, physical, and mechanical processes — the highly invested cerebral organ, where all the functions of soma and psyche are gathered, distributed, and resynthesized. A site, moreover, of phantasmatic projections and superegoical negotiations, the point of departure for "so-called epilepsy" forces an interrogation of the troubled unity of the subject's psychosomatic field upon which the unconscious intrudes. To speak in the sense of Ferenczi's findings, the drive at the core of the condition of epilepsy is neither entirely conscious nor exclusively unconscious but maintains its somatic heritage.[57] Too attentive simply to refute the postulate of an organic anchor, Freud seeks the connection to a determined mark of psychic prompting, which he locates in hysterical conversion. It should be pointed out that Freud is by no means alone in noting the mysteriously resistant nature of epilepsy when it comes to scientific investigation. Bouchard designates the condition as "one of the most unassailable citadels of neurology."[58]

Attentive to syncopic restatements thumping through mind and body, which are neither altogether conscious or unconscious yet are triggered by a sense of exteriority that seems lodged deep within, the condition of generalized epilepsy, when prompted out of its periods of latency, sends the subject out of consciousness, as it were, mechanizing the body by means of the robotic lurches that it encourages; configuring the automaton, it in a sense mineralizes a self that, according to the findings of a number of clinical studies, is sexuated indifferently, which is to say as asexual, seraphic, or often bisexual or androgynous. Wrung out by the punctual yet unpredictable manifestation of symptoms, the subject succumbs to the greatest extremes of passivity. The afflicted are plainly jerked around by a force that exceeds their control.

Epileptics, claim Freud and others, tend to be drawn into sadistic

231

scenes dominated, as it were, by a masochistic attachment; their sadism gets expressed outwardly in small doses but more consistently when turned against themselves. Hence the many greatly humiliated and offended subjects of Dostoevsky who repeatedly contend with infantile omnipotence. The sadomasochistic engagements to which Dostoevsky held are of consequence for Freud, and we will return to their various implications after the sketch of epileptoid attributes is completed. One aspect of the extreme passivity by which the subject submits is evidenced in the mechanical aspects of the seizure; already figuring the technobody, this eruption of corporeal mechanization is what Ippolit in The Idiot associates with unstoppable dumbness, enacted in the inevitable but stupid mimicry of convulsive acts.

The dumb repetitions of the sexual act are brought into contact with the epileptoid crisis, for there is a sexualized current running through the subjected body. Freud reminds us of the fact that the mechanisms of instinctual discharge unleashed in a seizure do not "stand remote from the sexual processes, which are fundamentally of toxic origin: the earliest physicians described coition as a minor epilepsy, and thus recognized in the sexual act a mitigation and adaptation of the epileptic method of discharging stimuli" (21:180–81). The sexual act, according to this argument by no means an original act, borrows from the "method" of epilepsy, which now occupies a field of epileptoid release. Coition is said to be modeled on the seizure.

The epileptic attack also stands at the beck and call of neurotic manipulation, becoming a symptom of hysteria. Freud continues: "The 'epileptic reaction,' as this common element may be called, is also undoubtedly at the disposal of the neurosis whose essence it is to get rid by somatic means of amounts of excitation which it cannot deal with psychically. Thus the epileptic attack becomes a symptom of hysteria and is adapted and modified by it just as it is by the normal sexual process of discharge" (21:181). This epileptic reaction can be recruited into service by the commanding neurosis in order to help the mind-body detox surplus stimulants. It corresponds to something of a cleansing mechanism, having converted an excess that cannot be coped with into a somatic chute.

At this point some light is shed on Dostoevsky's addictions, the most prominent of which were evidenced, of course, in his gambling binges. Freud interprets these compulsive and hysterical qualities in terms of Dostoevsky's need for great punishment, the requirement he exacted of the world to provide humiliation and tangible debt — needs that gambling satisfied. Not surprisingly, perhaps, the development becomes classically Freudian, linking the depleting addiction to the truth of castration. Gambling, which like all addictions derives from the "primal addiction" of masturbation,[59] pitches the subject toward the threat of castration while it raises the stakes of terrific guilt. Both the addiction and the epileptic attack are said to grow out of ambivalence toward a severe and sadistic father ("the boy wants to be in his father's place because he admires him and wants to be like him, and also because he wants to put him out of the way" [21:183]). Ambivalence puts the death drive in gear.

The attacks, which prime and mime the sexual act, also move beyond the pleasure principle to double for death. The lethargic, somnolent states that Dostoevsky documents "had the significance of death: they were heralded by a fear of death" (21:182) and produced what Freud subsequently calls "deathlike attacks." Several other sources underscore the extent to which Dostoevsky anxiously awaited death on an almost daily basis of rituals and preparations; among other stints, he left notes on his pillow to those who might find him dead the next morning, and he regularly ran over to his doctor's house, with whom he enjoyed nearly telepathic relations, to spend the night as his guest, in his care. The sleepovers staved off some fear but could not, in the long run, arrest the symptom. Back to Freud's couch. The attacks, in sum, indicate an identification with a dead person, "either with someone who is really dead or with someone who is still alive and whom the subject wishes dead" (21:183). This is how the attack, while identifying the subject with the dead center of the death wish, in fact carries the "value of a punishment." One has wished another person dead, "and now one is this other person and is dead oneself" (21:183). Hysterical epilepsy means that you have not gotten away with murder; you are the way. You have thrown your body in the way of the targeted object of a murderous impulse and will continue to trade positions with the intended other, dancing for the death commissioned by you. Freud makes the macabre dance contingent on a death wish, but not on the death wish of the other, as Sutterman subsequently contends — that is, on the likelihood, within the transmitted intimations of fantasy, that the infant has gotten the message of the near extinction wished upon her by the attending parent. Both views agree on the fantasy of an early murder scene, which the child, at once victim and perp, continues to perform into adulthood. Whereas Sutterman argues that the attack originates in the fantasy and dread of infanticide, Freud ages the infant and makes this a secondary effect of a projected death wish. Psychoanalytical theory asserts that the target for a boy is usually his father and that "the attack (which is termed hysterical) is thus a self-punishment for a death-wish against a hated father" (21:183). The punishing attack is the way of putting a restraining order on the part of oneself that is struggling to get the offending father and is already locked in identification with his demise.

There are two epileptic types, then. In order to pursue the interpretive line that casts Dostoevsky's illness into the domain of "our author's so-called epilepsy" (21:184), Freud has had to distinguish between an organic and an "effective," or functional (psychogenic), epilepsy: "The practical significance of this is that a person who suffers from the first kind has a disease of the brain, while a person who suffers from the second kind is a neurotic. In the first case his mental life is subjected to an alien disturbance from without, in the second case the disturbance is an expression of his mental life itself" (21:181). Freud ranges Dostoevsky's epilepsy within the second of the two options set forth, though hardly in the dogmatic sense that subsequent scholars have deplored. Freud's rhetoric of knowing will have relinquished the wish fulfillment of unassailable scientific proof. He writes: "This cannot, strictly speaking, be proved. . . . we know too little. . . . our information about the relations between [the attacks] and Dostoevsky's experiences is defective and often contradictory" (21:184). He proceeds on the basis of the "most probable assumption" according to which earlier, childhood symptoms assumed epileptic form on the heels of the shattering experience of the author's eighteenth year — the murder of his father.

Whether or not the assassination took place as Freud's sources have documented — he takes recourse to accounts offered by René Fülöp-Miller, Aimée Dostoevsky in her biography of her father, and Orest Miller — Freud pins the violent attacks on the father complex. Aggravated or confirmed by Dostoevsky's latent homosexuality, the father complex is largely responsible for the passive positions occupied by Fyodor Mikhailovich when faced with the massive existential insults leveled at him and informs, further, his inordinate submissiveness to the czar and God — to "little father" and big daddy. Dostoevsky's attacks are in imitation of the dead, of that which he wished dead and that now wishes him dead in a deadly karmic cycle according to which what goes around comes around to get you, especially because it stems from your unconscious (Freud: "So alien to our consciousness are the things by which our unconscious mental life is governed!" [21:184]). As

234

we know from other texts, father is more alive when (wished) dead than when living. Here the perished father stamps the coming to term of futurity, filling the meaning of a destiny. In a notable aside, Freud offers that destiny reverts in the end to paternal projection; the concept itself of fate is fatherly ("Even fate is, in the last resort, only a later projection of the father" [21:185]). The unavoidable resonances of fate and *father* have been fairly well set in place since at least the Nietzschean hints of a homonymic cooperation between *amor fati* and *amor vati*. All kidding aside, the kid's symptoms of deathlike attacks can thus be understood "as a father-identification on the part of his ego, which is permitted by his super-ego as a punishment" (21:185). The internalized desire of the father gets the upper hand over the ego-identified father in a rumble that has the subject falling to his death. The repetitive punishment, a punctual ritual, is the price exacted by superego's fury.

But how can two fathers rule and rumble? Freud narrates the splitoff of the father function. The so-called epilepsy of our author has arisen as a consequence of the repression of the hatred of the father in the Oedipus complex. The repression gets supplemented. "There is something fresh to be added: namely that in spite of everything the identification with the father finally makes a permanent place for itself in the ego" (21:184). Received into the ego, the identification establishes itself there as a separate agency, in contrast to the rest of the content of the ego. "We then give it the name of super-ego and ascribe to it, the inheritor of the parental influence, the most important functions" (21:185). If the father was hard, violent, and cruel, those attributes are taken over by the superego and, in the relations it holds with the ego, the passivity that was supposed to have been repressed is reestablished. The superego has become sadistic, and the ego becomes masochistic, passive, even "feminized" by superego's control systems. "A great need for punishment develops in the ego, which in part offers itself as a victim to fate, and in part finds satisfaction in ill-treatment by the super-ego (that is, in the sense of guilt). For every punishment is ultimately castration and, as such, a fulfillment of the old passive attitude towards the father" (21:185). To top it off, Freud writes: "'You wanted to kill your father in order to be your father yourself. Now you *are* your father, but a dead father' — the regular mechanism of hysterical symptoms. And further: 'Now your father is killing *you*.' For the ego the death symptom is a satisfaction in phantasy of the masculine wish and at the same time a masochistic satisfaction; for the super-ego it is a punitive satisfaction — that is, a sadistic satisfaction. Both of them, the ego and the super-ego, carry on the role of father" (21:185).

When Dostoevsky was put under arrest by the czar's police, his symptoms were arrested. The astonishing fact reported by Dostoevsky that in Siberia he was free from his attacks merely substantiates the supposition by Freud that these attacks served as his punishment. Serving time, serving father, Dostoevsky had no further need of the punishing attacks when humbled by fate in this extreme way. Still, Freud again offers a word of caution: "But that cannot be proved" (21:186). All that can be made out is that Dostoevsky was released from having to punish himself when he "got himself punished by his father's deputy. Here we have a glimpse of the psychological justification of the punishments inflicted by society. It is a fact that large groups of criminals want to be punished. The super-ego demands it and so saves itself the necessity for inflicting the punishment itself" (21:186–87).[60] A rigorous psychology of the institution of penal systems would have to contend with the point raised by Freud, namely, that superego casts about for strict external forms of punishment, the only condition under which ego can be relieved of unsparing symptoms. Lest one rush to authoritarian conclusions about the helpfulness of instituting systems of incarceration and the like, remember that Freud does not encourage the state to double for the punitive function or to satisfy its demands; it is no doubt important to observe, moreover, that Dostoevsky was innocent, even though superego and the police had collaborated on the necessity of deporting him.

Freud's contemplation of this case advances an explanation for the fact that Dostoevsky passed unbroken through the Siberian years of misery and humiliation: "Dostoevsky's condemnation as a political prisoner was unjust and he must have known it, but he accepted the undeserved punishment at the hands of the Little Father, the Tsar, as a substitute for the punishment he deserved for his sin against his real father. Instead of punishing himself, he got himself punished by his father's deputy" (21:186). The greater part of Freud's commentary refers to the epileptic criminal depicted in The Brothers Karamazov and the patricidal pact sealed by the dominant fraternity, which illustrate his theories. The affective qualities that he focalizes speak to The Idiot as well, though the paternal function is diffused and unruly in comparison with the one presiding over the Brothers. Both texts lead to ethical hesitations that urge a critical review of what we think we know about ethics, or what we have allowed ethics traditionally to exclude, discard.

On a number of occasions Freud appears to invite a comparison of the criminal with the epileptic. Dostoevsky has shown boundless sympathy, Freud observes, when it comes to criminals. A recurrent symptom in his works involves an immoderate display of sympathy for the evildoer associated with the tendency to forgive all. Freud attributes such adherence to the deviant on the part of the writer to "identification on the basis of similar murderous impulses — in fact, a slightly displaced narcissism" (21:190). Allowing parenthetically that he has little interest in undermining an ethics of sympathy — "(In saying this, we are not disputing the ethical value of this kindliness)" — he goes on to say that his inquiry concerns a general quality, which, to the degree that it underlies the mechanism of kindly sympathy toward other people, can be most readily gleaned from "this extreme case of a guilt-ridden novelist. There is no doubt that this sympathy by identification was a decisive factor in determining Dostoevsky's choice of material" (21:190). Symptoms of excessive sympathy and extreme kindliness pervade his work, where a steady decriminalization of the protagonist takes place (Myshkin has not yet supplanted Dmitri but belongs to the same constellation introduced by a rule of implicit analogy). Dostoevsky's sympathy for the criminal was found to be boundless, going "far beyond the pity which the unhappy wretch has a right to . . . [and] reminds us of the 'holy awe' with which epileptics and lunatics were regarded in the past. A criminal is to him almost a Redeemer, who has taken on himself the guilt which must else have been borne by others" (21:190).

The recuperation of the criminal soul and the overthrow of juridical evaluations become a theme later on in Jean Genet's essay "Une Lecture des Frères Karamazov," in which the indispensable criminal imposter modeled in the work is called a "bold instigation of souls."[61] The historical awe that greeted the epileptic and lunatic in the past is seen in both cases to have evolved in Dostoevsky into a cult of the glorified criminal. We detect signs of this mutation in progress in the figure of Myshkin, at once protected by a redemptive aura and capable of embracing the murderer, his soul's brother.

A complicated dossier has been opened. Freud takes some care to avoid destabilizing a possible ethics; even so, his article takes on the presumed virtue of kindliness. Under scrutiny, the qualities of overlarge kindliness, including courteousness and politeness, point to an improbable source in perversity. The reportedly Christian values of love and sympathy, viewed in terms of Dostoevsky's masochistic rap sheet, are connected to a very strong destructive instinct. Dostoevsky could easily have been a criminal, Freud says a number of times in a number of ways (for instance: "the extraordinary intensity of his emotional life, his perverse innate instinctual disposition, which inevitably marked him out to be a sado-masochist or a criminal, and his unanalyzable artistic gift" [21:179]). A similar type of claim and lineup has been made in the Rat Man case, where Freud admiringly notes the father's early charge that the son was destined to become a criminal or a genius — to which the analyst adds, in a footnote, "or a neurotic." Whereas he indulged the protaganist of the case study with his sympathy (and why not, since he was working out for the first time the countertransferential intensities of which his practice was capable, and the guy had read his work), Freud will have none of that in the study of Dostoevsky, where sympathy itself is submitted to interrogation. As Freud's later letter of April 14, 1929, to Theodor Reik avers, he was not writing out of admiration for Dostoevsky or particularly out of admiration for writing itself ("It was written as a favour to someone and written reluctantly. I always write reluctantly nowadays" [21:195]). If there is a question of countertransference here, it flows out of disdain; his transference onto the writer is a negative one.

Inevitably, Freud's uncompromising review of Dostoevsky's history earned him the resentment of more partisan literary critics. He had let little slide as concerned the author's personal defects or political inanities. This was no Rat Man to whom the analyst paid a debt of gratitude and whose demise in World War I he mourned in a note at the end of the case study. Dostoevsky's political demise followed another chart. When reckoning the debt, Freud was unwilling to pass over Dostoevsky's retrograde submission to nation or religion ("a position which lesser minds have reached with smaller effort. This is the weak point in that great personality. Dostoevsky threw away the chance of becoming a teacher and liberator of humanity and made himself one with their gaolers. The future of human civilization will have little to thank him for" [21:177]). Nor does he suppress mention of Dostoevsky's possible confession to a sexual assault upon a young girl (those who persist in accusing Freud of blurring the distinctions between hysteria and rape might look into this passage in conjunction with the many thematizations of child rape in Dostoevsky's writings, particularly in *Stavrogin's Confessions* and *The Life of a Great Sinner*). He skips over Dostoevsky's strident anti-Semitism, leaving it unaddressed. In the letter to Reik he confesses to a basic dislike of the guy ("You are right, too, in suspecting that, in spite of all my admiration for Dostoevsky's intensity and pre-eminence, I do not really like him" [21:196]). The reasons for the stated antipathy are rooted first in business, Freud assures Reik, and they are of a personal, nearly contingent nature: "That is because my patience with pathological natures is exhausted in analysis. In art and life I am intolerant of them. Those are character traits personal to me and not binding on others" (21:196). Exhausted, reluctant, doing someone (most likely Eitingon) a favor at about the same time he is thinking about *Civilization and Its Discontents,* "Fetishism," "A Religious Experience," *The Future of an Illusion,* Freud does not care for him precisely because Dostoevsky does not enjoy the privileges of a patient but locates himself on the side of life and art. If Fyodor Mikhailovich had been on the couch, the analyst's patience would have been considerable.

Dostoevsky, for his part, blew it as a political thinker, as a teacher, as a liberator; he threw away the key for unlocking painfully abrasive historical shackles. In any case, he doesn't get Freud out of the office. His intimacy with the criminal concerns Freud, who eventually lets him off because he does not match one determination of the criminal profile. Two traits are essential in a criminal: boundless egoism and a strong destructive urge. Both of these share as a necessary condition for their expression an absence of love, the lack of an emotional appreciation of (human) objects: "One at once recalls the contrast to this presented by Dostoevsky—his great need of love and his enormous capacity for love, which is to be seen in manifestations of exaggerated kindness and caused him to love and to help where he had a right to hate and to be revengeful, as, for example, in his relations with his first wife and her lover. That being so, it must be asked why there is any temptation to reckon Dostoevsky among the criminals" (21:178). The impulse to criminalize Dostoevsky is warranted by his choice of material, Freud offers. Yet Dostoevsky turned the criminal instinct against himself, in the form of a destructive pathos fueled by masochism. His personality retained sadistic traits "in plenty," which have shown themselves in his "irritability, his love of tormenting and his intolerance even towards people he loved, and which appear also in the way in which, as an author, he treats his readers. Thus in little things he was a sadist towards others, and in bigger things a sadist towards himself, in fact a masochist—that is to say, the mildest, kindliest, most helpful person possible" (21:178–79). It is no doubt of some importance that even the reader gets pulled into the dragnet of sadistic intention, becoming inscribed in the small print of a published contract and positioned as victim to the abuses of Dostoevsky's sadomasochistic indulgences.

Reaching beyond the particular instance provided by the self-tormentor, Freud keys into a quality that affects the underpinnings of sociality and binds community with the glue of perversion. As it turns out, courteousness and helpfulness — what resembles an outstanding ethical stance — involve a key feature of sadism turned inward. This apparent contradiction has not escaped current popular forms of expression according to which notorious sadists, historical and fictional, such as Hannibal Lector, supplement their anal sadistic sieges with princely postures of politesse. Consistent yet extreme forms of kindliness are traced back by Freud to the ironies of the sadomasochistic contract, possibly the most social of contracts.

Whiplash

Now that we have entered the realm of lectors and readers, we can ask once again what it might have meant for Prince Myshkin to select *Madame Bovary* as the one indisputable item on his reading list. The narrator, for his or its part, had fixed mainly upon Gogol, who, as object of Dostoevsky's frequent and intense ironizations, retained the position of spiritual father (a somewhat risky position for anyone within Dostoevsky's range).[62] Flaubert, on the other hand, was double, brother, father, feminized other, menace, object of tenderness, sadistic instigation, receptacle of a disavowed secret, an opening and liquidation. In a sense they shared the same corpses; the deathbeds, in any case, of Emma and Nastasya are set in the same austere prose milieu, watched over by two survivors, the living-dead remnants of a dubious vitality. Beyond the specular effects of thematic joinders and character assassinations, or the underlying destructive runs that both authors supervised, something else occurred when Dostoevsky attached himself to Flaubert, internalizing his great work but still maintaining its status as foreign body (it might have been a different matter if the Prince had contrived to *eat* the book, the way Emma, the addicted body, devoured literature). All we know is that when literature turns in on itself, cannibalizing, feeding on its own kind in a sort of reading frenzy, an irrefutable circuitry is reinstalled, something that, if it cannot be demonstrated directly, at least indicates the extent to which, despite it all, we are not alone; even in the instances of the most radical singularity — that of my own madness, the death of consciousness — we cannot claim to own our fate or fathers. It is not only the case that Freud, however reluctantly, took on Dostoevsky as an outpatient. *The Idiot* calls for Freud, even where it escapes the ER of psychoanalytical procedure. It is as if Dostoevsky had preinstalled a response to Freud's reading, summoning the possibilities of that reading in light of future innovation. Whether or not the unreadable condition of "so-called epilepsy" belongs to neurology or turns up as a specimen dream in the chronicle of hysterical conversion, it can only appear as double and other, either as an event of self-doubling or in the mirroring glare of a silent alterity.

When, in the last moments of consciousness, the Idiot hangs onto the other book, embodying it, he in a sense prepares a stage of the Freudo-Lacanian register of analysis: he legislates the insight according to which we are seen to be subjugated by signifiers (to stick with a worthy old term) — subjugated, that is, by the discourse of our predecessors and parents that determines our fate. The terms of this subjugation dictate termination or death even though we may go on living, surviving the recognition that our bodies, traversed by language, have been optioned out to death. This acknowledgment does not correspond to some naturalistic discovery; it normally occurs only through analysis or its likeness — the interminable scrutiny of literary process — culminating in the recognition that we are mortified by language. In part we stalk about as the undead. Pumped by language and written over, vampirized, stung by the mark of the other, we are exposed to Being inescapably as the living dead. With bodies overwritten, we are weighed down by language, which lives through us.[63] We have been grazed. Indented, epithetized, we become, we are surrounded by the compressive measure of citationality. Even in moments of greatest singularity, of ownmost disjunction, there is language, there was citation.

The novel has chronicled the effort on the part of Myshkin to read his body's language, to subjectify a mortal fate, owning it, if only in the mode of borrowing it, borrowing the book in this case, which allows him to assume the position of submission to the writing of the other — his true *Geworfenheit*. Depositing the book near or on his body, breaking the rule of the house and the law of lending circuitry in order to possess the book, now a purloined letter, Myshkin proffers his body as an impossible pre-scription, overwritten, as it were, and conscripted by a drive that comes from elsewhere. (There is no prescription for what he has.) Parasited and harassed, he, like anybody, finds himself borrowed and read as the map of extensive hospitality, an inscription pad where everyone crashes. He exhibits and tolerates the Lacanian insight, namely, "the body constitutes the Other's bed due to the operation of the signifier,"[64] which is to say that the signifier turns the body into the Other's territory, medium, or colony. The body contorts and collapses into a language site upon which the Other constellates — an understanding that Kafka would later share with the restive penal colonies under Dostoevsky's command. To be sure, this is another, if very effective, way of marking our alienation from the body to which we are wed and of emphasizing that, to the extent that body is overwritten by language, it is borrowed and possibly derivative, owed to the Other. Dostoevsky's exorbitant donations prompt Freud's reproach, for the Russian persists in acting out the derivative body, leasing it with equal subjection to the state and the holy kingdom of God. Unrelenting on this issue, Freud also opens a way for future reflections on a certain politics of pain.

Perhaps we can link these observations with Freud's remarks on masochism. To what extent, it may be asked, does Myshkin's determined integration of Madame Bovary participate in the acts of bondage and humiliation to which Freud's article points? Could the image of Emma Bovary be seen to function as the glacial, maternal, severe torturer of a gynocratic order? But the "woman torturer of masochism cannot be sadistic precisely because she is in the masochistic situation, she is an integral part of it, a realization of the masochistic fantasy."[65] For formal reasons she cannot be shunted to a presumed outside. She belongs in the masochistic world — not in the sense that she has the same tastes as her victim, "but because her 'sadism' is of a kind never found in a sadist; it is as it were the double of the reflection of masochism" (41). Brought together by specular alliance, a form of subjection occurs in which it is no longer clear who is parasiting whom, or what the economy of citationality linking the two texts is meant to control; still, they are evermore bound together within the irony of a masochistic claim. It is not as though Prince Myshkin clutches Madame Bovary to his breast because she is the dominatrix of choice, though a case could be made for such an arrangement (her masochistic world appears to bear down upon his, which it reflects, even duplicates at times). Sealing and concealing the book, Myshkin signs in and under the name of the other, binding himself irrevocably to this power that comes from elsewhere. He lends a countersignatory force to Madame Bovary by means of which he engages a reciprocal movement of countersigning, forming one body with the language of Flaubert. Henceforth Dostoevsky is bound up in Flaubert, who signs in turn and seals his fate.

When Krafft-Ebing gave Leopold von Sacher-Masoch credit for having refined a clinical entity, "not merely in terms of the link between pain and sexual pleasure, but in terms of something more fundamental connected with bondage and humiliation,"[66] he was also pointing to cases of masochism without algolagnia. The mobility of masochism on the grand chart of humiliation was established. The discovery, shared with regional differences by Dostoevsky and Sacher-Masoch, offers a motive for opening onto other courses and objects, different figures or experiences of subjection. The novel braces itself against the inevitability of such displacements, which it also prompts. It is necessary to note that the murder weapon will be taken from the pages of a book, a knife whose source and sorcery is located in the folds of a text. Dostoevsky's allowance for the book as a place of wounding, as the precise domain from which a knife can be drawn, a fatal blow incurred, reinforces the lacerating potential of the other book, whose retrieval is cleanly marked, even if the knife it wields remains as mysterious as it is untouchable. Feminized, even phallicized (no contradiction here), the book beckons and destroys, covers up and punishes.

Torture and Education

Reading *Venus in Furs*, Deleuze reveals how the rhetoric of masochism consists in persuasion and education, guided by an effort to get the other to "sign" (21), that is, to cosign a contract, to honor a reciprocal vow (the vow and disavowal are closely linked in the masochistic process). We are no longer in the presence, observes Deleuze, evidently reminiscing about de Sade, of a torturer seizing upon a victim and enjoying her all the more because she is unconsenting and unpersuaded. "We are dealing instead with a victim in search of a torturer and who needs to educate, persuade and conclude an alliance with the torturer in order to realize the strangest of schemes. . . . The masochist draws up contracts while the sadist abominates and destroys them" (20). In every respect the masochistic "educator" stands in contrast to the sadistic "instructor," the one who knows it all already and has only scorn for the rhetoric of persuasion, the method of wimps and dummies. The masochist, trying to enroll the other in a course of surrendered complicity, gets his clause on a contract and is ever on the lookout for the compliant signature. For whom is the other signing?

What the masochist carries in his heart, Deleuze argues, is the miniaturized image of the humiliated father; s/he has made contact with the secret of that humiliation. According to both Freud and Deleuze, though they are miles apart on key aspects of this analysis, the masochist remains prey to the paternal secret and is enlisted as a loyalist of the father's symptom. In the case of Dostoevsky, one could propose now that he effected the corporeal absorption of the letter: "symptom," we recall, comes from *syn* (together) and *piptein* (to fall). Succumbing to the symptom, the "falling sickness," he produces an act of commemoration, or punctual reiteration, of the father's humiliation. Yet too real, frozen out by trauma, father's secret had to travel, become symbolized, and even — in order to survive — redirected and fraternalized. To reclaim the safer bounds of the novel, the name or cryptaphor of Flaubert miniaturizes, folds; his fall is timed to occur together with the imminent collapse of Myshkin — or, more likely, he catches the fall. Dostoevsky, out and open, needs the guarded and humiliated Flaubert to cosign. Needing to secure for himself a partnership with the humiliated other, the masochist works from a place of harried destitution. This is why I have argued that the rapport to Flaubert is double (at least double) according to sadomasochistic protocols, involving the need to protect and the urge to expose. Tracked down for his signature at this crucial juncture, Flaubert is at once reassuring and disfranchising, the accomplice and persecutor. Yet his status in the novel is left rigorously suspended — remains a part, henceforth, of the suspense, even suspended on the body that carries the other writing to term. Suspense is not a stray shot, aleatory or random, but a strategic factor in the masochistic process. Masochism makes use of suspense. Deleuze points up the masochistic rites of torture and suffering, which imply actual physical suspension (the hero is hung up, crucified or suspended). His reliance on suspension may in part explain the terror that befell Dostoevsky and obsesses the text when facing the image of Christ taken down from the cross, where the masochistic process is disrupted and all lines of flight are frozen. It is as if the possibility itself of transcendence depended upon the masochistic process and the implicit contracts that draw up bodies.

* * *

It is perhaps of some significance to note one of Masoch's persistent fantasies. He liked to imagine that the Slavs were in need of a beautiful female despot, a terrible czarina, to ensure the triumph of the revolutions of 1848 and to strengthen the Pan-Slavic movement. "A further effort, Slavs, if you would become Republicans."[67]

Wordsworth

And by the moonlight, Betty Foy
Has on the well-girt saddle set
(The like was never heard of yet)
Him whom she loves, her Idiot Boy.
. . .
The moon that shines above his head
Is not more still and mute than he.
— William Wordsworth, "The Idiot Boy"

In such infernal circles round his door
Once when he shouted, stretched in ghastly shape.
I hurried by. But back from the hot shore
Passed him again . . . He was alone, agape.
— Hart Crane, "The Idiot"

Amid the daisies
Even the idiot boy
Has a dignity.
— Richard Wright, haiku #579

Satellite

I feel as though,
unattended by effects of historical
reference or the consolations of philosophi-
cal application, *The Idiot* risks getting lost in feral iso-
lation. The status of idiocy, grand and incomparable as it
has been made to appear in the text of the Russian masochist,
derives its undeniable weightiness from philosophical debates of
the eighteenth century. To a considerable degree, empirical philosophy depended upon idiocy in order to advance claims about the nature
of human understanding. In part a philosophical invention, idiocy did not
often stand alone but engendered a place for the elaboration of its own
meaning among asserted correlates. Thus the idiot appeared alongside
or at the head of the train of blind, deaf, or mute subjects (whose im-

plications for subjecthood, precisely, provoked crisis) and was most closely leagued with the prestige accorded to the construction of the wild child — the teachable idiot.

To ensure that *The Idiot* doesn't disappear into the night of its singularity, I am going to put a satellite in the space of its peculiar atmosphere, adding a moon above it to shed discreet light on its solitary path. To that end, turning steadily away from the solar systems of cognition that govern self-knowledge, we return to a moment in the moonlit poetry of Wordsworth, to an exorbitant site in his reflections that in fact has been largely shunned or, with a few stellar exceptions, politely overlooked. Nonetheless, this is a space that responds to the philosophical urgency bestowed upon the idiot. It historicizes the predicament of idiocy in language, prompting it, however tenuously, to take root in a milieu that is productive of historical significance. This emplacement occurs despite itself, for rarely does poetry show itself to be more casual about *Stiftung,* or historical instituting, than in these early experiments. One of the more remarkable scholars of Wordsworth in our time, Geoffrey Hartman, poignantly refers this poetry to the future of its interpretability.

Routinely excused from the table of worthy contents, the poems under consideration are given an uncommon edge by Hartman, who allows that their time may not have come. Asserting a distinction between a minor *poem* and a considered *text,* he writes: "We have to conclude either that such poems are weak, and redeemed only by the responsive interpreter, or that they have the sort of strength we are not yet fit to perceive: that our present image of great poetry stands in the way of their peculiar textual quality. . . . Time will tell. . . . The life of Wordsworth's lines is often uneasy and as if somewhere else: still to be manifested by the action of time or the utterance of future readers."[1] Awkward and untimely, this phase of Wordsworth's writing evinces something disturbing, and, despite the figural ascesis to which the poet himself admitted in a later preface to his own effort, the poems arrived, if they have arrived, as unreceivable, even unreadable. Well, some of them, at least, were put in the dead-letter box for future culling — or shredding.

Wordsworth, who collaborated on their publication with the great addict Samuel Taylor Coleridge, meant to offer these poems as an alternative drug. This is one register by which to read his stated intentions. The poems came on the scene as another, gentler stimulant intended to take the edge off street poetry or "popular Poetry of the day": "For the human mind is capable of being excited without the application of

248

gross and violent stimulants."[2] Men in cities, he notes, are jonesing for the rapid-fire technology of communication; they have become indentured to "a craving for extraordinary incident, which the rapid communication of intelligence hourly gratifies" (1:872–73). And language cartels exploiting such cravings are on the rise: "The invaluable works of our elder writers, I had almost said the works of Shakespeare and Milton, are driven into neglect by frantic novels, sickly and stupid German Tragedies, and deluges of idle and extravagant stories in verse" (1:873). Wordsworth's repressive forces will have been too weak, he fears, to counteract the new age of addiction, whose major dealers come from the neighborhood of "sickly and stupid" German texts: "When I think upon this degrading thirst after outrageous stimulation, I am almost ashamed to have spoken of the feeble effort with which I have endeavoured to counteract it" (1:873).

Now the great poet's efforts to counteract gross and violent textual crimes cannot be assimilated to a notion of repressive policing, as I may have suggested earlier, but operates more along those lines that justify the creation of a methadone clinic, if such a space could be converted to accommodate common addicts of German stimulants. Wordsworth counteracts these abuses with his own formula for dispensing stimulants; he at no point asks the reader to renounce stimulants as such or to destroy the premises underlying such a craving. The bad stimulants "blunt the discriminating powers of mind" and are viewed as "unfitting [the mind] for all voluntary exertion [and reducing] it to a state of almost savage torpor" (1:872). In order to prevent the general spread of stupefaction, Wordsworth, it seems, wants to supply and be the good drug, with no additives, no trace of a diction addiction: "There is little in these volumes of what is usually called poetic diction. I have taken as much pains to avoid it as others ordinarily take to produce it" (1:874). He has ditched the artifice and wants to get down with the lowlife. Even so, he in no way intends to get clean or to offer a proper poetic object, "because the pleasure which I have proposed to myself to impart is of a kind very different from that which is supposed by many persons to be the proper object of poetry.... it has necessarily cut me off from a large portion of phrases and figures of speech which from father to son have long been regarded as the common inheritance of Poets" (1:874). It is a matter of *pleasure* and equally, as we shall see, of improper objects. Having violated filial vows of transmission and broken a contract with the reader,[3] Wordsworth wished to keep his reader "in the company of flesh and blood" (1:874). On the side of life and body, he latches onto a "state of greater simplicity"; a "low and rustic life was generally chosen, because in that condition, the essential passions of the heart find a better soil in which they can attain their maturity, are under less restraint, and speak a plainer and more emphatic language" (1:869). He defends the peculiar outpouring in terms of rural simplicity, a low and rustic life of a pre-Heideggerian mold that he associates with essential passions, better soil. He seeks to stimulate — nonviolently. He takes pleasure in setting mellow (but passionate) simplicity against passionate (but mind-blunting) stupidity. To Coleridge's consternation, Wordsworth has defaced urban values to no discernible end.

These effects of aberrance, whether full-stop or future-oriented, may resonate in part with the mood of scandal with which the poet confronted readers of Milton, Pope, or Shakespeare. Perhaps we might pull a medium switch in order to illustrate his position. As it turns out, there has been a Wordsworth who dwelled beneath the surface of poetic respectability and whose independent poems, the experimental output of the *Lyrical Ballads,* betray a David Lynchian quality, if they are not to be viewed outright as slasher poems. To be sure, Wordsworth was "the first to establish a vulgate for the imagination."[4] Still, in such works as "Nutting" or *Peter Bell* he unleashes the forces of sheer predatory violence, depicting the unaccountable ecstasy of arbitrary destructive acts. In *Peter Bell* a dumb but loyal animal, the Ass, is beaten with punishing precision by the eponymous brute of the moonlit narrative. In "Nutting" a tree is incomprehensibly violated, shaken to its core by a country stalker. In another work, "The Somersetshire Tragedy," Wordsworth writes about the brutalization of Jenny, described by Thomas Poole as "a poor stupid creature, almost an ideot ... an ordinary squat person, disgustingly dirty, and slovenly in her dress."[5] This is worth going into, as the story will serve as the basis for "The Idiot Boy."

The remains of the "Tragedy" underscore Jenny's idiocy and vulnerability. One day a brute, John Walford, discovers her in the solitary woods. According to Poole's written account, which Wordsworth received in March 1798, Walford, a sign of savage predacity, had grown his animality on his body, as it were, for even Walford's clothes stuck to him, through continual wear, assuming the character of a second skin or animal covering. The detail of the wetted garments may be of interest to Wordsworth scholars to the extent that clothing serves as a trope in *The Prelude* for language that, from the start, concerns decayed or abused figures.[6] In the slasher poems, language is matted to bodies and affects,

as in *Peter Bell*, where the organs, crossing the liver, recall that language in Wordsworth invades the body and drives it to utterance, or in this case to "splutterance," to a figure worn down by painful literality. Pain, according to associationist psychology, instills reflective memory while in fact restructuring the bodily organs ("'Peter feels some ugly pains / Across his liver heart and reins / Just like a weaver's shuttle pass'").[7]

Back in the woods, a disfigured John takes Jenny by force (the convergence of their names will turn into "Johnny," the so-to-speak hero of "The Idiot Boy"). Jenny bears John an illegitimate child. Not the loyal kind, John moves on with his life, as we tend to say; he now sets his sights on Ann Rice, the miller's daughter. But Walford's mother forbids their marriage, "so Walford, in obstinacy and spite, [returns] to Jenny and, after once more making her pregnant, [marries] her" (323). Picking up the strands of this narrative, Wordsworth confronts us with the grim story of a battered wife. When her husband, whose name in the poem has been recast as Robert, was due to come home on Saturday nights, Jenny would linger elsewhere, at the home of neighbors, fearful of being near him. In the extant lines of "The Somersetshire Tragedy" the poet depicts her evasion, the way she was worn down by fear:

> Ill fared it now with his poor wife I ween,
> That in her hut she could no longer remain:
> Oft in the early morning she was seen
> Ere Robert to his work had cross'd the green.
> She roamed from house to house the weary day,
> And when the housewife's evening hearth was clean
> She lingers still, and if you chanc'd to say
> "Robert his supper needs," her colour pass'd away. (323)

The language of the poem tells us in so many ways that "she could no longer remain." The conjunction, supported by the poem, of Robert's asserted needs and her passing away predicts her ending. Less than three weeks after their marriage, Walford murders her in a wild and isolated spot and leaves her body lying beside the road, like roadkill: "He did it effectually; for all the muscles and great vessels on one side of the neck were divided, and a torrent of blood gushed out from the body."[8] Whereas Poole's account focuses on the fate of Walford — his conviction, his confession, execution, and gibbeting — he narrativizes a certain amount of violence into enactment, also leaving Jenny by the wayside. Wordsworth, for his part, seems to have been distressed essentially by the cruelty that Jenny was made to suffer and by the posthumous neglect she endured at the hands of her story's chronicler. The fate of the idiot, morphed and regendered, becomes the responsibility of the ballad "The Idiot Boy."

Wordsworth got into trouble for befriending the idiot, and though he proudly stood by his boy, Coleridge eventually slapped it out of him. He was not to write like that again. If *The Prelude* traces the growth of poetic consciousness, this idiot thing that Wordsworth was stuck on blunted consciousness, stunted growth. The poet had an uncanny capacity, Coleridge later wrote, for "ventriloquism," a self-confessed ability to project himself into his creations during short spells of time, "'perhaps . . . to let himself slip into an entire delusion, and even confound and identify his own feelings with theirs.'"[9] Wordsworth overly identified with his creations, was cannibalized by them, could not release but hung onto them. The fact that the poet was hung up on the idiot was an embarrassment (and we know how invested "hanging" as a figural pose for listening was to be in his work). Byron blasted the poem as one of Wordsworth's "Christmas stories tortured into rhyme";[10] Southey, a presumed friend, attacked it at length, and a seventeen year old named John Wilson wrote a highly critical letter to the poet — one of the very few letters to which Wordsworth responded. In any case, Wordsworth was finally enjoined to trade in the idiot boy for the boy of Winander, one babe for another, but it would be wrong to say that the new and improved, educable versions were not at least partly invaded and haunted by the violence that had accrued to Jenny and Johnny or to the animal humiliated and beaten in *Peter Bell* and the tree attacked in "Nutting." And not only for thematic reasons, for Wordsworth's other works would carry episodes of actual and rhetorical maiming, mutilation, drowning (the Ass stubbornly remains loyal to his drowned master, which precipitates Bell's savagery). On the question of the poet's nearly obsessive concern with mutilation, de Man observes the following, perhaps with an uncharacteristically placid positing of the existence of an "own poetic selfhood": "As is well known . . . figures of deprivation, maimed men, drowned corpses, blind beggars, children about to die . . . that appear throughout *The Prelude* are figures of Wordsworth's own poetic self."[11] In the less *Bildungs*-driven texts under consideration, these preludes to *The Prelude,* the notch of mutilation points to something that is unassimilable, stunted, incapable of being marked or mourned.

252

But rather than resist the way de Man harnesses such figures of deprivation to the poetic self, though they are properly attached to *The Prelude*, of which he writes, we should let the implicit question stand. What if these acts and figures belonged to the internal repertory of something like a poetic self? While the poetic self would in such a case cut a gruesome figure, to what extent is it responsive to its own *instincts* for disfigurement, capable of binding onto atrocity with troubling competence? Or, to rebalance the rhetoricity of this question, to what degree will the poetic inscription have been dependent upon an experience of destructive rage, random abusiveness, idiocy? These questions offer highly unlikely accompaniments to the now tranquil prestige and sublimity of Wordsworth's signature; yet his language persists in returning us relentlessly to the remains of poetic gibbeting. His language — at one point tinged by historical rage — follows the blood trail leading up to poetic (self-)discovery. He was, in Hartman's sense, the one to establish a vulgate for the modern imagination. Moreover, as Hartman allows, the work "makes us aware of the virtues of the vernacular, which Wordsworth brings back to dignity."[12] If dignity rises — and there is little doubt of the decidedly auratic pull of this poet's word — it does so on the basis of figures associated with horror and debasement, of which a number constantly open windows of opportunity for the winds of nonrepression. Sudden hate crimes and irredeemable squabbles with nature flare up only to return to what might be called the sublimated pastoral, a place of repressive silencing. His is not the effort of a Hölderlin to bring the mute gods out of their reticence and into language but is about another relatedness to muteness — to that which does not give of itself in world because, in part, it invades existence according to a different itinerary, coming from an unlocatable immanence.

"Mute" and "mutilation" operate homonymically for Wordsworth, pointing to a discontinuity in sameness. As poetic conditions in search of reference, they point to a deprived relation to language, a constitutive disorder in memory. The fate of the idiot is bound up in these tropes; he functions as a kind of holding pen for linguistic violence, unleashing only muffled signals of original erasure. Idiocy commences in disfigurement, as the mutilation over which the philosophers tried to write in an attempt to restore the proper, the literal, what is proper to man. Idiocy offered the sneak preview into a past that could not be known or experienced. To the extent that the "ideot" served in the eighteenth century

253

to shore up the origin of memory and the paradoxes of recalling origin (for Condillac the problem was that we cannot remember what is prior to language, which is why finding a creature who dwells prior to language could help recover the lost memory of humankind — but he cannot speak or describe that state and so is a poor investment, even when brought into language, for he erases a past uninhabited by speech), the "ideot" organized a stage of self that could not move beyond itself or its original alienation from nature. We shall return to the philosophical claims on idiocy shortly. For Wordsworth, the idiot, on leave from philosophical training camps, comes closer to the enigmatic stature accorded to him by Dostoevsky — this is a matter of concealedness, a sacred nondisclosure. Signaling from elsewhere, the idiot wanders in proximity to God ("I have often applied to idiots, in my own mind, that sublime expression of Scripture that, *their life is hidden with God*").[13] Such a holy alliance, at least, represents the claims made on his behalf when Wordsworth defended his idiot. A quasi-sacred being, the idiot put forth by the poet appalled his contemporaries, repelling and offending their sense of taste.

Beyond the strange survival of this figure in the poet for whom "the main region of my song" was located in "the Mind of Man —/ My haunt," there remains the question of Wordsworth's unexampled *pleasure* in writing "The Idiot Boy."[14] It was not just the case that his contemporaries, collaborator(s), and future readers encountered the ballad with a collective sense of dismay; they also had to accept the fact of the poet's own accredited delight when creating and regarding his work. There was to be no redemptive sign of repudiation, no reflective overcoming, no sign of remorse or indication of ever "getting over it." The poem owed its existence to a spontaneous outpouring that, in his view, required no revision, though its vulnerability did incite him to further defenses and explanatory immunizations. An editor's note to *Lyrical Ballads* remarks: "This poem was the subject of a long defense by Wordsworth in a letter to John Wilson (7 June 1802). Wordsworth always had a very high opinion of the poem." Wordsworth himself writes, "Let me add that this long poem was composed in the groves of Alfoxden, almost extempore; not a word, I believe, being corrected, though one stanza was omitted. I mention this in gratitude to those happy moments, for, in truth, I never wrote anything with so much glee."[15] Well, the glee club consisted of one member only, though we could add a few children's voices, and I would like to add my own, to populate the chorus of admirers.

The poet expresses his debt to the poem, which, recalling a sovereign

experience of joyous writing, is responsible for engendering further texts. His memory of joy is disseminated among a number of works, including the lines near the end of *The Prelude* in which, for example, the poet recalls to Coleridge "that summer" of 1798 when the two of them had wandered through the Quantock Hills of Somerset composing many of the poems in *Lyrical Ballads* and preparing what Gordon K. Thomas calls "the literary shot that would be heard round the world."[16] In this milieu of poetic remembrance, returning to the double-barreled *envoi* in preparation, Wordsworth yokes the impossible couple by joining Coleridge's "Christabel," a kind of supernatural lesbian fantasy, to "The Idiot Boy":

> *Thou in bewitching words, with happy heart,*
> . . . .
> *. . . rueful woes*
> *Didst utter of the Lady Christabel:*
> *And I, associate with such labour, steeped*
> *In soft forgetfulness the livelong hours,*
> *Murmuring of him, who, joyous hap, was found,*
> *After the perils of his moonlight ride,*
> *Near the loud waterfall [that is, the idiot boy].*[17]

In this rendering the poet associates the emergence of the poem with the murmuring benevolence of forgetfulness. The union of the two poems depends for its stability upon a certain distension that occurs within Wordsworth's modulation of his partner's utterance of words into his own murmuring, a murmur merging into the "loud waterfall" that fixes the idiot. Whereas Coleridge's poem belongs to the domain of language ("utter," "words") and work ("such labour"), Wordsworth, softened, is marked by a suspension of time, situated in a kind of accident-prone naturality ("joyous hap"). For once, accident and "hap" — happenstance, happiness, haphazard — collaborate in their findings. The boy was found; the poem, the moment were come upon rather than labored. We know from other sources that Wordsworth's composition was often accompanied by illness and pain ("the labor of composition which could make the poet physically ill").[18] What is remembered here, in explicit association with Coleridge's labor, is a kind of effortlessness, a release from the punitive charters of memory making. However "deluded" one might be tempted to judge this moment as being, the event of serenified forgetfulness allows something — someone — to arrive, to return after a trial by moonlight. It was a delusion, in any case, that lasted the livelong hours of a lifetime: Lady Christabel, evoked with rueful woes — she is to perish after the night with Geraldine — falls where the idiot boy elicits joy, because, magically protected, he will be found. Whatever that means.

When Wordsworth and Coleridge learned that Robert Southey was to be one of the early reviewers of *Lyrical Ballads*, they thought they were out of the woods. A friend who had been in contact with both authors during much of the previous year, Southey was thought to be particularly attuned to the work's ends and aims. Aim he did, principally at "The Thorn," "The Rime of the Ancient Mariner," but most critically at "The Idiot Boy." By accidental irony, considering that our poet claims to have done not a lick of work on the poem, Southey argues that "no tale less deserved the labour that appears to have been bestowed upon [it]."[19] Having cast Wordsworth and Coleridge as the Corregio and Raphael of the modern age, Southey sees them turning their attentions to unworthy, boorish objects:

> The majority of these poems, we are informed in the Advertisement, are to be considered as "experiments": "They were written chiefly with a view to ascertain how far the language of conversation in the middle and lower classes of society is adapted to the purposes of poetic pleasure."
>
> Of these "experimental" poems, the most important is "The Idiot Boy." ... No tale less deserved the labour that appears to have been bestowed upon this. It resembles a Flemish picture in the worthlessness of its design and the excellence of its execution. From Flemish artists we are satisfied with such pieces; who would not have lamented if Corregio or Raphael had wasted their talents in painting Dutch boors or the humours of a Flemish wake? (607)

Translated into other media and as the clash of two cultures, the poets, while recognizably Flemish in their ventures, have betrayed their transplanted Italian roots: What can be accepted from Flemish painters we have no receptors for should they prove to be Italian. This switch and betrayal inscribes the poet's name, translating and devaluating it as "worthlessness" within a precarious opposition (design/execution) that emphasizes the last term, the execution followed by the humors of a Flemish wake. What was Southey's design here? Duncan Wu conjectures that Southey felt particularly menaced by Wordsworth's ballad because he had himself claimed an idiot boy when on June 30, 1798, merely a

256

couple of months prior to the publication of *Lyrical Ballads,* he had anonymously printed "The Idiot" in *The Morning Post,* a newspaper to which Wordsworth and Coleridge also contributed.[20] The poem was attributed to Southey only in 1957. It corresponds to the few other poems or reflections that treat idiocy in that it focuses the maternal link — bringing to bear on consciousness a kind of unconditionality of care and correction that cannot be sundered. Here, as elsewhere, idiocy does not understand death. It is stranded in the condition of being "found," of being told and cajoled, of accepting limits like a leash — as that which remains uninternalizable and objectlike. But Southey, no doubt in his own estimation, goes one step further than Wordsworth, who had landed on foreign territory only to disappoint. Wordsworth should have stayed in his own neighborhood, at this point a mere development, of interiority and not strayed into Flemish, that is, Southey, territory.

What is the essential difference in their versions of the idiot? On the surface, Wordsworth keeps the mother alive. It is otherwise with Southey's boy, who, already lost, must encounter a loss past bearing. One day she perishes. After the funeral of his mother, Southey's idiot, having understood nothing of the burial rites, waits until nightfall and, under the witnessing moon, disinters her body. He brings her home with him. Both poets share maternal fusions, keeping the idiots with their oversized mothers, held by the devoted attachment where they place the refusal to mourn.

In the letter of June 7, 1802, to John Wilson, the poet re-emphasizes the experience of pleasure associated with this particular poem. As a breathless rush of writing time-released into an object of reading, the work doubled the dosage of pleasure: "I wrote the poem with exceeding delight and pleasure, and whenever I read it I read it with pleasure" (1:355). With the repetition compulsion written right into the utterance ("pleasure ... pleasure," "I read it I read it"), the poet elicits a double-take when it comes to his readers his readers. It is not certain whether the double "I read it"'s cancel out a reading or whether he is citing the rhythm and cadence of the idiot boy, who speaks by repetition, thus splitting the two instances of "I read it," saying essentially that I as idiot read the idiot's pleasure, which I wrote. It is in any case a gift that keeps on giving, repeating the pleasure in the experience of writing within the repeatability of reading. It suspends the manic-depressive couple that writing and reading often imply for the writer, but it also refuses the shame or sham of pleasurable writing by affirming the pleasure taken in reading and reading, in reading over and overreading so that nothing can overwrite the ecstatically temporizing poem. By positing the particularity of the I that reads, Wordsworth, moreover, prevents himself from generalizing this pleasure or imputing it to other readers. This is his pleasure, possibly as unshareable as it is unreadable.

The rapturous excess with which Wordsworth writes, reads, remembers the poem has understandably puzzled the critics and friends (often the same) of the poet. His unwavering loyalty to an apparently simplistic production when compared to the spare grandeur and reflective rigor of many of his other works made little sense. If his glee had been a momentary flash within the unfolding narrative of a sensibility, his critics might have let it go or pathologized and localized it, if need be, as part of his breakdown following the disappointment with the French Revolution, understanding his pleasure to inflect part of "a history only of departed things / Or a mere fiction of what never was,"[21] forgiving his attachment to the vulnerable boy who preceded the babe "who with his soul / Drinks in the feelings of his Mother's eye" (*Prelude* 2.236–37), a child who anticipates "the first / Poetic spirit of our human life" (2.260–61). And the tapping out of pleasure located to this poem was unabating, intractable. What could account for such an anomaly of spirit?

It was not the case simply that Wordsworth was blind to its vulnerability as poetic object, for he fully expected rejection, basing the inevitability of rejection on the poem being "so materially different from those upon which general approbation is at present bestowed."[22] The poem, if not roundly repudiated, was embraced, feared Coleridge, for reasons that remained altogether unflattering, for reasons that he described as stemming from "the gilded side" of "SIMPLICITY." Wordsworth was turned in the eyes of "some affected admirers [into] . . . a *sweet, simple poet!* and *so* natural, that little master Charles, and his young sister, are so charmed with them, that they play at 'Goody Blake' or at 'Johnny and Betty Foy!' "[23] Disturbed by the poem and its implications for his friend's reception, Coleridge enjoined Wordsworth to defend his "faery" vision against easy assimilations and inevitable accusations of "SIMPLICITY" — the "vulgarity of style, subject and conception" decried in *Biographia Literaria* (2:158) — and urged by means of prescriptive demand that he set about conceiving "the FIRST GENUINE PHILOSOPHIC POEM" (2:156). He tried to pull the friend away from the "Idiot Boy" by recalling, at one point, the divine status ascribed to his own son, Hartley,

in Wordsworth's "Immortality" ode. Coleridge asks: "at what time were we dipt in the Lethe, which has produced such utter oblivion of a state so godlike?" (2:138–39). Wordsworth capitulated. The power of Coleridge's truck with his co-writer has been gauged variously and according to different valences. In "The Idiot Boy as Healer," to cite a somewhat severe but sanctioned position, Ross Woodman argues that Wordsworth "makes the tragic mistake of attempting to answer Coleridge on his own ground, a ground which Coleridge himself admitted had crushed his own poetic spirit (he finally, in more than one sense, abandoned 'Christabel'). Unable on moral grounds to inhabit for long a mythopoetic world, when philosophy failed him, Coleridge was driven to theology where the guilt-ridden poet finally offered himself upon the altar of the 'infinite I AM.'"[24] According to this view, Wordsworth will have begun the long haul into conservative constriction when the poet advisor moved in on him. "The Idiot Boy" was the last wild ride on poetic license.

A fugitive, the "Idiot Boy" had momentarily escaped Coleridge's detection systems and was spared his castrative legislations; from then on Wordsworth was put on probation and had to report to his probation officer, probing and testing for approval, refining the machinery by which, according to Hartman, "each poem becomes a new test of the imagination."[25] "The Idiot Boy," sprung from the test drive and off probation, had enacted its thematic register, wandering off "from eight o'clock till five" (l. 446) into an enchanted forest preserved by the lunar realm of maternal light. If the poem had been released "almost extempore" in a mood of "glee" during what the poet calls "those happy moments," returning to him ever as the "glad animal movements," "arching joys," and "dizzy raptures" of an earlier period of his life that, as he recognizes in "Tintern Abbey," are "now no more,"[26] it is surely in no small way because the poem rigorously performs what it tells, holding Wordsworth by the maternal injunction — or if such a yoking of the maternal and law be implausible, then by the seductions of unconditional devotion: the poem itself, flawed and vulnerable, ever in his affectionate custody, *is* his idiot child, "so materially different," etc. And so the idiot poem, corresponding to the idiolect of his heart, the babe of babes, older and younger at once, in perpetual need of protection if its survival were to be ensured, had special claims upon the poetic bosom. If there was to be a community of the isolated ones — a community of solitudes, as Nietzsche might say — it would be gathered together in the safehold of maternal care. "Care," however, also means and unleashes anxiety, which the poem follows down to its suicidal umbilicus. When Betty Foy momentarily lets go of her boy, her anxiety ("Unworthy things she talked, and wild; / Even he, of cattle the most mild, / The Pony had his share" [ll. 239–41]) swiftly translates into murderous rage, and, guided by a sense of unappeasable loss, she gradually turns the rage against herself ("O woe is me! O woe is me! / Here will I die; here will I die /.../.../.../ O! what a wretched Mother I!" [ll. 262–66]). Losing the boy, she risks losing her mind ("Her thoughts are bent on deadly sin /.../.../ Lest she should drown herself therein" [ll. 293–96]). But he will be found. In fact, he functions as the refusal of loss, as the very opposite of the experience of deprivation for which he has been made to stand. This refusal has little to do with mere denial, tracing as it does affirmatory possibilities of deprivation.

Though isolated, Wordsworth's Boy is not alone. The idiot boys penned in the eighteenth century by poets tend to dwell in the reserve of uninhibited maternal love. As absolute phallus and devotional object, they inhabit a maternally demarcated zone where father's mighty objections are not let in. The mothers, often widows, in any case form a uniquely fused couple with the idiot child. Wordsworth, as mother, does not come to his station naturally but models the spontaneity of unbounded affection on political difference. The poet has witnessed, he writes, loving parents of idiot children: he speaks of the softened and open hearts of the so-called lower classes. Samuel Taylor Coleridge, Wordsworth's partner in rime, had no access to the space of this relatedness, upon which he would break and enter with a massive "non du père," instituting law and severing the maternal Wordsworth from her little idiot poem. The severance was to be sealed and supplemented with the introduction of a paternal phallus, that of PHILOSOPHY.

Under Coleridge's influence Wordsworth endeavored to explain, in the 1800 preface to the poem, his turn toward "humble and rustic life." Instead of clearing his name and pinning his fame, he further exposes himself to the kind of criticism aimed at him by Coleridge when he asserts, contravening the phallic order, that the rustic's language is "a more permanent, and a far more philosophical language, than that which is frequently substituted for it by Poets."[27] The subversion is subtle, for he has recruited philosophical language to his cause rather than abandon, as Coleridge might have hoped, the rustic lexicon. Still, as he defends the poem with Coleridge looking over his shoulder, the poet lets up, allowing it to be read as a mock-heroic poem, what in Woodman's view amounts to a kind of Worthsworthian *Dunciad*. Coleridge had nailed the

designation when describing the poem's effect upon the "general reader" as "a laughable burlesque."[28] While the preface, offering a compromise formation Intended to protect the poem and appease the critics, operates as a concession to Coleridge, Wordsworth, though led to other projects and a philosophically more legitimated use of language, never really lets his partner at the "Idiot Boy." The poem-child remains defended from his incursions, secured against his insertions. Thus, the exceptional letter written to John Wilson — a way of (not) writing a letter to father — bypassing Coleridge yet binding Wilson to the same destination as the one more or less patched into the dispatch, avers: "A friend of mine knowing that some persons had a dislike to the poem, such as you have expressed, advised me to add a stanza describing the person of the Boy [so as] entirely to separate him in the imaginations of my readers from that class of idiots who are disgusting in their persons; but the narration in the poem is so rapid and impassioned, that I could not find a place in which to insert the stanza without checking the progress of it and [so leave] a deadness upon the feeling" (1:357–58). The passage to the Boy is blocked off from Coleridge, for, as the letter implies, stating its dread to the letter, the insertion of Coleridge would be death; it would spread a deadness of feeling, strike a castrative blow against the poem: his addition would amount to a subtraction. What was meant to fill gaps and blanks would take away from the poem; his entering the body of the poem would signify a depletion, a check in its (my) progress. Coleridge has legislated severance and separation ("entirely to separate him," etc.), which Wordsworth resists integrating; he cannot even separate out disgust but seeks to dissolve in the reader "every feeble sensation of disgust and aversion." The maternal figure of Betty Foy grows into the space of the poem without allowing for editorial excursion or incursion. She expresses "the great triumph of the human heart." "It is there," offers Wordsworth, "that we see the strength, disinterestedness, and grandeur of love" (1:357). The poet essentially sticks with the threat of the disgusting that does not scruple to support an emphatic attachment to the idiot child. A "deadness upon the feeling" will check in later, sealing more successful installations of an overseeing superego.

The letter — in a sense meant for Coleridge but sent to his proxy, Wilson, though not an idiot but still a boy — breaks with Wordsworth's noted inability to write letters, an inability stemming partly "from some constitutional infirmities, and partly from certain habits of mind." He tended not to write any letters "unless on business, not even to [his] dearest friends." In fact, he adds, that "except during absence from my own family I have not written five letters of friendship during the last five years" (1:353). Whether or not the letter addressed to Wilson constitutes such a letter of friendship is not stated but implied, and this ambiguity serves to complicate the itinerary of connections and missing links attaching Wordsworth to Coleridge. The death threat to the poem had to be averted, and Wordsworth pulled himself together and into his body in order to launch the missive. We know from Wordsworth's letter to Thomas De Quincey that writing attacked his body, distressing his organs: "I have a kind of derangement in my stomach and digestive organs which makes writing painful to me, and indeed almost prevents me from holding correspondence with any body: and this (I mean to say the unpleasant feelings I have connected with the act of holding a Pen) has been the chief cause of my long silence."[29] The maternalizing sister, Dorothy, his amanuensis, who long held the pen for the poet, was not sent for. The anxiety snaked up his digestive organs. This John Wilson, a placeholder, was not just any body. So on this occasion Wordsworth had to write the letter himself.

He holds his body together and writes back to Wilson and his friends. "The poem has, I know, frequently produced the same effect as it did upon you and your friends," he writes, "but there are many also to whom it affords exquisite delight, and who, indeed, prefer it to any other of my poems" (1:298). The many others, here unaccounted for, are pulled by Coleridge in the wake, traced in *The Prelude,* that will have translated infant joy into an elegy for a dead child — a memorializing act that enshrines the beloved Boy.[30] The mother in Wordsworth must mourn, let go. *The Excursion* follows, controlled in the first book by the figure of a mother who abandons her children to her despair, leaving them "in the impotence of grief."[31] He, the poet, makes her an offering of his blessing, detaches himself, turning away to wander another path, with difficulty: " — An irksome drudgery seems it to plod on" (l. 322). Turning away, he does not efface; nor does he see repression of past attachment as an option, for "Dumb yearnings, hidden appetites are ours," Wordsworth maintains in *The Prelude,* "And they *must* have their food" (5.509). This would revoke the law laid down by Coleridge, posing a counterlaw that provides for incontrovertible appetitive prerogatives, hidden and dumb though they may be, over and against the steel-fisted laws of philosophical reflection. Wordsworth, for her part, serves the dumb yearnings some food.

We know where we have friends. Ye dreamers, then,
Forgers of daring Tales! we bless you then,
Imposters, drivellers, dotards, as the ape
Philosophy will call you: then *we feel*
With what, and how great might ye are in league,
Who make our wish our power, our thought a deed,
An empire, a possession. (*Prelude*, 5.525–31)

Turning away, detaching, Wordsworth mourns the passages in *The Excursion* that make way for the "pale despair" of the solitary. He was not alone in mourning the meaning that his earlier works would hold. Shelley, in *Alastor*, reads *The Excursion* in terms that suggest the defeat of Wordsworth as a visionary poet; he laments the willingness to sacrifice to Christian faith the "dumb yearnings, hidden appetites."

"The Idiot Boy" stood up against the cultural sedimentations of Christianity. The boy is neither saved nor miraculated; he becomes the object of a mother's hysterical anxiety, tormenting her in the accidental enactment of separation. The scene of his being found does not host the theme of redemption but conjures up magical wonder. Though her name might indicate faith (*foi,* in French), Betty Foy has no recourse to such metaphysical comforts as a religious narrative might bestow. It has been suggested that the evacuated skies and magical cures of Betty Foy disappear, degenerate in the poet's oeuvre, as age and insight progress into the codified miracles of the Christian faith. Wordsworth, according to Shelley, finally failed in his effort to approach the "inmost sanctuary" of "our great Mother."[32]

These remarks have been made in response to the incomparable pleasure with which Wordsworth associated the writing and reading of "The Idiot Boy" and that continued to restore to the poet the memory of a time when his body embraced the poem, excribed joy. The disjunction between pleasure and poetic value cannot be overlooked; nor are we meant to stabilize a reading that laments the quality or tenor of the poetry to come. The painful acts of severance that Wordsworth was condemned to repeat appear to be related to the constraints of writing — Coleridge, in a word — that he welcomed. "The Idiot Boy" occupied a unique place for the poet and never lost its affective stature; yet it was not alone in terms of where it was going. The ballad belongs to a repertoire of poetic concerns organized around the political blight of "legalised exclusion." Deeply sensitive to what must be classed as social injustice, Wordsworth reflected on his past involvement with the French Revolution, a cause to which he became strongly committed under the influence of Michel Beaupuy. His sense of horror was provoked on one occasion by what became an unforgettable image of destitution to which he devoted a passage in *The Prelude*. "And when we chanced / One day to meet a hunger-bitten girl," the poet writes of her,

> Who crept along fitting her languid gait
> Unto a heifer's motion, by a cord
> Tied to her arm, and picking thus from the lane
> Its sustenance, while the girl with pallid hands
> Was busy knitting in a heartless mood
> Of solitude, and at the sight my friend
> In agitation said, "'Tis against that
> That we are fighting," I with him believed
> That a benignant Spirit was abroad
> Which might not be withstood, that poverty
> Abject as this would in a little time
> Be found no more, that we should see the earth
> Unthwarted in her wish to recompence
> The meek, the lowly, patient child of toil.
> All institutes for ever blotted out
> That legalised exclusion, empty pomp
> Abolished, sensual State and cruel Power,
> Whether by edict of the one or few;
> And finally, as sum and crown of all,
> Should see the People having a strong hand
> In framing their own Laws; whence better days
> To all mankind. (9.509–32)

Ever focused on that which has been excluded, minoritized and abjected by institutions capable of producing effects of power, the poet turns his forces against those practitioners of "legalised exclusion" evinced in the higher ranks of poetic vision or philosophical analysis. Wordsworth does not relinquish the neighborhood of moods in which the Idiot Boy dwells but continues in his endeavor to evoke sympathy where he has provoked disgust. In the case of "The Idiot Boy," he has stacked the codified levels of disgust, meaning deliberately to flood "every feeble sensation of disgust and aversion" with his poetic "deluge."[33]

His poetic activism, he wrote to Wilson, consisted in the intent to awaken in his readers what he had often observed in "lower classes of society": "the conduct of fathers and mothers ... towards Idiots" (1:357). The reading classes were to be educated by the lower classes, whose conduct, exemplified in Betty Foy, gave unique access to "the great triumph of the human heart." Having witnessed such love — strong, disinterested, grand — Wordsworth describes himself as "hallowed" by it. He has experienced something about which he feels it crucial that "people in our rank" encounter. "[It] is not enough for me as a Poet," he offers, "to delineate merely such feelings as all men *do* sympathize with: but it is also highly desirable to add to these others, such as many men *may* sympathize with, and such as there is reason to believe they would be better and more moral beings if they did sympathize with" (1:358). Poetico-political activism converges with a healing art. Hallowing and healing, the poetic experience traverses a danger zone like a fever, by which sensibility is somehow cleansed, restored, bettered. In order to feel, in order to heal, one instills feelings of what one does not feel, and in feeling what one may feel, which is a hypothetical feeling bodyguarded by reasoned morality, one acquires a feeling for the future of feeling — a turn, the poet indicates, for the better of feeling.

Unwilling to repress the instances of disgust that formed the basis for Coleridge's concern, Wordsworth has prepared an emetic formula. Poetry circumscribes the site of a healing crisis, making room for the convulsive contortions of a massive readjustment. In poetry the poet induces a fever meant to cleanse or realign; s/he administers disgust as *pharmakon*. It is all a matter of dosage. In his article naming the poet as healer, Woodman sees Wordsworth's purpose as healing the reader, much as the Idiot Boy heals Susan Gale, who, forgetting her own debilitating ailment, has turned her mind to the boy and his mother: "I'll to the wood," she cries. "The word scarce said," the poem goes on, "Did Susan rise up from her bed, / As if by magic cured" (ll. 424–26). The poem makes known its intention in these lines and articulates the law of its resurrectionist desire: it means to effect such healing powers over the reader. Woodman never interrogates the concept itself of healing or of a restorative poetics, though his interpretation remains tempting to adopt. While Wordsworth refrains from offering an elaborate account according to whose terms we can consider his readers as ill or in need of spontaneous healing rituals — moreover, he shows that the feelings targeted by the poem do not, as such, exist in the present — it is the case that Susan Gale is a figure for sudden recovery. When she turns her thoughts to one who is lost, possibly dead on her account, she makes a resolve, and energy — inexplicably — returns. How does the poem effect the magical recuperation? Naming her resolve, she is healed. If this designates a magical occurrence, as the poem insists it does, then perhaps we are asked to decipher a magic formula.

The inexplicable wave of magic wandering — the suggestion of a magic saying or formula — is another way of being exhorted to read the unreadable, in other words, to read the action of a poem. How has the language of the resolve entered her body, performed a cure? What was injected to allow her to rise? This serum — it is a matter of a diachronic mark. "I'll to the wood" underscores the fragile mark that separates a self from the condition of being ill, that which contracts the will, the apostrophe: I(')ll. Susan Gale, prepared to follow the Idiot Boy into the wood, splinters her illness into an "I'llness," inserting a wedge into the signifier from which she's sprung. As if by magic. Susan Gale is resurrected not by miracle but by magic, by something that cannot be assimilated to determined systems of another, often Christian, logic of healing. Wordsworth is manifestly less concerned with depicting the history of a redemptive crisis or monitoring a conversion hysteria pulled by transcendental strings than with the immediate effects of an utterance that regroups the body under its unpredictable command. Susan Gale is magically cured; this may not be identical to a healing, which implies a process that can be engaged with no cure in sight. (Or a cure can occur, as in some of Freud's insertions, without process, by means of a decisive intervention, with the introduction of a signifier — even on the order of an apostrophe.)

Language is body; it enters the body, forming or deforming it, putting up a force field to which organs respond. The wedge introduced into the "ill" body opens up the space for a certain experience of selfhood where there has been a transfer, among the three actors, of care. Betty Foy had been caring for her sick neighbor, Susan, when she felt called upon to risk her son by sending him off to find the doctor. The story, structured as a feminine Abrahamic one, offers up the beloved son, who, in mute compliance, accepts without question the sacrificial fate. (He cannot question, but then neither could Isaac.) This time the sacrifice is revoked. By the panicked mother. The test called off, Ms. Foy reclaims her boy after intense and harrowing backtracking. There is no God to guide her. In the poem the grandeur of love engenders more love, staging the pursuit of the double maternal figures that enable movement and recovery in a nearly comical hierarchy of the infirm helping the infirm, the illiter-

ate helping the idiot, the hopeless helping the helpless. The only stable being of reliable solidity is the pony, the designated "thinker" and driver upon which the Idiot Boy is propped — literally set up ("But then he is a horse that thinks! / And when he thinks, his pace is slack …" [ll. 112–13]).

The women follow the boy into the woods, losing him and finding him, interrogating his whereabouts and destination. When, after enduring a night of calamitous anxiety, she finally discovers him, Betty Foy becomes for a moment the questioning philosopher of the eighteenth century who comes upon the wild child, an entity of her own invention: "Tell us true. … Where have you been?" Well, in the first place the idiot has been in the custody of the empiricists. So, in a sense, it was wrong of Coleridge to inveigh against a poem that would require, in his view, a philosophical correctional facility, or wrong of us to think that Coleridge had not found tracks in this woods to indicate that Wordsworth was already on the trail of philosophical investigation. The Idiot Boy has been plucked from philosophy and transported on the back of a more thinking animal to poetical fields.

In the sixteenth or seventeenth century the idiot blended in with the rest of the passengers on the ship of fools, a character among many tucked haphazardly in the margins of knowledge, unnoted as category and *Dasein* or meshed into madness. They — idiots — emerged in the discourse on knowledge, being held distinct from the insane, in Locke's *Essay Concerning Human Understanding*. They were pressed into service, assigned to uphold the mythic assurances of a humanly clean slate, presenting such a possibility, in theory, at least, to the extent that they — idiots — donated their bodies to the cause of a science that staked everything on what appeared to constitute observable traits of human origins. Essentially an essay on memory, Locke's treatise drafts the idiot for the purposes of supporting his polemic against the doctrine of "innate impressions." "All *Children,* and *Ideots,*" Locke observes, "have not the least Apprehension or thought of them."[34] Because these impressions cannot be said to exist as the purity of origin that the child or idiot approximates, Locke infers that memories cannot be deemed "natural" or innate to man but are rather effects and must be produced. The idiot betokens the inability to produce or retain memories. If idiots, to the contrary, proved to possess innate memories, these would "shine out in their full lustre, and leave us no more doubt of their being there. … But alas, among *Children, Ideots, Savages,* and the grossly *Illiterate,* what general maxims are to be found? What universal principles of knowledge?" (1.II.§27). The idiot, along with the other members of the lineup, not only annuls memory from the start but can be seen to threaten the premises of philosophical inquiry to the extent that it exhibits an originary force that, cutting through generality, repels universal principals of knowledge. Recruited into philosophy to make a philosophical point, the idiot belongs outside the philosophy whose cause it promotes. Locke, essentially inventing the "Ideot," remembers the forgotten idiot in order to produce a discourse on originary forgetting. In any case — and to generalize — Locke has produced the function and place of the idiot from which the empiricist inquiry into the conditions of memory proceeds.[35] The figure of the idiot henceforth inserts an imaginary lesion in philosophy — a condition that calls out for endless symbolic repair. A provisional conclusion to be drawn from these observations is that Wordsworth's resolute embrace of such determined marginalization cannot be limited to a program imagined to consist of romantic wistfulness, exalted primitivism or sentimentalism, or even peculiar affective investment, but it responds to the call of philosophy in terms that spell out the empiricist claim on an original subjectivity. When the Idiot Boy forgets the rules prescribed by his mother as he is sent off to find the doctor, the receptacle of codified knowledge in the poem, he breaks away from the instructions and strictures of his philosophical container, which mother momentarily embodies. She temps for empirical philosophy. He, on the other hand, he's carried away by the thinking animal in a direction prompted by another instinct or, more precisely, by another drive.

Viewed in large strokes, empiricism was a critical force that braved itself to any authority that claimed to be situated beyond what is available to observation and experience. As concerns its need to observe and experience the idiot, it crashed against the wall of the real. In keeping with a more familiar register, we can say that it encountered an aporetic limit. What could be said, strictly speaking, to be observable in the mute resistance or the nondisclosive docility of the idiot? How could idiocy responsibly answer to the quest for the origin of human memory or serve as a solid example of a state of forgetting, "where sensations pass by without ever being retained, [which] would seem to indicate that such a state existed for men in general, prior to their development of the ability to remember and, later, to record events and impressions"?[36] Tracking man in his transit from a state of nature to culture, language, and memory is not something that can be accomplished by observation. A concession to the aporetic snag heads up Condillac's em-

piricist *Treatise on the Sensations:* "We cannot recollect the ignorance in which we were born. It is a state which leaves no traces behind it. We remember our ignorance only when we remember what we have learned. We must already know something before we can attend to what we are learning. We must have ideas before we can observe that we were once without them. Reflective memory, which makes us conscious of the passage of one cognition to another, cannot go back to beginnings: it supposes them."[37] Reflective memory places us before contradictory tensions, what one critic has called a "structural infirmity,"[38] for memory can find no trace and has no memory of its emergence; memory is unable to remember the conditions that made it possible and cannot account for its own genesis to the extent that such a gesture assumes the existence of those faculties it seeks to explain. Because no observable traces of prehistory or of the earliest stirrings of consciousness can be reasonably ascertained, Condillac, for his part, reverted to a notion of "hypothetical" or "conjectural" history, which, prevalent among the empiricists of the latter half of the eighteenth century, handled the problem with philosophical urgency but elicited the dismay of social scientists. One such being, an Adam Ferguson, protested that it confounded "the provinces of imagination and reason, of poetry and science."[39]

Empiricism did not counter the objection but recognized that, as a discursive practice beholden to factual ground, it could not construct much of an argument by relying solely upon hypothetical demonstration. Casting about for empirical support, Condillac took recourse to the story of a "wild child" discovered in the forests of Lithuania in 1694 and incorporated this particular form and performance of idiocy into eighteenth-century philosophy. Leaving aside the fact that the wild child is constituted as story, its inclusion in the philosophical text was seen to function as an empirical supplement to speculation. A fable of origins, it supplied the missing links to cover the transit between the state of nature and man, between original forgetting and culture. Making a fairly typical reference to such a child, Lord Monboddo states, "I consider his history as a brief chronicle or abstract of the history of progress of human nature, from the mere animal to the first stage of civilised life."[40] While Condillac's inclusion of the wild child of Lithuania allows for the appearance in his demonstration of a metaphorical lure of the state of nature, he situates him within a hypothetical history. Condillac observes that when the child learned to speak, the prospects faded for his giving a retrospective account of his experience in the forest prior to and without language: "As soon as he could speak, he was questioned concerning his former state, but he could remember no more about it than we can remember what happened to us in the cradle" (225). Drawing a blank about the events preceding his initiation into speech, the child, no longer an *infans* (i.e., incapable of speech), demonstrated that memory is an effect of culture; indeed, "it was perfectly natural for him to forget his first state.... His life was a sleep interrupted only by dreams" (226). If we were pursuing another path, we would feel compelled to enter the scene of this interruption, to interrogate the status of dreams in terms of their inherent linguisticity. But let us remain within the flow of unhampered interruptions, with this eighteenth-century dream team, and leave the other team in the future of this unanalyzed, if seamed, dream. Given that the wild child cannot remember his origins, the philosopher has found legitimation in reverting to hypothetical history. Hence the section on the wild child of Lithuania, being of no more use to a philosophy of memory than a wild child of lithium might be, concludes with a chapter, "The Memory of One Who Has Been Given the Use of His Senses in Succession" — centering Condillac's famous imaginary statue capable of giving a complete account of itself, of "that dark scene in which memory and consciousness struggle into being out of pure sensation and pleasure and pain" (225–26).

There was a hierarchy of wild children. One of the most celebrated of the wild children was Peter of Hanover, whose discovery — he was caught in a tree in the woods outside Hamelin in 1724 — made him "an instant celebrity": "Soon after his appearance, it was learned that he was a congenital idiot, the son of a widower named Krüger, who had recently remarried.... many philosophers and natural scientists saw Peter as exactly the person for whom they were searching."[41] Yet another prestigious signatory weighed in on this matter. In *Mere Nature Delineated,* Daniel Defoe, who had been reluctant to endorse the myths surrounding wild children — that they ran on all fours like animals and climbed trees, or, for us, swinging Tarzan-style — nonetheless confirms Peter's importance. Defoe reminds his readers that philosophy and its like had not simply "brought an Ideot upon the Stage, and made a great Something out of Nothing."[42] The wild child responds to a specific philosophical need, being "the very Creature which the learned World have, for many Years past, pretended to wish for, viz., one that being kept entirely from human Society so as never to have heard any one speak, must therefore either not speak at all, or, if he did from any speech to himself, then they should know what Language Nature should first form

for mankind" (17). Philosophy will have found what it was looking for, which is to say that it more or less invented the lost object that was meant to confirm its theories. A philosophical wish fulfillment, the creature inserts itself into an imaginary trajectory.

In accord with the understanding of eighteenth-century empiricists, Defoe sees idiocy as that which, enjoying no access to language, is furthermore bereft of feeling, soul, or passion. Disabled in terms of feeling, the idiot exemplifies language deprivation, marking a loss that according to Defoe abolishes the scale of human affect and a basic relatedness to things. "Words are to us, the Medium of Thought," he writes. "We cannot conceive of Things, but by their names, and in the very Use of their names . . . we cannot muse, contrive, imagine, design, resolve, or reject; nay we cannot love or hate, but in acting upon those Passions in the Very Form of Words, and we have no other way for it" (39). The idiot conjures the blind man when compared to a being incapable of even receiving, much less retaining or remembering, visual impressions: "Nature seems *to him,* like a fine Picture to a Blind Man, ONE UNIVERSAL BLANK . . . he sees the Surface of it but seems to receive no Impression from it of one Kind, or of another"(27). There occur aporias that are not touched by the blind philosopher: if the idiot belongs to and is inextricable from nature — that is, to the extent that the idiot *is* nature — why would he have to receive impressions from nature as if it were other, say (to stay with the provocatively perverse rhetoricity of the example), as if nature were artifice, "a fine Picture"? Nature, like idiocy, is an effect of the erasure of naturality, a figure of lost literality. This is where Wordsworth could come in, but the defective cornerstone of his demonstration already shows up for Defoe as the logic collapses in on itself, knocking out a wall in the empirical house of idiocy.

Now, much more can be said about the induction of wild children, savages, idiots, and children into the realm of philosophical speculation, and it would be important to investigate more fully the peculiar yet crucial status of these minorities as philosophy conducts its adult raids. From Socrates' predatory urges to Kant's racist assignments, philosophy has demonstrated a need to impound those who cannot speak for themselves, who have not reached a certain legislated majority, though Nietzsche may be seen to have turned this around when he invited the animals to participate in a new tropology.[43]

In the case of Wordsworth, and including Dostoevsky, we are faced with the figure of the idiot for whom language is not entirely foreclosed, though absences, the predominance of muteness, and a repertoire of stammers govern the scene of idiocy. Still, there are reprieves and the event of memory; language, however jumbled, mimetic, deregulated, occurs and belongs to the existence to which idiocy is fitted. Something like interiority does not appear to take hold. Yet even when these idiots are finally silenced there is no doubt that they have been traversed by something that resembles feeling — maybe a pinch of joy, a sting of regret, a body memory that trembles. With no language of interiority to vouch for feeling, they are more or less stranded, bared to colonializing projection. Vaulted and shut, their subjectivity — if there is one — offers little in the way of an account; even so, in both cases they surpass or at least scramble the master codes of philosophical claims made on their behalf and occupy a space that is liminal in terms of sheer idiocy — they are touched, however fleetingly, by language. And speech, when it fades, resolves into the written codifications for which their bodies stand.

How did they stumble into philosophical headquarters? How did they enter a contract according to whose fine print they could suddenly be "found"? Their very deprivation engenders desire, produces an unavowable nostalgia. Why else would the idiots be pushed toward the sacred or sicced on God? How is it that they have God on their side even where He is disavowed?

They are gloriously deprived of the real — a condition, says Lacan, reading the troubadour, that answers to the demand of the being we call man.[44] At the moment when empiricism puts out a search for that which can establish some reality behind the speculative drive, when it seeks to brush aside the fictions and fancies of prior philosophical maneuvers bolstered by imaginary armament, it claims to discover itself in those beings that, held in the real and resistant to symbolizing acts, somehow *pose* the real in its extreme unreadability. There is something that empiricism gets close to when it encounters a nearly traceless path prior to the inscriptions of language. Yet if the idiot were made to represent the proper beginnings of language, the place where the first hints of symbolizing urges could be detected, it would be wrong to think that the experience of deprivation simply ended with the introduction of nonmimetic language. For, as Wordsworth has taught us, like the body, language as trope is always privative.[45]

The Idiot Boy, propped up on a horse like a troubadour, will never arrive at his determined destination. The poem shows his mother strapping him in and prescribing directions to the doctor's house. She gives the

pony instructions, she reminds Johnny to return to her ("Johnny! Johnny! mind that you / Come home again, nor stop at all — / Come home again, whate'er befall, / My Johnny, do, I pray you, do" [ll. 58–61]). Susan Gale's life depends upon it. As you already know, Johnny gets lost, his mother wigs out, Susan Gale magically resurrects, the doctor knows from nothing, and Johnny is finally found in the woods, near a loud waterfall. Betty and Susan, overwhelmed with joy, bring Johnny home with them. They ask him where he's been, how he's spent the night. There's a narrator in there who suggests that his own talents are not up to the task; he may even be mentally impaired. It has taken him fourteen years (rather than the customary seven) to complete his apprenticeship. He is slow to comprehend. In fact, he is incapable of telling the story, on which he draws a blank. The muses are not his friends. Nor are Wordsworth's editors. Jack Stillinger, in his 1965 edition of selected Wordsworth poems, indicates that fourteen years is intended to "show that the narrator is a bit slow-witted."[46] The secondary drama of narrative stupidity is not aleatory or incidental, a hiccup along the path of poetic recounting. (Where poetry does not demonstrate its stupefaction, halt or falter, it sometimes sends the empirical shadow of the poet to the Hölderlin-Turm, on Lenz's walks or through Artaud's howls.)

The narrative stall around the events that take Johnny away recapitulates the initiatory drama of not knowing: Susan, who dwells alone, is making a "piteous moan" (l. 20):

No hand to help them in distress;
Old Susan lies a-bed in pain,
And sorely puzzled are the twain,
For what she ails they cannot guess[.] (ll. 23–26)

They are caught in the spiraling despair of naming her illness; it is a task that makes them a couple, Susan and Betty, as it sunders them in two, in twain. The effort of deciphering her condition is itself associated with pain; they are *sorely* puzzled, stumped, unable to guess. Cut to the narrator, who also is caught in the predicament of guessing, or of having his guessing powers disabled. We learn by so many inroads that we have before us a tale that cannot be told. It is a matter of a story whose center is missing, given over to hypothetical conjuring. It is a story, organized around a missing story, that by necessity produces speculative excess. The repetition of "perhaps," which occurs when the narrator attempts to puzzle together the clues of an absent center, throws the voice against the winds of scientific knowledge or narratorial authority. Abandoned

273

by the muses, the narrator abandons any assurance of knowing his narration. Indeed, the only thing the poem has claimed to read, to be able to know, is Betty Foy's face ("But Betty, poor good woman! she, / You plainly in her face may read it, / Could lend out of that moment's store / Five years of happiness or more / To any that might need it" [ll. 132–36]). The narrative function disabled, the secret of the story remains with the beloved Idiot Boy, locked in his silence ("The moon that shines above his head / Is not more still and mute than he" [ll. 80–81]). Still, we have a proliferation of *perhapses* to hold onto, a distant relative of the same *perhaps* that Nietzsche says brought metaphysics to its knees. For who can live in the sphere of the perhaps?[47] It designates, in the poem, the milieu of maternal undoing, opening onto the abyss of wild speculation. It loosens the destiny of the boy — he has slipped into the terrifying realm of the perhaps. There is so little to hold on to when you are traveling at the speed of perhaps. The narrator turns in any case to me, as if asking for clemency, as if bowed by the burden of a confession:

> Oh Reader! now that I might tell
> What Johnny and his Horse are doing!
> What they've been doing all this time,
> Oh could I put it into rhyme,
> A most delightful tale pursuing!
>
> Perhaps, and no unlikely thought!
> He with his Pony now does roam
> The cliffs and peaks so high that are,
> To lay his hands upon a star,
> And in his pocket bring it home.
>
> Perhaps he's turned himself about,
> His face unto his horse's tail,
> And, still and mute, in wonder lost,
> All silent as a horseman-ghost,
> He travels slowly down the vale.
>
> And now, perhaps, is hunting sheep,
> A fierce and dreadful hunter he;
> Yon valley, now so trim and green,
> In five months' time, should he be seen,
> A desert wilderness will be!

Perhaps, with head and heels on fire,
And like the very soul of evil,
He's galloping away, away,
And so will gallop on for aye,
The bane of all that dread the devil!

I to the Muses have been bound,
These fourteen years by strong indentures:
O gentle Muses! Let me tell
But half of what to him befell;
He surely met with strange adventures.

O gentle Muses! is this kind?
Why will ye thus my suit repel?
Why of your further aid bereave me?
And can ye thus unfriended leave me;
Ye Muses! whom I love so well? (ll. 312–46)

Now here is what's maddening, truly scary about the poem. Dunked in idiocy, avowing impairment, it, on the level of *saying,* mimes the balladeer's upgrade of the nursery rhyme. As intelligible utterance goes, this seems manageable, a critical piece of cake. Offsetting the deceptive ease with which it goes about its way, that is, about its say, something occurs that, namely, does not occur. On the level of *doing* it enacts the poetic predicament par excellence, so that the stutter or stammer around the event that cannot be told reverberates from Hölderlin to Mallarmé, traveling in the first place from the loud waterfall near poem's end to "Der Rhein." Determined to tell a story about idiocy, the poem hovers on the edge of aphasia (or "pure idiom"). Even when it has Johnny speak, it cites a whirring sound to which affect can be only arbitrarily assigned: "His lips with joy they burr at you" (l. 14); "And Johnny burrs, and laughs aloud; / Whether in cunning or joy / I cannot tell" (ll. 377–79). Part of the poem recognizes itself in Johnny's nonsignifying language, at the limit of saying, and holds with him vigilance over the silent experience of poetry. What it does as a poem is to relate to his flight without relating; it cannot tell what has happened — it cannot become story — but can only tell of an ungraspable event, a missing present, the enigma of its source. It can follow its theme and object into the disappearance of the present, but it remains constrained by idiocy when called upon to render present "what happened." The poem is mute when it comes to assuming the burden of its central assignment. It cannot get to the doctor's house, the analyst's couch, the empiricist's lair. Escaping containment, it shrinks from observability. Unable to master the enigma of its source, the poem gets lost on its drive to tell, to recount; the poem wrenches the story away from itself. In its moment of catastrophic truth-telling, nothing occurs but the serialization of the *perhapses*. The ineffectual narrator can point at most to the pure suspension of occurrence: a caesura or a syncope. "This is what 'drawing a blank' means. What is suspended, arrested, tipping suddenly into strangeness, is the presence of the present (the being-present of the present). And what then occurs without occurring (for it is by definition what cannot occur) is — without being — nothingness, the 'nothing of being.'"[48] The poem cannot tell where the Idiot Boy has been, where he has come from, or even what it means for him to be. It has the mother call for truth, ask for narration:

> *Tell us, Johnny, do,*
> *Where all this long night you have been,*
> *What you have heard, what you have seen;*
> *And, Johnny, mind you tell us true.* (ll. 438–41)

One has the sense that the poem wants to say but can't. It cannot answer to the mother's call; it cannot coax Johnny into telling the truth of his experience or any other version of his experience, for that matter. It desists, in other words, from explaining the adventure of idiocy or following it to wherever it has been in the nocturnal turn of mind. In this sense, where sense is dimmed, the poem travels in the spare light of its own lunar muteness, for it has pressed its object against the limit of poeticity: it has tried to articulate singularity, the absolute singularity for which the idiot stands and stutters — burrs, in the glacial silence of discursive stubbornness. What could the idiot have experienced or lived? it asks us. What is there to say of his absence, his flight? Poetry can't go there (the muses withdraw), but poetry must go there, indeed, has already been taken there. For poetry, as the tremor in existence that draws a blank — poetry is the idiot boy.

"The end of meaning — hiccuping, halting."[49] And so the poem, true to the ethics of singularity around which it necessarily falters, leaves the last word to the one who cannot produce sense or craft meaning, who tells in the end "all his travel's story" — the totality of a story that cannot be told but elicits a mimetic tumble down the cold path of a missing sun/son. It is no doubt of some consequence to recall here that, more than a natural object, the sun, an emblem in his later poetry of "the mind

with absolute sovereignty upon itself," becomes for Wordsworth a figure of knowledge — an eye, in de Man's rendering, that reads the text of the epitaph.[50] Here the sun turns a cold eye on the question of reading story:

> And thus, to Betty's question, he
> Made answer . . .
>
> . . . .
>
> "The cocks did crow to-whoo, to-whoo,
> And the sun did shine so cold!"
> — Thus answered Johnny in his glory,
> And that was all his travel's story. (ll. 447–53)

At once inviting and resisting figurative interpretation, Johnny's answer cites the literalists, the mimics who produce sounds that "render a faithful copy" of what they imitate.[51] In an act that turns from simplicity to seeming duplicity, he sounds the mutual mimicry of the boy and the owls that will return with the Boy of Winander, as from a distant mountaintop. But he does not speak merely from the realm of poetic monkeys, owls, and parrots, for his language tries to describe the solar withdrawal, the constancy of the other sun that left him counting out the linguistic rations of his burrs, the measure of his vacantly glacializing ecstasy. His story, a two-liner at poem's end, of barely decipherable cast, also launches the question of destiny and destination, deriving the contours of a possible identity that cannot yet be puzzled out: "to-whoo, to-whoo" (l. 450). This is the answer he made. It is also a question, poised precariously with an agrammatical abandon that repeats the irrecuperably improper essence of its object.

Socrates: Why, take the case of Thales, Theodorus. While he was studying the stars and looking upwards, he fell into a pit, and a neat, witty Thracian servant girl jeered at him, they say, because he was so eager to know the things in the sky that he could not see what was there before him at his very feet. The same jest applies to all who pass their lives in philosophy. For really such a man pays no attention to his next door neighbor; he is not only ignorant of what he is doing, but he hardly knows whether he is a human being or some other kind of creature. — Plato, *Theatetus* (174a–b)

Kant

Satellite

THE FIGURE OF THE RIDICULOUS

PHILOSOPHER;

OR, WHY I AM SO POPULAR

A. The Popularity Contest of the Faculties

This satellite is set to gather information on the paradoxes and aporias of world-class popularity. As the device that tracks its findings, I can only open the dossier on this problem. A mere copier and data bank attached invisibly to a larger apparatus, I am programmed to situate the problem and respond to its call. Scanning and recoding, I regulate the flow and generate further signals. There is something they're trying to tell me about an ancient complicity among Kant, Kierkegaard, and Kafka, and this consortium, they maintain, is related to the coordinates of what has passed for French theory. A matter of top planetary priority, high maintenance: high as Mount Moriah. Archival anxiety turning the clock back to what it never finished telling.

Backing up to the scene of a primal kind of inscription, Kafka and Kierkegaard shared an insight into the ridiculousness of Abraham. Kierkegaard's example of foolish faithfulness, which he takes up at length in *Fear and Trembling,* is Abraham: "Abraham believed and did not doubt, he believed in the preposterous."[1] Kafka's parable "Abraham," which ponders the deconstitution of the primal patriarch, evokes Kierkegaard (and Don Quixote). Multiplied and serialized, his several Abrahams are ridiculous creatures — the world, it is said, would laugh itself to death at the sight of them, one of whom is a harried waiter taking an order. Their performance of insurmountable foolishness binds them to an unforgettable saga, dividing while sealing a first letter to the Father.[2]

The data, I admit, is arriving out of sequence. Certainly not of the genre of chronological orders that scholars have endeavored to maintain. An effect of the newer technologies, the course of information flow needs first to be unscrambled and decoded. I am going to have it scan the entirety of the argument as it sifts and sorts, putting the information into a new order. It passes over the failure of cognition in Paul de Man and his secret obsessions with stupidity, ignorance, imbecility, the nitwit, and the way linguistic positing outwits the positing or suppositing subject. It continues o plot out the fractured lineage of the uninterrogated question of stupidity — the fears, the phobias, the apotropaic strategies used to cope with ≪ ≫

Entity French Theory

So there is a sequence on Schlegel's work entitled "On Unintelligibility," where a response to eighteenth-century theory bashers essentially defends the rights and necessity of unintelligibility as a basis for all creative and interpretive activity. They want to hook up Schlegel with

Bataille in terms not only of their rigorous, often courageous resistance to sense, ever bucking the production of codifiable sense but also because they were linked, if not simply historically then as pornographers of the cogito. They were fated to read each other, Bataille and Schlegel, according to pulses of a new chronicity. Friedrich Schlegel got in trouble for the pornographic code he installed in philosophical discourse. (Bataille would follow in this noncanonical act.) These incompatible codes — the pornographic and philosophical, side by side — got Friedrich disowned by all the serious Germans from Hegel to Kierkegaard and Dilthey (and Georges B., by such serious Germans as Sartre). In a sense, to sum and speed it up, Friedrich the philosophical pornographer was too French. And worse than that, he signed his name to his most offending text, *Lucinde*. Prior to that no one in his right mind had signed a work of pornography.

The memory graph of Friedrich cues a different though related kind of history: that of figuring the philosopher as ridiculous. Not as such stupid but, with an interesting displacement, perhaps an intensification — this remains to be seen — *ridiculous*. In our day the peculiar prestige of this lot has fallen to nearly everyone aligned with the destinerring of "French theory" (itself an interesting and suspiciously invested displacement of philosophy). They don't need to go after them; they do it to themselves. One thinks of Kristeva's treatment, in her roman à clef, of Foucault, who is figured as a smiling idiot, and the many images disfiguring or subjecting to ridicule Derrida, Lacan, Deleuze, Irigaray, and others. This tendency, the tendency of a certain type of human writer to be picked out of a lineup as that which is ridiculous, is not an accident or something contingent that befalls the philosopher: it has a history, one that culminates in a provocative sense in Nietzsche and the way he bounces ridicule off his corpus, nonetheless absorbing stray effects of deliberate hits: why I write such good books, why I am so clever — why I pose as ridiculous, one might add, or why I love and affirm the buffoon. Nor was Heidegger spared the claim (made by Adorno and others) of being ridiculous before he was found guilty of other, decidedly less rhetorically based charges. Who was the first ridiculous philosopher in modernity, the one who subjected himself to ridicule, deliberately abject-ng himself? This form of deliberation is what we have to explore, because his abjection is part of a calculated economy — or, to be more precise, it belongs to a *sacrificial* economy according to whose laws the philosopher will be crucified on the altar of literature. So, "Where were we?" asks the scholar.

"French Theory," given its fades and returns, is a way of avoiding having to decide or tell between literature and philosophy. Only since Kant has it become possible and necessary to distinguish between philosophy and literature. Kant presented himself and signed his work as a failed writer. This had consequences for the destiny of critical philosophy, for metaphysics, and, in a peculiar but deliberate way, for the fate of literature. Modern literature adopted Kant and participated in making Kant a popular if also a punctually ridiculed hero. For Kant, wrote Kant, could not write. He was the first to inscribe the desire of the philosopher to be *an author,* to achieve a certain literary transcendence, that is to say, to pack elegance and claim style. The problems of Kant the writer versus Kant the philosopher became everybody's business, for he prefaced the critiques and loaded his thoughts with the anxiety of failed literariness — his inability to write. He was no David Hume, he couldn't compete with this one or that one, was doomed to inelegance, and Moses (Mendelssohn) really had it over him in terms of sheer power of expression.

That Kant writes like a pig is stated repeatedly by Jean Paul, by Heine, by Nietzsche, by Musil, and by other beautiful writers, mostly ironists, but first of all by Kant himself: Kant's inability to write wounds and embarrasses the philosopher. He imposes on philosophy a mortifying ascesis. He couldn't help it. He lacked the luminous talent of elegant writing, he wrote. He couldn't help it, and it wasn't his fault. Philosophy cannot present itself directly; it is fragile, the exposition (*Darstellung*) vulnerable because it is philosophical. Time and again Kant contends that he is lacking in talent, unable to present his thought; these negative attributes invariably place his judgment and talent at issue. Yet, as Jean-Luc Nancy points out, without talent there is no transcendental constitution of knowledge.[3] A lot rides on Kant's inability to get with the program, in which talent, linked to judgment, performs crucial functions. In order to philosophize, Kant has had to lose the talent. The implications of a disabled talent are manifold for the history of metaphysics, since talent, among other things, viewed as a gift of nature and consisting in the faculty of understanding, would not depend on instruction but on the natural disposition of the subject. There is always the risk that, in the absence of talent thus understood, philosophy might lose its object and miss its point. Kant, however, claims at several junctures in his oeuvre to lack the talent that, according to the *Anthroplogy,* crowns the superior faculties of knowledge and is at one point recognized as

the acme of reason. Let us consider how Kant works this relinquishing act, for even though he can't help it and it isn't his fault and she (philosophy) started it, he relinquished, which is to say, he effected a choice, made a decision to blow off talent.

Putting together a solid motive for giving up the talent, he will have turned the negativity of the lack of talent around by switching on the transvaluating machine. Because, don't forget, ever since Kant, as Heine and Nietzsche remind us, in order to be a philosopher one has to write badly. This became part of the contract, an obtrusive imperative of the Kantian text. Owing to Kant's legacy a true philosopher henceforth will have to be a poor writer or rhetorically strung out, syntactically boorish, impoverished in terms of diction — in sum, decisively unliterary. The concept could not be made to appear in pink ballet slippers: it was to show up scientifically, that is, rhetorically unadorned. There is a powerful advocacy on Kant's part for the substitution of art by science, of the values of a readable *displeasure* of the scientific elaboration with its attendant markers of dry, laborious, bitter working through: "The *truth* thus demands science, laborious and without style, without sugar coating [*sans miel*]."[4] This procedure, which cannot even metabolize a sugar substitute, promotes itself as the necessity of the structure and essence of knowledge. Philosophical exposition was to be downed without honey or the similarly sweet but troubling enticements of art. It became somewhat of an epistemic resolve to acquit oneself honorably, to recognize and embrace the manly duty of the philosophical act. The legacy will have affected so-called French Theory, which, following Nietzsche's finishing school, practices style and carries thinking elegantly, with rhetorical finesse. It is small wonder that the bouncers of serious and manly philosophical schools would get rid of, under the sign of ridiculous, anyone practicing the talent that Kant the writer had renounced. Since Kant, beautiful writing has been feminized and homosexualized, as so many attacks on theory reveal (or try to conceal). Kant, for his part, openly struggled with two heterogeneous entities: philosophy, on the one hand, style and elegance, on the other, feminine, one.

Kant has relinquished talent; he can't write beautifully. He complains, he denounces himself, he confesses as if it were a matter of revealing, in the manner of de Sade, a sexual perversion. There is some pleasure over the displeasure he inflicts on the philosophical body, though he does not hold the de Sadean line for long, preferring momentarily to explore its masochistic underbelly. Kant, he only goes so far before backtracking. For, he asserts, laying down the other soundtrack, It is a sacrifice for me to give up talent; in fact, I have had to sacrifice myself. He goes even further, or even further back, when he recognizes that this sacrifice is not without its benefits. So in the end Kant will appropriate the failure to write well, displace its value, insert a will — it's now fixed as an act of renunciation; he *has* to do it for the sake of philosophy — and explains the renunciation of elegance, locating the critical position it forces him to occupy. Besides which, it is a matter not merely of talent but of advancing age, because time is creeping up on Kant and he has to rush to the finish line, even if he is slowed down by the limitations of age and a relentless biological clock (he is not Abraham; he cannot expect to multiply his texts at a very old age). If it is a matter of his time and his age, then we are not simply isolated in the sphere of his disabled talent. Maybe he does have the talent but not the time; he has to get on with the task, which does not permit him to honor a temporality proper to talent. Finitude puts the squeeze on him. Harried and pinched by time, he has no patience for the seductive call of talent. He martyrs himself to the exigencies of philosophical writing. One need only read the delicious passages in the second preface to the *Critique of Pure Reason,* where Kant explains why he has to sacrifice himself. But it still adds up, by means of a tortuous logic, to asserting the desire to write a book. As Nancy insists, this is the first time that a philosopher wanted to be an author and to sign his proper name as the name proper to a book. A book. No other philosopher has wanted so badly to be bound by a book.

Because he cannot deliver the book that he could and would have written, Kant has to accept, he says, the inescapable predicament of being unpopular; "the critiques can never become popular," he avers.[5] But he will go on to subvert this claim as well, and here I ask that we think about Kant's various contests — to begin with, the contest of the faculties, the popularity contest, as he implied, and another contest to which we will come — according to their allegorical possibilities, in terms of the paradoxes and aporias of popularity that have also befallen what I am receiving as "French theory."

How did Kant, despite it all, become a popular hero? The failure of Kant as writer affected literature as regards its self-conception, in terms, indeed, of its self-possession, pumping up its historical narcissism. The great breakthrough thinker who broke down before the literary phallus mapped out the sphere of the literary as that which remains elusive, inaccessible, painfully desirable. With Kant, philosophical exposition became fragile, opening an experience of a self-doubting writing that proves unable to measure up to its task. Philosophical exposition can-

not be entirely independent or even heterogeneous with regard to the content the philosopher endeavors to present. The only invulnerable exposition would be that of mathematics, which proffers the sole domain of presentation adequate to both the concept and the intuition. Mathematics comprises "the only site of presentation (*Darstellung*) in the full and proper sense of the term."[6] Fallen short of self-adequate mathematical knowledge, philosophical exposition has been thrown into perpetual crisis; henceforth it will bear the marginal, accidental, biographical, and provisional allure that it takes on with Kant. The crisis of *Darstellung* exposes the up-close and personal profile of a trembling philosopher necessarily estranged from the autonomy of knowledge that has been ascribed to mathematical science. The vulnerability of exposition will seem to be the problem of Kant the writer, not of the philosophy of Kant. Finding himself in a problem set, Kant in a sense kept on repeating, "Why I write such bad books." Nietzsche's refrain, "Why I write such good books," is a response intended to break with the Kantian curse of which it is nonetheless an addressee. Nietzsche, repeating the gesture of posing his "I" before the challenge of a text, had to put up all sorts of apotropaic spells to shield his work against the Kantian curse of bad writing. It was a matter of self-respect and dignity.

Kant, despite it all, became popular, a cult figure. His work, tremendously difficult, uncompromising, awkward, dry, rhetorically cramped, made it to the top of everyone's list — and despite what he said, Kant had installed a program for this eventuality in his own work: he programmed the very popularity he claimed to renounce. Well, strictly speaking, it is not the same popularity, for Kant ends up assigning two valences to the concept of popularity. There are two ways of being popular. In a word, you can be common or you can refuse to be common — but the refusal has to be rigorous. And don't forget how very invested Kant is in registering different levels of commonality, the communitarian and community, what Nancy elsewhere calls literary communism.[7] In any case, Kant has a double rapport to popularity.

In the first place, it is a matter of the sheer impossibility or danger of being popular. Popular philosophy would resemble what, opposing it to speculative philosophy, Hume describes in the *Inquiry*. Popular philosophy offers advice, dogmatic exhortation, and proceeds by example; moreover, it is written in popular language, "coloring" its pretensions without having established foundation. In the critique nothing is colored in — Kant is explicit about this — but operates according to a design, a trace, a plan, a scheme, or a sketch. Popular style is, on the other hand, filled in, accessorized, color coded. There is the matter of style, then, before which Kant shies. For style to be style, it has to be popular, even in the case of ostensibly unique style. Popular style *is* style, then. By contrast, the Kantian critique is stripped down to a kind of cloddy minimalism. In this regard Kant has surrendered all hope of being popular; in fact, he has shown only anxiety over such a possibility. Here's how he wins out in the long run — for Kant is betting on the long run and is playing, as he says, for keeps.

There are two values of the popular at play. There is mere popularity and then there is genuine, real popularity. Real popularity belongs to the domain of reason, to the concerns of philosophical exposition. Kant famously appealed to *sensus communis,* to a community of reasonableness, in his critical work. Here he indicates a distinction between *sensus communis* and *sensus vulgaris.* Pure practical reason absolutely requires, for its unfolding and demonstration, a popular presentation. The question of popularity ranges in Kant from that of literary elegance to the concerns of reason itself. There is a point, then, where reason *is* popular and does not need the cloak of elegance in order to present itself. This circumstance has everything to do with the autonomy of reason.

There's a catch, though. It would not amount to such a problem if you could choose an authentic mode of popularity over a vulgar one. Who would hesitate over which choice to make? That's not how it works in Kant. Both kinds of popularity are disclosive of philosophical value, so that by choosing one kind of popularity you are excluding the other and are thereby running a sacrificial economy. To put it all too schematically: if you renounce a more vulgar popularity, you are sacrificing for philosophy a beautiful, seductive, and welcoming presentation, a writing capable of inviting and delighting. If, however, you sacrifice the more transcendent type of popularity, you not only renounce the concept and autonomy of reason but risk diminishing the future returns of philosophy. There is a knot of undecidability: How can one choose one over the other kind of popularity? Notice that by now there is no question of not being popular. Philosophy *is* popular and that, in fact, is its problem, its internal control issue. The inaptitude, writes Kant, to choose your popularity reveals a lack of taste. There is an ethics of exposition upon which Kant's elaboration relies and which has had to overcome the at once desired yet suspicious lure of elegance. It turns out that, for Kant, after a number of aporetic claims and disclaimers, the truly and really popular figure, the pop that rules, is, without question, the genius. Genius achieves uncanny proportions of popularity. Hence the inescapable

popularity of Einstein, Rembrandt, Shakespeare, Charlie Chaplin, Mozart (fill in the blank of a commonly held property)...............................
....

This is not where the signals should have been interrupted. Genius is a troubled and troubling figure that cannot be supported simply but that, as Kant already noted in the *Third Critique,* bears the mark of monstrosity. An aberration in nature, genius uneasily straddles the limit between sheer simplicity and the excess — an unaccountable natural force — by which the exceptional talent carries out its inscriptions. In fact, the poetic genius, while regularly sponsored and celebrated, is often depicted by Kant as suspect, puerile, hopelessly out of it. The poet, irremediably split between exaltation and vulgarity, between the autonomy that produces the concept within intuition and the foolish earthly being, functions as a contaminant for philosophy — a being who, at least since Plato, has been trying to read and master an eviction notice served by philosophy. The poet as genius continues to threaten and fascinate, menacing the philosopher with the beyond of knowledge. Philosophy cringes. Excluding and appropriating to itself the poeticity by which it is harassed and shadowed, philosophy has provoked a crisis on its own premises as a result of which these premises will henceforth be shared by the antics of the popular poet: "Paradoxically, then, it is perhaps owing to Kant that there can be neither philosophy nor literature, only a permanent scrambling, ever searching to write itself ..."[8] .... brouillage permanent scrambling ....
....

B. And Sarah Laughed

Abraham, the great patriarch, the *Erzvater,* the one and only, still remembered, nearly as popular as God — he, as Kafka reminds us, from whom we descend, shares decisive motifs with Kant's self-conception as ridiculous. Though it may appear to amount to something of a sacrilege to take these fathers down, or, paradoxically, even to take them at their word, this is neither my intention nor my doing. (I just transcribe.) They take themselves down the very mountains they endeavor to scale. More precisely, the logos takes them down. Kant says in one of his theological works that reason itself is responsible for the fall into foolishness.[9]

Questions of poor style and bad appearance inform Kafka's parable of Abraham, who is turned into so many hypotheses of ridiculousness. Inevitably set to provoke the world's laughter, these retakes of Abraham in ridiculous poses grapple with the emergence of a certain popularity. The text tries to resist his popularity while at the same time accounting for it. It begins by naming the spiritual poverty of the patriarch ("Abrahams geistige Armut") and the inertia it spreads, his inability to see the diversity of world. And then, outrageously, as if capable of sustaining a competition with the Almighty, the text itself conjures and calls up the man, the primal one, creating for itself another possibility of Abraham ("I could think up another Abraham").[10] The "I" thinks up an Abraham who, though prepared to satisfy immediately the demand for a sacrifice, first freezes upon receiving his marching orders. This one stumbles, namely, over the constative utterance in the Bible that unleashes a performative necessity: "He set his house in order." The narrative can't get past the fact of this house, the ordering of which it posits (the Bible does not set great store in having Abraham clean house; Kafka read it off some wall).[11] The parable insists: Abraham had some property. He had a house; moreover, it had to be set in order. The house of being or a small estate, the house already contained Abraham, bestowed upon him specific worldly properties and established somewhat of a prescriptive routine. He was bound by this house. It had to be put in order before any other, higher orders could be followed, much less heard. Housebound, this Abraham, who "certainly would have never gotten to be a patriarch or even an old-clothes dealer," was prepared to answer the call with the promptness of a waiter but was unable to bring it off "because he was unable to get away, being indispensable; the household needed him, there was perpetually something or other to put in order, the house was never ready" (41). The issue of sacrifice implicates readiness, a giving up of property. The concern evinced by Kafka is presacrificial. How can a house be ready when the call comes through? A house needs to be ready so that a call can be received. The reception of the call would deliver the host to an outside that is more intimate than the hearth. What is the link between the call and the order of the house? There is the insinuation of a state of house arrest: he'll never leave the house, not even by leaping out the window. There is the other issue of the leap, Abraham's leap, which does not appear to have taken place.

The problem with this Abraham, says the narrator, is that he already had the house, something to fall back on, something to leave: "if he had not had a house, where would he have raised his son, and in which rafter would he have stuck the sacrificial knife?" This Abraham, who displays greater evidence of style than the more popular, the impoverished one, becomes his substitute, becomes the more "real Abraham" who, how-

288

ever, is "an old story not worth discussing any longer" (43). So why are we discussing it?

There is something about the old story that cannot be put to rest; it calls us, repeating itself ever as an old story whose recurrence marks it as a founding story, the story of Abraham, the one who received the call. This one "had everything to start with, was brought up to it from childhood — I can't see the leap" (43). The narrator supplies a logic where the leap is missing. If this Abraham already had everything, then something had to be taken away from him, "at least in appearance: this would be logical and no leap" (43). Where is the famous leap of faith, the rumor, promoted by Kierkegaard, of a sudden, unaccountable narrative breakaway? The logic of sacrifice seems too close to calculative simplicity here, resembling in a prefigurative way the sacrifice of Job, from whom so much was taken. "It was different for the other Abrahams, who stood in the houses they were building and suddenly had to go up on Mount Moriah; it is possible that they did not even have a son, yet already had to sacrifice him. These are impossibilities, and Sarah was right to laugh" (43). But Sarah's laughter is not addressed to the most ridiculous of possibilities, only to impossibilities that make sense and fail to produce a leap. What makes sense? There were Abrahams who were called before they were ready, that is, before their houses were readied, much less built. These were pure sacrificial beings who were prepared to surrender that which they did not have. This sacrifice, following the logic of the parable, is greater even than that of the Abraham who had someone to give up to a higher power. These Abrahams gave what they could not offer. Hence Sarah laughs at the gift that, never having been given, is already, "suddenly," given away and somehow redeemed. She laughs at the peculiar nothingness of the gift, the danger and disruption of the gift that bears no present. Laughing, she doubles the gift's unfathomable givens, for, according to Freud and Nancy, laughter "itself" would be gift as well — the *Geschenk* (present) or *Gabe* (gift) inhering in the surrender of *Aufgabe* (giving up).[12] Laughing, she surrenders an unnameable gift. According to the program notes provided by Baudelaire, her laughter would be that of a she-devil, breaking and entering into the house of limits, bursting and busting (she bursts into laughter) the steeliness of man's calculative grid.

The narrator continues: "But take another Abraham" ("Aber ein anderer Abraham"), in which the *aber,* and *abra,* and *aba* (*abba*) converge (43), an other father, one who inhabits the leap and passes through a loop of warping disjuncture. This other one got everything straight; he "wanted to perform the sacrifice altogether in the right way and had a correct sense in general of the whole affair" (43). There was a problem of address, however, scorched by an impossible presentation, the sheer negativity of exposition. He had the right sense of things "but could not believe that he was the one meant, he, an ugly old man, and the dirty youngster that was his child. . . . he would make the sacrifice in the right spirit if only he could believe he was the one meant" (43). It is not the case that this one, he does not believe in God; no, what he does not believe is that the call was meant for him to take. He does not believe in himself as destination; he cannot believe that the call will have arrived if he were to respond to its demand. This might be an intercept, a matter of mistaken identity in the divine call-forwarding system. In fact, this Abraham, old and capable of presenting only his ugliness, fears mainly the metamorphosis. "He is afraid that after starting out as Abraham with his son he would change on the way into Don Quixote" (43). He would turn into the ridiculed figure of the seeker, the improbable hero of thought, a fabulously bumbling tourist of the imaginary. Worse still, he would have turned into literature; that is, he would have turned himself into the authority of literature that strip searches the sacred, consistently enraging world. "The world would have been enraged at Abraham could it have beheld him at the time, but this one is afraid that the world would laugh itself to death at the sight of him" (43; "die Welt werde sich bei dem Anblick totlachen" [45]). The other side of the world's rage at Abraham consists in this laughter, a laughter-to-death that threatens extinction. Kafka's text thus presents another version of *Totem and Taboo* where, instead of producing a blood-and-guts murder of the primal father, the world horde emerges as capable of laughing itself to death, to his death, in a broad sweep of castrative derision. The trope of ridiculousness subverts the gravity of biblical patriarchy or shows what was always there, left untouched. It prepares the grounds for a world-class masochistic introject, for another internalization of the first father, humiliated and steadily miniaturized. Freud's horde got theirs, too. Conscience-bitten, they were felled by remorse in the end; or, rather, they were henceforth to stand by remorse and a father for whom love arrived in the ambivalent aftermath of an immemorial murder. Their father, however, stood tall, with haunting authority.

We learn from Kafka's narrator that ridiculousness has the power of agency and aging. It is not merely the case that Abraham's ugliness makes him ridiculous but, more to the point, that ridiculousness increases his age and ugliness, further sullying his son. Ridiculousness is imbued with divine powers of negation, and so a subtle tautology enters into a popularity contest that resounds with laughter: "However, it is not ridiculousness as such that he is afraid of — though he is, of course, afraid of that too and, above all, of his joining in the laughter — but in the main he is afraid that this ridiculousness will make him even older and uglier, his son even dirtier, even more unworthy of being really called" (45). The ridiculous is exposition: it will expose him, nearly eating into his skin, *making* him older and uglier, transforming him as it presents him, rendering unsightly as it inspects. It is, moreover, hereditary, for it exposes the son to even more dirt on his father, "his son even dirtier," tainted, destitute. An improper sacrifice acts in fact as the destruction of sacrifice (something that Kafka accomplishes but that, as we shall see, God could not: the end of sacrifice). The son, Isaac, if he is to be offered, must be given up as a clean sacrifice, as that which is clean in itself, a clean cut, a proper offering. The parable takes up the other side of the biblical obsession with cleanliness, zooming in on a stain that cannot be removed: the possibility that Abraham was dirty, his son even dirtier. The proper mode of responsiveness depends upon erasing the stain that, however, proves to be ineffaceable. Under the circumstances, how can Abraham make the cut? Ridicule stalks him like a ghost.

Abraham finds himself in a bind: he must of course answer the call because it addresses him; but when rising to answer the call, he becomes ridiculous for responding to it as if it had been meant for him, Abraham. Ridiculousness, which comes after the call, reverses the charges, turning temporality around on itself, for it bestows upon Abraham the predicament of having not been called — not "really being called" (44; "wirklich gerufen zu werden" [45]). It has the ability to return the call on itself and reoriginates it as mistaken, off range. The ridiculous diverts and cancels the call. So that God "really" could have made the call to this Abraham, the call "intended only for you" ("nur für Dich bestimmt," as the doorkeeper in another parable says to the man from the country).[13] This Abraham could have been God's intended, the intended destination of His call, which was to be canceled when the ridiculous supervened as a kind of devil on the line of divine transmission. But ridiculousness has effected a mutation in the addressee, who is no longer the same as the one called. Abraham did not become ridiculous until he answered the call. Answering the call, he annuls it: "An Abraham who should come unsummoned!" (45).

The narrator of the parable fades the sequence into a pedagogical analogy of contemporary consequence, deriving a scene wherein the class dummkopf hears his name called on commencement day. An institutional ritual has been disrupted: the student body writhes in laughter. "It is as if, at the end of the year, when the best student was solemnly about to receive a prize, the worst student rose in the expectant stillness and came forward from his dirty desk in the last row because he had made a mistake of hearing, and the whole class burst out laughing" (45). The dumbest of the dumb rises to the occasion of solemn bestowal, having heard his name and felt himself addressed. A notably Christian moment can be seen to occur when the meek comes up from educational death row, the last row and lowest rank, to inherit, unaccountably, the prize. He is crucified by class difference; betrayed within a different hierarchical standard by which he is downgraded, his insufficiency provokes a unanimous peal of laughter. The class dummkopf is too dumb to know that he cannot be the smart one beckoned forth on this day; he leaps up — here, finally, comes the leap — to claim the prize meant for the best student according to a scorecard that he cannot decipher. All he knows is that he heard his name called. Again, this morphed Abraham is associated with the improper: his desk, dirty, has not been put in order, yet he hears himself called. There is a film of disgust trailing Abraham, a minor dust storm kicking up in the wake of the father. The solemnity of the event is broken. The unclean father, a constant Kafkan obsession, returns to its once-auratic source exposing the father as reflected in a dirty child or lame student. There is one thing, *the Thing,* that occupies a shared imago and shatters its integrity. It arrests the stain, inevitably disfiguring the face of authority without lessening the severity of that authority — lending it, rather, the power to induce even more anxiety. Crumbs on a newspaper, dirty sheets, a tear in a picture: these lesions in being whose precise punctuation already marked Abraham. The presentation has been absolutely sacrificed, appearances materialized and degraded, beginning with the dirty desk in the back row, the loser's place. How could an Abraham, stained and disheveled, originate in the back row except by hearing impairment or random draw — the deformity — of an improper address?

One possibility remains constant: that his name has been called out if only, the text says, in punishment. The contest of the faculties enfolds the question of contesting faculties, for if he can believe his ears maybe the teacher's understanding is at stake: "And perhaps he had made no mistake at all, his name really was called, it having been the teacher's intention to make the rewarding of the best student at the same time a punishment for the worst one" (45). Kafka does a retake of the great

Book, displacing and condensing the value of reward, the necessity of punishment. How was the truth of Abraham tested? There are two parts to this test. In the Bible Abraham's obedience was tested — he passed the test, won back the boy, got God on his side; in Kafka's parable the test, though schooled and standardized, is scrambled, the test results rendered inconclusive. Did he pass? Did he fail? Did he not need always already to have failed in order to pass? Or did he think he passed but was failed by the multiplication of Sarah's laughter booming through the chorus of his classmates? Did he accidentally skip a grade when he was supposed to be left back?[14]

His faculties contested, little dumb dirty Abraham answers to the call of the faculty, a call meant as punishment but where no one can be entirely sure anymore who is being rewarded as best student or punished as the worst one. All we know is that the punished and rewarded are collapsed into the same figure that accounts for the fiction of the father. The most exalted and secretly ridiculed of beings owes his existence to the undecidable nature of the call, its meaning or address, its intention and value. By answering to his name, he has already offered his sacrifice, whether or not the teacher will call it off — whether or not it is even in the power of the faculty to recognize the difference. The final irony is that, having been called, Abraham comes unsummoned. As unforgettable source, seared by the trauma of universal laughter, he is measured in Kafka by the consistent shedding of self-worth, bowed by the incursion of unrelenting indignities. He remains hostage to those subliminal acts — they are a matter largely of passivity, of following a sacrificial order — that risk exposing him primordially to the most naked core of sheer ridiculous being.

The teacher, the master, or God, plays a part in the destitutionalization of the boy, Abraham, our father. What we learn from Kafka's parable, if the teacher means us to learn anything, concerns the failure of presentation. Ineffaceable, the lesion surfaces, as in "A Country Doctor," in the struggle over presentation. There is always a smudge of dirt where anointment occurs. As much a sign of the missed appointment as of a missed anointment — the appointment is made dependent in Kafka on having missed the point — the calling of Abraham disarranges hierarchy, subverts class expectation (why should the poorest student inherit the prize?), so that the good student is always tainted by the worst student, who can come around, according to the order of a new curve, and be commended as the most prizeworthy. Yet the text at no point effects a dialectics or a genealogical switch as it swings over the breakage of singularity. The bad student does not turn into the good one according to a logic of secret negotiations with a higher power. He wins the divine lottery, but as a loser.

A lot depends in the parable on Kafka's use of the term *gleichzeitig*, on the simultaneous wish of the teacher to present reward and punishment. How can simultaneity be instituted and observed? Even God cannot practice simultaneity and must call out Abraham's name twice, if it is indeed Abraham's name that is being called — the question mark around which the parable rotates. We have a hard time imagining the voice that summons as a stammering one, resembling the syncopated speech pattern of Moses. The voice of God has been reported to be clear, though not always, and there is some probability that somewhere voice can be cracked, split, even in His case. Kafka does not say whether the voice summoning Abraham was disarticulating or hoarse, whether, on the contrary, it rang out with unparalleled acuity. In a sense it doesn't matter. God was not heard on the first try. God Almighty, for the most part, must submit His calls to the laws of temporization, which, in order to be heard, have to be repeated to begin with. Not to speak of what could have been *meant* when the call was made. Intention, when the name is called, remains rigorously unreadable. The best student may be Abraham — yes, maybe, but this story, the old one, we are told, has lost all interest. Neither God nor the teacher can have access to the intention that motivates the calling of the name since both are limited by the one name, by the oneness of a name that strictly defies spontaneous serialization. However mastered the intention, it does not in the end allow one to know which or who was called, for even in the utterance of the one name He can always think another Abraham ("Ich könnte mir einen anderen Abraham denken"). As for the name, it cannot be reduced to the same or difference. To the extent that it remains impossible to call out two names at once, the intention must be split, as with the cut that binds Judeo-slash-Christianity.

C. Kant's Anthro: The Case against "Stupid but Honest"; or, Goys 'R' Us

When introducing the passages devoted to disorders of mind in the *Anthropology*, Kant makes a general statement before zeroing in on those most subject to ridicule. "Simpletons, idiots, morons, conceited asses, fools, and buffoons," he writes, "are distinguished from the mentally disturbed not only in degree, but also in the quality of their mental disorders; and the former do not yet, because of their disorders, belong in a

mental institution."[15] The group portrait gathers together figures who occupy, much as does Kafka's country hick in the parable "Before the Law," a liminal space at the portals of the institution. They are before the institution, both prior to and in front of its doors but already set in relation to it, whether or not the borders can be stabilized. They remain before the institution to the degree that Kant institutes the "not yet" — they do not yet belong yet are on their way to the institution. Being on their way, they may never arrive, but they are already located on its premises. Inasmuch as they are "not yet" in the institution, they cannot be said absolutely to occupy an outside-the-institution.[16] They face it, are before it, neither having gained admission (not yet) nor having been expulsed. But to have been spared institutionalization means they are not entirely within Reason's grasp, they do not belong to the system of choices that determines the codes of the lockup. Somewhere between reason and madness, in the space of disorder, the simpletons, idiots, morons, etc., hold a convex mirror to Kant's philosophy of mind.

It is not easy to clamp down on these aberrant figures, and Kant skids a bit as he tries to control their direction and implications. These figures are other, but perhaps not other enough. At times they are not even recognizable as what they are, as his reflections on stupidity indicate, for even if one is basically stupid, "through misfortune, one becomes shrewd" (5). Then there are those who are seen as stupid because, believe it or not, they are overreaders. They have studied too much — a habit that can burn your brain. Not to worry, says Kant in a somewhat skewed footnote, because while merchants are known to overextend themselves, in the case of overreading students, "nature herself well provides against such overloading of knowledge, by this means: that those things disgust the student over which he has pored to the point of head- breaking, and yet all in vain" (24n.32). Mind is shielded by disgust. Where knowledge has strained the student, something intervenes to block out the threat of becoming stupid. Or, indulging some overreading, there is something on the order of knowledge that the mind cannot bear and of which it is relieved. Kant calls the protective intervention "disgust." Invoked here as a natural and benevolent energy, disgust averts the risk of becoming stupid, an eventuality prompted by over-studying and excessive reading. What cannot be stabilized is the timing of this "yet," which determines that all has been in vain. At which point of the terminable-interminable exercise of reading stupidity sets in is left indeterminable. The possibility exists that all has been in vain, from the start. Disgust protects against exorbitance, outsmarting the overreader who incessantly reads over a text, becoming dumber and number by the minute. Where the question of surplus arises, nature restores balance by dosing out disgust. This marketing of disgust, situated in the neighborhood of some greedy merchants, will return to Kant in an as yet understudied footnote.

An effect, indeed, of moderation, safeguarding against the irreversible onslaught of stupidity, the famous issue of Kant's disgust arrives on the scene on yet another expository occasion, without escort or explanation. Dashing from one thought to the next, he asserts this about the cognitive pretender: "He who only pretends to have either of these qualities, cleverness or smartness, is a disgusting creature."[17] We are not clued in to the kind of mimetic logic by which one can imitate being smart or clever and pull off this ruse in a significant manner; we are merely shown that, for Kant, such pretense can function as an emetic, arousing disgust as nonnatural valence.[18] This instance of disgust goes against nature, settling on the side of artifice, pretense, making and faking up. Faking smartness stirs the judgment of taste in Kant to the point of excessive distaste and provokes revulsion. But how smart does one have to be in order to fake being smart? Why does Kant leave aside all discussion of faculty realignment when it comes to affecting a quality of mind? Kant couples this kind of duplicity — faking smartness or acting clever — with an arraignment of the "disgusting subject," thus imputing to the pretender a subjectivity tainted in the procedures initiated by the judgment of taste. The smart ass (der Witzling) or wiseguy (der Klügling) is the one in the back row with the dirty desk, the one who gets up in obedience to some inaudible roll call, pretending to be smart.

Disgust creeps up. The weight of the ridiculous is linked by Kant to old age, much as it was in the 1787 preface to the *First Critique*. In that context he was producing excuses for his ridiculous poses and poor style by way of his advancing age. He was, in sum, getting old and had no time to clean up the style pile he had left behind. In the *Anthropology* we learn that the ridiculous is associated with the "mildest of all deviations beyond the limits of sound reason" (4). The minor deviation has something to do with reaching a high majority, a time when one may establish an inner retirement colony, namely, the "hobbyhorse" (*Steckenpferd*): "an inclination to occupy oneself diligently, as with a business, with creatures of the imagination, which the mind pursues simply for entertainment, like a busy idleness" (4). The promotion of a bustling passivity recaptures for the aging a trace of freedom, redeeming the being-carefree of childhood. The world of occupied leisure borders but ap-

pears to fall short of the aesthetic experience; it bestirs something like disinterested pleasure for the elderly, particularly for those with means: "For old and wealthy people, settled in retirement, as if they had once again fallen back into carefree childhood, this state of mind is not only healthful, as an agitation always keeping their vitality astir, but also agreeable" (4). Kant's comments focalize that which lightly stimulates pleasure and belongs on the side of health; he opens the dossier on a realm of passive agitation, a balancing of vital forces that he situates among the wealthy, recalling here the moral probity of Jean-Jacques.[19] Retiring and rich, these old people (Sarah laughs) have their house in order and their retirement plan in place; these old folks are now occupied diligently with creatures of their imaginations. They are running phantom businesses, making important calls, answering to other demands — all of which is organized at the brink of nothingness. Though Kant pronounces this healthy and "also agreeable," he swiftly stops the pleasure and calls in a judgment: "as an agitation always keeping their vitality astir, but also agreeable; at the same time, however, it is also ridiculous: so much so that the person being ridiculed can good-humoredly laugh at himself" (4). This kind of repetition of early pleasure and later busyness, redolent with easy aesthetic self-gathering, descending on this side of the pleasure principle (this luxury aberration does not display qualities of compulsion, nor is one prodded by the death drive but pleasantly propped on a hobbyhorse), shows how one can go out in style, having let go of it, on the crest of a surplus, following the lead of sheer purposiveness without purpose. It all amounts to nothing, to a planned bout of child's play at death's door.

Kant does not establish with great precision why this purposive passivity should earn the label of ridiculous, even when applied self-consciously, except by indicating that such a form of geriatric mimesis exposes itself as being dependent on a fiction of doing. One is doing *as if* one were still in business, working diligently but with imaginary objects ("creatures"), managing at a remove. This kind of activity of the *als ob*, bereft as it is of ground and goal, of reality and purpose, compares, if one wanted to go in that direction — Kant doesn't — with the freeplay of the poetic faculties, with the principal activity of "suspect and puerile" *Dichter*. The poetic-driven aesthetic has always threatened to inch up to the ridiculous. In the *Nachlass* Kant offers a thought on that which pleases, which he puts close to aesthetics: beauty is for the weak and children, and the aesthetic is a way of accustoming those who are delicate to the rigors of proofs and explications, is a spoonful of honey on the rim of a child's cup.[20] But eventually, when one grows up, adding honey becomes excessive and one must in any case effect the substitution of art by science — a necessity has been established for preferring, in the long run, the bitterness and labor of science to the sugar-coated yummy taste of aesthetics. One grows up and learns to prefer the displeasure of science, its painstaking bitterness, much in the same way as, later on in Freud, one grows to like spinach and ends up swallowing, without coercive prodding, the bitter pill of an internalized superego. Science offers no retirement benefits, no social security for the earnest laborer who cannot embrace the artificial sweeteners for which advancing age may call. The philosopher as scientist in fact renders himself ridiculous by surrendering the aesthetic *Darstellung*, an act that is then recuperated by the imperative of conceptual positing. Here we run the risk of repeating ourselves, as if stuck riding a hobbyhorse that isn't really going anywhere, so let me offer another angle.

What would the threat of the ridiculous be to the philosopher? In the second place the ridiculous represents only a mild deformity, so it could swing on either side of the boundary on which sound mind is mapped. You can get away with being ridiculous without having to pay a penalty or show up in a court or institution. In the first place, however, being ridiculous and, given the riders upon which his texts appear to insist, *knowing* one is being ridiculous nails you as a philosopher or at least targets the philosophical component of your *Dasein*. Being ridiculous already involves a philosophical insert, because it implies the act of laughing at oneself. In "L'Essence du rire" Baudelaire defines this ability to laugh at oneself falling (on one's ass, back into childhood, forward into old age) as the moment constitutive of philosophical consciousness. What de Man interprets as irony — the philosopher splits in two, accelerating time while collapsing on the self — is set up by the fall designating a split between the dumb buddy, on the one hand, and the one who ridiculizes the faltered ego, on the other hand. When the philosopher falls, prompting the opening act in the ur-scene of philosophical consciousness, this produces the double effects of ironic consciousness. (De Man does not so much concern himself with the ridiculization of the body in the fall, the butt of mockery, though Kant and Baudelaire are felled by the body's sudden but inevitable lapse and collapse, by the way it lurches out of control, splattering dignity, becoming unrecoverably enfeebled.) The subject laughs at himself falling; indeed, the fall announces the moment the subject becomes a philosopher by means, precisely, of laughing at himself, making himself ridiculous, *sich lächerlich*

298

machen, thus in falling *making* himself performatively. Affected by the laughter of the other, as this other, the philosophical consciousness makes itself happen by passing through the constituting moment of making itself ridiculous. The laugh-along distinguishes the philosopher from the nonphilosopher to the extent that a position is taken outside the self, beyond which the self, detached, can be observed. The moment savagely accelerates the history of the self and its fall: to laugh at oneself is to laugh at oneself dying from an improbable position beyond or on the other side of a life that has disjoined by dint of the sudden slip in consciousness.

Let these hobbyhorses, says Kant citing Sterne, tarry on the roadside while we speed past them on the highway of nonimaginary pursuits. They are harmless. But are they? They "probably" deserve to be defended, particularly when one considers that the young and seriously busy also pursue hobbies ("But even with young and busy people, this riding of a hobby serves as recreation; and their little follies probably deserve Sterne's defense against pendants: 'So long as a man rides his Hobby-horse peaceably and quietly along the King's highway, and neither compels you or me to get up behind him, — pray, Sir, what have either you or I to do with it?'" [5]). Why does Kant, riding Sterne, have to pass them, those who have gone to pasture, and leave them in the dust? How are we to be certain that the philosophical highway is not just another country road for those lingering in the precincts of finitude and sheltered principally by the imagination? Does not "the philosophical life" imply retirement, *Entzug,* withdrawal from the values of practical business? In other words, does not the philosophical life always accept its fate as a mindful relation to death, whether imposed and inscribed (Socrates) or repelled and inscribed (Kant, Nietzsche)?

Kant goes to a literary source to bring forth the harmlessness of the scene he has depicted. It is literature that marks out the otherness of a threatening enterprise, that is made to console philosophy about what can be ignored in the field of the real. So Kant invokes fiction to tell the truth about the bypassability of the fictional endeavor that the poets of retirement practice in phantom poses. Why would Sterne be the authority and border patrol for deciding what can pass for a real or mimed occupation, what can be seen as contraband or gently left aside, even laughed at? The retirees whom Kant runs down are laughing at themselves; miming disinterested pleasure, they are in a healthful rapport with the imaginary. Kant is not laughing, and he cannot afford the supplement of honey to make it go down more easily. He's out of money, honey, and out of time. Ever going out of style (Kant is still going out of style), he has little patience for pleasure, having given it up along with the honey-rimmed frame of exposition; in fact, his pleasure is displeasure: more interested, sacrificial — indeed, saccharoficial — Kant has opted for another order of the ridiculous.

In the section of the *Anthropology* entitled "On the Weaknesses of the Cognitive Faculty," where he discusses the relative differences that abide in the case of the dullard (*obtusam caput*) and that of stupidity (*stupiditas*), Kant observes: "A mind of slow comprehension is . . . not necessarily a weak mind, just as one of quick comprehension is not always profound but is often very superficial" (5). This admonition militates against the technostandard by which we set those values of intelligence assumed to be aligned with quick-wittedness, speed of comprehension — in general, with the high velocity mind of our modernity. The mind capable of quick comprehension may be a calculative mind, agile in performing mechanical operations that, however, are not interiorized or broken but smooth and unproblematic in terms of the results they yield. It could be that fast is slow, where mind hasn't stopped or been stopped, made to give pause over some imponderable or stumped by an effect of paradox. The worst student could turn out to have been Abraham.

Kant introduces a distinction between simple-mindedness and stupidity that involves the understanding: "Simple-minded is he who cannot take much into his mind; but he is not on that account stupid, unless he misunderstands what he does take in" (5). So stupid has a larger capacity for absorption but will misconstrue what has been absorbed; it is as if stupidity were to be located in a more interior zone of mind, at a place or function where understanding gets mobilized. Because a margin of interiority implicates the faculty of understanding, the matter of a fair and just assessment comes into play. The question of a just locution emerges with the common observation that one can be "honest but stupid," as has been frequently said of Pomeranian, that is, Prussian, servants. This represents "a false and highly reprehensible expression" (6). It is false, asserts Kant, because honesty (observance of duty as a rule of conduct) issues from and is practical reason. It is reprehensible "because it presupposes that everyone would cheat, if only he felt that he was clever enough to do so, and that his not cheating stems only from his incompetence" (6). To bring home his point, Kant recalls the proverb "He didn't invent gunpowder, he won't betray his country, he isn't a master-magician," which, he argues, reflects a misanthropic attitude: "namely, that we cannot, assuming the good intentions of the people we know,

300

be sure of them, but only of their incompetence. — Thus, as Hume says, the Grand Sultan does not entrust his harem to the virtue of those who guard it, but to their impotence (as black eunuchs)" (6). It is metaphysically wrong to assert the conjunction of honesty and stupidity, thus devaluing humanity and insulting practical reason. Honesty cannot be made to depend on incompetence or racialized castration narratives. (Interestingly, the assertion attributed to Hume cannot be found anywhere in his works, so Kant's harem comes from another place, another space or phantasm of castration. This time the impotentiated other is not the ridiculous retiree but the emasculated guard who mimes virtue but is too enfeebled to act otherwise, so that virtue cannot be said to have been pure or an effect of practical reason.) Needless to say, the example jars the discursive intent, though not inconsistently so for the philosopher Kant. At the very moment when he censures an insult to humankind, he bolsters his argument on an insult to humanity, enlisting double enslavement in the figure of a black eunuch.

The racialized undermap continues to grow in Kant's hands as he moves on to a shade of stupidity typified by those who let themselves get ripped off. He establishes a relationship between the cheater and the cheated, pitting those who cheat — the ability to cheat others derives from cunning, wiliness, slyness (*versutia, astutia*) — against those who are cheated. "Now the question is, whether the cheater has to be smarter than the person who can easily be cheated, or whether the latter is the stupid one. Because he is an easy prey for rascals, the warm-hearted person who really trusts (believes, gives credit) is sometimes, although very erroneously, called a fool, too" (6). Down for the count, the cheated will have already established an account; they are the ones who really trust beyond the strictures of negotiation, which is to say, they give credit and credence by offering a surplus to another. To trust is to open for another the temporality implicit in a credit account, to receive the other on credit, whereas to cheat means to have already withdrawn the account. "It is true and sensible that I never again trust a man who has once cheated me; for he is corrupt in his principles. But on that account, because one man has cheated me, to trust nobody else is misanthropy. The cheater is actually the fool" (6). This presents one considerable case of desistance when it comes to the subsumption of the particular under the general; the particular instance of being cheated must remain isolated or else we risk having to write up something like a misanthropology. Kant's declaration that the cheater is actually a fool is pushed out there like a lamb to slaughter — appearing in his argument as isolated as the particular experience of being cheated ought to have been. He offers no demonstration or explanation as to how he arrived at this affirmation, though the cheater seems to have taken the place of the one who trusts no one and can offer no credit. Always on the take, the cheater (of whom it is not determined, finally, whether he is smarter than the cheated), when he is the object of fraud ("the cheated cheater"), becomes ridiculous.

As if cheated of an opportunity to supply an example, the text inflates into a huge footnote at this point, one in which the tendential urge to generalize is shown to do an injustice to a noted tribe of cheaters, the Jewish people. The logic of the footnote doubles over on itself, warning at once of naturalizing and totalizing the cheating impulse onto a whole people while providing the evidence for doing so according to more historicizing protocols. When prodded allegorically, the passage leads one to question whether the people of Abraham are not being constructed, in this instance, as the synthesizing figure of the cheated cheater, the historical embodiment of the concept of the ridiculous. Kant's surplus footnote gives these people a kick in the ass while at same time endeavoring to rehabilitate or at least relocate them within a general economy of cheating that "can by no means be counted as evidence of a curse pronounced upon these people, but must rather be regarded as a blessing, especially since their wealth, in personal property, probably now exceeds that of any other people of like numbers" (23n.21). What looked like the deficit of a curse turns into its opposite according to a structure of credit bestowed upon the Jewish people, a historical trust fund approved by divine force ("a blessing") that now appears to be coming, the footnote estimates, to maturity. The Jewish people, set off by the prejudice of state, have responded to their restrictive civic limits with a kind of competitive passion. This passion maxes out in an excess of "outdoing" the neighboring goys "and even," writes Kant, "in outdoing each other" (22n.21). The proximity of cheating to outdoing is left uninterrogated, but the slippage allows for a relaxed hold on the nation of cheaters, who are doing it to one another as well as to "us." By these means the cheating impulse gets rerouted into a competitive frame, a contest of the Jewish faculties that increases their stock.

Kant begins by stating the improbability of ascribing to a whole nation a negative attribute but eventually swings into the litotic free-style concession, "now this cannot be otherwise for a whole nation composed entirely of merchants," though he continues to temper the rheto-

ric of generality that persecutes the Jew. In order not to cheat the footnote of its account, I offer it here in full:

> The Jews living among us have attained the not unfounded reputation of being to a great extent given to cheating [in den nicht unbegründeten Ruf des Betruges], because of their usury since their exile. As a matter of fact, however, it seems odd to think in terms of a whole nation of cheaters; and it is just as odd, surely, to think in terms of a nation wholly of merchants, of whom the great majority, segregated on the basis of an old, established prejudice of the state in which they live, seek no respectable reputations but try to compensate for the lack of them by means of the profits gained in outdoing the people among whom they have found refuge, and even in outdoing each other. Now this cannot be otherwise for a whole nation composed entirely of merchants, of non-productive members of society (e.g., the Jews in Poland); hence their contracts, sanctioned by the old charters of us among whom they live (and who have certain holy scriptures in common with them), cannot be abrogated by us without our becoming guilty of contradiction, even though they undoubtedly make it the cardinal principle of their morality, in dealing with us: "Let the buyer beware" ["Käufer tue die Augen auf"]. Instead of idle plans to preach to these people, in terms of cheating and honesty, I would rather state my suppositions as to the origins of this strange situation (namely, of a people consisting entirely of merchants). — Wealth was carried in the earliest times, by trade, to India, … the Mediterranean Sea, … Palestine, … [blahblahblah.] … So it appears that their dispersion throughout the world, with their unity of a religion and of language, can by no means be counted as evidence of a curse pronounced upon these people, but must rather be regarded as a blessing, especially since their wealth, in personal property, probably now exceeds that of any other people of like numbers. (22–23n.21)

I cheated. The footnote was not given its full due. When Kant effects a momentary switch from cheating to outdoing, the rhetorical glitch makes one consider whether Kant has slipped in an autobiographeme. One has to wonder which Jew has outdone, if not cheated him. I'm not sure, but I have a hunch. It brings us, via the Nietzschean hold on gratitude, to the figure of Moses Mendelssohn, to whom Kant has repeatedly shown the aggression of gratefulness — he gives him "*gr*attitude" — for his ability to philosophize without losing the essential surplus of style. Will Mendelssohn not have outdone him in the matter of the beautiful *Darstellung*? Kant himself has said as much. Yet it is not possible to get into Kant's head (or lower extremeties) at this point of entry in terms of the irruptive footnote, which by no means matches footprints with other assertions about the people of the Book ("of us among whom they live [and who have certain holy scriptures in common with them]").[21]

One can only read the footnote to observe how it violates the logic by which it is set up and proceeds by anacoluthon to prove the very opposite of what it intially states: the beginning, namely, goes in one rhetorical direction, urging a resistance to generality, and then interrupts itself in order to profile the righteous necessity of that generality. In fact, Kant will not "preach to these people in terms of cheating and honesty," refusing them the commerce of morality. He cannot "deal" with them. Since when has Kant been a preacher? Why does philosophy recede and regress to the skewed desire of preaching before these nonreading readers who share certain holy scriptures with "us"? In a way that remains unmarked, the argument has shifted from Kant's dispute with the "stupid but honest" syntagm evoking misanthropy to a secret syntagm of "smart but cheaters," a local branch of misanthropy. A stealth divide begins to take shape in terms of the honest stupidity of the "us" who are invaded by the clever cheaters of the "them." The issue, in fact, was incited by the fear that all of us could be cheaters — in other words, according to the essential argument, all of us could be Jews.

The footnote is beset with contradiction, the very thing of which Kant does not want to be found guilty and on which the entire note is centered. The beginning, then, aims to go in one direction but then repeals its intention. Unsupported assertions are made, organized around the stated hope that these can be put forth "without our becoming guilty of contradiction." I'll name a few such assertions in the form of questions. How do we recognize "the Palestinians living among us" (Kant is rigorously [anti-]Semitic about this designation: "Die unter uns lebenden Palästiner")? Having begun with a generality that undercuts generality, he then says that the generality exists in a particular location of the general: Poland. What motivates the referential gesture that determines an example in support of the impossible generality ("z.B. der Juden in Polen" [e.g., the Jews in Poland])? If this concerns all of them yet establishes a totality in need of an example that localizes and limits, isolating them, then it cannot be about *all of them*. Indeed, what kind of an uninterrogated generality is "us among whom they live" — what founds and legitimates the "us"? Kant does not decide who or where "they" among (or beneath, *unter*) us are, except for allowing that they quickly get globalized and simultaneously local, in the end creating only the

spectral security of an "us." And so forth. The particularized example of a Jewish site becomes consistently delocalized, as does the place from which Kant ostensibly writes: Königsberg, which, according to conventional mappings, is not in Poland, not in Germany, and not in Prussia, though nonetheless in Prussia, as it begins to seem possible that, in a Kafkan sense, Kant is himself underwriting a "minor literature."

In the end this note, which could have borne the title "Why I Am So Anti-Semitic," produces a logic according to which the "us" and "them" can be distilled to separate entities: it is finally on the basis of the values of smart and stupid, though there exist internal fissures within each of these terms, that the distinctness of Aryan and Semite is marked. A simple chiasmus reinscribes the cross or double cross that informs the relation of the one to the others: the Jews outdo us and one another; they are on the fast track of a kind of malignant smartness, whereas "we" are, if not outright stupid, then fundamentally honest, though shadowed by the misanthropic habit that continues, despite it all, to associate honesty with stupidity. The footnote wants to hold on to the solidity of this distinction at all costs.[22]

Something, however, destabilizes the sureness of the hold, something that we share with them and of which they may even be the origin, cheating us of the moral distinction that we seek to assert. If X marks the spot as that by which we are bound, then it may indeed name the place where They 'R' Us, where letters get scrambled before they are separated out into meaningful segregates. There exists, namely, a commonality, an inscription of cobelonging prior to any separation. It is a matter of record, and Kant gives place to this testimony, which recounts a more original identity preceeding the split between us and them. To the extent that the fundamental identity is based on writing, it urges the necessity of difference from the start, but nothing that could lead to the gross naturalizations and sullen historicization to which Kant gives vent. This may be why Kant needed to introduce two events of writing in order to advance his case. Thus the scripture held in common disrupts the distinction between us and them but becomes hidden under a contract that, in the name of noncontradiction, cannot as such be abrogated. There would be a holy script that binds and, on the other hand — the hand played by the state — a bind that cuts, a binding contract that ought to be respected. Two texts, then, one in which the us was them in the first place and another that ensures that the us was not them but the possibility of which needed to be instituted as possibility and impossibility at once.

Despite scripture and its contractual supervention, which appear to guarantee very little, a fundamental differend abides, disabling a shareable morality. *Their* morality "undoubtedly" urges an eleventh but cardinal and single commandment when "dealing with us." *Their* one commandment reads, "Let the buyer beware." Kant is buying this. He has even invested in this other morality. He does not want to be cheated and wants to understand why he would be cheated, necessarily, by this whole nation of cheaters. Instead of engaging idle plans ("Statt der vergeblichen Pläne") to moralize on deception, betrayal, or cheating (*Betrug*) in relation to honesty (*Ehrlichkeit*), he prefers to give a fantastical history lecture. The impulse to actualize such an "idle plan" would amount to a ridiculous effort, a vain attempt to throw morality at those who still worship the golden calf. Why moralize at the emptiness? To do so would mean that he was prepared to conduct himself as though he were a retiree, vainly miming a consequential act. Rather than talk to them, he will seek understanding for himself, he will take recourse to reason and history, powerful allies in reckoning the deficit by which they are recounted. The final contradiction, of which there are numerous other examples, concerns the curse that Kant turns at the end of the note into a blessing. It is not certain whom the philosopher addresses in this instance or whose perspective he appropriates in order to make his point, and to what end. The point gives the appearance of a conciliatory gesture but is not one. For if the Jews have regarded their fated wealth as a curse, this must be due to the fact that they do not regard money as a blessing — it is Kant who does.

※ ※ ※

The more general structure making what constitutes a curse or a blessing indeterminable has informed the economy of this elaboration and disposes a complex politics of sacrifice. Is philosophy without style to be viewed as a curse or a blessing? Do Kafka's Abrahams, with their tattered, dirty stains of being, belong to the sphere of the cursed or the blessed, or do they rather figure both at once, equally ridiculous, in dissonant rhyme with the solemn ordeal of the primal father? Is there a scale of cheating that has been historically removed from speech and sight but projected onto the "unter uns lebenden Palästiner"? For, after all, what was the deal cut between God and Abraham? Who was cheating whom in terms of the tremendous credit account that was opened on behalf of the man, Abraham? And what about the down payment? Abraham answered the call on credit, in sheer belief. No questions asked. (Sarah laughed.) Isaac came along silently. Prepared to offer a sur-

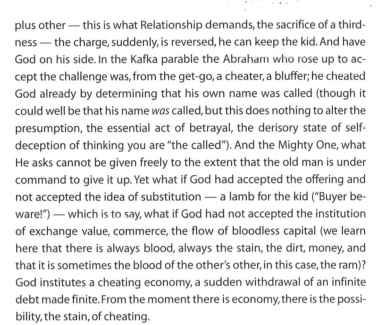

plus other — this is what Relationship demands, the sacrifice of a third-ness — the charge, suddenly, is reversed, he can keep the kid. And have God on his side. In the Kafka parable the Abraham who rose up to accept the challenge was, from the get-go, a cheater, a bluffer; he cheated God already by determining that his own name was called (though it could well be that his name *was* called, but this does nothing to alter the presumption, the essential act of betrayal, the derisory state of self-deception of thinking you are "the called"). And the Mighty One, what He asks cannot be given freely to the extent that the old man is under command to give it up. Yet what if God had accepted the offering and not accepted the idea of substitution — a lamb for the kid ("Buyer beware!") — which is to say, what if God had not accepted the institution of exchange value, commerce, the flow of bloodless capital (we learn here that there is always blood, always the stain, the dirt, money, and that it is sometimes the blood of the other's other, in this case, the ram)? God institutes a cheating economy, a sudden withdrawal of an infinite debt made finite. From the moment there is economy, there is the possibility, the stain, of cheating.

Why did God enter into commerce with Abraham, bidding on the thing of highest value, on that which surpasses any calculable value, only in order to introduce value by the act of substitution and holocaust (the ram proffered as burnt offering)? It is thought that God is He who transcends economy. Even so, God wanted an estimate of His own value — demanding the incalculable, he wanted to enter into the calculation. He demanded to be reckoned with. A bad move on God's part, if I may say so. Henceforth they will call each other's bluff; they will play chicken and see who first desists, betting on survival. (Since He got drawn into economy, it is a matter of survival for Him as well, for there remains the possibility that He would not have survived the offering, that He could not have founded the primal father to guarantee His survival, and in this regard He is Abraham's son and creation, ever about to be sacrificed.)[23]

The economy of cheating was there from the start, which is why Sarah laughed. Abraham was too old; he was cheated of progeny, could not reproduce himself. God makes an offer. Cheating time, they bear the firstborn, of whom he, Abraham, is soon enough prepared to be cheated. How can God not be a cheater if He wants to take away what it seems He has given? Is this not an essential trait of God, to dispossess, to be the cause of one fall after another and, in so doing, to render ridiculous the very possibility of (self-)possession? (The junk bonds proliferate. Later on Abraham cheats God of the take-no-prisoners deal with

Sodom — he bargains God down to a few righteous men in exchange for the town's survival.)

When Kafka retrieves Abraham in order to serialize and submit him to ridicule, it is with a view to pondering the very possibility of possession, which the initiative of God undermines (the serialization of the primal patriarch is ridiculous because it shatters his singularity and the stability of the *ur,* the *Erz,* but also because, as spontaneous multiplication, it answers immediately, as only God can do, to the promise that he will reproduce, that is, mutate and populate). How can Abraham have a house? How can he "have" anything, even the certainty of the call up? If there are to be many and other Abrahams, contested Abrahams, this is because the concept of imposture inheres in his name; insofar as he hears his name called, he has already operated a switch, he rises to the call as impostor. To the extent that one can answer the call, one can do so only as an impostor, at best as one's own alternate, the other of oneself — the one who is called. In any case, the one who answers the call is other than the one who had not yet been called.[24] Answering the call (which you must do; this is not a question of "choice"), you become an impostor: do you seriously think you are the Messiah? And even if it is you, you will be wracked with doubt and asking questions when they crucify you. The switch occurs at the beginning when Abraham thinks he is Abraham, the one, the only being called, and from this moment onward the law of substitution will have been instituted (Abraham for Abraham — which may be why each time God calls out his name twice: "Abraham! Abraham!" — Isaac for Abraham, the ram for Isaac). The one God for the other gods. Lacan reminds us in his thought on the Thing that the monotheistic God does not assert his unicity — that He is the only God — but that he is the best among the gods and deserves to get out of the series. On the other hand, the name Abraham was to become coextensive with the concept of cheating to the extent that in England the "Abraham-man" designated one of a class of impostors who wandered about the country pretending lunacy. To "sham Abraham" means to feign sickness, to substitute an infirm for a capable presentation of self.

How the primal father became associated with sham, imposture, and cheating at the level of the letter calls for an elaborate genealogical investigation of the sort Freud undertakes in *Moses and Monotheism.* Among other things, it would delve into the unsolved mystery of Sarah's death — though left behind, she does not survive the trip to Mount Moriah. For all she knows, and this is what she thinks she knows, Isaac was sacrificed, and she perishes of a broken heart. For all we know, Sarah

was murdered and the father reenacted the scene before the Law. But being in analysis with God, he did not yield unflinchingly to the repetition compulsion and this time let his victim go. Assuming that Abraham was cured and did not sacrifice Isaac (though according to one midrash the son was executed),[25] the question remains of how and whether Isaac survived the near-death experience — how he survived a psychotic father, that is, everybody's primal father, Kafka's, yours, and mine, even, or *especially,* when they are in sync with the Law.

Isaac became a figure of traumatic repetition; he dug holes in the earth where his father had done the digging before him, puncturing mother earth, producing holes already marked by Abraham. The son reproduces holes, digging and emptying, as if responsible for a dumb show whose sense Hamlet subsequently imposed on Western consciousness. What Isaac was "getting at" we still do not know or cannot tolerate knowing. In any case, he turned out to be a bit of a loser, if he was anything at all in the end, the almost-sacrificed son. It cannot be said with certitude that he survived. One supposes that he would have been better served had his destiny not been summed up in the Dostoevskyan freeze-flash of the nearly executed. Deprived of a martyr's grandeur, relieved of his stake in establishing an unprecedented contract between God and man — he had been a wager, he was dealt out — Isaac was condemned to live in the trauma zone of empty repetition, digging for a truth trove that was never to be found. The serial digger displaces the dagger, punctuating earth with the unreadable hieroglyphs of another story, that of another, untold Abraham. There could have been, there must be, yet another Abraham.[26]

So God introduces a discrepancy between intention and doing. Abraham's intention to offer his son does not need to be sealed by an act (or even ratified by a material boy). Intention is act enough. Proneness to intention would suffice, a certain numbness that answers to a name prior to the constitution of any subject or any faculty of understanding. Understanding, then, does not even come into the picture, unless Isaac's silence betrays his understanding and complicity.[27] Somnambulent intention can be act enough, so the act itself can be renegotiated, modified. The moment renegotiation becomes possible, this also means that man, Isaac, is substitutable or already acts as substitute, as an index of value, for Isaac exists in his essence as substitute for something else, greater than himself, as a disjointed synecdoche of that part of Abraham which is most prized. Isaac, at once irreplaceable and substitutable, functions as a sign of God's insatiable demand but is never the "thing itself" that God wants (God does not want Isaac as such but [something from] Abraham). Nor is it the case that Abraham says, "Take me! I offer myself; I convert myself into sign and wager." In not offering himself (he may be dirty, unworthy), Abraham is also prepared to offer something greater than himself. All we know at the end of the day of intended sacrifice is that, given the implicit hierarchies of value and estimations, God will settle for less. He can be, so to speak, and with no further harm meant to the animals that have been made to stand in for our *Dasein,* a being with whom one can bargain: this would be the compact. You want my son, I'll give you a ram. Can you live with that? Neither Sarah nor Isaac could. For our purposes, suffice it to say that what appears to have been meant to suspend human sacrifice — Isaac reprieved — in fact has introduced a structure that perpetuates sacrifice and substitution. As though the tribes were made ever more to pay the difference, and the sacrifice, once demanded, was reset and futured — tendered, so to speak, as that which was yet to come. Isaac, knowing what he cannot say, keeps on digging holes into the old story, preparing new plots.

✳ ✳ ✳

The biggest bluff, for all that, may have occurred when the delusion was implanted, the hope nurtured, of a chosen people. Isaac, he was and was not called. More radically uncertain than persecution (when you know they're after you, you're already dead meat; you *are* the ram caught in the bushes) is being cheated by the call. Too stupid to know whether your name was called, you are ridiculous. You are ready to go up for the sacrifice, but in the last moment you are benched. They don't need you. An animal will serve the purpose, your purpose. This call, it told you that you were the one, the chosen. You set yourself up to receive it, you were set up. A cheated cheater. It was no longer recognizable whether the call meant to serve as punishment or reward. Your father took the call. You inherited it, with all the expected static; you inherited his burden, which you thought you could lighten. You followed your father in mute complicity. As you were walking, as he was preparing to give you up, you could not tell, you simply could not decide, whether this call that expelled you from your house was a blessing or a curse.

Notes

INTRODUCTION

1. Friedrich Schiller, *Jungfrau von Orleans* (act 3, sc. 6), in *Werke Nationalausgabe*, ed. Julius Peterson and Hermann Schneider, 42 vols. (Weimar: Böhlau, 1942), 9:257; Hannah Arendt and Karl Jaspers, *Correspondence, 1926–1969*, ed. Lotte Kohler and Hans Saner, trans. Robert Kimber and Rita Kimber (New York: Harcourt Brace, 1992), 439; Alain Grosrichard, *The Sultan's Court: European Fantasies of the East*, trans. Liz Heron (London: Verso, 1998); Jacques Lacan, *The Seminar of Jacques Lacan*, bk. 7: *The Ethics of Psychoanalysis, 1959–1960*, ed. Jacques-Alain Miller, trans. Dennis Porter (New York: W. W. Norton, 1992). The same concern over the sheer stupidity of Eichmann's positions is voiced in Hannah Arendt and Mary McCarthy, *Between Friends*, ed. Carol Brightman (New York: Harcourt Brace, 1995), 296–98. One might additionally consider in this context the remarks made by Ernst Cassirer to open his political contemplation *The Myth of the State* (New Haven, Conn.: Yale University Press, 1946): "But in man's practical and social life the defeat of rational thought seems to be complete and irrevocable. . . . Imagination itself cannot account for all its incongruities and its fantastic and bizarre elements. It is rather the *Urdummheit* of man that is responsible for these absurdities and contradictions. Without this 'primeval stupidity' there would be no myth" (4).

2. "When Catoblépas, a black buffalo with the head of a pig that drags on the ground, addresses him, he [Saint Antoine] is sorely tempted: 'Sa stupidité m'attire'" (Jonathan Culler, *Flaubert: The Uses of Uncertainty* [Ithaca, N.Y.: Cornell University Press, 1985], 183).

3. Friedrich Nietzsche, *Beyond Good and Evil: Prelude to a Philosophy of the Future*, trans. Walter Kaufmann (New York: Random House, 1989), no. 188.

4. Ibid., no. 228.

5. Among the few who did not ignore its potential significance in modernity was Schopenhauer, for whom stupidity implied, together with vulgarity, a complete reversal of the will-understanding relation. In "On the Sublime and Naive in the Fine Sciences," Moses Mendelssohn devotes several paragraphs to a description of stupidity as embedded in facial features. The face imparts different levels of stupidity: "if the simplicity in the movements betrays thoughtlessness and lack of sensitivity, then it is called 'stupidity' and if it is accompanied by listlessness, then we have . . . *niais* [silliness]" (*Philosophical Writings*, trans. Daniel O. Dahlstrom [Cambridge: Cambridge University Press, 1997], 226–27).

6. Friedrich Hölderlin, *Sämtliche Werke: Frankfurter Ausgabe*, 20 vols., ed. D. E.

Sattler (Frankfurt am Main: Verlag Roter Stern, 1975), 4:261, 336–40; 5:683–700.

7. Rainer Maria Rilke, "Das Lied des Idioten," in *Werke*, 4 vols., ed. Manfred Engel et al. (Frankfurt: Insel Verlag, 1996), 1:327; Richard Wright, haiku #579, in *Haiku: The Other World* (New York: Arcade Publishing, 1998), 132; Joseph Conrad, *Tales of Unrest* (New York: Penguin Books, 1977), 57.

8. Walter Benjamin, "Zwei Gedichte von Friedrich Hölderlin. 'Dichtermut' — Blödigkeit," in *Gesammelte Schriften*, 7 vols., ed. Rolf Tiedemann and Hermann Schweppenhaüser (Frankfurt am Main: Suhrkamp Verlag, 1972), 2(1): 105–26 (for English-language translations see Benjamin, "Two Poems by Friedrich Hölderlin: 'The Poet's Courage' and 'Timidity,'" trans. Stanley Corngold, *Selected Writings*, 2 vols., ed. Michael Jennings [Cambridge, Mass.: Harvard University Press, 1996], 1:18–36); Gershom Scholem, *Walter Benjamin — die Geschichte einer Freundschaft* (Frankfurt am Main: Suhrkamp Verlag, 1975), 26.

9. On the avoidance of personal agency see Stanley Corngold, *Complex Pleasure: Forms of Feeling in German Literature* (Stanford, Calif.: Stanford University Press, 1998), 153.

10. Bart Philipsen, "Herz aus Glas — Hölderlin, Rousseau und das 'blöde' Subjeckt der Moderne," in *Bild-Sprache: Texte zwischen Dichten und Denken*, ed. L. Lamberechts and J. Nowé (Louvain: Presses Universitaires, 1990), 177–94; Michael Jennings, "Benjamin as a Reader of Hölderlin: The Origins of Benjamin's Theory of Literary Criticism," *German Quarterly Review* 56.4 (Nov. 1983): 544–62; Corngold, *Complex Pleasure*, 150–70; Friedrich Hölderlin, *Selected Verse*, trans. and ed. Michael Hamburger (London: Anvil Press Poetry, 1986), 238.

11. Corngold, *Complex Pleasure*, 162.

12. Wolfgang Pfeifer, in *Etymologisches Wörterbuch des Deutschen* (Berlin: Akademie-Verlag, 1989), s.v., "blöd(e)," dates the use of the term as "dumm, schwachsinnig [dumb, feeble-minded]" to the sixteenth century. It clearly carried this connotation — if not the outright denotative value — for Hölderlin.

13. Philipsen, "Herz aus Glas," 192 (my translation).

14. Corngold, *Complex Pleasure*, 168. Reverting to a position of relative safety, Corngold places stupidity in quotation marks.

15. Benjamin, "Two Poems," 1:22 (subsequent citations occur parenthetically in the text).

16. Benjamin, "Zwei Gedichte," 2(1): 125 (subsequent citations occur parenthetically in the text).

17. Hölderlin, *Sämtliche Werke*: "Drum! so wandle nur wehrlos / Fort durchs Leben, und sorge nicht!" ("Dichtermut," 4:261); or "Drum, mein Genius! tritt nur / Baar ins Leben, und sorge nicht!" ("Blödigkeit," 5:699).

18. Pierre Alferi, "Un Accent de vérité," *Revue des Sciences Humaines: Maurice Blanchot* 253.1 (1999): 153–71.

19. Henry James, *The Sacred Fount* (New York: New Directions, 1983), 17.

20. Roland Barthes, "Barthes to the Third Power," trans. Matthew Ward and Richard Howard, in *On Signs*, ed. Marshall Blonsky (Baltimore, Md.: Johns Hopkins University Press, 1985), 189.

21. Another text, "Images," repeats Barthes's obsessive anxiety over Stupidity: "In the arena of language, constructed like a football field, there are two extreme sites, two goals that can never be avoided: Stupidity on the one end, the Unreadable at the other. . . . Stupidity is not linked to error. Always triumphant (impossible to overcome), it derives its victory from an enigmatic power: it is 'Dasein' in all its naked splendor. Whence a terror and a fascination, that of a corpse. (Corpse of what? Perhaps of truth: truth as dead.) . . . Stupidity 'is there,' obtuse as death. Exorcism can only be a formal operation which confronts it 'en bloc,' from outside. . . . Here I am back at the same panic that Stupidity inspires: Is it me? Is it the other? Is it the other who is unreadable (or stupid)? Am I the one who is limited, inept, am I the one who doesn't understand?" (Roland Barthes, *The Rustle of Language*, trans. Richard Howard [Berkeley: University of California Press, 1989], 351–52).

22. The resemblance of a rock to stupidity's hard place ends there, for the recourse taken by Flaubert to a natural object is a desperate one, designed mainly to offset the grasp of understanding and to allow stupidity to borrow from inorganic nature the attributes of its hardness. The imperturbable inertia characteristic of some forms of stupidity in fact unsettles any rhetorical resolution into an object. If Flaubert deploys an unreliable analogy to get a hold on the traits of stupidity, it is to show the limits of understanding: "One can understand facts about [a stone or a mountain] or problems that are posed when a human project or discourse operates on them, providing a focus, asking a question" (Culler, *Flaubert*, 175).

23. Gustave Flaubert, *Correspondance*, 9 vols. (Paris: Louis Conard, 1926–33), 2:398 (my translation, all such; subsequent citations occur parenthetically in the text).

24. Culler, *Flaubert*, 176.

25. Flaubert, *Correspondance*, 2:485: "A Alexandrie un certain Thompson, de Sunderland, a sur la colonne de Pompée écrit son nom en lettres de six pieds de haut. . . . Il n'y a pas moyen de voir la colonne sans voir le nom de Thompson, et par conséquent sans penser à Thompson."

26. Jacques Derrida, "An Idea of Flaubert: 'Plato's Letter,'" trans. Peter Starr, *Modern Language Notes* 99.4 (Sept. 1984): 758–59, translating Derrida, "Une idée de Flaubert: La lettre de Platon," *Revue d'Histoire Littéraire de la France* 4–5 (July–Oct. 1981): 666: "(et pour Flaubert la bêtise est toujours monumentale, de la taille du monument pierreux couvert d'inscription)."

27. Playing on the name of his close friend, Erasmus dedicated his *Moria* (as he usually called the work) to More — Thomas More, in whose house the

work was written. For a discussion of *morosophos*, see the translator's introduction in Desiderius Erasmus, *The Praise of Folly*, trans. Clarence H. Miller (New Haven, Conn.: Yale University Press, 1979), xiii.

28. Flaubert, *Correspondance*, 2:243: "La bêtise est quelque chose d'inébranable; rien ne l'attaque sans se briser contre elle. Elle est de la nature du granit, dure et résistante."

29. Quoted in Culler, *Flaubert*, 174.

30. Jean Paul, "Von der Dumheit," *Werke*, pt. 2, ed. Norbert Miller, 4 vols. (Munich: Carl Hanser Verlag, 1974), 1:266–75 (subsequent citations occur parenthetically in the text).

31. Ibid., 1:270: "Der Dumkopf ist meistens glücklich, wenn er den aufgeklärten Kopf angreift."

32. Ibid.: "Nie sind diese Geschöpfe allein. Sie . . . fülen ihre gegenseitige Anziehung am stärksten im Kriege gegen den Klugen."

33. Ibid.: "Der grosse Man verachtet die Mükkenstiche der kleinen Geister; er betrügt sich."

34. Ibid., 1:269: "Sein Ideensystem beschränkt sich auf eine kleine Anzal Begriffe, die tief in ihm haften, weil sie in seiner Jugend ihren Weg durch den Rükken namen, die er für heilig hält, weil sie die Reliquien von dem Geiste seines Vaters sind und einen Teil seiner Erbschaft ausmachen."

35. Ibid., 1:268: "Die Gedanken des andern interessieren ihn mehr als seine eigne."

36. Ibid., 1:267: "Das Gedächtnis ist die einzige Fähigkeit, die der Dumme vor dem klugen Tier voraushat."

37. Ibid.: "Ein besserer Kopf merkt weniger auf einmal aber eine einzige Sache erinnert ihn an tausend ähnliche."

38. See Jean Paul, "Siebenkäs," *Werke*, 2:7–565.

39. Jean Paul, "Von der Dumheit," 1:275: "Überall sind reiche und mächtige Dunsen gepflanzt."

40. Ibid.: "Der zum Orden der Dunsen gehört und verbant den Aufgeklärten als einen Rebel aus den friedlichen Reiche der Esel."

41. Ibid. (my translation): "— Man irt sich — der Spiegel ist längst da — gebt dem Dummen erst Augen zum hineinsehen, d.h. macht ihn klug!"

42. Also, Jean Paul, "Übungen im Denken," *Werke*, 1:95 (my translation): "Ich mus also aufhören — vom Narren zu reden."

43. Derrida's recent works have been devoted to the unfinished aspects of responsibility. See also Thomas Keenan, *Fables of Responsibility: Aberrations and Predicaments in Ethics and Politics* (Stanford, Calif.: Stanford University Press, 1997), and Drucilla Cornell, *The Philosophy of the Limit: Justice and Legal Interpretation* (New York: Routledge, 1992).

44. See Emmanuel Levinas, "Responsibility for the Other," *Ethics and Infinity: Conversations with Philippe Nemo*, trans. Richard A. Cohen (Pittsburgh: Duquesne University Press, 1985), 93–101. Levinas's reading of responsibility points to powerful political events in his discussion of the massacres at

Sabra and Chatila in 1982. See his "Ethics and Politics," trans. Jonathan Romney, in *The Levinas Reader*, ed. Seán Hand (Oxford: Blackwell, 1989), 289–97.

45. Gilles Deleuze, *Difference and Repetition*, trans. Paul Patton (New York: Columbia University Press, 1994); originally *Différence et Répetition* (Paris: Presses Universitaires de France, 1969) (subsequent citations occur parenthetically in the text).

46. Deleuze, *Différence et Répetition*, 196: "la bêtise ne peut plus être qu'une détermination empirique, renvoyant à la psychologie ou à l'anecdote — pire encore, à la polémique et aux injures — et aux sottisiers comme genre pseudo-littéraire particulièrement exécrable" (196).

47. Robert Musil, "The Ruminations of a Slow-Witted Mind," in *Precision and Soul: Essays and Addresses*, ed. and trans. Burton Pike and David S. Luft (Chicago: University of Chicago Press, 1978), 224.

48. See Arnold I. Davidson, "1933–1934: Thoughts on National Socialism," *Critical Inquiry* 17 (Autumn 1990): 35–45.

49. Musil, "Ruminations," 224.

50. Consider Jean-François Lyotard, "The Tomb of the Intellectual," *Political Writings*, trans. Bill Readings and Kevin Paul Geiman (Minneapolis: University of Minnesota Press, 1993). Lyotard's attack on intellectuals, Big Brother, and other experts generally concerns the presumption to authority in politics. "The responsibility of 'intellectuals' is inseparable from the (shared) idea of a universal subject" (3). In his introductory comments, Readings argues that the intellectual, exiled from the particular in order to reach the universal, is a citizen of the universe who speaks to everyone and to no one in particular. "The intellectual, as a modernist creature, rationalizes history by means of abstraction, constructing a grand narrative of the liberation of a subject as self-realization. The end of history is thus the liberation of mankind as essentially free from ignorance (Enlightenment), essentially capable of providing material needs in a free market (capitalism), or essentially laboring (Marxism). Actual events are merely the raw materials for a metadiscursive reflection upon the progress of this narrative of self-realization" (xxii).

   For a discussion of the crisis in the legitimation of knowledge after the "death" of the subject, after the failure of Enlightenment liberalism, see Chantal Mouffe, "Deconstruction, Pragmatism and the Politics of Democracy," in *Deconstruction and Pragmatism*, ed. Chantal Mouffe (New York: Routledge, 1996), i–x, and *The Return of the Political* (New York: Verso, 1993).

51. Stanley Cavell, *Pursuits of Happiness: The Hollywood Comedy of Remarriage* (Cambridge, Mass.: Harvard University Press, 1981), 42.

52. See Theodor W. Adorno, *Minima Moralia: Reflexionen aus dem beschädigten Leben* (Frankfurt am Main: Suhrkamp Verlag, 1993), 263.

53. Jean Améry, *Radical Humanism: Selected Essays*, trans. and ed. Sidney Rosen-

feld and Stella F. Rosenfeld (Bloomington: Indiana University Press, 1984), 136. See also his *At the Mind's Limit: Contemplations by a Survivor on Auschwitz and Its Realities*, trans. Sidney Rosenfeld and Stella F. Rosenfeld (Bloomington: Indiana University Press, 1998). For a discussion of history and its relation to hallucination (to that which "does not belong to the domain of knowledge"), see Eduardo Cadava's reading of Bergson's *Matter and Memory* in *Words of Light: Theses on the Photography of History* (Princeton, N.J.: Princeton University Press, 1997), 95–97.

54. According to the *Oxford English Dictionary*, a dope is "a stupid person, a simpleton, a fool," and in U.S. slang, "a person under the influence of, or addicted to, some drug."

55. Paul de Man, *The Rhetoric of Romanticism* (New York: Columbia University Press, 1984,) viii: "Such massive evidence of the failure to make the various individuals coalesce is a somewhat melancholy spectacle." In the foreword to *Blindness and Insight: Essays in the Rhetoric of Contemporary Criticism*, 2d rev. ed. (Minneapolis: University of Minnesota Press, 1983), de Man sets up the melancholic practice of self-review in the mode of disavowal: "I am not given to retrospective self-examination and mercifully forget what I have written with the same alacrity I forget bad movies — although, as with bad movies, certain scenes or phrases return at times to embarrass and haunt me like a guilty conscience. When one imagines to have felt the exhilaration of renewal, one is certainly the last to know whether such a change actually took place or whether one is restating, in a slightly different mode, earlier and unresolved obsessions" (xii).

56. Thomas Pynchon, *Slow Learner* (New York: Little, Brown, 1984), 3 (subsequent citations occur parenthetically in the text).

"I HAVE IN THE PAST . . ."

1. Deleuze, *Différence et répétition*, 43–44.

2. Samuel Beckett, *Samuel Beckett: The Complete Short Prose, 1929–1989*, ed. S. E. Gontarski (New York: Grove Press, 1995), 189.

CHAPTER 1: THE QUESTION OF STUPIDITY

1. For a compelling discussion of Hegel's appropriation of Schelling on this point, see Marc Froment-Meurice, "Du Pareil au même," in *De la bêtise et des bêtes* (special issue of *Le temps de la réflexion*), ed. J.-B. Pontalis (Paris: Gallimard, 1988), 127–58.

2. Max Horkheimer and Theodor W. Adorno, "The Genesis of Stupidity," *Dialectic of Enlightenment*, trans. John Cumming (New York: Continuum, 1986), 157, 257. The section asserts that in "its early stages the life of the mind is infinitely fragile" (256). "Dummheit ist ein Wundmal," a kind of

monument of wounding: "Such scars lead to deformities. They can build hard and able characters; they can breed stupidity — as a symptom of pathological deficiency, of blindness and impotency if they are quiescent; in the form of malice, spite and fanaticism if they produce a cancer within" (257–58). Eventually the scarred body of stupidity turns to stone (Versteinerung), becoming unmoveable, hard. The phrase "Dummheit ist ein Wundmal" is from Max Horkheimer and Theodor W. Adorno, Dialektik der Aufklärung: Philosophische Fragmente, ed. Rolf Tiedemann (Frankfurt am Main: Suhrkamp Verlag, 1972), 296–97.

3. Lacan, Ethics of Psychoanalysis, 1959–1960, 107.

4. Gustave Flaubert, Le Dictionnaire des idées reçues (Paris: A. G. Nizet, 1990), 246; published in English as Flaubert's Dictionary of Accepted Ideas, trans. Jacques Barzun (Norfolk, Conn.: New Directions, 1954), 47. A more literal rendering would be "IDDIOTS: Those who do not think like us."

5. In "Toward an Ethics of Reading: Levinas and American Literature" (Ph.D. diss., University of California at Berkeley, 2001), Shireen R. K. Patell writes of the double-edged enigma of the slave's historically presumed stupidity. On the one hand, designated as not quite human, the slave was thought to be ineducable (Bildungsunfähig); on the other hand, laws against teaching slaves to read and write seem to belie this assertion. Projecting their own anxieties, the slaveowners deflected the dangers of literacy back onto the slave, who might be able to learn the mechanics of language without proper interiorization and yet be exposed to the depths of a suffering consciousness. On the surface, Frederick Douglass seems to have appropriated this paternalizing logic of protection: "I would at times feel that learning to read had been a curse rather than a blessing. . . . In moments of agony, I envied my fellow slaves their stupidity" — a purely rhetorical appropriation, for this exclamation of despair appears in Douglass's published narrative of his escape from slavery (Narrative of the Life of Frederick Douglass, quoted in Patell, "Toward an Ethics of Reading," 179).

6. See François Hartog, "Bêtises grecques," in De la bêtise et des bêtes (special issue of Le temps de la réflexion), ed. J.-B. Pontalis (Paris: Gallimard, 1988), 63.

7. Martin Heidegger, "Schöpferische Landschaft: Warum bleiben wir in der Provinz?," Aus der Erfahrung des Denkens, 1910–1976 (Frankfurt am Main: Vittorio Klostermann, 1983), 9–15. This brief essay was prompted by the second job offer (Ruf) made to Heidegger by the University of Berlin in 1933. Transmitted as part of a radio program by the Berliner Rundfunk, it was first published in 1962 without permission ("ohne Genehmigung") by Guido Schneeberger in Nachlese zu Heidegger (Bern, 1962), 216–18. On March 2, 1934, the piece had been published without revision by the National Socialist newsletter (Kampfblatt) Der Allemanne. The text, which thematizes Heidegger's rejection of the Berlin offer, argues that his work (Arbeit) is essentially linked to the possibility of the landscape in a relation-

ship of codisclosiveness: "Die Arbeit öffnet erst den Raum für diese Berg-
wirklichkeit. Der Gang der Arbeit bleibt in das Geschehen der Landschaft
eingesenkt" (10). A major point is scored in the name of loyalty (Treue),
which places the peasant above the urbanite (der Städter). Such loyalty is
often expressed by silence and helps Heidegger make his decision to remain in the provinces. He recounts a visit to a seventy-five-year-old peasant friend who had read in the papers about the offer from Berlin. What
will he say? Heidegger wonders. The peasant gazes with his clear eyes at
Heidegger, places his loyal-truthful, his thoughtful hand ("seine treu-
bedächtige Hand") on Heidegger's shoulder, and shakes his head in a
barely perceptible way. The meaning of this quasi gesture is, "No!" ("[er]
legt mir seine treu-bedächtige Hand auf die Schulter und — schüttelt
kaum merklich den Kopf. Das will sagen: unerbittlich Nein!") Beyond the
ideologically laden weight of authenticity sketched by Heidegger in the
war of these worlds (including the world of journalism versus that of the
peasant's knowing silence), Heidegger's way of arriving at the decision
would have to be read against the horizon of decision, Entschlossenheit, in
Sein und Zeit. For our purposes, it should suffice to observe that the decisive
moment occurs in contrast to the city and its relatedness to language, intelligence, media, and institution. The truth-loyalty of peasant-being is
rooted in a resolute muteness (though it speaks elsewhere), a paucity of
language, in immobility, and a profound resistance or dumbness as concerns Wissenschaft (science) and learning — in short, a certain if unavowable dumbfoundedness, a pious stupidity that sustains Heidegger, making
his work possible, determining his site.

8. Heidegger spoke in private of the greatest act of stupidity ("die grösste
Dummheit") of his life when referring to his political commitment of
1933–34 (quoted by Heinrich W. Petzet in his preface to Martin Heidegger,
Erhart Kästner, Briefwechsel, 1953–1974, ed. Heinrich W. Petzet [Frank-
furt am Main: Insel Verlag, 1986], 10). See also Philippe Lacoue-Labarthe,
"Heidegger's Affair," Heidegger, Art, and Politics: The Fiction of the Political,
trans. Chris Turner (Oxford: Blackwell, 1990), 12.

9. The French term denoting stupidity is of course bête, tying dumbness to
the animality of animals. You don't have to be vegan or an animal rights
activist to note how unfair this is to animals. Only humans can be, or be
predicated as, bête.

10. Friedrich Schlegel, Friedrich Schlegel's "Lucinde" and the Fragments, trans. Peter Firchow (Minneapolis: University of Minnesota Press, 1971), 277.

11. Henri Michaux, "Bonheur bête," in La Nuit remue, quoted in Froment-
Meurice, "Du Pareil au même," 127 (my translation).

12. Louis Birner, "The Shlemiel and the Shlep: A Psychoanalytic Note on Two
Masochistic Styles," Modern Psychoanalysis 9.2 (1984): 180. An essay on the
distinct qualities of the simpleton, the hard-luck type, and the born loser,
it also devotes several pages to enforced passivity and the display of inad-

equacy. The masochist is shown to "use the shlemiel or shlep posture and role as a neurotic cover for his masochism" (179). Psychic helplessness and pseudo-inadequacy are their ways of remaining with mother. "Let the analyst be wary of the shlep and the shlemiel; they are artful manipulators longing for the old maternal relationship" (187).

13. Froment-Meurice casts a compelling moment in his argument in terms of the relatedness of stupidity to the metaphysics of fulfillment ("Du Pareil au même," 127–58).

14. See Jean-Marie Goulemot, "Philosophie des Lumières au Royaume de la Nuit," in De la bêtise et des bêtes (special issue of Le temps de la réflexion), ed. J.-B. Pontalis (Paris: Gallimard, 1988), 102. In keeping with the title of this essay, one might offer as a figure for bêtise in the Lumières Mozart's Papageno, who, as part animal and associate of the Queen of the Night, participates in Tamino's Enlightenment hazing, consistently displaying the principal qualities of stupidity: prejudice, mendacity, and fear for his life.

15. Jean-Luc Nancy, "Fragments de la bêtise," in De la bêtise et des bêtes (special issue of Le temps de la réflexion), ed. J.-B. Pontalis (Paris: Gallimard, 1988), 16 (my translation): "Le grec-juif connaît une folie, la démesure de l'insensé. Le chrétien connaît la foi comme une folie (qui répond à celle de son Dieu), et cette folie humilie la raison et la sagesse du monde. La bêtise appartient donc à l'essence de la déchéance, et à la nécessité du salut."

Nancy's discussion of Christianity's investment in stupidity offers one context in which to situate the history of contempt for those who are constructed as being smart — smart-alecky, that is, clever and evil, the historically targeted wiseguys who are seen to be asking for trouble. In terms of dominant tendencies and their inescapable consequences, it is stupid to be smart, even in sites conventionally thought to uphold values of learning. For interpretations that relate intelligence and race (dare I say intelligently?), see Sander L. Gilman, Smart Jews: The Construction of the Image of Jewish Superior Intelligence (Lincoln: University of Nebraska Press, 1996). A 1994 New York Times article on Jacques Derrida quotes a prominent Harvard professor lamenting, in a manner that still needs to be decoded, the fact that in order to understand deconstruction students have to be really intelligent; this fact is offered as the downside of admitting deconstruction to college. I hope I have made it clear by now that there is no reason to assume that universities fall on the other side of stupidity. However, it is important to note that stupidity takes no sides. And the other way around, intelligence is not always opposable to stupidity but can become its manifest symptom.

On the other coast, Laurence A. Rickels (The Vampire Lectures [Minneapolis: University of Minnesota Press, 1999], xiv–xv) explicates the native pedagogy of California, "one that is as dumb and unforgettble as god and dog." See also his discussion of adolescent hermeneutics: "Give them what they already know and leave them there, feeling good about themselves."

16. Nancy, "Fragments de la bêtise," 16: "le retournement simple de l'optimisme dans son contraire pas plus intelligent, le pessimisme nihiliste."

17. Nicholas de Cusa, *Opera omnia: Issu et auctoritate Academiae Litterarum Heidelbergensis ad codem fidem edita*, 17 vols. to date (Hamburg: Meiner, 1959-), 1.88.16-20 (my translation, all such; subsequent citations, which occur parenthetically in the text, are to volume, part [if any], page, and line). See his *De visione dei*, 6.51.4-8 and 6.67.7-8.

18. Jasper Hopkins, *Nicholas of Cusa on Learned Ignorance: A Translation and an Appraisal of "De docta ignorantia"* (Minneapolis: Arthur J. Banning, 1981), 4 (subsequent citations occur parenthetically in the text).

19. Hopkins (*Nicholas of Cusa*, 2-3) shows that the *De docta ignorantia* went through a number of translative operations that point to the theoretical instability of the title. According to Hopkins, Paul Wilpert argues that the title is more correctly translated as "*Die belehrte Unwissenheit*" (Learnt Ignorance) than as "*Die gelehrte Unwissenheit*" (Learned Ignorance). By contrast, again according to Hopkins, Erich Meuthen opts for the title "*Das gelehrte Nicht-Wissen*" (Learned Not-Knowing). Hopkins writes: "Wilpert feels that the unknowing which Nicholas discusses is not so much an erudite or a wise unknowing (i.e., an unknowing which confers a kind of erudition or wisdom on the one who does not know) as it is simply a recognition-of-limitedness that has been achieved (i.e., an unknowing which has been learned, so that the one who has learned of his unknowing is now among the instructed, rather than remaining one of the unlearned). Wilpert is certainly right that in DI the emphasis is upon instruction in the way-of-ignorance and that the man of learned ignorance is not thought by Nicholas to be a man of erudition.... Yet, it is equally clear from I, 1 (4:16-17: 'the more he knows that he is unknowing, the more learned he will be') that Nicholas also sometimes understands '*docta ignorantia*' as an ignorance which renders its possessor wise. Indeed, in *Apologia* 2:9-10 Socrates is said to be wise precisely because he knows that he does not know" (2-3).

20. Jean-Jacques Rousseau, *The Confessions*, trans. J. M. Cohen (New York: Penguin Books, 1953), 112 (subsequent citations occur parenthetically in the text); for the French, see Rousseau, *Les Confessions*, in *Oeuvres complètes*, ed. Marcel Raymond and Bernard Gagnebin, 5 vols. (Paris: Gallimard, 1959), 1:1-656 (subsequent citations occur parenthetically in the text).

21. Rousseau, *Les Confessions*, 1:113: "Le résultat de ses observations fut que, malgré ce que promettaient mon extérieur et ma physionomie animée, j'étais, sinon tout à fait inepte, au moins un garçon de peu d'esprit, sans idées, presques sans acquis, très borné en un mot à tous égards, et que l'honneur de devenir un jour curé de village était la plus haute fortune à laquelle je dusse aspirer."

22. In *Allegories of Reading: Figural Language in Rousseau, Nietzsche, Rilke, and*

Proust (New Haven, Conn.: Yale University Press, 1979), Paul de Man writes: "What Rousseau really wanted is neither the ribbon nor Marion, but the public scene of exposure which he actually gets" (285). Mobilizing a theatrical figure, de Man continues: "This desire is truly shameful, for it suggests that Marion was destroyed, not for the sake of Rousseau's saving face, nor for the sake of his desire for her, but merely in order to provide him with a stage on which to parade his disgrace" (286).

23. Robert Musil, "Sheep, as Seen in Another Light," *Posthumous Papers of a Living Author*, trans. Peter Wortsman (Hygiene, Colo.: Eridanos, 1987), 21–22 (subsequent citations occur parenthetically in the text).

24. See Hartog, "Bêtises grecques," 52.

25. J. E. Erdmann, *Ernste Spiele: Vorträge, theils neu, theils längst vergessen* (Berlin: Verlag von Wilhelm Hertz, 1875), 319.

26. Ibid., 319 (my translation): ". . . und nicht nur von der eigenen Mutter, wie Jener, sondern von der Mutter aller Menschenkinder ward man so regalirt von Fortuna, deren Vorliebe für die Dummen sprüchwörtlich ist. Nicht mit Unrecht, denn daß er ohne Umsicht handelt, wie der Nachtwandler auf dem Dach oder Blondel auf dem Seil, gar nicht um sich sieht, oft sein Ziel erreicht, daß die Dummen, gerade wie die Kinder, auch wenn sie auf die Nase fallen, sie nicht verletzen, während mancher Gescheidte sie bricht, wenn er auf den Rücken fällt, das ist bekannt."

27. I have explored the logic and valuations of immunodeficiency in Nietzsche in "Queens of the Night," *Finitude's Score: Essays for the End of the Millennium* (Lincoln: University of Nebraska Press, 1994), 41–61.

28. Werner Hamacher, "Working through Working," trans. Matthew T. Hartman, *Modernism/Modernity* 3.1 (1996): 23–55.

29. Wolfgang Fritz Haug, ed. *Historisch-Kritisches Wörterbuch des Marxismus*, 4 vols. (Hamburg: Argument, 1995), 2:859: "Neben Gewalt und Ökonomie zählt Dummheit demnach zu den Geschichtsmächten" (subsequent citations occur parenthetically in the text; translations are mine). I thank Professor Robert Cohen for reviewing with me the focus in Marxist literature on the historical weightiness of *Dummheit*.

30. Karl Marx and Friedrich Engels, *Marx-Engels Werke*, 40 vols. (Berlin: Dietz, 1956–), 2:861 (my translation): "Wir wissen jetzt welche Rolle die Dummheit in Revolutionen spielt und wie sie von Lumpen exploitiert werden."

31. Stephen J. Gould, *The Mismeasure of Man* (New York: Norton, 1981). Gould sets up a fight against scientific racism. Mobilizing a history of scientific attitudes in order to offer a devastating critique of intelligence testing and its forebears, "American polygeny and craniometry," he at one point quotes Condorcet: "[They] make nature herself an accomplice in the crime of political inequality" (21). He also recalls Léonce Manouvrier, the nondeterminist black sheep of Paul Broca's craniologist's fold, who commented on Broca's data on the small brains of women: "Women displayed their

talents and their diplomas. They also invoked philosophical authorities. But they were opposed by *numbers* unknown to Condorcet or to John Stuart Mill. These numbers fell upon poor women like a sledge hammer, and they were accompanied by commentaries and sarcasms more ferocious than the most misogynist imprecations of certain church fathers. The theologians had asked if women had a soul. Several centuries later, some scientists were ready to refuse them a human intelligence" (26). Gould's initiatory contention is that what "craniometry was for the nineteenth century, intelligence testing has become for the twentieth, when it assumes that intelligence (or at least a dominant part of it) is a single, innate, heritable, and measurable thing" (25). He invalidates the two components of this approach to mental testing, the hereditarian version of the IQ scale as an American product and the argument for reifying intelligence as a single entity by the mathematical technique of factor analysis.

32. Jean-Michel Kantor, "Bêtes et savants," in *De la bêtise et des bêtes* (special issue of *Le temps de la réflexion*), ed. J.-B. Pontalis (Paris: Gallimard, 1988), 225. The works of Gould, Spearman, Jensen, and other sociobiologists are discussed elaborately in Kantor, "Bêtes et savants," 223–31. In a section of *The Mismeasure of Man* entitled "Preventing the Immigration and Propagation of Morons," Gould reviews the influential works of H. H. Goddard, including *The Kallikak Family: A Study in the Heredity of Feeble-mindedness* (New York: Macmillan, 1912); "The Binet Tests in Relation to Immigration," *Journal of Psycho-Asthenics* 18 (1913): 105–7; and "Mental Tests and the Immigrant," *Journal of Delinquency* 2 (1917): 30–32. In a parenthetical remark, Gould writes: "(I am continually amazed by the unconscious statements of prejudice that slip into supposedly objective accounts. Note here that average immigrants are below normal, or at least not obviously normal — the proposition that Goddard was supposedly testing, not asserting a priori)" (165). Here is an example of how Goddard rigged the results of the Binet tests, meant to show "the menace of moronity" (168) among immigrants: "Binet tests on the four groups [of selected immigrants] led to an astounding result: 83 per cent of the Jews, 80 per cent of the Hungarians, 79 per cent of the Italians, and 87 per cent of the Russians were feeble-minded — that is, below age twelve on the Binet scale. Goddard himself was flabbergasted: could anyone be made to believe that four-fifths of any nation were morons? 'The results obtained by the foregoing evaluation of the data are so surprising and difficult of acceptance that they can hardly stand by themselves as valid.' ... Perhaps the tests had not been adequately explained by interpreters? But the Jews had been tested by a Yiddish-speaking psychologist, and they ranked no higher than the other groups. Eventually, Goddard monkied about with the tests, tossed several out, and got his figures down to 40 to 50 per cent, but still he was disturbed" (166). Gould goes on to expose some of the more absurd dimensions of the test

and to explain the conditions under which they were taken — immigrants just off the boat, often after months of horrendous seafaring in subhuman conditions, arriving half-starved, frightened, confused. As a welcoming gesture on the part of Miss Liberty, they were ushered to their places and made to take lengthy tests. Perhaps this is why, in *Amerika*, Kafka imagined her to be holding a menacing sword rather than an illuminating torch.

CHAPTER 2: THE POLITICS OF STUPIDITY

1. "Postmodernism of the 1920s: Robert Musil, Writer and Philosopher for Our Time," conference held at the Deutsches Haus of New York University, December 1–2, 1995.
2. Robert Musil, "The German as Symptom," *Precision and Soul: Essays and Addresses*, ed. and trans. Burton Pike and David S. Luft (Chicago: University of Chicago Press, 1978), 156; originally published as *Schriftenreihe "Ausblicke"* (Vienna: Bermann-Fischer Verlag, 1937).
3. Robert Musil, "The Serious Writer in Our Time," *Precision and Soul*, 253.
4. Ibid., 254.
5. Robert Musil, "The Ruminations of a Slow-Witted Mind," *Precision and Soul*, 214–15 ("Blahblahblah" is mine).
6. Musil, "Serious Writer," 260.
7. Immanuel Kant, *Anthropologie in pragmatischer Hinsicht*, in *Immanuel Kants Werkausgabe*, ed. Wilhelm Weischedel, 12 vols. (Frankfurt am Main: Suhrkamp Verlag, 1982), 12:516: "Der Mangel der Urteilskraft ohne Witz ist Dummheit (stupiditas). Derselbe Mangel aber mit Witz ist Albernheit."
8. Robert Musil, "On Stupidity," *Precision and Soul*, 268 (subsequent citations occur parenthetically in the text). The original reads: "Was ist eigentlich Dummheit?" (*Schriftenreihe "Ausblicke*," 214).
9. Quoted in Jerry Mayer and John P. Holms, eds., *Bite-Size Einstein* (New York: St. Martin's, 1996), 38.
10. Schiller, *Jungfrau von Orleans*, act 3, sc. 6 (my translation): "Mit der Dummheit kämpfen Götter selbst vergebens."
11. Nancy, "Fragments de la bêtise," 23 (my translation): "Il aurait pu dire aussi: c'est une compréhension 'toute bête.'"
12. Lacan, *Ethics of Psychoanalysis, 1959–1960*, 308.
13. Kant, *Anthropologie*, 12:470: "Weiber, Geistliche und Juden betrinken sich nicht, wenigstens vermeiden sie sorgfältig allen Schein davon, weil sie bürgerlich schwach sind und Zurückhaltung nötig haben (wozu durchaus Nüchternheit erfordert wird)."
14. Michel de Montaigne, *Complete Essays of Montaigne*, trans. Donald M. Frame (Stanford, Calif.: Stanford University Press, 1965), 37–39.
15. Friedrich Nietzsche, *The Gay Science: With a Prelude in Rhymes and an Ap-*

pendix of Songs, trans. Walter Kaufmann (New York: Random House, 1974), 131. In a recent typescript on the history of nonknowledge in Musil and Döblin, Bernd Hüppauf discusses Musil's indebtedness to Nietzsche's militancy ("Literatur nach der Skepsis").

16. Charles Baudelaire, *Intimate Journals*, trans. Christopher Isherwood (San Francisco: City Lights Books, 1983), 112.

17. Paul Valéry, *Monsieur Teste*, trans. Jackson Matthews (Princeton, N.J.: Princeton University Press, 1989), 30; see also Valéry, *Monsieur Teste* (Paris: Gallimard, 1972), 49: "L'amour consiste à pouvoir être bêtes ensemble — toute licence de niaiserie et de bestialité."

18. In an altogether other context, Giorgio Agamben (*The Coming Community*, trans. Michael Hardt [Minneapolis: University of Minnesota Press, 1993]) treats the whateverness of existence.

19. I read this childhood utterance of Nietzsche's in "Hitting the Streets: *Ecce Fama*" (*Finitude's Score*, 81).

CHAPTER 3: THE RHETORIC OF TESTING

1. See Jacques Derrida, "Psyché, invention de l'autre" in *Psyché: Inventions de l'autre* (Paris: Galilée, 1987), 11–61.

2. For more on the de Manian machine and the unresolvable aporias of cognition, see Geoffrey Bennington's development of the blind performances of the archiperformance machine in "Aberrations: De Man (and) the Machine," in *Reading De Man Reading*, ed. Lindsay Waters and Wlad Godzich (Minneapolis: University of Minnesota Press, 1989), 209–33; and Rodolphe Gasché, "'Setzung und Übersetzung': Notes on Paul de Man," *Diacritics* 11 (1981): 36–57. Also note Wlad Godzich's introduction in de Man's *Blindness and Insight*: "De Man's rhetorical inquiry consists in recognizing the finiteness of the text and in bringing out its rhetorical machine" (xxvii).

3. De Man, *Allegories of Reading*, 3, 16 (subsequent citations occur parenthetically in the text).

4. See Cynthia Chase, "Trappings of an Education," in *Responses: On Paul de Man's Wartime Journalism*, ed. Werner Hamacher, Neil Hertz, and Thomas Keenan (Lincoln: University of Nebraska Press, 1989), 44–80. On the broken trajectories of reference, see Andrzej Warminski's introduction, "Allegories of Reference," in Paul de Man, *Aesthetic Ideology*, ed. Andrzej Warminski (Minneapolis: University of Minnesota Press, 1996), 1–33; and Cathy Caruth, *Unclaimed Experience* (Baltimore, Md.: Johns Hopkins University Press, 1996), 76–91. In the section entitled "Excess of Rigor" in his introduction to *Aesthetic Ideology*, Warminski cites the opening of de Man's 1982 seminar "Aesthetic Theory from Kant to Hegel," which indicates the cognitive and performative standards of testing under which de Man subsumes critical philosophy, "'which involves a testing of a variety of cate-gories against an

epistemological truth and falsehood. Critical philosophy here is thus the testing of the categories in terms of questions of epistemology'" (21n.23).

5. Chase, "Trappings of an Education," 48.

6. Ibid., 43.

7. De Man, Rhetoric of Romanticism, 285.

8. Ibid., 287.

9. Chase, "Trappings of an Education," 54.

10. De Man, Rhetoric of Romanticism, 282; de Man, Aesthetic Ideology, 36.

11. Barbara Johnson, The Critical Difference: Essays in the Contemporary Rhetoric of Reading (Baltimore, Md.: Johns Hopkins University Press, 1980), 97 (subsequent citations occur parenthetically in the text).

12. Hans-Jost Frey, "Undecidability," trans. Robert Livingston, in The Lessons of Paul de Man, ed. Peter Brooks, Shoshana Felman, and J. Hillis Miller (special issue of Yale French Studies 69 [1985]), 132, 133.

13. E. S. Burt, "Developments in Character: Reading and Interpretation in 'The Children's Punishment' and 'The Broken Comb,'" in The Lesson of Paul de Man, ed. Peter Brooks, Shoshana Felman, and J. Hillis Miller (special issue of Yale French Studies 69 [1985]), 192–210 (subsequent citations occur parenthetically in the text).

14. Of Aristotle, Heidegger sternly said that it was sufficient to note that the philosopher was born, had written, died. See Hannah Arendt, "Heidegger at Eighty," in Heidegger and Modern Philosophy, ed. Michael Murray (New Haven, Conn.: Yale University Press, 1978), 297.

15. De Man, Blindness and Insight, 207.

16. For a thorough discussion of allegory's mournful relation to the unknowable in Benjamin, see Christopher Fynsk, Language and Relation . . . That There Is Language (Stanford, Calif.: Stanford University Press, 1996).

17. Tom Cohen, Ideology and Inscription: "Cultural Studies" after Benjamin, de Man, and Bakhtin (Cambridge: Cambridge University Press, 1998), 224 (subsequent citations occur parenthetically in the text).

18. Walter Benjamin, The Origin of the German Tragic Drama, trans. John Osborne (London: NLB, 1977), 233.

19. Ibid., 176.

20. Paul de Man, The Resistance to Theory, ed. Wlad Godzich, (Minneapolis: University of Minnesota Press, 1986), 76.

21. Emmanuel Levinas, "The Trace of the Other," trans. Alphonso Lingis, in Deconstruction in Context, ed. Mark C. Taylor (Chicago: University of Chicago Press, 1986), 356.

22. Benjamin, Origin of the German Tragic Drama, 183.

23. See Jacques Derrida's discussions of the always allegorical dimension of mourning and de Man's "true 'mourning'" in his Mémoires: For Paul de Man, rev. ed., trans. Cecile Lindsay, Jonathan Culler, Eduardo Cadava, and Peggy Kamuf (New York: Columbia University Press, 1989), 3–39.

24. Benjamin, *Origin of the German Tragic Drama*, 116.

25. Ibid., 113.

26. De Man, *Blindness and Insight*, 191.

27. Michael MacDonald, "Rigorous Mortis: Allegory and the End of Hermeneutics," *Studies in the Literary Imagination* 28.2 (Fall 1995): 108. The thinking of allegory in Benjamin, de Man, and Levinas is carefully and persuasively exposed in this illuminating essay.

28. Benjamin, *Origin of the German Tragic Drama*, 167.

29. De Man, *Allegories of Reading*, 75.

30. Rodolphe Gasché, "In-Difference to Philosophy: de Man on Kant, Hegel, and Nietzsche," in *Reading de Man Reading*, ed. Lindsay Waters and Wlad Godzich (Minneapolis: University of Minnesota Press, 1989), 267.

31. To class de Man with the dummkopfs of in-difference is, on first review, a serious charge. For, as Gasché argues, the object of philosophy is a function of a cognizing subject, which he, in accordance with the tradition, defines as "a subject whose possibility presupposes difference, and whose object is the whole in its difference to what it is the whole of. . . . philosophy . . . must be said to be concerned with the enigma of difference" ("In-Difference," 260). De Man's thought, in other words, has not experienced the first Hegelian tear, an effect of *thaumazein*: "philosophical questioning starts in thaumazein, i.e., in wonder, and marvel. In wonder, indeed, man stands back from the immediate and from his most elementary and purely practical relation to it, as Hegel explains at one point in the *Aesthetics*. In wonder he is torn free 'from nature and his own singularity and now seeks and sees in things a universal, implicit, and permanent element'" (260). See G. W. F. Hegel, *Aesthetics: Lectures on Fine Art*, trans. T. M. Knox. 2 vols. (Oxford: Clarendon, 1975), 1:134. On stupefaction and philosophical wonder, see also Stanley Cavell, *Must We Mean What We Say?* (Cambridge: Cambridge University Press, 1976).

32. Gasché, "In-Difference to Philosophy," 287 (subsequent citations occur parenthetically in the text).

33. The last sentence of Gasché's essay reads: "In this sense [de Man's readings] are 'different,' idiosyncratic to a point where, by making no point, they will have made their point — so singular as to make no difference but, perhaps, in that total apathy a formidable challenge to philosophical difference" (293).

34. Paul de Man, "Phenomenality and Materiality in Kant," in *Hermeneutics: Questions and Prospects*, eds. Gary Shapiro and Anthony Sica (Amherst: University of Massachusetts Press, 1984), 135 (subsequent citations occur parenthetically in the text).

35. De Man, "Kant's Materialism," *Aesthetic Ideology*, 127, 128.

36. See Derrida's treatment of phenomenality and materiality in Kant in *Mémoires*, 91–153. Consider also in this context MacDonald's discussion in

"Rigorous Mortis" of the rapport between materiality and inscription, allegory and writing, in terms of *différance* (110–11).

37. Rodolphe Gasché, *The Wild Card of Reading: On Paul de Man* (Cambridge, Mass.: Harvard University Press, 1998), 1–2 (subsequent citations occur parenthetically in the text).

38. Werner Hamacher, "LECTIO: de Man's Imperative," trans. Susan Bernstein, in *Reading de Man Reading*, ed. Lindsay Waters and Wlad Godzich (Minneapolis: University of Minnesota Press, 1989), 171 (subsequent citations occur parenthetically in the text).

39. Carol Jacobs, "Allegories of Reading Paul de Man," in *Reading de Man Reading*, ed. Lindsay Waters and Wlad Godzich (Minneapolis: University of Minnesota Press, 1989), 108.

40. Chase, "Trappings of an Education," 48.

41. Shoshana Felman, "After the Apocalypse: Paul de Man and the Fall to Silence," in Shoshana Felman and Dori Laub, *Testimony: Crisis of Witnessing in Literature, Psychoanalysis, and History* (New York: Routledge, 1992), 120.

42. Hamacher, "LECTIO," 174.

43. Thomas Pepper, *Singularities: Extremes of Theory in the Twentieth Century* (Cambridge: Cambridge University Press, 1997), 141.

44. De Man, "The Concept of Irony," *Aesthetic Ideology*, 181 (subsequent citations occur parenthetically in the text).

45. Ibid., 181, in part quoting Friedrich Schlegel, *Kritische Friedrich Schlegel Ausgabe*, ed. Ernst Behler. 35 vols. (Paderborn, Germany: Verlag Ferdinand Schöningh, 1967), 2:364.

46. Quoted in de Man, "Concept of Irony," 183.

47. Hamacher, "LECTIO," 199.

48. On performative acts and virtuoso performances, see Susan Bernstein, *Virtuosity of the Nineteenth Century: Performing Music and Language in Heine, Liszt, and Baudelaire* (Stanford, Calif.: Stanford University Press, 1998).

49. De Man, *Resistance to Theory*, 16.

50. Wayne Booth, *A Rhetoric of Irony* (Chicago: University of Chicago Press, 1974), 59n.14. Cyrus Hamlin, citing Ernst Behler, comments on the place of the *eiron* in romantic irony, which is seen to reflect "a modern attitude of mind (*moderne Geisteshaltung*), where the author steps out of his work. Such an attitude or mode of behavior is acknowledged to derive ultimately from the role of Socrates as *eiron* — both in the Platonic dialogues and in other instances of this type of comic character, as in the plays of Aristophanes or the treatise on character by Theophrastus" (Hamlin, *Hermeneutics of Form: Romantic Poetic in Theory and Practice* [New Haven, Conn.: Henry R. Schwab, 1998], 290).

51. Booth, *Rhetoric of Irony*, 59.

52. Schlegel's fragment 53 in the *Athenäum* is quoted in de Man, "Concept of Irony," 176n.17 (my translation).

53. Quoted in ibid., 177.
54. Quoted in ibid., 170–71.
55. De Man's draft translation is given in ibid., 171n.11.
56. Johann Wolfgang von Goethe, "Parabase," *Goethes Werke*, Hamburg edition, ed. Erich Trunz, 14 vols. (Hamburg: C. Wegner, 1974), 1:358; the translation is from *Goethe: Selected Poems*, trans. Christopher Middleton (Boston: Suhrkamp/Insels, 1983), 155. I offer two colloquial renditions that capture the gist of the poem's argument and underscore the surprise effect that Goethe conveys: (1) "Always changing, holding tight; / Near and far and far and near; / Now in one shape, now another; / I am here to astonish you." (2) "Always changing, grasping itself firmly; / Close and distant, distant and close; / Choosing a form, then transforming it; / I have come to surprise you."
57. De Man, "Concept of Irony," 178. Tom Keenan, who, according to a headnote in *Aesthetic Ideology* (163), transcribed and edited "The Concept of Irony" from the audiotape of de Man's 1977 lecture at Ohio State University and also provided the notes, points out that "Proust's text reads: 'Ce n'était pas elle qui était le sujet de l'action' and has 'grammairiens' for 'rhétoriciens'" (178n.19). See Marcel Proust, *À la recherche du temps perdu*, 3 vols. (Paris: Gallimard, 1954), 3:153.
58. Quoted in ibid., 180.
59. Quoted in ibid., 180–81.
60. Quoted in ibid., 181.
61. Here de Man refers the reader to Schlegel's *Lyceum*, fragment 42, in *Kritische Ausgabe*, 2:151.
62. Quoted in de Man, "Concept of Irony, 182.
63. Ibid., 183, quoting in part Benjamin, *Gesammelte Schriften*, 1:86.
64. De Man's generalizations concerning the uses of history to block irony are useful. Nonetheless, it should be noted that Kierkegaard's itinerary is considerably more complicated than de Man allows for and links the question of history to prophecy, sacrifice, and irony; this is a question that must be raised again in terms of a later segment of Schlegel's essay "Über die Unverständlichkeit," as well as some of de Man's own tonal variations on that which is impending and, I would not hesitate to say, in terms of the whole prophetic dimension of the Nietzschean corpus. Discussing the turning point in history, Kierkegaard moves from the tragic hero (who battles for the new and strives to destroy what for him is a vanishing actuality, "but his task is still not so much to destroy as to advance the new and thereby destroy the past indirectly. . . . the old must be superseded" [200]) to the ironic subject, who does not posses the new. "In one sense the ironist is certainly prophetic, because he is continually pointing to something impending, but what it is he does not know. He is prophetic, but his position and situation are the reverse of the prophet's. The prophet walks arm in

arm with his age, and from this position he glimpses what is coming. . . . The ironist, however, has stepped out of line with his age, has turned around and faced it. That which is coming is hidden from him, lies behind his back, but the actuality he so antagonistically confronts is what he must destroy; upon this he focuses his burning gaze. . . . The ironist is also a sacrifice that the world process demands, not as if the ironist always needed in the strictest sense to fall as a sacrifice, but his fervor in the service of the world spirit consumes him. Here, then, we have irony as the infinite absolute negativity. It is negativity, because it only negates; it is infinite, because it does not negate this or that phenomenon; it is absolute, because that by virtue of which it negates is a higher something that still is not. The irony establishes nothing, because that which is to be established lies behind it. . . . To a certain degree, every world-historical turning point must have this formation also, and it certainly would not be without historical interest to track this formation through world history" (Søren Kierkegaard, *The Concept of Irony, with Continual Reference to Socrates,* ed. and trans. Howard V. Hong and Edna H. Hong [Princeton, N.J.: Princeton University Press, 1989], 260–61).

65. See Ernst Behler, "Introduction," *Friedrich Schlegel: Dialogue on Poetry and Literary Aphorisms* (University Park: Pennsylvania State University Press, 1968): "The artist, more precisely the poet, assumes the extraordinary position which was held in former times by the mystic and priest. . . . Romantic authors like Friedrich Schlegel had already posited an unconsciousness which underlies conscious thought. In his *Dialogue* Schlegel called this principle poetry or a part of the divine poet, 'a spark of his creative spirit' which lives in us and 'never ceases to glow with secret force.' Elsewhere the unconscious yet creative force within man is called the 'unconscious genius within man,' or 'instinct,' or 'productive intuition'" (16).

66. Quoted in Eckhard Schumacher, "Die Ironie der Unverständlichkeit. Zur Problematisierung von Lesen und Verstehen bei Johann Hamann, Friedrich Schlegel, Jacques Derrida, und Paul de Man" (Ph.D. diss., Fakultät für Linguistik und Literaturwissenschaft, University of Bielefeld, 1996), 193 (my translation).

67. Quoted in ibid. (my translation): "es müsse gewiss einer von den beyden Schlegeln geschrieben haben. Es ist nämlich für ihn wie für mehrere Philister Axiom: Was man nicht versteht, hat ein Schlegel geschrieben."

68. Schlegel, *Kritische Ausgabe,* 2:366 (my translation): "Die Französische Revolution, Fichtes Wissenschaftslehre und Goethes Meister sind die größten Tendenzen des Zeitalters. Wer an dieser Zusammenstellung Anstoß nimmt, wem keine Revolution wichtig scheinen kann, die nicht laut und materiell ist, der hat sich noch nicht auf den hohen weiten Standpunkt der Geschichte der Menschheit erhoben." Schlegel briefly discusses this statement, the "meistdiskutiere[n] Text aus dem ersten Jahrgang des

'Athenäum,'" as an example of unintelligibility, which he does not, however, bother to disentangle (see Heinz Härtl, "'Athenaeum'-Polemiken," in *Debatten und Kontroversen: Literarische Auseinandersetzungen in Deutschland am Ende des 18. Jahrhunderts*, vol. 2, ed. Hans-Dieter Dahnke and Bernd Leistner [Berlin: Aufbau-Verlag, 1989], 286).

69. Carl Schmitt, *Politische Romantik* (Munich: Duncker und Humblot, 1925), 113 (my translation): "aus der Unklarheit ein Prinzip zu machen sucht."

70. It should be noted that Jean-Luc Nancy has devoted the powerful communitarian aspect of his thought both to Schlegel and to Bataille without necessarily connecting them. Nonetheless, they coexist convincingly in the body of his political and philosophical reflections. See Nancy, "'Literary Communism,'" *The Inoperative Community*, ed. and trans. Peter Connor (Minneapolis: University of Minnesota Press, 1991), 71–81.

71. "Romantik als Lebens- und Schreibform" in *Deutsche Literaturgeschichte*, ed. Wolfgang Beutin et al. (Stuttgart: J. B. Metzlersche Verlagsbuchhandlung, 1992), 177 (my translation): "Rollenaustausch und Androgynität und das Postulat freier Liebe." The editors continue: "Skandalträchtiger noch als die erotischen Passagen im Roman wirkte die Tatsache, daß Schlegel und seine Freunde das, was als 'freie Liebe' im Roman gefeiert wurde, in Lebenpraxis umzusetzen versuchten. Gerade die Frühromantiker um die Brüder Schlegel experimentierten mit neuen Formen des Zusammenlebens und fühlten sich nicht an die bürgerlichen Konventionen gebunden, die Schiller etwa in seinen Gedichten *Männerwürde* und *Würde der Frauen* beschwor. Auch im alltäglichen Umgang versuchten sie, ein antibürgerliches, bohemienhaftes Leben zu führen" (Even more pregnant with scandal than the erotic passages in the novel [*Lucinde*] was the fact that Schlegel and his friends tried to put into practice in their own lives what was celebrated as "free love" in the novel. It was exactly these early Romantics around the Schlegel brothers who experimented with new forms of living together and who did not feel bound to the middle-class conventions that, for example, Schiller invokes in his poems "Men's Dignity" and "The Dignity of Women." Even in circumstances of everyday life, they tried to lead an anti-bourgeois, bohemian existence).

72. Friedrich Schlegel, *Sämmtliche Werke, zweite Original-Ausgabe*, 15 vols. (Wien: Klang, 1846), 15:56 (my translation): "Die wahre Ironie [. . .] ist die Ironie der Liebe" (subsequent citations occur parenthetically in the text).

73. Schlegel, *Kristische Friedrich Schlegel Ausgabe*, 2:531 (my translation): "die Frage, ob sie überhaupt möglich sei."

74. Ibid. (my translation): "Und wo hätte man nähere Gelegenheit, über die Möglichkeit oder Unmöglichkeit dieser Sache mancherlei Versuche anzustellen, als wenn man ein Journal wie das Athenäum entweder selbst schreibt, oder doch als Leser an demselben teilnimmt."

75. Ibid. (my translation): "die ganze Kette meiner Versuche durch(zu)gehen."

76. For a comparable point of view, consider in this regard Behler's discussion of language loss in the Romantic form of irony and the always fragmentary character of poetic intuition: "According to Schlegel, irony reflects the eternal conflict between the ideal and the real; it derives from the artist's awareness of the 'necessity and impossibility of complete communication.' (Schlegel, *Lyceum*, 1797) . . . The awareness of the necessary incompleteness of poetic achievements, moreover, leads to literary criticism" (Behler, "Introduction," 18).

77. There was a good bit of friendly fire, which seems somewhat inevitable in intellectual circles. In the correspondences among August Wilhelm Schlegel, Schleiermacher, and Novalis there is abundant evidence of the difficulties his buddies and brother had with Friedrich's texts, which they in part held to be altogether . . . unintelligible. The implications of the inner and outer levels of difficulty organized around Schlegel's work on unintelligibility is discussed at length by Schumacher. I am most taken, however, by Friedrich's response to Schleiermacher's evident anguish over not understanding his best friend's work. To console his friend, and to reassure him, Friedrich constructs a theory of friendship based on nonunderstanding. Nonunderstanding has everything to do with the personal domain, Schlegel emphasizes. In his personal relationship to Schleiermacher he marks the necessity of frequent "Anerkennung ewiger Verschiedenheit, Scheidung und Nichtverstehung" (recognition of eternal difference, separation and nonunderstanding; Schlegel to Schleiermacher, July 3, 1798, in Schlegel, *Kritische Ausgabe*, 24:140). Responding to Schleiermacher's uncomprehending reception of the fragments, Schlegel shows his friend compassion: "Daß Du sie nicht so gleich frisch weg verstanden hast, nimmt mich nicht Wunder, besonders da Du meynst, man könne einige einzelne daraus verstehen, ohne das Ganze. Es ist schon viel und gut, daß Du sie nicht verstanden hast, und noch besser, daß Dir einiges was Du schon klar glaubtest, wieder dunkel dadurch geworden ist" (It doesn't surprise me that you didn't understand them right away, especially since you think that one can understand individual fragments without understanding the whole. It's quite all right that you didn't understand them, and even better that the little that you believed to be clear has become obscure again) (Schlegel to Schleiermacher, September 13, 1799, in Friedrich Schleiermacher, *Kritsche Gesamtausgabe*, pt. 5, ed. Hans-Joachim Birkener et al., 5 vols. to date (Berlin: De Gruyter, 1980–), 3:180.

78. The argument goes further, expressing the daily dose of pain he feels when confronted with the rage for understanding: "Mit Schmerzen sehe ich es täglich, wie die Wut des Verstehens den Sinn gar nicht aufkommenläßt" (I see this painfully every day — the rage of understanding doesn't allow for sense to come through) (Schleiermacher, *Über die Religion. Reden an die Gebildeten unter ihren Verächtern* [Stuttgart: Reclam, 1969], 96). Schleiermacher

more or less opposes the "yoke of understanding" and those *Verständigen* who depend upon it to the yearnings of younger sensibilities for the marvelous and supernatural, a secret premonition that determines the first stirrings of religion.

79. Schlegel, *"Lucinde" and the Fragments*, 6.

80. Quoted in ibid., 3–4.

81. Ibid., 8.

82. Peter Tracey Connor, *Georges Bataille and the Sin of Mysticism* (Baltimore, Md.: Johns Hopkins University Press, 2000), 156 (subsequent citations occur parenthetically in the text). See also Connor's discussion of Bataille's *Inner Experience*, particularly with regard to Bataille's essay "Jean-Paul Sartre: A New Mystic" (31–38).

83. Schlegel, *Kritische Ausgabe*, 2:539 (my translation): "gegen die anerkannte Unverständlichkeit des Athenäums."

84. Ibid. (my translation): "Welche Katastrophe! Dann wird es Leser geben, die lesen können. Im neunzehnten Jahrhundert wird jeder die Fragmente mit vielem Behagen und Vergnügen in den Verdauungsstunden genießen können, und auch zu den härtesten, unverdaulichsten keinen Nußnacker bedürfen."

85. Quoted in ibid., 2:540.

86. Ibid., 2:536 (my translation): "Ein großer Teil von der Unverständlichkeit des Athenäums liegt unstreitig in der Ironie, die sich mehr oder minder überall darin äußert."

87. On the "Ambivalenz zwischen 'Unverständlichkeit' und Prophetie, Ironie und Pathos," see Karl Heinz Bohrer, *Das absolute Präsens: Die Semantik ästhetischer Zeit* (Frankfurt am Main: Suhrkamp Verlag, 1994), 20.

88. Schlegel, *Kristische Ausgabe*, 2:538 (my translation): "Welche Götter werden uns von allen diesen Ironien erretten können?"

89. De Man, *Allegories of Reading*, 301.

90. Pepper, *Singularities*, 145. Pepper decisively reviews the failed introjection that irony marks in a text.

91. Hamacher, "LECTIO," 199.

92. Pepper, *Singularities*, 153.

93. See Pepper's brilliant discussion of the structure of irony in de Man's work (ibid., 88–172).

94. Ibid., 106.

95. Benjamin, *Origin of the German Tragic Drama*, 233.

96. Friedrich Schlegel, *Zur Philologie II*, no. 95, *Kritische Ausgabe*, 16:96 (my translation): "Es gibt einen hermeneutischen Imperativ."

97. In *Premises: Essays on Philosophy and Literature from Kant to Celan*, trans. Peter Fenves (Cambridge, Mass.: Harvard University Press, 1996), Werner Hamacher writes: "If understanding understands itself, it has already forgotten the devastation, the astonishment, the wonder, and the eavesdropping

from which it took its point of departure" (10). I would have to add, in terms of Schlegel's lexicon, that the very force that stands at the base of authentic language would have been forgotten, namely, stupidity. Hamacher continues: "Understanding is possible only between these two impossibilities of understanding — the hermeneutic parousia in its autoposition and de-posing *sans phrase* — only *between* them, hence only insofar as the movement of self-positing must always be exposed and once again discharged by another understanding, and thus only insofar as its standing suspends itself in this unposited, groundless 'between'" (10-11). The aporia that incites understanding remains incomprehensible — "and with this abyss of understanding, so too does understanding itself" (10).

98. Friedrich Schlegel, *Tranzentdentalphilosophie* (Jena, 1800-1801), in *Kritische Ausgabe*, 12:102 (my translation): "Ein absolutes Verstehen ist nach unserer Ansicht gar nicht möglich. . . . Gäbe es eine absolute Wahrheit, so gäbe es auch eine absolute Verständlichkeit." The exact wording is not absolutely reliable as the lecture text has been reconstructed based on the notes of a student ("Aufzeichnungen eines nicht zu ermittlenden Hörers"). See Schumacher, "Die Ironie der Unverständlichkeit," 285, and Jean-Jacques Anstett's introduction in Schlegel, *Kritische Ausgabe*, 12:xxi.

99. Quoted in Schumacher, "Die Ironie der Unverständlichkeit," 195 (my translation). This could also be translated as "Entirely perfect and complete understanding, however."

KIERKEGAARD SATELLITE

1. Kierkegaard, *Concept of Irony*, 286 (subsequent citations occur parenthetically in the text).

CHAPTER 4: THE DISAPPEARANCE AND RETURNS OF THE IDIOT

1. Quoted in Joseph Frank, *Dostoevsky: The Miraculous Years, 1865-1871* (Princeton, N.J.: Princeton University Press, 1995), 249 (subsequent citations occur parenthetically in the text).

2. Fyodor Dostoyevsky, *The Idiot*, trans. David Magarshack (New York: Bantam, 1955), 597 (subsequent citations occur parenthetically in the text).

3. Walter Benjamin, "Der Idiot," in *Gesammelte Schriften*, 4:277 (my translation): "D[er] metaphysische[n] Identität des Nationellen wie des Humanen in der Idee der Schöpfung Dostojewskijs."

4. Frank, *Dostoevsky*, 6.

5. Quoted in ibid., 305.

6. See the discussion of "the Russian equivalent of the Germanic 'reiner Tor' (pure fool)" in Avrahm Yarmolinsky, *Dostoevsky: Works and Days* (New York: Funk and Wagnalls, 1971), 262.

7. Benjamin, "Der Idiot," 239: "Das unsterbliche Leben, vom dem dieser Roman das Zeugnis ablegt"; "unsterblich aber ist Fleisch, Kraft, Person, Geist in ihren verschiedenen Fassungen."
8. Ibid.: "So hat Goethe von einer Unsterblichkeit des Wirkenden in seinem Wort zu Eckermann gesprochen, wonach die Natur verpflichtet sei uns einen neuen Wirkungsraum zu geben wenn dieser hier uns genommen sei"; "Das unsterbliche Leben ist unvergeßlich"; "Es ist das Leben, das ohne Denkmal und ohne Andenken, ja vielleicht ohne Zeugnis unvergessen sein müßte. Es kann nicht vergessen werden."
9. Quoted in Frank, *Dostoevsky*, 274.
10. Anthony J. Cascardi, *The Bounds of Reason: Cervantes, Dostoevsky, Flaubert* (New York: Columbia University Press, 1986), 37 (subsequent citations occur parenthetically in the text).
11. Miguel de Cervantes, *Don Quixote*, trans. Samuel Putnam (New York: Modern Library, 1949), bk. 1, i.
12. Cascardi, *Bounds of Reason*, 37.
13. The Prince is startled by a remarkable copy of the painting when he visits Rogozhin (209–14) and refers to the experience of having seen the original abroad. (If the Prince comments on the copy, this no doubt is because the first viewing of Holbein's painting — it may be that there can be only a first, because blinding, view — occurs in the mode of shock, which is to say that the novel lays no claim to having seen anything, and yet, like Dostoevsky, the Prince stares in stupefaction, as if what he saw were the "real" body, which had been promised to transcendence).

A third party, Ippolit, offers a commentary on Holbein's painting in the course of his "Explanation": "In Rogozhin's picture there was no trace of beauty. It was a faithful representation of the dead body of a man who has undergone unbearable torments before the crucifixion, been wounded, tortured, beaten by the guards, beaten by the people, when he carried the cross and fell under its weight, and, at last, has suffered the agony of crucifixion, lasting for six hours (according to my calculations at least). It is true, it is the face of a man who has only *just* been taken from the cross — that is, still retaining a great deal of warmth and life; rigor mortis has not yet set in, so there is still a look of suffering on the face of the dead man, as though he were still feeling it (that has been well caught by the artist); on the other hand, the face has not been spared in the least; it is nature itself, and, indeed, any man's corpse would look like that after such suffering.... In the picture, the face is terribly smashed with blows, swollen, covered with terrible, swollen, and bloodstained bruises, the eyes open and squinting; the large, open whites of the eyes have a sort of dead and glassy glint (391–92).

Cascardi writes of the problems inherent in what Ippolit says: "There is every likelihood that the physical suffering of Christ may be taken as grounds to doubt His Godliness. To accept his suffering as real and not merely as symbolic may lead one to repeat the challenges of the skeptics who asked why Christ, if he were God, did not come down from the cross. To see the body of the God-man destroyed by natural forces may prompt doubts about His claims to divinity" (*Bounds of Reason*, 150).

14. G. P. Fedotov, *The Russian Religious Mind*, 2 vols. (Cambridge, Mass.: Harvard University Press, 1946), 1:130; see also chapter 4, "Russian Kenoticism," in volume 1.

15. Ernst Bernst, *Nietzsches Ideen zur Geschichte des Christentums und der Kirche* (Leiden: n.p., 1956), 98 (my translation).

16. I realize that such assertions concerning our stupid bodies may sound nonprogressive, particularly in the face of such movements as Positive Action, Positive Choices, and the marks of similar tags of empowerment that issue from the hope that we know what we're doing, that we can take charge and act up and affirm our bodies, our selves, that we can now stop being victims and relinquish passivity. One need only read Mark Doty's elegiac memoir to be reminded of our unshelteredness in the face of the hopelessly stupid language of health care and all the AIDS acronyms (AZT, ARC, DDI, HIV, etc., etc.), signs of the severely impoverished, technologized idiom of the late twentieth century. Part of the memoir addresses the ruses of knowledge as concerns the afflicted body, in this case subjected to "viral activity" — an expression systematically used by doctors when they do not know what to call or how to describe, much less heal, the enigmatic symptom. Anyone who claims to know the body, who responds solely with prescription and denies the factum of stupidity when it comes to bodies in their unbearable singularities, anyone suspending suspense — from torturer to healer — has become entangled in a political dilemma of significant ethical proportions. "There is no relief in long illness, which suspends us in not-knowing. Every case of AIDS is unique; each person has AIDS in his or her own way. We couldn't know what was coming, we could only hold our breaths as it began, slowly, it seemed then — though so swift now, in retrospect's compression — to make itself known" (*Heaven's Coast: A Memoir* [New York: HarperCollins, 1996], 204). While the course of the disease will have made something ("itself") known, there was never a present attestable by Doty in which such knowledge was at hand.

In a catalog of recent paintings by Titina Maselli (Galleria Giulia, April 15, 1998), Alexander Garcia Düttmann, whose philosophical reflection on AIDS is well known (*At Odds with AIDS* [Stanford, Calif.: Stanford University Press, 1996]), comments on a poem by Tom Carey that begins, "'I watch my body like I watch someone else's pet / It lives in my peripheral vision / Poor dumb thing, it can't see, speak or hear / it grunts, blows and weeps.'" Even, or especially, the so-called healthy body, not entirely there, trails stupidly behind, as in Dennis Cooper's *Frisk* (New York: Grove Press, 1991): "Usually I don't notice my body. It's just there, working steadily. I wash it,

NOTES TO PAGES 180–91

feed it, jerk it off, wipe its ass, and that's all. Even during sex I don't use my body that much. I'm more interested in other guys'. Mine just sort of follows my head and hands, like a trailer" (50).

17. Dostoevsky's relationship to the intensities of such suffering prompts further reflection. On the masochistic stirrings of the humiliated, see, for instance, his depiction of the character of little Nellie in *The Insulted and Injured*. Having been "ill-treated," she is "'purposely trying to aggravate her wound by this mysterious behavior, this mistrustfulness of us all; as though she enjoyed her own pain, by this *egoism of suffering*, if I may so express it. This aggravation of suffering and this revelling in it I could understand; it is the enjoyment of many of the insulted and injured, oppressed by destiny and smarting under the sense of injustice'" (quoted in Frank, *Bounds of Reason*, 323).

18. Alex de Jonge, *Dostoevsky and the Age of Intensity* (New York: St. Martin's, 1975), 145.

19. The place of epilepsy in poetry and the history of thought is elaborated in Marie-Thérèse Sutterman, *Dostoïevski et Flaubert: Écritures de l'épilepsie* (Paris: Presses Universitaires de France, 1993). For an outstanding analysis of epilepsy and temporality, see Kimura Bin's *Écrits de psychopathologie phénoménologique* (Paris: Presses Universitaires de France, 1992), which is based on the existential analysis (*Daseinsanalyse*) of Ludwig Binswanger. Epilepsy, of which Bin writes that "personne ne sait ce qu'il en est au juste" (no one knows exactly what it is [58]) — it remains an enigma — is understood here as that which most closely approaches death in life, the *morbus sacer* that brings the subject to the most extreme disorder and destructuration. The epileptic episode is located by Bin as the originary anxiety (*Urangst*) that determines all other crises of anxiety. He analyzes the perturbation of temporality introduced by the epileptic episode, what he calls the reduction of temporality "au présent instantané ponctuel" (to the indivisible, instantaneous present [92]). In the chapter "Le Temps et l'angoisse," Bin focuses on the ethical constitution of the afflicted, who display an exasperated sense of obligation, a heightened consciousness of duty in relation to others. See also Ludwig Binswanger, *Über Ideenflucht* (Zürich: Orell Füssli, 1933); H. Tellenbach, "Zur Phänomenologie der Verschränkung von Anfallsleiden und Wesensänderung beim Epileptiker," *Jarbuch der Psychologie, Psychotherapie, und medizinischer Anthropologie* 14.57 (1966); and V. E. von Gesattel, "Störungen des Werdens und des Zeiterlebens im Rahmen psychiatrischer Erkrankungen," in *Prolegomena einer medizinischen Anthropologie* (Berlin: Springer Verlag, 1954).

20. Jean-Luc Nancy, *Birth to Presence*, trans. Brian Holmes et al. (Stanford, Calif.: Stanford University Press, 1993), 193 (subsequent citations occur parenthetically in the text).

21. It would be tempting to imagine Nancy invoking the nostalgic trophies of

an original wound, after which there would be only serial replication or the buildup of a hysterical mimesis — endless counts of wounding that could never coincide with the originary spirituality of those lacerating Christ's body. At times Nancy's propositions appear to betray a tendency to share with Bataille a longing for past states and histories that are capable of relaying us back to an epoch when blood flowed with purpose and meant something — when, as in the case of Hegel, war (to cite one example) was still wageable because it was productive of sense. However, Nancy disdains the nostalgic inflections to which a number of Bataille's interpretations have pointed. Unless I am mistaken in this assumption, it is not part of Nancy's insight or intention in this text to make Christ's body the referent, though it becomes somewhat difficult to deny that such a movement or tendency is afoot.

What can be original about a wound, especially if it is susceptible to hysterical mimicry? The seriousness of Nancy's interventions has always involved the retrieval of lost continuities and their syncopic returns. In other words, Nancy reads the opaque historicity of woundedness from a consideration of Western thrownness — what he has called elsewhere "our history" — and, as always, his work rigorously capitulates to the ambiguities on which Western thought continues to be based. If we were engaged in military strategy or metaphor, capitulation might not be a good thing. Here it indicates acceptance, the marked passivity of a vigilance that demands a certain number of inclusions and remembrances without re-establishing the values they have held or continue to hold in a forgetful and metaphysically laden world. It is useful to bear in mind that there are different kinds of wounds involving archetypes of wounds that won't heal: Prometheus, Philoctetes, the Fisher King, and the sudden wounding of Kafka's "Country Doctor." Derrida discusses the referent to "Corpus" from yet another point of view in *Le toucher, Jean-Luc Nancy* (Paris: Galilée, 2000).

22. Jean-Luc Nancy, "La douleur existe, elle est injustifiable," *Revue d'éthique et de théologie morale* 95 (Dec. 1995): 91–96 (all English translations are mine).

23. Ibid., 95: "le travail, la patience, et la douleur du concept."

24. Ibid.: "La douleur n'est peut-être rien d'autre que ce refus de soi."

25. Ibid.: "une sorte de j'ai mal, donc je suis."

26. Ibid.: "et de telle façon que je ne suis plus 'moi,' mais ce mal même, cette folie."

27. Ibid., 96: "Mais ce ne-pas-avoir-lieu est aussi bien la certitude même, et la réalité."

28. Elaine Scarry writes in *The Body in Pain: The Making and Unmaking of the World* (New York: Oxford University Press, 1985): "Physical pain does not simply resist language but actively destroys it, bringing about an immediate reversion to a state anterior to language, to the sounds and cries a human being makes before language is learned" (4). Consider also her dis-

cussion of analogical verification and the resistance to language, the
unshareability of pain (5–20). For a compelling reflection on the quality of
language and illness, see Susan Sontag, *"Illness as Metaphor" and "AIDS and
Its Metaphors"* (New York: Doubleday, 1990).

29. See Slavoj Žižek, *The Metastases of Enjoyment: Six Essays on Woman and Cau-
sality* (London: Verso, 1994), 171ff.

30. See Sutterman, *Dostoïevski et Flaubert.*

31. "This painting, by Hans Holbein, depicts Jesus Christ after his inhuman
agony, after his body has been taken down the Cross and begun to decay.
His swollen face is covered with bloody wounds, and it is terrible to be-
hold.

"The painting had a crushing impact on Fyodor Mikhailovich. He
stood before it as if stunned. And I did not have the strength to look at it —
it was too painful for me, particularly in my sickly condition — and I went
into other rooms. When I came back after fifteen or twenty minutes, I
found him still riveted to the same spot in front of the painting. His agi-
tated face had a kind of dread in it, something I had noticed more than
once during the first moments of an epileptic seizure.

"Quietly I took my husband by the arm, led him into another room
and sat him down on a bench, expecting the attack from one minute to the
next. Luckily this did not happen" (Anna Dostoevsky, *Dostoevsky: Reminis-
cences*, trans. and ed. Beatrice Stillman [New York: Liveright, 1975], 133–34).

32. Michel Foucault, *Madness and Civilization: A History of Insanity in the Age of
Reason*, trans. Richard Howard (New York: Pantheon Books, 1965), ix. To
my mind this work has been consistently undervalued — New Historicist
reclamations serve only to underscore its neglect.

33. On the somatophobic tendencies of Western philosophy, see the elabor-
ations of Elizabeth Grosz in *Volatile Bodies: Toward a Corporeal Feminism*
(Bloomington: Indiana University Press, 1994). Consider also the complications introduced by the Spinozist account of the body as an entity that
cannot be "known" since it is not identical with itself across time. "The
body does not have a 'truth' or a 'true nature'" (Moira Gatens, "Towards
a Feminist Philosophy of the Body," in *Crossing Boundaries: Feminism and
the Critique of Knowledges*, ed. Barbara Caine, Elizabeth Grosz, and Marie de
Lepervanche [Sydney: Allen and Unwin, 1988], 68–69).

34. "They want to put you under control. Can you believe it? With everything,
your freedom and your money — that is, the two objects which distinguish everyone of us from a quadruped!" Finally, though: "On leaving
Myshkin the doctor said to Lebedyev, if everyone like that were to be put
under control, who would be left to control them?" (*The Idiot*, 570–71).

35. "Anyway, when after many hours the doors were opened and people came
in, they found the murderer completely unconscious and raving. Myshkin
was sitting beside him motionless on the floor, and every time the deliri-

ous man broke into screaming of babble, he hastened to pass his trembling hand softly over his hair and cheeks, as though caressing and soothing him" (ibid., 594).

36. See Friedrich Hölderlin, "Andenken" (Remembrance), in *Hymns and Fragments*, trans. Richard Sieburth (Princeton, N.J.: Princeton University Press, 1984), 106–9. See also Heidegger's reading of the poem in *Erläuterungen zu Hölderlin's Dichtung* (Frankfurt am Main: Vittorio Klostermann, 1971), 78–151, where he trips over the foreigner held in the figure of the brown ladies — a figure of what might be seen as the "native foreigner," at once intimate and improper, original and expropriated.

37. See Jacques Derrida, "Eating Well," trans. Peter Connor and Avital Ronell, in *Points*, ed. Elisabeth Weber (Stanford, Calif.: Stanford University Press, 1995), 260. On gift giving and the relation to time, see Derrida's *Given Time: I. Counterfeit Money*, trans. Peggy Kamuf (Chicago: University of Chicago Press, 1992), where the links between *geben* ("to give") and *vergeben*, ("to forgive") and between *don* ("gift") and *pardon* ("pardon") are established.

38. It would be interesting to follow up the suggestions of Dostoevsky and Nietzsche (in the *Genealogy of Morals* and elsewhere) with the thought of Heidegger, who in *What Is Called Thinking?* (trans. J. Glenn Gray and Fred D. Wieck [New York: Harper and Row, 1968]) links thinking to thanking. The well-known piety of the thinker-thanker no doubt establishes him as a distant relative of the Idiot. In other figurations of idiocy, such as one proposed by Hart Crane's poem "The Idiot," the idiot becomes the site for pure reflection.

39. See Derrida's chapter "'Counterfeit Money' II: Gift and Countergift, Excuse and Forgiveness (Baudelaire and the Story of the Dedication)" in *Given Time* (108–72). In Baudelaire's text, moreover, the narrator's disgust with his friend centers on the fact of his stupidity. For recent readings of Baudelaire and time, see Ulrich Baer's *Remnants of Song: Trauma and the Experience of Modernity in Charles Baudelaire and Paul Celan* (Stanford, Calif.: Stanford University Press, 2000) and Elyssa Marder's *Dead Time* (Stanford, Calif.: Stanford University Press, forthcoming).

40. Seminar on hospitality held at Deutsches Haus, New York University, October 1997. The figure of the stranger has been explored in the works of Blanchot and Levinas and has been poignantly reinscribed in Jean-Luc Nancy's "L'intrus," *Dédale* 9–10 (1999): 440–50.

41. Friedrich Schiller, "Über naïve und sentimentalische Dichtung," in *Schillers Werke und Brief*, ed. Otto Dann et al., 12 vols. (Frankfurt: Deutsche Klassiker Verlag, 1992), 8:706–811.

42. "He told him he had been a long while, over four years, away from Russia, that he had been sent abroad for his health on account of a strange nervous disease, something of the nature of epilepsy or St. Vitus's dance, attacks of twitching and trembling. The dark man smiled several times as

he listened, and laughed, especially when, in answer to his inquiry, 'Well, have they cured you?' his companion answered, 'No, they haven't.' 'Ha! You must have wasted a lot of money over it, and we believe in them over here,' the dark man observed, sarcastically" (*The Idiot*, 4–5).

43. More precisely, he recalls the Corinthian imperative, the attribute of the apostles: "We are fools for Christ's sake" (1 Cor. 4:10). Jacqueline Leonhardt-Aumüller has read the genre of the fool for Christ's sake in both Dostoevsky and Gerhart Hauptmann, among others, in *Narren um Christi willen: Eine Studie zu Tradition und Typologie des "Narren in Christo" und dessen Ausprägung bei Gerhart Hauptmann* (Munich: Tuduv, 1993).

44. For another burst of laughter, consider Jean-Luc Nancy's observations in "Laughter, Presence": "Laughter is thus neither a presence nor an absence. It is the offering of a presence in its own disappearance" (*Birth to Presence*, 383).

45. "And as he answered, the young man looked intently and searchingly at the omniscient gentleman.

"Such omniscient gentlemen are to be found pretty often in a certain stratum of society. They know everything. All the restless curiosity and faculties of their mind are irresistibly bent in one direction, no doubt from lack of more important ideas and interests in life, as the critic of to-day would explain. But the words, 'they know everything,' must be taken in a rather limited sense: in what department so-and-so serves, who are his friends, what his income is, where he was governor, who his wife is and what dowry she brought him, who are his first cousins and who are his second cousins, and everything of that sort. For the most part these omniscient gentlemen are out at elbow, and receive a salary of seventeen rubles a month. The people of whose lives they know every detail would be at a loss to imagine their motives. Yet many of them get positive consolation out of this knowledge, which amounts to a complete science, and derive from it self-respect and their highest spiritual gratification. And indeed it is a fascinating science" (*The Idiot*, 6).

46. "And how many Pirogovs there have been among our writers, savants and propagandists! I say 'have been,' but of course we have them still" (ibid., 449).

47. Besides offering a scene of writing, Ippolit, the other sick body covered by the novel, stakes out another rapport to illness. The resident nihilist, he abhors the simplistic, unconscious acceptance of the body's degradation. Dostoevsky notes even "an immense satisfaction in his very degradation," meaning, it seems, a triumphal narcissism propped on absolute destruction. "Can't I just be devoured without being expected to praise what devours me? Let me tell you, there is a limit of ignominy in the consciousness of one's own nothingness and impotence beyond which a man cannot go, and beyond which he begins to feel immense satisfaction in his

very degradation. . . . Can there really be Somebody up aloft who will be aggrieved by my not going on for a fortnight longer? I don't believe it; and it's a much more likely supposition that all that's needed is my worthless life, the life of an atom, to complete some universal harmony; for some sort of plus and minus, for the take of some sort of contrast, and so on, just as the life of millions of creatures is needed every day as a sacrifice, as, without their death, the rest of the world couldn't go on (though that's not a very grand idea in itself, I must observe). Say what you like, it's all impossible and unjust. . . . I do not want this life! If I'd had the power not to be born, I would certainly not have accepted existence upon conditions that are such a mockery. But I still have power to die, though the days I give back are numbered. It's no great power, it's no great mutiny" (ibid., 401–2).

48. In the interest of containment we leave aside the issues of sexual difference that mark these passages. Madame Bovary is spread open, Myshkin takes (her) but then he, in turn, is inseminated, and so forth.

49. Jean-Paul Sartre, L'Idiot de la famille: Gustave Flaubert de 1821 à 1857 (Paris: Éditions Gallimard, 1971), 612.

50. Ibid., 17 (my translation): "l'idiotie d'abord, l'alarme du père . . . les années stériles de Paris et, pour finir, la crise de Pont-l'Evêque, le haut mal, enfin la séquestration volontaire et l'oisiveté."

51. Ibid., 17–18 (my translation): "Toutes ces infortunes lui semblaient liées par un fil secret: dans le cerveau du petit, quelque chose c'était détraqué, peut-être dès la naissance: l'épilepsie — c'etait le nom qu'on donnait à la "maladie" de Flaubert — c'était, en somme, l'idiotie continuée."

52. I have tried to show in Crack Wars: Literature, Addiction, Mania (Lincoln: University of Nebraska Press, 1992) that Flaubert was performing surgery on the name of his brother, a name shared with the father and located in the Achilles tendon. The fraterno-paternal name that enacts the textual mutilation is Achilles.

53. Gustave Flaubert, Madame Bovary, trans. Lowell Blair (Toronto: Bantam, 1981), 156.

54. See Ronell, Crack Wars, 140–44.

55. Quoted in Sutterman, Dostoïevski et Flaubert, 199 (my translation): "'C'est le genre épileptique! C'est un bruit répandu que Flaubert est épileptique.'"

56. Sigmund Freud, The Standard Edition of the Complete Psychological Works of Sigmund Freud, ed. James Strachey and Anna Freud, 26 vols. (London: Hogarth Press, 1964), 21:180 (subsequent citations occur parenthetically in the text).

57. In On the Drive (special issue of UMBR(a): A Journal of the Unconscious 1 [1997]), Joan Copjec's editorial asserts a "hope to forge a new path to the body" (13). Freud's theory of drives, she writes, "is a theory that sacrifices neither the signifier nor the flesh, but unites them through a transform-

ing montage. Drive is a kind of demand that awakens us to our bodily existence. Because this awakening takes place in us through drive, rather than as in animals through instinct, our bodily being is out of whack with our physical environment. *Our bodies battle biology.* . . . The barrage of books on embodiment has evidenced almost total ignorance of the body and its self-inhibited destinies, of the distinctions among the different vicissitudes of its drives" (13). Her aim is "to help reattach the body to that which generates it — the drive — and thus to give life back to the body" (13). A paradoxical conceit, as most discussions of the body come in a body bag. Before that, Lacan wrote more generally of "a point whose importance does not seem to have been noticed, namely, that the Freudian project has caused the whole world to reenter us, has definitely put it back in its place, that is to say, in our body, and nowhere else" (*Ethics of Psychoanalysis, 1959–1960*, 92).

58. R. Bouchard, J. Lorillous, C. Guedeney, and D. Kipman, "L'Épilepsie essentielle de l'enfant," in *Psychiatrie de l'enfant* (Paris: Presses Universitaires de France, 1975), 117 (my translation): "une des citadelles les plus intouchables de la neurologie."

59. Strachey notes that Freud's letter to Fliess of December 22, 1897, suggests that masturbation is the "primal addiction, for which all later addictions are substitutes" (Freud, 1950a, Letter 79, *Complete Works*, 21:193n.1).

60. Gilles Deleuze discusses the aggressive and hallucinatory return of the father in a world that has symbolically abolished him. The aggressive return of the father disrupts the masochistic situation. See *Coldness and Cruelty: Masochism* (New York: Zone Books, 1989), 40.

61. Jean Genet, "Une Lecture des *Frères Karamazov*," *Nouvelle Revue française* 405 (1986): 69 (my translation): "audacieuse instigation des âmes."

62. "Dostoevsky ironisa souvent et parfois frénétiquement sur le compte de Gogol que l'on appela pourtant — et à sa suite — son 'père spirituel'" (Sutterman, *Dostoïevski et Flaubert*, 131).

63. Bruce Fink, in "Desire and the Drive" (*UMBR[a]* 1 [1997]: 36, 48), considers Jacques-Alain Miller's view that desire concerns the body as dead, as mortified or overwritten by the signifier ("Donc," unpublished seminar, 1993–94). See also Fink, "Commentary on Lacan's Text," in *Reading Seminars I and II: Lacan's Return to Freud*, ed. Bruce Fink, Richard Feldstein, and Maire Jaanus (Albany: SUNY Press, 1996), 422–27.

64. Jacques Lacan, "De la psychanalyse dans ses rapports avec la réalité," *Scilicet* 1 (1968): 58.

65. Deleuze, *Coldness and Cruelty*, 40 (subsequent citations occur parenthetically in the text).

66. Quoted in ibid., 16.

67. Quoted in ibid., 38.

1. Geoffrey H. Hartman, *The Unremarkable Wordsworth* (Minneapolis: University of Minnesota Press, 1987), 116.

2. William Wordsworth, "Preface to *Lyrical Ballads, with Pastoral and Other Poems* (1802)," in *William Wordsworth: The Poems,* ed. John O. Hayden, 2 vols. (New Haven, Conn.: Yale University Press, 1977), 1:872 (subsequent citations occur parenthetically in the text).

3. Wordsworth writes of an implicit contract binding the author to a readership, which in this case he can be seen to have violated: "It is supposed, that by the act of writing in verse an Author makes a formal engagement that he will gratify certain known habits of association; that he not only thus apprises the reader that certain classes of ideas and expressions will be found in his book, but that others will be carefully excluded. . . . I will not take upon me to determine the exact import of the promise which by the act of writing in verse an Author, in the present day, makes to his Reader; but I am certain, it will appear to many persons that I have not fulfilled the terms of an engagement thus voluntarily contracted. . . . they will look round for poetry, and will be induced to inquire by what species of courtesy these attempts can be permitted to assume that title" (1:868–69).

4. Hartman, *Unremarkable Wordsworth,* 9.

5. Thomas Poole, "John Walford," *Bath and Bristol Magazine; or, Western Miscellany* 2 (1883): 168–79 (subsequent citations occur parenthetically in the text).

6. On the divestment of figural meanings in the literal recurrence of the noun "garments," see Cynthia Chase, "The Accidents of Disfiguration: Limits to Literal and Figurative Reading of Wordsworth's 'Books,'" *Decomposing Figures: Rhetorical Readings in the Romantic Tradition* (Baltimore, Md.: Johns Hopkins University Press, 1986), 16.

7. Quoted in Alan J. Bewell, "Wordsworth's Primal Scene: Retrospective Tales of Idiots, Wild Children and Savages," *English Literary History* 50.2 (Summer 1983): 339.

8. Poole, "John Walford," 173.

9. Quoted in Patrick Campbell, *Wordsworth and Coleridge: Lyrical Ballads* (Houndmills, U.K.: Macmillan, 1991), 20. Campbell continues: The "notion of a creative symbiosis, systematically and cordially fostered during those thirteen months and initiated by Coleridge's leap over the gate to greet his friends in June 1797, was already under fire from Stephen Parrish, the first to take seriously Coleridge's retrospective avowal that 'a radical Difference' of opinion about 'the language appropriate to poetry' existed between them (letter to Southey, 13 July 1802). For Parrish the key word, reemphasized in subsequent discussions, is 'ventriloquism,' Coleridge's pejorative epithet" (20).

10. Quoted in Gordon K. Thomas, "Letters: 'Christabel,' 'The Idiot Boy,' and Paraphrasia," *Encyclia* 58 (1981): 64.

11. De Man, *Rhetoric of Romanticism*, 73.

12. Hartman, *Unremarkable Wordsworth*, 9.

13. Wordsworth to John Wilson, June 7, 1802, in *The Letters of William and Dorothy Wordsworth*, 2d ed., ed. Ernest de Selincourt, rev. Chester L. Shaver, 8 vols. (Oxford: Oxford University Press, 1967) 1:357 (subsequent citations occur parenthetically in the text).

14. William Wordsworth, "Preface to the Edition of 1814," *The Excursion*, in *Poetical Works*, ed. Thomas Hutchinson, rev. Ernest de Selincourt (Oxford: Oxford University Press, 1969), 590, ll. 40–41.

15. Wordsworth, *The Poems*, 1:946n.

16. Thomas, "Letters," 64.

17. William Wordsworth, *The Fourteen-Book Prelude*, ed. W. J. B. Owen (Ithaca, N.Y.: Cornell University Press, 1985), bk. 14, 270, ll. 400–408 (subsequent citations occur parenthetically in the text).

18. Hartman, *Unremarkable Wordsworth*, 13.

19. Robert Southey, "Review of William Wordsworth and S. T. Coleridge, 'Lyrical Ballads' [excerpt]," reprinted in *Romanticism: An Anthology*, ed. Duncan Wu (Oxford: Oxford University Press, 1994), 607 (subsequent citations occur parenthetically in the text).

20. Duncan Wu, "Looking for Johnny: Wordsworth's 'The Idiot Boy,'" *Charles Lamb Bulletin* 88 (1973): 166–176.

21. William Wordsworth, "The Recluse," in *The Poems*, 1:697.

22. William Wordsworth, "Preface to the Second Edition of . . . 'Lyrical Ballads,'" in *Poetical Works*, 734.

23. Samuel Taylor Coleridge, *Biographia Literaria*, ed. James Engell and W. Jackson Bate, 2 vols. in 1 (Princeton, N.J.: Princeton University Press, 1983), 2:158–59 (subsequent citations occur parenthetically in the text).

24. Ross Woodman, "The Idiot Boy as Healer," in *Romanticism and Children's Literature in Nineteenth-Century England*, ed. James Holt McGavran Jr. (Athens: University of Georgia Press, 1991), 76 (quoting in part *Biographia Literaria*, 1:304).

25. Hartman, *Unremarkable Wordsworth*, xxv. Of considerable interest to an intersecting thematic, Hartman makes Wordsworth's poetical production a matter of the latent technology of testing: "Each poem becomes a new test of the imagination, or where the world fits in. Such testing, however, is inevitably comparative and temporal, and opens Wordsworth to latent memories of childhood and adolescence. This temporal complexity shapes a poetic instrument containing very subtle eddyings that cannot be fixed in the amber of neoclassical verse. The poem of this mind reacts on itself, composing even 'blind thoughts' that usurp the attempt to write, and compel Wordsworth to revise his self-understanding" (xxv).

26. William Wordsworth, "Tintern Abbey," ll. 84, in *Poetical Works*, 164.

27. Wordsworth, "Preface . . . 'Lyrical Ballads,'" *Poetical Works*, 734, 735.

28. Coleridge, *Biographia Literaria*, 2:48: ". . . the idiocy of the *boy* is so evenly balanced by the folly of the *mother*, as to present to the general reader rather a laughable burlesque on the blindness of anile dotage, than an analytic display of maternal affection in its ordinary workings." For his part, Coleridge would have wanted the maternal sphere submitted to analytic rigor.

29. Wordsworth to Thomas De Quincey, March 6, 1804, in *Letters*, 1:368.

30. See Woodman, "Idiot Boy as Healer," 81.

31. William Wordsworth, *The Excursion*, l. 963, in *The Poems*, 2:49 (subsequent citations occur parenthetically in the text).

32. Quoted in *Shelley's Poetry and Prose*, ed. Donald H. Reiman and Sharon B. Powers (New York: Norton, 1977), 71.

33. Wordsworth to Wilson, *Letters*, 1:357. See also Woodman, "Idiot Boy as Healer," 79.

34. John Locke, *An Essay Concerning Human Understanding*, ed. Peter H. Nidditch (Oxford: Clarendon, 1975), 1.II.§27 (subsequent citations occur parenthetically in the text).

35. See, for example, Bewell's article on the subject, where Locke's *Essay* is viewed in terms of "a family of privileged epistemological subjects — of which the idiot is but one member — who play a central role in the empiricist discourse of the human conditions of memory" ("Wordsworth's Primal Scene," 327).

36. Ibid.

37. Étienne de Condillac, *Treatise on the Sensations*, trans. Geraldine Carr (Los Angeles: University of Southern California, 1930), xix (subsequent citations occur parenthetically in the text).

38. Bewell, "Wordsworth's Primal Scene," 328.

39. Adam Ferguson, *Essay on the History of Civil Society* (Edinburgh: A. Milar and T. Caddell, 1767), 4. See also Bewell's discussion of the discomfiture of social scientists ("Wordsworth's Primal Scene," 328).

40. Lord Monboddo, *Ancient Metaphysics* 3 vols. (London, 1799), 3:57; Bewell, "Wordsworth's Primal Scene," 329.

41. Bewell, "Wordsworth's Primal Scene," 329, 330.

42. Daniel Defoe, *Mere Nature Delineated; or, a Body Without a Soul . . .* (London, 1726), 4 (subsequent citations occur parenthetically in the text); Bewell, "Wordsworth's Primal Scene," 330.

43. Nietzsche's zoography in light of Heidegger's essay on Nietzsche's animals is discussed in my *Finitude's Score: Essays for the End of the Millennium* (Lincoln: University of Nebraska Press, 1994), 63–82.

44. See Jaques Lacan, *The Seminar of Jacques Lacan: Book VII, The Ethics of Psychoanalysis, 1959–1960*, ed. Jacques-Alain Miller, trans. Dennis Porter (New

York: Norton, 1992): "That is to say, that what man demands, what he cannot help but demand, is to be deprived of something real" (150).

45. See de Man, *Rhetoric of Romanticism*, 75.

46. Stillinger is quoted in the notes to *Lyrical Ballads*, in Wordsworth, *The Poems*, 1:946n. The state of the narrator's stupefaction, his utter stupidity before the poetic facts, is another way of telling us that the poetic act is ecstatic, exorbitant, pointing to a place without a place of the advent. The poetic act is catastrophic (see Lacoue-Labarthe reading Heidegger), "an upsetting relation to what is an upset, in being, in the direction of nothingness (the abyss)" (Philippe Lacoue-Labarthe, *Poetry as Experience*, trans. Andrea Tarnowski [Stanford, Calif.: Stanford University Press, 1999], 67). In this sense poetry acts to interrupt art, that is, mimesis; it is the interruption of mimesis. The poetic consists in probing the limits of the perceptible, not in representing, which would only be a way of saying that it tries to tape what is already present. The narrator, trying to catch (up with) the Idiot Boy on tape, has precisely nothing to go on. In the process of appearing and disappearing, the idiot cannot be represented, cannot be followed to his secret sites, but must be interrupted or, rather, marks the interruption of mimesis. The entire poem can be seen as playing on the difficult registers of mimesis that poetry assumes.

47. See also Jacques Derrida's discussion of the Nietzschean "vielleicht" in *Politics of Friendship*, trans. George Collins (London: Verso, 1997), 26-48.

48. Lacoue-Labarthe, *Poetry as Experience*, 19.

49. Ibid., 18.

50. De Man, *Rhetoric of Romanticism*, 71.

51. See the discussion of Wordsworth's literalists and mimics and how we "mimic the misreading we discover" in Chase, "Accidents of Disfiguration" (29).

KANT SATELLITE

1. Søren Kierkegaard *"Fear and Trembling" and "The Sickness unto Death,"* trans. Walter Lowrie (Princeton, N.J.: Princeton University Press, 1981), 35.

2. Franz Kafka, "Abraham," in *Parables and Paradoxes* (New York: Schocken, 1958).

3. Jean-Luc Nancy, *Le Discours de la syncope* (Paris: Aubier-Flammarion, 1976).

4. Jean-Luc Nancy, "Logodaedalus (Kant écrivain)," *Poétique* 21 (1975): 42 (my translation): "La *vérité* exige donc la science laborieuse et sans style, sans miel." When discussing the matter of Kant's poor style, Willi Goetschel assimilates it to notions of coquetry and irony. See *Kant als Schriftsteller* (Wien: Passagen Verlag, 1990).

5. Immauel Kant, preface to the second edition, *The Critique of Pure Reason*, trans. and ed. Paul Guyer and Allen W. Wood (Cambridge: Cambridge University Press, 1998), 106-24.

6. Nancy, *Le Discours de la syncope*, 42 (my translation): mathematics "est ainsi le seul lieu de la *présentation (Darstellung)* au sens propre et plein du terme."

7. Jean-Luc Nancy, "Literary Communism,'" in *The Inoperative Community*, ed. Peter Connor (Minneapolis: University of Minnesota Press, 1991), 71–81.

8. Nancy, "Logodaedalus," 51 (my translation): "Paradoxalement, c'est peut-être aussi à partir de Kant qu'il ne pourra plus y avoir ni philosophie ni littérature. Mais un brouillage permanent, et cherchant en permanence à s'écrire, de ces catégories."

9. Immanuel Kant, *Lectures on Philosophical Theology*, trans. Allen W. Wood and Gertrude M. Clark (Ithaca, N.Y.: Cornell University Press, 1978), 117.

10. Kafka, "Abraham," 40: "Ich könnte mir einen anderen Abraham denken" (subsequent citations occur parenthetically in the text).

11. While the Bible does not make Abraham clean his room before he can go out, it turns out that Kierkegaard does: "It was early in the morning, and everything in Abraham's house was ready for the journey" (Søren Kierkegaard, "Exordium," in *Fear and Trembling/Repetition*, trans. and ed. Howard V. Hong and Edna H. Hong [Princeton, N.J.: Princeton University Press, 1983], 14).

12. For Freud and his analysis of the "*Geschenk*," see his *Jokes and Their Relation to the Unconscious*, in *The Standard Edition of the Complete Psychological Works of Sigmund Freud*, ed. James Strachey and Anna Freud, 26 vols. (London: Hogarth, 1964), 8:166. On the connectedness of the gift and laughter, see Jean-Luc Nancy's "Laughter, Presence," in *Birth to Presence*, trans. Brian Holmes et al. (Stanford, Calif.: Stanford University Press, 1993): "Laughter is thus neither a presence nor an absence. It is the offering of a presence in its own disappearance. It is not given but offered" (383).

13. Franz Kakfa, "Before the Law," *Parables*, 64–65.

14. See also Kafka's parable "Die Prüfung (The Test)," in *Parables and Paradoxes*, 180: "'Bleib,' sagte er, 'das war ja nur eine Prüfung. Wer die Fragen nicht beantwortet, hat die Prüfung bestanden'" ("'Hold on,' he said; 'That was just a test. Anyone who didn't answer the question passed it'").

15. Immanuel Kant, "The Classification of Mental Disorders," in *Anthrolopology from a Pragmatic Point of View*, trans. Charles T. Sullivan (Doylestown, Pa.: Doylestown Foundation, 1964), 3 (subsequent citations occur parenthetically in the text).

16. It is of some interest to note that it was Foucault who translated the *Anthropology* into French. See *Anthropologie du point de vue pragmatique*, trans. Michel Foucault (Paris: J. Vrin, 1979).

17. Kant, "Classification of Mental Disorders," 5. The original reads: "Der, welcher eine dieser Eigenschaften bloß affektiert ... ist ein ekelhaftes Subjekt" (Kant, *Anthropologie im Pragmatischer Hinsicht*, in *Immanuel Kants Werkausgabe*, 12:516).

18. For more on the motif of disgust in Kant, see Derrida's essay "Economime-

sis," trans. R. Klein, in *The Ghost of Theology: Readings of Kant and Hegel* (special issue of *diacritics* 11.2 [Summer 1981]), 3–25. For a reading of Kant's use of the term *Ekel*, see Winfried Menninghaus's "Zwischen Überwältigung und Widerstand: Macht und Gewalt in Longins und Kants Theorien der Erhabenen," *Poetica: Zeitschrift für Sprach- und Literaturwissenschaft* 23.1–2 (1991): 1–19.

19. In the *Third Critique*, Kant is reminded, when sketching palatial grounds, of the workers and labors that such beauty always entails, "auf gut Rousseauistich" (Kant, *Kritik der Urteilskraft*, in *Immanuel Kants Werkausgabe*, 10:116).

20. Ak. XVI, 1753, as cited in Nancy, *Le Discours de la syncope*, 69n.44.

21. In his essay "Interpretations at War: Kant, the Jew, the German," trans. Moshe Ron, *New Literary History* 22 (1991): 39–95, Derrida mentions this note in the context of Kant's philosemitism: "Kant's thought, whose Protestant descendance is so evident, has very rapidly been interpreted as a profound Judaism. It may be recalled both that he was saluted as a sort of Moses [Hölderlin had referred to Kant as "the Moses of his nation"] and that Hegel saw in him a shameful Jew. . . . The fact that the *Anthropology from a Pragmatic Point of View* contains at least one properly anti-Semitic note (literally anti-Palestinian) is not incompatible with Kant's quasi Judaism. Besides, what is anti-Semitism not compatible with? This is a terrible question, for it is directed at Jews, at those who call themselves such, as well as at non-Jews, at the anti-Semites and at those who are not such, still more perhaps at the philo-Semites" (69).

22. On Kant and the Jews, see Sander L. Gilman, *Smart Jews: The Construction of the Image of Jewish Superior Intelligence* (Lincoln: University of Nebraska Press, 1996), 15. For a probing discussion of the role language plays in Kant's philosophy, see Peter Fenves, "Introduction," in *Raising the Tone of Philosophy: Late Essays of Immanuel Kant, Transformative Critique by Jacques Derrida*, ed. Peter Fenves (Baltimore, Md.: Johns Hopkins University Press, 1993), 1–48.

23. Such a reversal of the function of primacy is a hallmark of the poet's relation to the god in the work of Hölderlin. The poet, the one who answers the call, brings the god into being or establishes the god's existence in temporality and as future, on earth. God's dependence on the one called implies fragility in the constitution of divine being.

24. In Kafka's parable "The Test," the servant avers: "the main thing is that I am not called upon to serve, others have been called yet they have not tried harder than I, indeed perhaps they have not even felt the desire to be called, whereas I, at least sometimes, have felt it very strongly" (*Parables and Paradoxes*, 181). The test hinges on being called, as does K.'s predicament in *The Castle* — his drama revolves around the ordeal of being called but without title, and gets substantialized in the telephone call that confers his title.

25. In *The Last Trial: On the Legends and Lore of the Command to Abraham to Offer Isaac as a Sacrifice: The Akedah*, trans. Judah Goldin (Woodstock, Vt.: Jewish Lights, 1993), Shalom Spiegel describes the way in which the rabbinic tradition has engaged the puzzle of Abraham descending — to all intents and purposes *alone* — from Mount Moriah ("So Abraham returned to the young men" [Gen. 22:19]). Spiegel shows how significant was the interpretation that considered Isaac to have been wounded or indeed killed by Abraham, an interpretation that began to emerge in early rabbinic commentaries. By the twelfth century Abraham Ibn Ezra saw a need to defend the verse against this interpretation: "'And Abraham returned — And Isaac is not mentioned.... But he who asserts that Abraham slew Isaac and abandoned him, and that afterwards Isaac came to life again, is speaking contrary to writ'" (quoted in Spiegel, *Last Trial*, 8).

26. Take still another Abraham, one who stages a collusion between the imaginary and real fathers — the depriving and castrating ones, the father, according to Lacan, elevated to the rank of Great Fucker. ("If we are sufficiently cruel to ourselves to incorporate the father, it is perhaps because we have a lot to reproach this father with. ... It is this imaginary father [the one associated with the experience of privation] and not the real one which is the basis of the providential image of God. And the function of the superego in the end, from its final point of view, is hatred for God, the reproach that God has handled things so badly.") Finally: "What is in question is the moment when the subject quite simply perceives that his father is an idiot or a thief, as the case may be, or quite simply a weakling or, routinely, an old fogey, as in Freud's case." Or Abraham's. (*The Ethics of Psychoanalysis*, 307–8).

27. In *Donner la mort* (Paris: Galilée, 1999), Derrida writes about the irrevocable heritage assigned to us by Abraham, the one locked in silence and secrecy, about which no knowledge can be asserted: "On ne sait plus le réinterpréter. On ne sait plus, car ce n'est plus une question de savoir" (flysheet).

Index

and *Denkfaulheit*, 64; "Zwei Ge-
dichte von Friedrich Hölderlin,"
7, 8
Bernhard, Thomas, 66, 79
Bernst, Ernst, 178–79
Bernstein, Susan, 329n
Beyond Good and Evil (Nietzsche),
3–5
Billy Budd (Melville), 100–102
Binet, Alfred, 324n
Binswanger, Ludwig, 338n
Biographia Literaria (Coleridge), 258,
347n
Birth to Presence (Nancy), 186–90,
338–39n, 349n
Blanchot, Maurice, 5, 10, 29, 64
Bleuler, Eugen, 79
Blindness and Insight (de Man), 106
Bloch, Ernst, 59
"Blödigkeit" (Hölderlin), 5–9, 28
Bloy, Léon, 21, 45
Body in Pain, The (Scarry), 339–40n
"Bonheur bête" (Michaux), 42, 44
Booth, Wayne, 127, 128, 130–31
Bossuet, Jacques-Bénigne, 188
Bouchard, R., 231
Brecht, Bertolt, 43, 73
Broca, Paul, 323–34n
Brothers Karamazov, The (Dosto-
evsky), 236, 237
Buddha, 184, 212
Bunker, Archie (TV role), 27, 69, 110
Burt, E. S., 103–4
Byron, Lord (Gordon), 184, 252

Cadava, Eduardo, 318n
Campbell, Patrick, 345n
Camus, Albert, 83
Candide (Voltaire), 11–12
Carey, Tom, 337n
Caruth, Cathy, 326n
Cascardi, Anthony J., 336–37n
Cassirer, Ernst, 313n

Castle, The (Kafka), 350n
Cavell, Stanley, 22–23
Cervantes, Miguel de: *Don Quixote*,
175–76, 280, 290
Chaplin, Charlie, 287
Charcot, Jean-Martin, 229
Chase, Cynthia, 118, 345n
Chernyshevsky, Nikolay Gavrilo-
vich, 172
"Christabel" (Coleridge), 255–56, 259
Christianity: Bataille on, 194, 339n;
and death of God, 151, 152; Dostoevsky on, 14, 17, 178–79, 188,
191, 206–7, 209, 254; Feuerbachian
atheism and, 172; Nancy on, 45,
189, 339n; Nietzsche on, 17–18, 39,
46, 81, 178–79, 203; pain and, 190;
relationship to God in, 54; Roman Catholicism, 171; stupidity
and redemption in, 41, 45–47, 53–
54; Wordsworth on, 263, 266
Christ Taken from the Cross (Holbein), 176–77, 187, 188, 195, 225,
244, 336–37n, 340n
Civilization and Its Discontents
(Freud), 239
Cohen, Tom, 106–7, 109
Coldness and Cruelty (Deleuze), 344n
Coleridge, Hartley, 258–59
Coleridge, Samuel Taylor: *Biographia Literaria*, 258, 347n;
"Christabel," 255–56, 259; *Lyrical
Ballads*, 248, 256–57; Wordsworth
and, 248, 250, 252, 255–59, 260–62,
263, 265, 345n
"Commentary on Lacan's Text"
(Fink), 344n
"Concept of Irony, The" (de Man),
85, 111, 118, 121–31, 134, 136–37,
139–46, 150
Concept of Irony, The (Kierkegaard),
125–26, 127–28, 130, 144, 164, 330–
31n

Condillac, Étienne Bonnot de, 254, 268–70

Condorcet, Marquis de, 323–24n

Confessions (Rousseau), 47–53, 96, 103, 104, 121

Confidential Letters on Schlegel's Lucinde (Schleiermacher), 153

Connor, Peter, 154–55

Conrad, Joseph, 6

Conversations with Eckermann (Goethe), 174, 336n

Cooper, Dennis, 337–38n

Copjec, Joan, 343–44n

Corngold, Stanley, 7

"Counterfeit Money" (Derrida), 204, 206, 341n

"Country Doctor, A" (Kafka), 211–12, 293, 295, 339n

Crane, Hart, 6, 247, 341n

Critique of Judgment (Third Critique; Kant), 113, 287, 350n

Critique of Pure Reason (First Critique; Kant), 152, 284, 296

Culler, Jonathan, 12

De Docta ignorantia (Nicholas de Cusa), 46

Defoe, Daniel, 270–71

Deleuze, Gilles: *Coldness and Cruelty*, 344n; *Difference and Repetition*, 20–21, 32; Kristeva on, 281; on the rhetoric of masochism, 243–44

de Man, Paul, 108–44; *Aesthetic Ideology*, 121; "Aesthetic Theory from Kant to Hegel," 326–27n; *Allegories of Reading*, 69, 98, 108–9, 118, 119, 158–59; on anacoluthon, 139–40; author's connection with, 120–21; *Blindness and Insight*, 106; "Concept of Irony," 85, 111, 118, 121–31, 134, 136–37, 139–46, 150; "Excuses," 52; Gasché on, 110–17; guilt feelings of, 25; Hamacher on, 117–19;

life and death of, 104–6, 132; parabasis defined by, 138, 140; "Phenomenality and Materiality in Kant," 112–14; on the philosopher as ridiculous, 298; *Resistance to Theory*, 107, 125; *Rhetoric of Romanticism*, 96, 99, 100–103; "Rhetoric of Temporality," 121; on technology, 97–100, 109, 121–22; on Wordsworth, 252–53, 272, 277

De possest (Nicholas de Cusa), 46

De Quincey, Thomas, 262

Derrida, Jacques, 281, 321n, 339n; on Abraham, 351n; "Counterfeit Money," 204, 206, 341n; *Donner la mort*, 351n; "Eating Well," 341n; "Economimesis," 349–50n; on Flaubert, 13; on hospitality, 206; on Kant, 349–50n; on mourning, 327n; *Politics of Friendship*, 348n

Descartes, René, 155

"Desire and the Drive" (Fink), 344n

Dialectic of Enlightenment (Horkheimer and Adorno), 37

Dialogue on Poetry and Literary Aphorisms (Schlegel), 145, 331n

Dialogues (Plato), 40

Diary of a Writer (Dostoevsky), 197

"Dichtermut" (Hölderlin), 5–9

Dictionary of Accepted Ideas (Flaubert), 39

Diderot, Denis, 44, 138

Die neue Rundschau (journal), 21

Difference and Repetition (Deleuze), 20–21, 32

"Dignity of Women, The" (Schiller), 332n

Dilthey, Wilhelm, 153, 281

Dionysius, 47, 81, 179

Donner la mort (Derrida), 351n

Don Quixote (Cervantes), 175–76,
   280, 290
Dostoevsky, Aimée, 234
Dostoevsky, Anna Grigoryevna,
   171, 177, 195, 340n
Dostoevsky, Fyodor, 6; addictions
   of, 232–33; *Brothers Karamazov*,
   236, 237; on Christianity, 14, 17,
   178–79, 188, 191, 206–7, 209, 254;
   criminalization of, 238–39; *Diary
   of a Writer*, 197; epilepsy of, 177,
   183–84, 193, 194, 195, 228–30, 232–
   37, 241, 340n; on ethical liability,
   19–20; Flaubert and, 222–26, 227–
   29, 240, 242, 244; Foucault on,
   197; Freud on, 177, 193, 227, 229–
   40, 242; fundamentalism of, 172;
   The Idiot, 169–96, 198–226 (see
   also *Idiot, The*); *Insulted and Injured*, 180, 338n; on the intelligentsia, 213–14; latent homosexuality of, 234; *Life of a Great
   Sinner*, 238; as political prisoner,
   236, 238; sadomasochistic engagements of, 232–34, 236, 239–
   40, 242–44; *Stavrogin's Confessions*,
   238; *Underground Man*, 191
Dostoïevski et Flaubert (Sutterman),
   194, 338n
Doty, Mark, 337n
Douglass, Frederick, 319n
Düttmann, Alexander Garcia, 337n

"Eating Well" (Derrida), 341n
Eckermann, Johann Peter, 174,
   336n
"Economimesis" (Derrida), 349–50n
Education sentimentale (Flaubert), 15
Eichmann, Adolf, 3
Einstein, Albert, 73, 287
Engels, Friedrich, 58, 59
Enlightenment: as Age of Reason,
   44; Améry and, 23–24; Horkhei-

mer and Adorno on, 37; Musil
   and, 19, 23; occult in, 45; Paul
   and, 19; Readings and, 317n;
   thought detached from stupidity in, 23–24
Epicurus, 57–58
Epimetheus, 40
Erasmus, Desiderius, 14, 15, 66
Erdmann, J. E., 54–55; on ethical
   principles, 166; scorned by audience, 68, 76, 77, 78; *Serious Play*,
   55; "Über Dummheit," 76–77, 85
Essai sur les moeurs (Voltaire), 44
*Essay Concerning Human Under-
   standing, An* (Locke), 267–68, 347n
Eve: cleverness of, 86–87; punishment of, 46
Excursion, The (Wordsworth), 262,
   263
"Excuses" (de Man), 52

"Fall of Hyperion, The" (Keats), 115
Fausse Monnaie (Baudelaire), 204,
   341n
Faust, Johann, 196
Fear and Trembling (Kierkegaard),
   280
Fedotov, G. P., 178
Felman, Shoshana, 118
Ferenczi, Sándor, 194, 231
Ferguson, Adam, 269
"Fetishism" (Freud), 239
Feuerbach, Ludwig Andreas, 172
Fichte, Johann Gottlieb, 122, 143,
   144, 147, 151, 153, 154
Fichtean system, 122, 126, 133–34,
   136, 140, 143, 148
Fink, Bruce, 344n
Finnegans Wake (Joyce), 85
Fisher King, 339n
Flaubert, Gustave, 3, 6, 142, 213; on
   Candide, 11–12; on closure, 70;
   Derrida on, 13; *Dictionary of Ac-*

Heidegger, Martin, 19, 25, 65, 154;
anxiety in work of, 107; *das Man*
in works of, 73–74; on destruction vs. devastation, 122; Freiburg lectures, 111; on Hölderlin,
341n; Lacoue-Labarthe and, 348n;
on mediocrity, 74; minimalism
of, 105, 327n; Nancy on, 74; on
philosophy vs. thinking, 116,
187, 281; on readiness, 211; and
self-determination, 63; on technology, 97, 98; *What Is Called
Thinking?*, 341n; "Why Do We Remain in the Provinces?," 41, 42,
319–20n
Heine, Heinrich, 282, 283
Herder, Johann Gottfried von, 147
Histoire de la folie (Foucault), 197
*Historisch-Kritisches Wörterbuch des
Marxismus* (ed. Haug), 56–59
Holbein, Hans: *Christ Taken from the
Cross*, 176–77, 187, 188, 195, 225,
244, 336–37n, 340n
Hölderlin, Friedrich, 14, 26, 212,
253, 273, 275; "Andenken," 75;
Benjamin on, 7, 8; "Blödigkeit,"
5–9, 28; "Dichtermut," 5–9;
Heidegger on, 341n; on Rous-
seau, 48; on the poet's relation to
God, 350n; on the "sacred alien,"
200, 341n
Homer, 5
Hopkins, Jasper, 46, 322n
Horkheimer, Max: *Dialectic of En-
lightenment*, 37
Hume, David, 44, 282, 285, 301
Hüppauf, Bernd, 326n
Hustler (magazine), 154

"Idiot, Der" (Benjamin), 174, 335n
"Idiot, The" (Crane), 6, 247, 341n
Idiot, The (Dostoevsky), 20, 167, 169–
96, 198–226, 254, 271; apology in,

215–17; cry of abandonment in,
177–85; end of Europe in, 198–200;
epileptic seizure in, 177, 184–85,
192–96, 230, 232, 341–42n; forbidden body in, 185–92, 196; intelligentsia in, 213–15; *Madame Bovary* and, 222–26, 227–29, 240, 242,
244; Prince Christ in, 14, 17, 173,
174–77, 178–79, 182, 185, 192, 194,
200–206, 207, 208, 210–11, 212, 214–
15; readiness expressed in, 210–12;
rupture and modernity in, 206–8;
smile or laughter in, 212–13; the
stupids in, 217–26; trust depicted
in, 208–12; Wordsworth and, 247–
48, 254; writing of, 171–73
"Idiot, The" (Southey), 257
"Idiot Boy, The" (Wordsworth), 9,
246, 251–52, 254–57, 258–62, 263–
68, 271–77
"Idiot Boy as Healer, The" (Wood-
man), 259
"Idiots, The" (Conrad), 6
Illness as Metaphor (Sontag), 340n
"Images" (Barthes), 315n
"Immortality" (Wordsworth), 259
"In-Difference to Philosophy"
(Gasché), 110–17
Infinite Conversation (Blanchot), 64
Inner Experience (Bataille), 154–55
In Praise of Folly (Erasmus), 66
*Inquiry Concerning the Principles of
Morals* (Hume), 285
Insulted and Injured, The (Dosto-
evsky), 180, 338n
IQ testing, 59–60, 324–25n
Irigaray, Luce, 281
Isaac, as sacrifice, 291, 306–10, 351n

Jacobs, Carol, 118
Jacques le Fataliste (Diderot), 138
James, Henry, 9–10, 12, 38
Jaspers, Karl, 3

Designed by R. Eckersley
in Enschedé's Trinité types
Manufactured by Thomson-Shore, Inc.
University of Illinois Press
1325 South Oak Street
Champaign, IL 61820-6903
www.press.uillinois.edu

DATE DUE

HIGHSMITH #45115